TRACK SUPPLIES
RAILWAY MATERIAL

CATALOGUE N⁰ 110

This catalogue contains many additions to our regular lines as well as new departures. The lines covered include Scales; Hand and Push Cars; Velocipedes; Rail Drilling Machines; Tool Grinders; Rail Benders; Track Gauges and Levels; Switch Stands; Ratchet, Friction and Ball-Bearing Jacks; Car Replacers; Stoves; and Special Track Work which is handled by our Paige Iron Works Department

1907 EDITION

©2008-2010 PERISCOPE FILM LLC
ALL RIGHTS RESERVED
ISBN #978-1-935700-08-1
WWW.PERISCOPEFILM.COM
This book has been digitally watermarked to prevent illegal duplication.

THE BUDA FOUNDRY & MFG. CO.
MAIN OFFICE: CHICAGO   WORKS: HARVEY, ILL.

New York, 26 Cortlandt Street   St. Louis, Frisco Building

WORKS OF THE BUDA FOUNDRY & MANUFACTURING COMPANY, HARVEY, ILL.

H ARVEY is twenty miles from Chicago and all shipments from that point obtain Chicago freight rates. The Buda Works are located on two trunk and a belt line connecting with all roads entering Chicago. Its shipping facilities are therefore complete and service prompt. ¶ The shops are equipped with modern machinery and appliances so that all goods are produced in a manner which enables the best values to be offered throughout the entire line of manufactures.

To Purchasers

THE Buda Company believes it has a distinctive claim upon the favorable consideration of all railroads desirous of reducing costs. In the face of constantly increasing prices of raw materials and of labor during the past three years, the Buda Company has devised ways and means of reducing selling prices of finished goods throughout the largest line of railway appliances made by any one manufacturer in the country.

We believe that this condition is remarkable and unique and that we are entitled to considerable credit for the efforts and the success of those efforts all along the line—**Scales, Hand Cars, Push Cars, Wheels, Velocipedes, Drills, Gauges, Levels, Rail Benders, Ratchet Jacks, Friction Jacks, Ball-Bearing Jacks, Cone-Bearing Jacks and Car Replacers.**

The material entering into the construction of these goods has advanced from twenty to forty per-cent (the latter in the cost of malleable castings, which enter largely into the manufacture of these goods); and labor has, as all are aware, at the same time been gradually increasing in cost, and yet the Buda Company is furnishing all these articles, with many improvements added during the past three years, at prices considerably lower than those of three years since.

This has been accomplished through our adoption of the policy some three years ago to revolutionize the ordinary methods of conducting this business, and to direct our attention at the Factory and in the Sales Department to see how LOW and not how HIGH, our goods could be sold. In steadily working toward this end many economies have contributed, but the two great factors are:

First—The sale and shipment of our goods direct from the factory to users, thus eliminating the great burden of warehouse and selling expense; and

Secondly—Through improved methods and machinery in the Manufacturing Department.

We are pleased to advise that our efforts appear to be appreciated—our business having more than trebled within a period of three years; and as, naturally, this increased volume has aided us in the making of our LOWER prices, so also, naturally, increased orders in the future will likewise assist in that direction; and, for this reason, we confidently hope for the orders of those who favor this policy.

Buda U. S. Standard Scales

Additional Styles and Capacities

Since the publication of our last catalogue, we have added, it will be noted, a number of styles of scales to the list we formerly made. These varieties are manufactured in a number of capacities each with platforms in standard measurements and cover all general weighing requirements of railroads and enterprises contiguous to them, such as coal and ore mines, grain elevators, warehouses and industrial plants.

In designing these additional scales, we have followed the lines of reinforced construction along which our other types have been built. This improved construction adds largely to the life and general durability, as described in pages following, making an economical investment as against other makes of lighter general design which are expensive to maintain on account of replacements made necessary by breakages, and the time lost waiting for them to arrive.

We guarantee the quality of Buda scales. They are of correct mechanical design and are to be thoroughly relied on as to weights.

Points to Consider When Purchasing

Three considerations should influence the buyer of scales: **Quality; First Cost; Maintenance.**

The qualifications that place Buda Scales first in these three respects are as follows:

Quality, i. e.: Material --- Workmanship

Connected with the Buda Company are men of large experience in the manufacture and sale of scales. This experience has demonstrated to them the desirability of building a distinct line of scales, especially for railroad service, which should be superior to those made for ordinary commercial use.

The requirements of railroads are so much more constant and exacting that it is evident, to meet these requirements adequately, something better is needed than has heretofore been provided.

Buda Scales were, therefore, designed especially for railroad work, made of the best material, of exceptional strength throughout, those parts subjected to the greatest strain re-inforced and strengthened, reducing to a minimum the liability of getting out of order and needing repairs.

Practical men who have used scales extensively are best aware of the importance of this, for they know that although the repairs are expensive, the cost of repairs is but a small fraction of the loss frequently incurred in such cases, due to the scales being unusable for the time.

First Cost

Using larger amounts of the best grades of material, the cost of manufacturing and real value of Buda Scales is greater than others, but we are able to make reduced prices because Buda Scales go direct from manufacturer to consumer. The large toll that is necessary to maintain stores, show rooms and their concomitants is, therefore, eliminated from the selling price of Buda Scales.

Cost of Maintenance

For reasons above mentioned, the Buda Scales will not require repairs as early or often, and when repairs are needed (we ask your special attention to this) they will be furnished at greatly reduced prices, also, you will find it advantageous to purchase our re-inforced repair parts for other makes of scales which you may have in use, on account of both price and strength.

Steel Main Levers

Attention is called to the fact that when desired we are prepared to furnish steel main levers in place of the usual cast iron levers. Although our cast iron levers are of a special mixture of high grade and run particularly for scale levers, the use of steel levers provides additional security where scales are likely to be subjected to excessive loads or where the service is unusually severe.

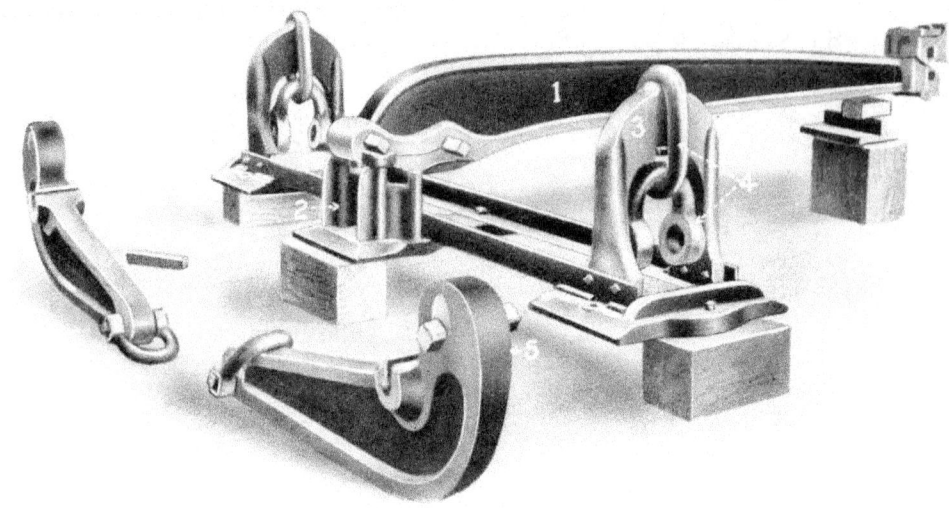

The Necessity of Stronger Scales

Within a few years the weight of rolling stock has considerably increased, while, in our opinion, there has not been an adequate increase in strength of track scales. The result of this is that scales frequently break in one part or another and there is incurred, not alone the expense of repairs, but a more important loss which results from the scales being useless while waiting for repair parts to arrive; and, as there is always a likelihood of delay in shipment and transit, the evident economy of purchasing scales with re-inforced levers will be recognized once the attention has been directed to it.

Our object in offering our scales is to overcome these contingencies and, with this in view, we have strengthened the construction of those levers and parts subjected to the greatest strains at points where breakage most often occurs. This means an addition from 450 to 650 pounds of metal in a track scale, and, while this represents at least an increase of ten per cent in weight, the metal has been so placed where re-inforcement is the most needed that the strength of the scale has been added to by at least 25 per cent.

It is not possible to precisely calculate the advantages derived from the additional 25 per cent to be found in Buda track scales. We think it is fair to estimate 50 per cent decrease in the cost of maintenance and an increase in the life of the scale of at least 50 per cent. When it is considered that the cost of maintenance is reduced by one-half, it is possible also to imagine the saving effected by a correspondingly increased use of the scales; for we have already mentioned the loss incurred by scales being out of use while waiting for repairs to be made.

For the benefit of the prospective purchaser, who may feel interested in more thoroughly understanding the improved features of our scales, we point out, by the aid of the illustrations, some of the parts which have been strengthened. Obviously, it would be tedious to the average reader to go extensively into all minute details, therefore we are brief. The parts are numbered to correspond with the following description:

Main levers often break from too heavy loading. See part No. 5 in first illustration showing manner in which we strengthen our main levers.

1. Extension Levers. These have been made heavier, having been widened and ribs on top and bottom made thicker.
2. Stands, on which extension levers rest, have been strengthened by the addition of more metal in the posts, and by the extra wide and thick rib at back of post.
3. All arches are considerably heavier than heretofore.
4. Links and loops, as well as all our forgings, made of double refined iron instead of the common bar iron used by others.
5. Main levers. Where these break is shown in a separate illustration. Note that we have well fortified our main levers by adding metal where needed.
6. All pivots and knife edges are heavier throughout.
7. Bearing Feet. These, perhaps, more than any other thing are most often broken; for upon them first rests the load. We show, in separate illustration, how bearing feet break. To overcome this we have made ours thicker, as can be seen.

Other Buda Scales Also Made Stronger

While reference has been made in the foregoing to our track scales only, we have strengthened the levers of all the styles and sizes we offer which includes depot, coal-hopper, wagon, stock, grain, portable and others, and with these, as with our track scales, we believe the cost of maintenance will be reduced at least 50 per cent.

This cut illustrates how bearing feet break. Note below how we have made ours much thicker and stronger.

Buda Re-inforced Repair Parts Fit Other Makes of Scales

Bearing feet for Buda Railroad Track Scales are much stronger than others. Note above cut showing where breakage occurs from too light construction.

Our re-inforced levers may be used to repair other makes of scales. They not only, owing to their heavier nature, tend to do away with future trouble, but we can supply them at reasonable prices, and in this respect solicit your inquiries.

Concrete foundation with Five-Section Scale partially erected; also iron stands for dead rail

Scale Foundations

For many years stone, brick and timber were used in the building of foundations for railroad track scales, and these materials are extensively employed even at the present time.

A manifest improvement, which has to commend it both duration and reduced cost of construction, is shown in the cut illustrating a concrete foundation on the opposite page. This style of scale foundation was originated by the superintendent of our scale department who has, for many years, been closely connected with all the details which enter into the manufacture and building of scales.

By the use of the concrete foundation all timber below the scale levers and that which enters into the framework around the top of the brick or stone foundation is done away with, effecting a saving of from $75.00 to $100.00, according to the locality. When it is remembered that the timber work must be restored every five to seven years, it will be seen that the economy does not end with the installation. Then, too, if competent masons and good materials have not been employed the foundation of brick or stone will doubtless require repairs from time to time. Concrete, on the other hand, is superior in the way of permanency—lasting, as it does, an indefinite period and requiring no attention after being built.

The only timber required with the concrete foundation outside of what is used in the platform, is that which composes the large 12x18 inch beams extending the entire length of the scale which rest upon the bearing feet and which support the platform. In place of these we recommend the use of steel "I" beams for the support of the platform. While these cost more to install they are so much stronger and satisfactory, not requiring to be renewed as does timber, that the eventual economy outweighs by far any additional first cost they might represent.

We are pleased to furnish blue-prints of any of these styles of construction giving dimensions and complete building directions.

The Buda Foundry & Manufacturing Company

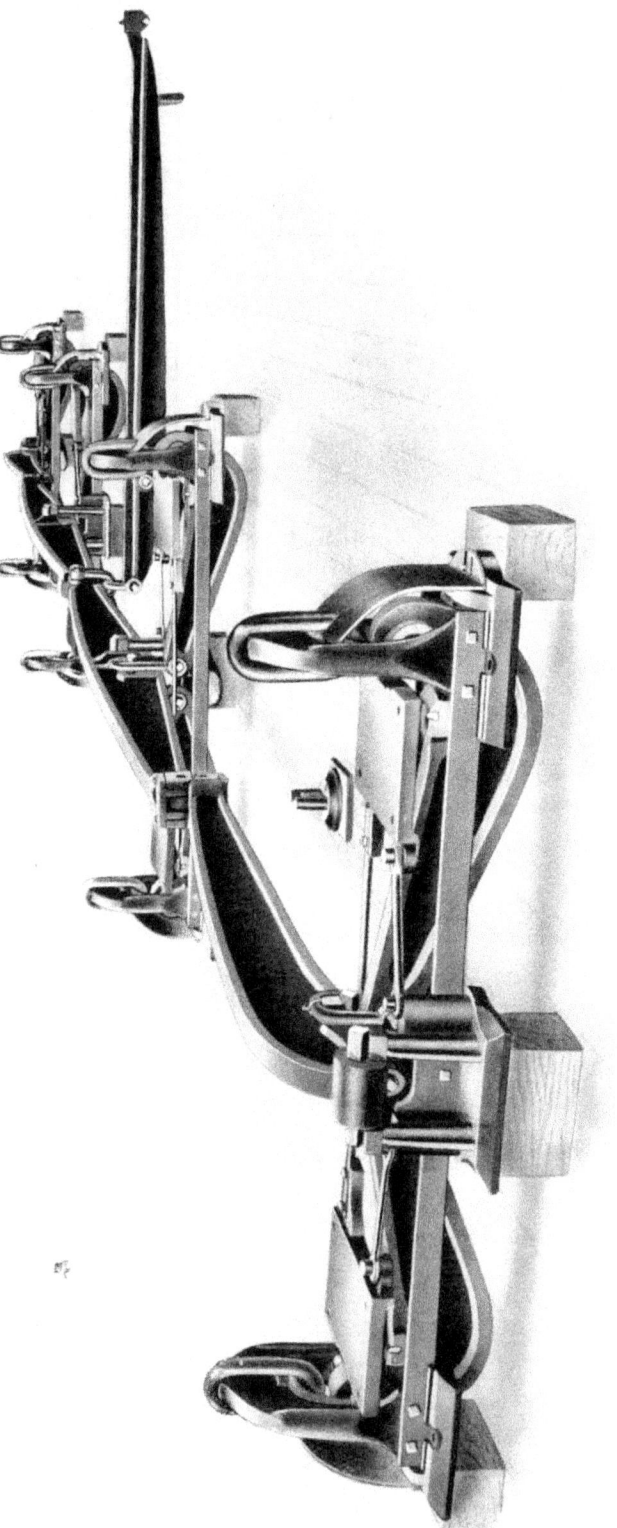

Buda Four-Section R. R. Track Scale

The above scale is assembled and set up on floor for photographic purposes. Description of same, with list of sizes and prices, are on pages following.

A five section pattern is shown on page 10.

Buda Railroad Track Scales

These scales are constructed to meet the demands of the increased weight of rolling stock. All levers subjected to the greatest strains have been designed in a heavier manner, the added metal being used at points where breakages have been frequent. Thus, while the levers contain about 10 per cent. more metal, it has been located in such a way that the total strength has been increased at a conservative estimate about 25 per cent. This should decrease the cost of maintenance at least 50 per cent. and add a like percentage to the life of the scale.

These and other improvements offer advantages which will appeal to railroads, any of which have doubtless had experience enough with scales which break frequently and involve heavy losses by being useless until repaired.

Our manufacturing facilities enable us to produce these scales with the additional metal they contain and offer them at no advance in the first cost over similar scales of lighter construction. The evident economy to be secured by the use of our re-inforced scales, from first cost to longer length of life, with the unintermittent service, cannot fail to interest the prospective purchaser to the extent of investigating the merits of what we have to offer before definitely deciding on any make whatever.

A brief illustrated description of our improved designs of levers and other parts is to be found on pages 8 and 9.

Unless specified, all scales are for standard gauge, 4 ft. 8½ inches. We can furnish them for any gauge, however.

Track scales are usually supplied with single beam which is included in the list of prices shown on next page. Where double or where recording beam is desired, we furnish same at prices shown on pages 16 and 17.

Railroad Track Scales

The prices shown in this list do not include timber and foundations, which are to be supplied by the purchaser, though we furnish building directions and bill of timber required, together with blue prints.

The prices include the single beam. Double beams and recording beam are extra, as shown on pages 16 and 17.

No.	Platform	Capacity	List Price	No.	Platform	Capacity	List Price
4268	30 ft.	30 tons	$ 925.00	4316	38 ft.	40 tons	$1,050.00
4270	30 "	40 "	950.00	4318	38 "	50 "	1,075.00
4272	30 "	50 "	975.00	4320	38 "	60 "	1,100.00
4274	30 "	60 "	1,000.00	4322	38 "	70 "	1,125.00
4276	30 "	70 "	1,025.00	4324	38 "	80 "	1,150.00
4278	30 "	80 "	1,050.00	4357	38 "	100 "	1,200.00
4280	32 ft	30 tons	$ 950.00	4326	40 ft.	50 tons	$1,100.00
4282	32 "	40 "	975.00	4328	40 "	60 "	1,125.00
4284	32 "	50 "	1,000.00	4330	40 "	70 "	1,150.00
4286	32 "	60 "	1,025.00	4332	40 "	80 "	1,175.00
4288	32 "	70 "	1,050.00	4363	40 "	100 "	1,225.00
4290	32 "	80 "	1,075.00	4334	42 ft.	50 tons	$1,125.00
				4336	42 "	60 "	1,150.00
4292	34 ft.	30 tons	$ 975.00	4338	42 "	70 "	1,175.00
4294	34 "	40 "	1,000.00	4340	42 "	80 "	1,200.00
4296	34 "	50 "	1,025.00	4369	42 "	100 "	1,350.00
4298	34 "	60 "	1,050.00				
4300	34 "	70 "	1,075.00	4342	44 ft.	50 tons	$1,150.00
4302	34 "	80 "	1,100.00	4344	44 "	60 "	1,175.00
				4346	44 "	70 "	1,200.00
4304	36 ft.	30 tons	$1,000.00	4348	44 "	80 "	1,225.00
4306	36 "	40 "	1,025.00	4375	44 "	100 "	1,375.00
4308	36 "	50 "	1,050.00	4350	46 ft.	50 tons	$1,175.00
4310	36 "	60 "	1,075.00	4352	46 "	60 "	1,200.00
4312	36 "	70 "	1,100.00	4354	46 "	70 "	1,225.00
4314	36 "	80 "	1,125.00	4356	46 "	80 "	1,350.00
4351	36 "	100 "	1,175.00	4381	46 "	100 "	1,400.00

The Buda Foundry & Manufacturing Company

No.	Platform	Capacity	List Price	No.	Platform	Capacity	List Price
4358	48 ft.	50 tons	$1,200.00	4414	62 ft.	60 tons	$1,600.00
4360	48 "	60 "	1,225.00	4416	62 "	70 "	1,625.00
4362	48 "	70 "	1,250.00	4418	62 "	80 "	1,650.00
4364	48 "	80 "	1,375.00	4429	62 "	100 "	1,700.00
4387	48 "	100 "	1,425.00				
4366	50 ft.	50 tons	$1,325.00	4420	64 ft.	70 tons	$1,650.00
4368	50 "	60 "	1,350.00	4422	64 "	80 "	1,675.00
4370	50 "	70 "	1,375.00	4435	64 "	100 "	1,725.00
4372	50 "	80 "	1,400.00				
4393	50 "	100 "	1,450.00	4424	66 ft.	70 tons	$1,675.00
				4426	66 "	80 "	1,700.00
4374	52 ft.	50 tons	$1,350.00	4441	66 "	100 "	1,850.00
4376	52 "	60 "	1,375.00				
4378	52 "	70 "	1,400.00	4428	68 ft.	70 tons	$1,700.00
4380	52 "	80 "	1,425.00	4430	68 "	80 "	1,725.00
4399	52 "	100 "	1,475.00	4447	68 "	100 "	1,875.00
4382	54 ft.	50 tons	$1,375.00	4432	70 ft.	70 tons	$1,825.00
4384	54 "	60 "	1,400.00	4434	70 "	80 "	1,850.00
4386	54 "	70 "	1,425.00	4453	70 "	100 "	1,900.00
4388	54 "	80 "	1,450.00				
4405	54 "	100 "	1,600.00	4436	72 ft.	70 tons	$1,850.00
				4438	72 "	80 "	1,875.00
4390	56 ft.	50 tons	$1,400.00	4459	72 "	100 "	1,925.00
4392	56 "	60 "	1,425.00				
4394	56 "	70 "	1,450.00	4440	74 ft.	70 tons	$1,875.00
4396	56 "	80 "	1,475.00	4442	74 "	80 "	1,900.00
4411	56 "	100 "	1,625.00	4465	74 "	100 "	1,950.00
4398	58 ft.	50 tons	$1,525.00	4444	76 ft.	70 tons	$1,900.00
4400	58 "	60 "	1,550.00	4446	76 "	80 "	1,925.00
4402	58 "	70 "	1,575.00	4471	76 "	100 "	2,075.00
4404	58 "	80 "	1,600.00				
4417	58 "	100 "	1,650.00	4448	78 ft.	70 tons	$1,925.00
				4450	78 "	80 "	1,950.00
4406	60 ft.	50 tons	$1,550.00	4477	78 "	100 "	2,100.00
4408	60 "	60 "	1,575.00				
4410	60 "	70 "	1,600.00	4452	80 ft.	75 tons	$2,075.00
4412	60 "	80 "	1,625.00	4454	80 "	85 "	2,100.00
4423	60 "	100 "	1,675.00	4483	80 "	100 "	2,150.00

Prices on Scales with longer or shorter platforms than shown in this list, furnished on request.

Beams for Railroad Track Scales

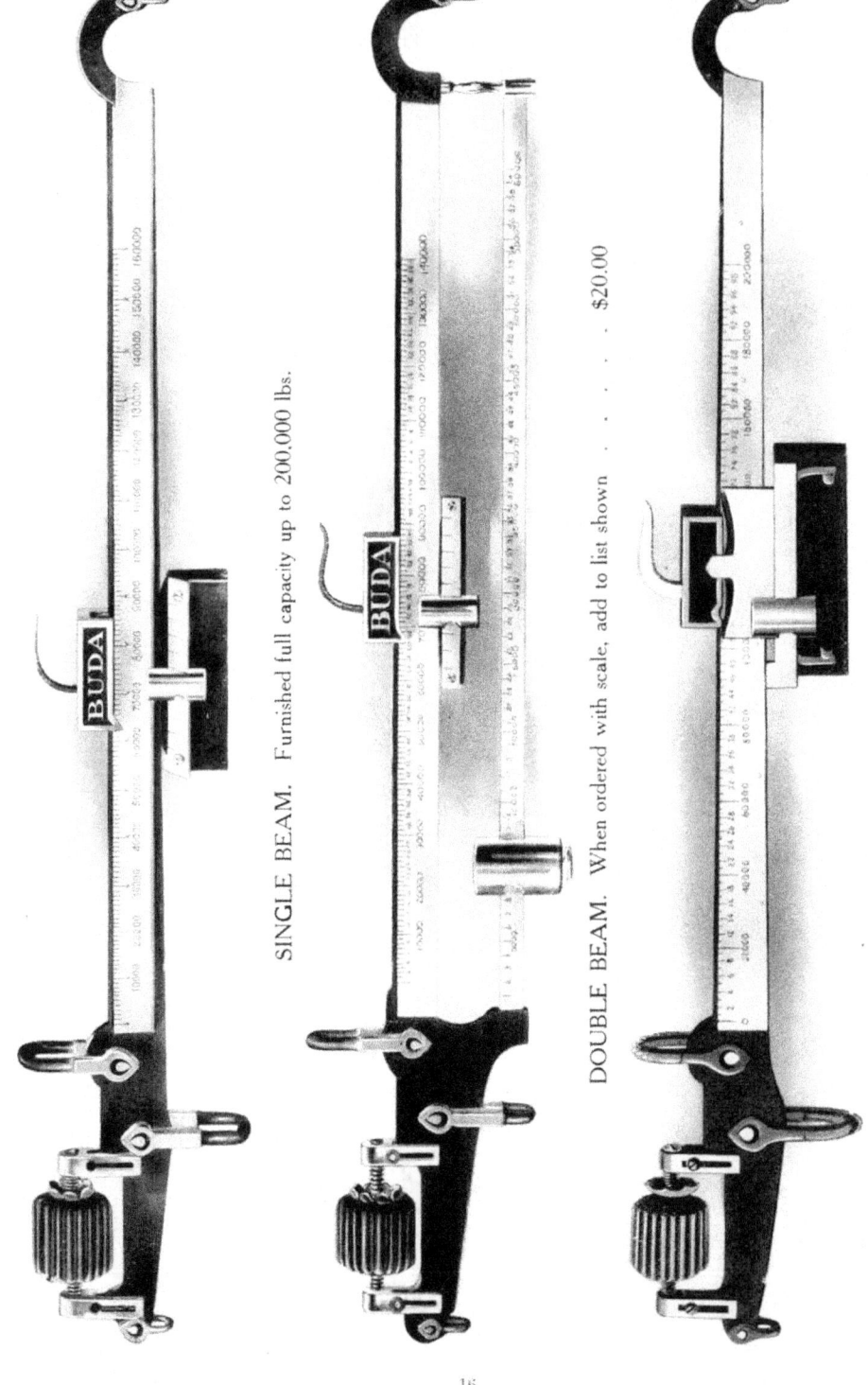

SINGLE BEAM. Furnished full capacity up to 200,000 lbs.

DOUBLE BEAM. When ordered with scale, add to list shown $20.00

RECORDING BEAM FOR R. R. TRACK SCALE. For quickly weighing and accurately recording number of pounds on ticket. Full description given on opposite page. When ordered with scale, add to list shown $140.00

Beams for Railroad Track Scales

Single Beam for Railroad Track Scales

On opposite page is shown the beam which is furnished with railroad track scales without extra charge. It has rolling poise and is graduated up to full capacity of 200,000 lbs.

Double Beam for Railroad Track Scales

These beams are used to show tare weights. The main beam is graduated to a capacity of 60,000 lbs.; the tare beam 35,000 x 50 lbs. If necessary, both beams can be furnished for greater capacity. The double beam is not included in the prices of track scales, and if scale is to be supplied with same, $20.00 should be added to the list shown.

Recording Beams for Railroad Track Scales

The use of the recording beam has spread widely on account of the quick and accurate reading obtained which is punched in the ticket and forms a valuable record in case of disputed weights.

This beam has nothing complicated about its construction; nothing to get out of order and cannot be affected in any way by wear or by the weather. It performs all requirements in the most accurate manner and there is no possibility of making any errors whatever in registering the weight.

Two or three tickets may be punched at a time—the operation is simple. The tickets are placed in the receiver attached to the poise. When the proper weight is obtained, the holder is pressed lightly forward—or toward the beam, which causes the exact weight to be punched instantly.

We furnish tickets which are printed to show date, car number, contents, marked weight, gross, tare and net. The simplicity of the arrangement will appeal to anyone who investigates it.

The list price of recording beam when ordered with scale is $140.00.

Track Scales

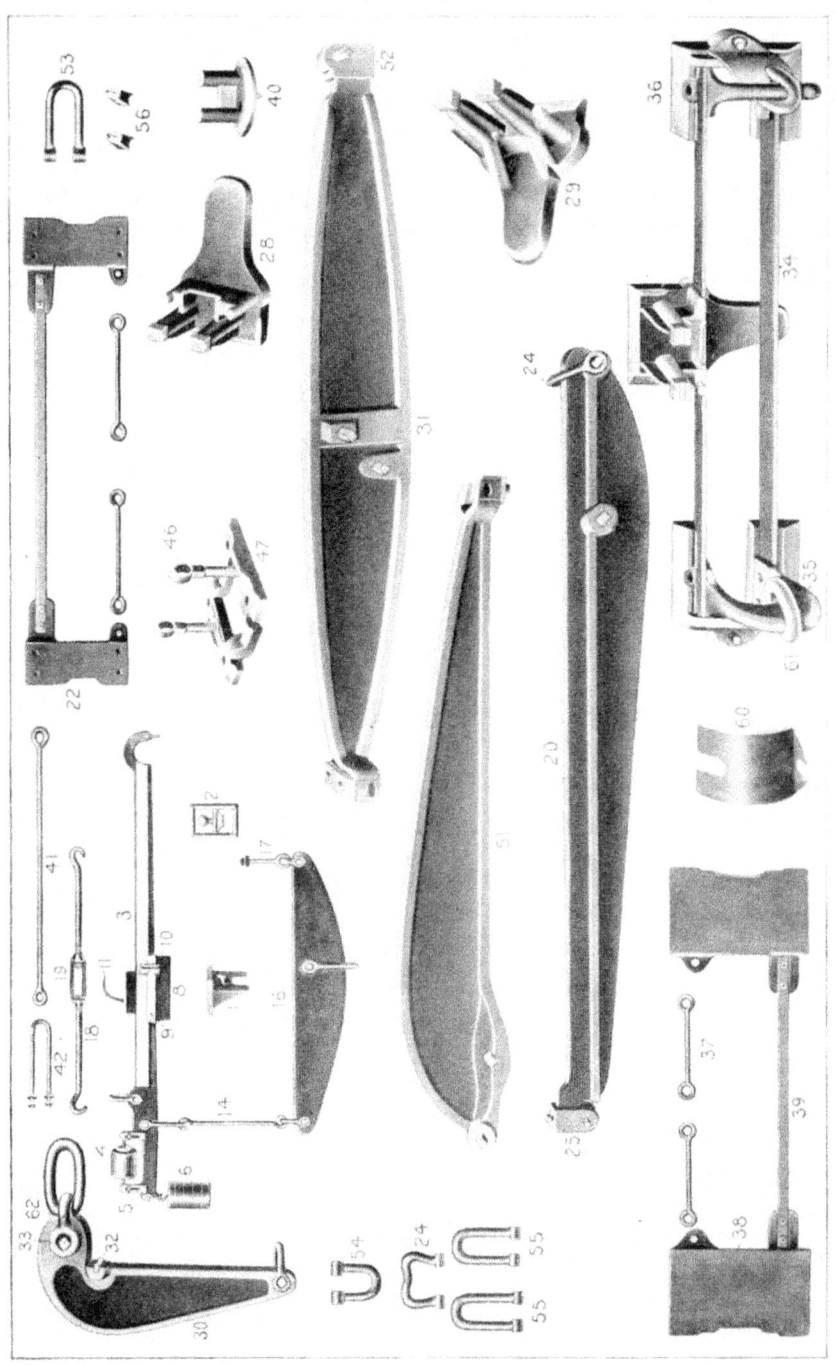

Repair parts of Railroad Track Scales

Railroad Track Scales

List of Parts

In another place we have called attention to the fact that our scale parts have been much strengthened at points subjected to the greatest strain. Inasmuch as our parts will fit scales of other makes the advantage of ordering repairs from us will be apparent.

We are in a position to make attractive prices and aside from the economy secured in this direction you will receive the benefit of the re-inforced features.

1. Beam Hook.
2. Trig Loop.
3. Beam.
4. Balance Ball.
5. Ball Slides.
6. Back Balance.
8. Poise.
9. Fractional Beam.
10. Fractional Poise
11. Dog.
14. Beam Rod.
16. Shelf.
17. Eye Bolt.
18. Steelyard Bolt.
19. Turnbuckle.
20. Fifth Lever.
22. Platform Bearing for "I" beams.
24. Double Loop.
25. Nose Iron Fifth Lever.
28. End Extension Stand.
29. Middle Extension Stand.
30. Main Lever.
31. Middle Extension Lever.

32. Flat Pivot.
33. Main Pivot.
34. Angle Iron.
35. Yoke.
36. End Piece.
37. Cross Check Chain.
38. Platform Bearing.
39. Bearing Rod.
40. Round Stay Iron.
41. Long Check Chain.
42. Check Staple.
46. Stud Loop.
47. Fifth Lever Stand.
51. End Extension Lever.
52. Box Nose Iron.
53. Middle Extension Lever Nose Iron Loop.
54. Short Square Top Loop.
55. Long Square Top Loop.
56. Saddle Block.
60. Bonnet or Shield.
61. Link.
62. Main Loop.

The Buda Foundry & Manufacturing Company

Railway Depot Scales

For use on railway and steamship freight platforms; in baggage rooms; in storehouses, warehouses, etc.

All sizes of these scales have been re-inforced by making the levers heavier and adding considerably to those points where the greatest strain falls. Furnished with single or with double beams at prices shown in following list. The prices given do not include foundations or material for erecting.

No.	Capacity Tons	Size of Platform	Price Single Beam	Price Double Beam
2264	6	10 ft. 0 in. x 9 ft. 2¼ in.	$280.00	$295.00
2266	4	9 ft. 0 in. x 6 ft. 11 in.	230.00	245.00
2268	3	6 ft. 0 in. x 4 ft. 11¼ in.	210.00	218.50
2270	2	7 ft. 6 in. x 4 ft. 8⅛ in.	168.00	176.50

Short Iron Pillar Beam Outfit for Railroad Track Scales

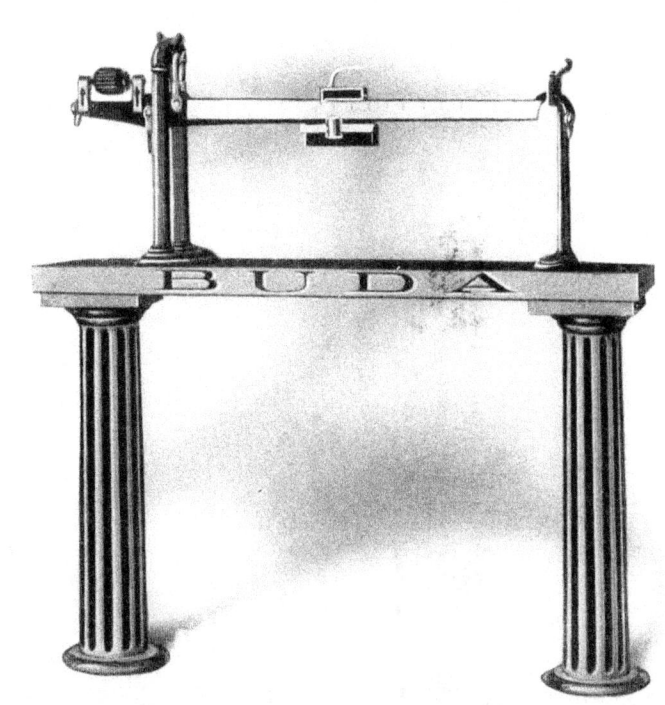

This style of beam arrangement is very convenient where the weighing is done inside an office.

Beam not included in price. Price $35.00

Short Iron Pillar Outfit for Wagon or Stock Scales

Similar to the style used for railroad track scales, but has a differently designed beam support, and has lighter pillars and shelf.

Prices given do not include beam, counterpoise and weights.

Price for 4 to 5 ton scales $25.00

Price for 6 to 15 ton scales $30.00

The Buda Foundry & Manufacturing Company

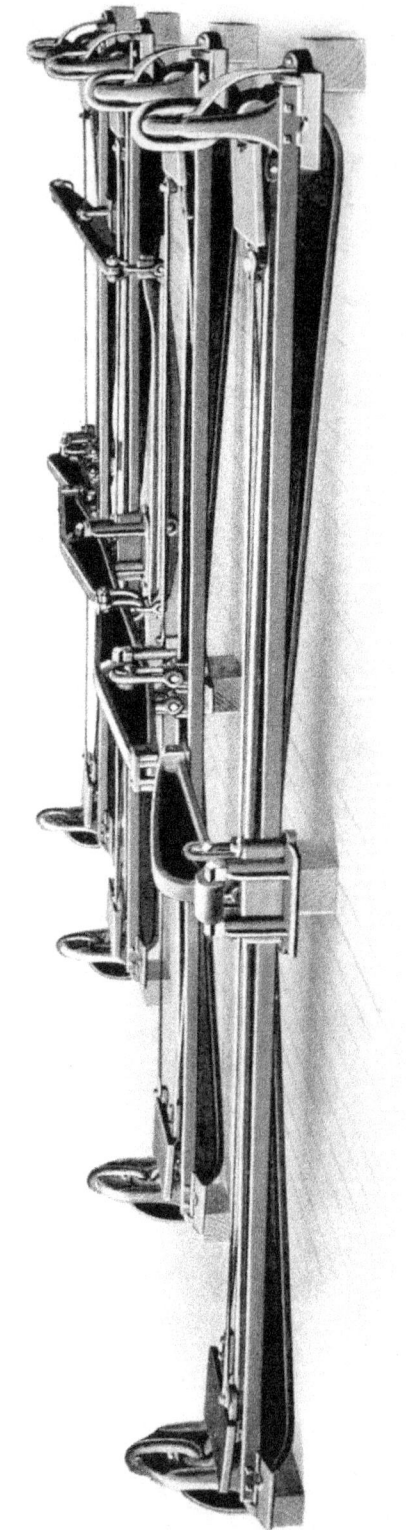

Coaling Station Hopper Scales

The parts above shown were assembled for photographic purposes. These scales are of 100 tons capacity and are strongly built, every part subjected to strain being especially re-inforced. Description follows on next page.

Coaling Station Scales

Modern coaling stations are now being equipped with hopper scales of 100 tons capacity, the length of the station determining the number of hoppers and likewise the number of hopper scales. The above is a sectional illustration of a coaling station, outfitted with three hoppers, each of 100 tons capacity, arranged to discharge on both sides of station; though they are often built with chutes on one side only.

The beams supporting the hopper have been re-inforced, after the manner of our railroad track scales, a description of which is given in the first pages of this booklet. This is a particularly desirable feature in this form of scale, as there is usually a constant load of 100 tons upon the levers at all times.

The beam boxes are located on the ground below the levers. In connection with coal hopper scales, we furnish double poise registering beam. The main beam registers the total amount of coal in hopper, while the subsidiary beam registers the amount to be let out the chute, and a simple arrangement punches the exact number of pounds on one or more tickets with a single operation, thus furnishing an accurate record of coal taken by engines.

Suspension Coal Tipple Scales

This style of scale is for weighing coal at mine or breakers as it comes from screens. Beam can be located above or below scales. Automatic quick weighing outfit may be used in connection, if desired.

The size of platform is ordinarily 14 x 8 feet. Price does not include material for erecting.

No.	Capacity Tons	Platform	Distance from edge of Platform to Beam	Price Single Beam	Price Double Beam
2147	4	14 x 8 ft.	1 ft. 9 in.	$175	$185
2155	5	14 x 8 ft.	1 ft. 9 in.	200	210
2149	6	14 x 7½ ft.	1 ft. 9 in.	235	250
2151	10	14 x 7½ ft.	1 ft. 9 in.	285	300
2152	12	14 x 7½ ft.	1 ft. 9 in.	305	320

Miners' and Transportation Scales

For Use also on Small Railways and in Factories

This scale is shown in use at mine where lorry cars are weighed in tipple. The No. 2145 has extra wide platform permitting two tracks so that one man can weigh from both cages.

The other sizes are also used for weighing small truck loads of ore and are likewise used on industrial and other small railways, factories, etc.

Full capacity for beam for 2 to 5 ton scale, extra $20.00; 6 to 10 ton scale, extra $30.00.

Quick weighing device may be fitted to any of these sizes.

Prices do not include material for erecting.

No.	Tons	Platform	Single Beam	Double Beam
2176	2	6 ft. x 4 ft. 11¼ in.	$135.60	$143.50
2192	2	5 ft. x 4 ft.	135.00	143.50
2166	3	5 ft. x 4 ft.	155.00	163.50
2190	3	6 ft. x 4 ft. 11¼ in.	155.00	163.50
2188	4	6½ ft. x 4 ft. 10⅜ in.	170.00	180.00
2162	5	7 ft. x 4 ft. 9¼ in.	185.00	195.00
2186	5	5 ft. x 4 ft.	185.00	195.00
2184	6	7½ ft. x 4 ft. 8⅛ in.	205.00	215.00
2158	8	7½ in. x 4 ft. 8⅛ in.	240.00	250.00
2156	10	8 ft. x 4 ft. 6½ in.	270.00	280.00
2145	4	6 ft. x 9 ft. 11½ in.		160.00

Wagon and Stock Scales

Very durable in all parts and those levers upon which greatest strains fall have been re-inforced by the addition of more metal, properly placed, and by desirable changes in design of strengthening ribs.

For weighing stock a rack is placed on platform.

Should certain changes in size of platform be desired, this can be arranged, as can also extension of distance from beam box to platform. If this extension does not exceed 18 inches over distance shown in the list, we make no charge; over 18 inches special price will be quoted. We furnish with each scale a neat beam box without charge. Should short iron pillar outfit be desired—for use inside of office—the price of same and illustration will be found on page 21. The prices shown do not include timber, foundations, or stock rack, which are to be furnished by purchaser.

For description of beam outfits, see pages 30-31.

No.	Capacity Tons	Size of Platform	Distance from Edge of Platform to Beam Rod	Price Single Beam	Price Double Beam	Price Comp'd Beam
1801	15	22x10 ft.	2 ft. 4½ in.	$440.00	$455.00	$470.00
1824	15	22x7 ft. 11 in.	3 ft. 1⅜ in.	420.00	435.00	450.00
1838	15	22x7 ft. 3 in.	3 ft. 10 in.	420.00	435.00	450.00
1829	10	22x7 ft. 11 in.	3 ft. 1⅜ in.	360.00	375.00	390.00
1843	10	22x7 ft. 2⅞ in.	3 ft. 9½ in.	350.00	365.00	380.00
1845	8	22x7 ft. 2⅞ in.	3 ft. 9½ in.	315.00	330.00	345.00
1924	15	16x7 ft. 9⅝ in.	1 ft. 10⅞ in.	390.00	405.00	420.00
1928	10	16x7 ft. 10 in.	1 ft. 10½ in.	300.00	315.00	330.00
1930	8	16x7 ft. 10 in.	1 ft. 10½ in.	275.00	290.00	305.00
1932	6	16x7 ft. 10 in.	1 ft. 10½ in.	250.00	265.00	280.00
1926	12	14x8 ft. 4¼ in.	2 ft. 1 in.	320.00	335.00	350.00
1928	10	14x8 ft. 4⅝ in.	2 ft. 0¾ in.	300.00	315.00	330.00
1930	8	14x8 ft. 4⅝ in.	2 ft. 0¾ in.	275.00	290.00	305.00
2110	6	14x8 ft.	2 ft. 2½ in.	225.00	240.00	255.00
2112	5	14x8 ft.	2 ft. 2½ in.	200.00	210.00	220.00
2114	4	14x8 ft.	2 ft. 2½ in.	170.00	180.00	190.00

Extra Heavy Railroad Pattern

Full Capacity Railroad Beam

No.	Capacity Tons	Size of Platform	Price R. R. Beam	Price Doub. Beam
6580	15	14 x 8	$450.00	$470.00
6582	20	14 x 8	475.00	495.00
6602	20	16 x 8	500.00	520.00
6622	20	18 x 8	525.00	545.00
6624	30	18 x 8	550.00	570.00
6642	20	20 x 8	600.00	620.00
6644	30	20 x 8	625.00	645.00
6683	25	24 x 8	700.00	720.00

Stock Scales

Exceptionally strong and calculated to withstand heavy usage; we are also in position to supply larger sizes than shown here, so that full carloads may be weighed at one time. On the large sizes we are pleased to quote special prices.

The prices shown do not include timber for rack or for construction of scale or cost of foundation.

No.	Capacity Lbs.	Size of Platform Over-all	Size of Platform Inside Cattle Rack	No. Cattle Platform Will Hold	Price
1802	30,000	22 ft. x 10 ft. 4 in.	20 ft. 10 in. x 9 ft. 2 in.	20 to 25	$440.00
1804	24,000	22 ft. x 10 ft. 4 in.	20 ft. 10 in. x 9 ft. 2 in.	20 to 25	395.00
1806	20,000	22 ft. x 10 ft. 4 in.	20 ft. 10 in. x 9 ft. 2 in.	20 to 25	365.00
1824	30,000	22 ft. x 7 ft. 11 in.	20 ft. 10 in. x 6 ft. 9 in.	15 to 20	420.00
1843	20,000	22 ft. x 7 ft. 3 in.	20 ft. 10 in. x 6 ft. 1 in.	10 to 15	350.00
1840	24,000	18 ft. x 8 ft. 3 in.	16 ft. 10 in. x 7 ft. 1 in.	10 to 15	365.00

Dump Scales

At grain elevators and warehouses it is often desired to facilitate the unloading of wagons by dumping as shown in the illustrations. This scale has specially designed levers and controllable dumping arrangement so that the incline of wagon may be regulated. This is a very convenient arrangement and one which saves a great deal of time and facilitates weighing.

Prices given do not include cost of foundation or material for erecting.

				Price	
			Distance from Edge of	Single	Double
No.	Capacity	Platform	Platform to Beam Rod	Beam	Beam
2051	4 tons	14 x 8 ft.	2 ft. 3 in.	$170.00	$180.00
2065	5 tons	14 x 8 ft.	2 ft. 3 in.	200.00	210.00
2053	6 tons	14 x 8 ft.	2 ft. 3 in.	225.00	240.00
2055	4 tons	15 x 8 ft.	2 ft. 3 in.	175.00	185.00
2067	5 tons	15 x 8 ft.	2 ft. 3 in.	205.00	215.00
2057	6 tons	15 x 8 ft.	2 ft. 3 in.	230.00	245.00
2059	4 tons	16 x 8 ft.	2 ft. 3 in.	180.00	190.00
2069	5 tons	16 x 8 ft.	2 ft. 3 in.	210.00	220.00
2061	6 tons	16 x 8 ft.	2 ft. 3 in.	235.00	250.00
2063	6 tons	22 x 8 ft.	2 ft. 3 in.	250.00	265.00

Iron Dealers Scales

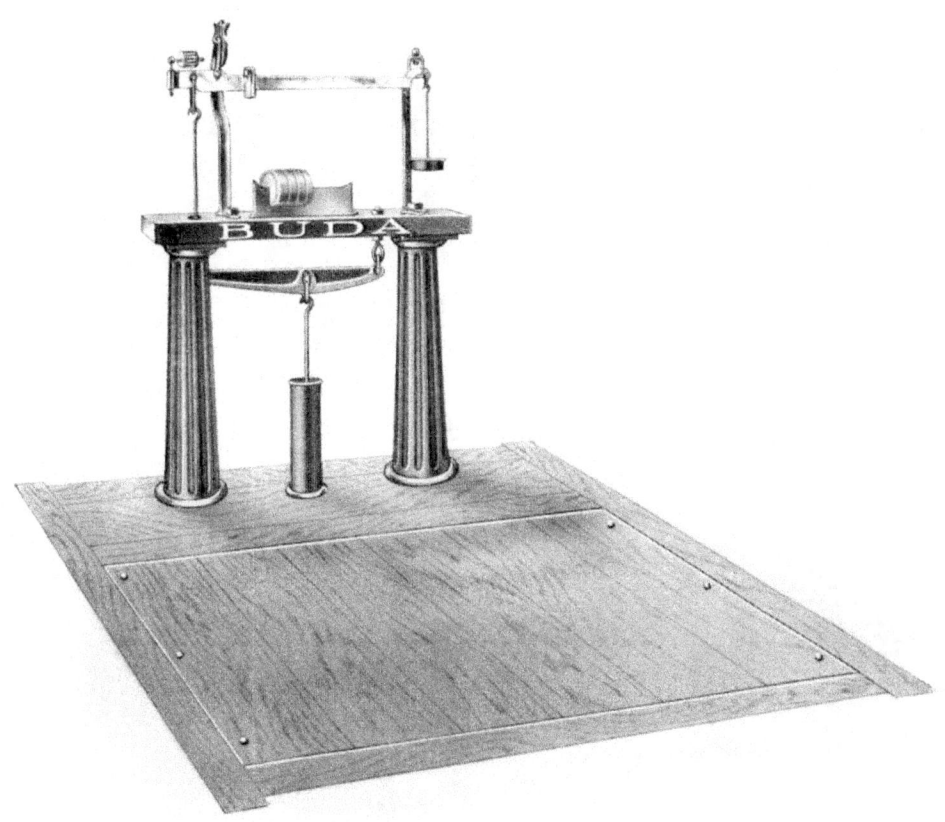

The weighing of metals requires scales that are not only unusually strong, but are sensitive as well, and this latter is particularly necessary where metals of higher value are handled. Inaccuracy and variation are expensive and often entailed unaccountable losses. Any of our scales may be depended upon in all seasons.

If double beam is desired an extra charge of $10.00 to list shown will be made. Full capacity beam, doing away with use of weights may be ordered as follows: 4 tons, $20.00 extra; 6 to 10 tons, $30.00 extra.

No.	Capacity, Tons.	Size of Platform.	Price.
2185	4	5 ft. x 4 ft. 6 in.	$235.00
2153	4	6 ft. x 4 ft. 8 in.	265.00
2171	6	6 ft. x 3 ft. 5 in.	300.00
2175	6	6 ft. x 4 ft. 8 in.	315.00
2179	10	6 ft. x 4 ft. 8 in.	350.00

Beams for Wagon and Stock Scales

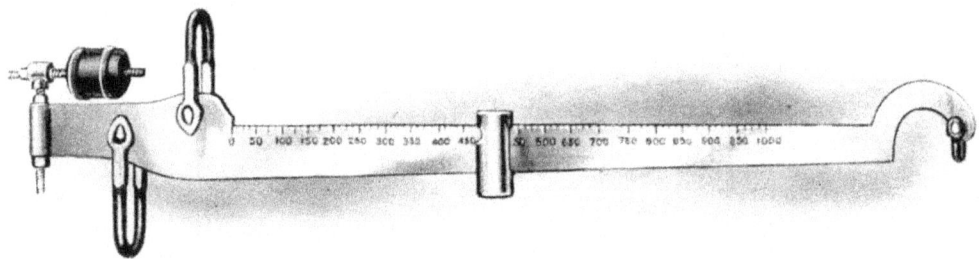

SINGLE BEAM

This beam has 1000 pounds capacity shown, on the graduations, the full capacity being made up by counterpoise and loose weights.

DOUBLE BEAM

The advantage of the double beam is that tare weights may be readily taken.

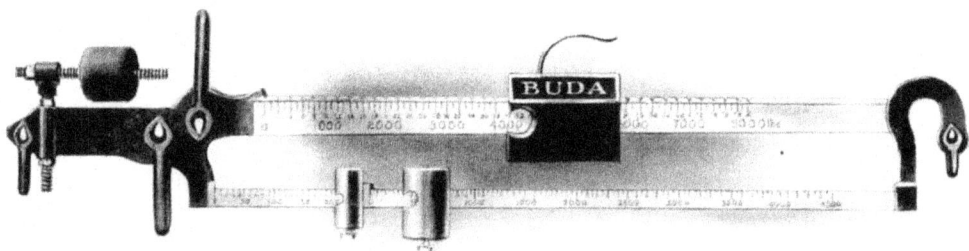

COMPOUND BEAM

This beam has full capacity of scale and requires no weights.

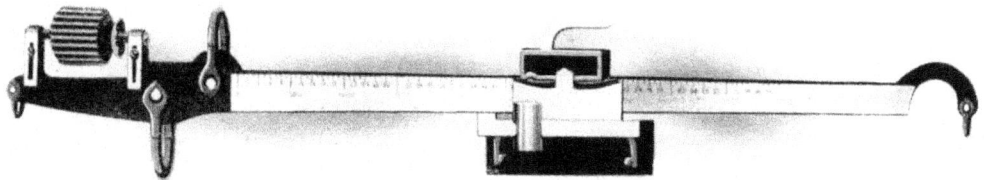

Recording Beams for Wagon Scales

The purpose of this beam is to provide an arrangement for recording accurately the number of pounds on the scale.

It is often desirable to have such records in the event of disputed weights. By a simple device the weigher is enabled to punch the exact weight on one or more cards, the operation occasioning no delay, in fact saving much time over any other method.

This beam is exactly the same in principle as that used with railroad track scales, the only difference being in the size and capacity with ticket to correspond.

In construction, it is perfectly simple. There is nothing to be affected by wear, dirt or by climatic conditions. Prices quoted on request.

Recording Beams for Grain Hopper Scales

The advantages obtained by the use of recording beams in connection with grain hopper scales, are indentical with those of railroad track and of wagon scales. As is the case with our other recording beams, the weights are registered on a card in an indisputable manner, and form a valuable record. The design of this beam differs slightly from that of the wagon scale, but the general principle is the same.

Prices quoted on application.

Quick Weighing Beams

Quick weighing beams are intended largely for use in weighing cars in motion, such as at mines, and docks.

A special beam is provided which is made steady by means of a dash pot. The beam is also connected with a dial and indicator, the latter showing the weight at once, and when load is discharged, the indicator goes back to zero.

It is a useful device in connection with coal hopper scales, as the weight is quickly ascertained, enabling an immediate discharge of coal, and refilling, the vibration of levers and beam being arrested by dash pot.

The quick-weighing dial may also be used in connection with wagon, depot and other scales, where quick work and reasonable accuracy is more desirable than fine adjustments.

Wagon and Stock Scales

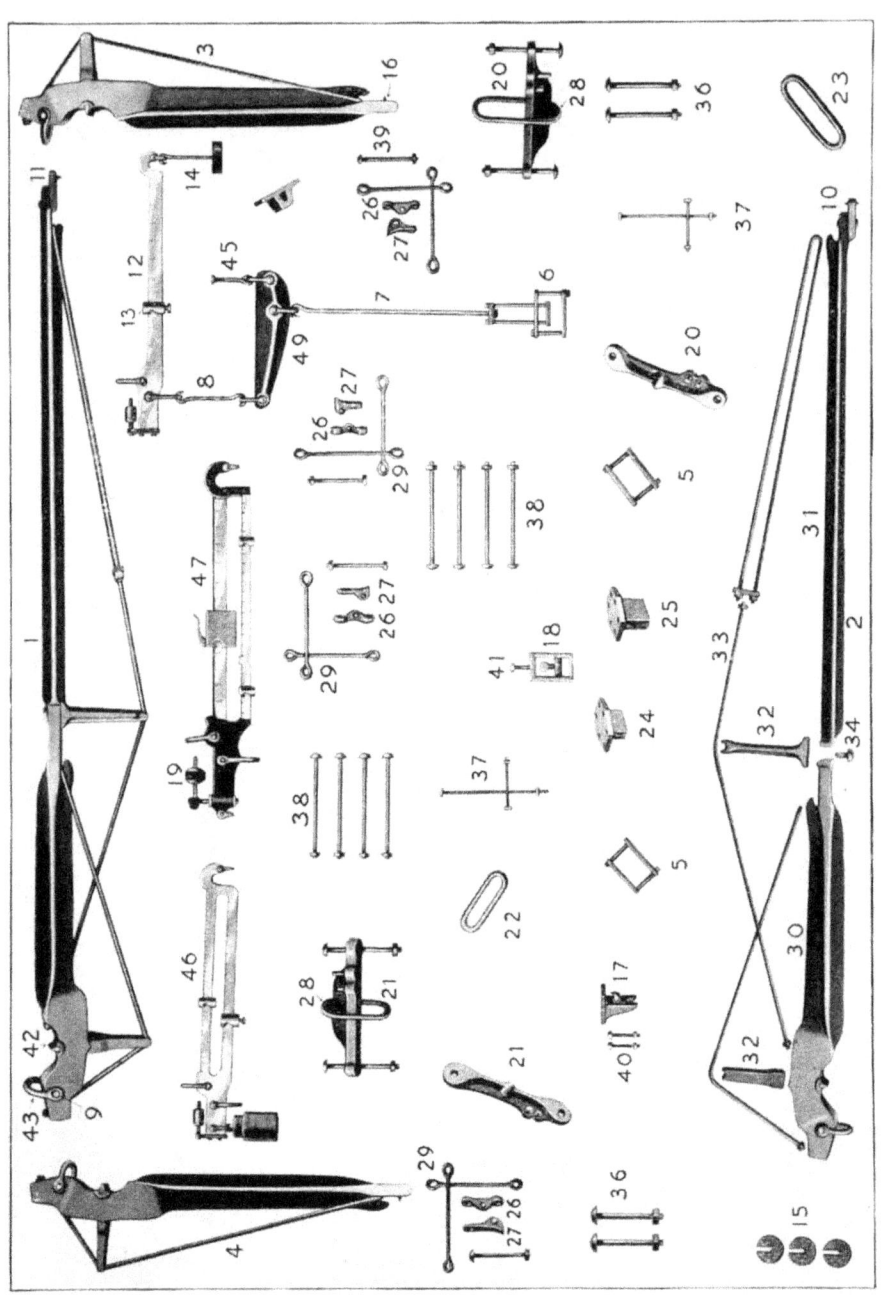

Repair parts of Wagon and Stock Scales

Wagon, Stock and Depot Scales

LIST OF PARTS

As in our other styles, we have here strengthened, by the proper placing of metal, all parts subjected to greatest strains. These parts fit scales of other makes, and by ordering repairs from us you can secure the advantage of our re-inforced features, and favorable prices as well.

1. Left-hand Lever.	24. Bearing 1 and 2.
2. Right-hand Lever.	25. Bearing 3 and 4.
3. Right-hand Short Lever.	26. Flat Stay Irons.
4. Left-hand Short Lever.	27. Square Stay Irons.
5. Center Loops.	28. Swivel Blocks.
6. Shackle.	29. Check Rods.
7. Steelyard Rod.	30. Butt Lever.
8. Beam Rod.	31. Splice Lever.
9. Main Pivot.	32. Truss Posts.
10. Nose Iron No. 2.	33. Truss Rods.
11. Nose Iron No. 1.	34. Truss Post Bolt.
12. Beam.	36. Corner Iron Bolts.
13. Poise.	37. Cupboard Bolts.
14. Counterpoise.	38. Platform Bolts.
15. Weights.	39. Stay Iron Bolts.
16. Button Nose Iron.	40. Beam Hook Bolts.
17. Beam Hook.	41. Trig Loop Bolt.
18. Trig Loop.	42. Bearing Pivot.
19. Balance Ball.	43. Main Loops.
20. Corner Iron 2 and 4.	44. Shelf Lever.
21. Corner Iron 1 and 3.	45. Eye Bolt.
22. Links 1 and 2.	46. Double Beam.
23. Links 3 and 4.	47. Compound Beam.

Hopper Scales for Grain

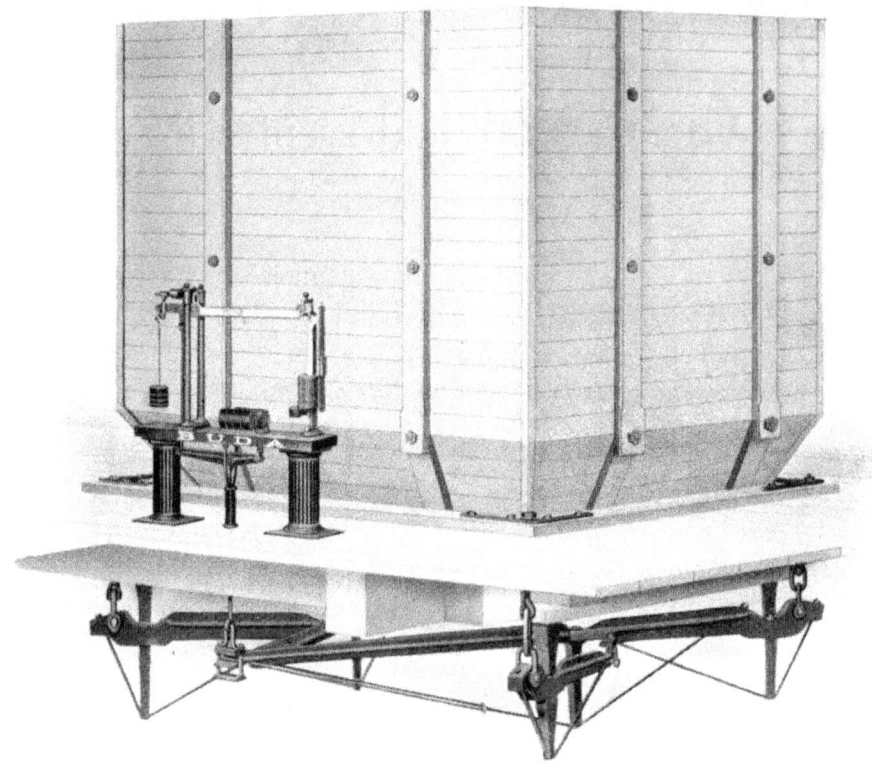

Trussed Lever Pattern

The scales here illustrated while shown with wood framing are intended for use with metal framing also and in the large sizes we recommend the latter.

The levers are of strengthened design, aside from the truss reinforcements, and are perfect in adjustment and action, so that there is no variation in weights. This style is principally used in grain warehouses, elevators, breweries, etc., and being unusually well built, as compared with other scales of this class, we recommend that their merits be considered when purchasing. Adjustable check rods and corner irons are provided to compensate for settled buildings, thereby preserving at all times a perfect level.

Recording beam for grain hopper scales is mentioned on page 31. Prices do not include hopper, or timber, or steel for framing.

Trussed Lever Pattern—Wood Framing

No.	Cap. Bush.	Opening for Hopper.	Price.
1746	100	3 ft. 0 in. x 3 ft. 0 in.	$155.00
1748	150	3 ft. 0 in. x 3 ft. 0 in.	205.00
1750	200	4 ft. 0 in. x 4 ft. 0 in.	225.00
1752	300	3 ft. 8 in. x 3 ft. 8 in.	285.00
1762	400	4 ft. 6 in. x 4 ft. 6 in.	320.00
1764	500	4 ft. 6 in. x 4 ft. 6 in.	350.00
1768	600	5 ft. 10 in. x 5 ft. 10 in.	390.00
1770	700	5 ft. 6 in. x 5 ft. 6 in.	430.00
1772	800	5 ft. 6 in. x 5 ft. 6 in.	475.00
1794	1000	6 ft. 3 in. x 6 ft. 3 in.	600.00
1796	1200	6 ft. 3 in. x 6 ft. 3 in.	700.00

Trussed Lever Pattern—Steel Framing

No.	Cap. Bush.	Opening for Hopper.	Price.
1739	1400	6 ft. 10 in. x 6 ft. 10 in.	$800.00
1741	1600	6 ft. 10 in. x 6 ft. 10 in.	900.00
1731	1800	10 ft. 9 in. x 11 ft. 9 in.	1100.00
1733	2000	10 ft. 9 in. x 11 ft. 9 in.	1200.00

Hopper Scales for Grain

Iron Frame Pattern

Where vertical space is limited the iron frame pattern is extremely desirable. Instead of levers being located beneath floor they are arranged to set on floor itself. Like our trussed lever patterns, these scales are fitted with adjustable check rods and corner irons to preserve a perfect level where located in buildings that tend to settle.

The hopper openings given below have reference to wood framing and scales will be so furnished unless otherwise ordered. For the larger sizes, however, we recommend the steel framing as shown in illustration. The prices shown do not include hopper, or timber, or steel for framing.

If recording beam is desired, same can be furnished. This beam is mentioned on page 31.

No.	Bush.	Opening for Hopper.	Price.
1701	200	6 ft. 7 in. x 6 ft. 7 in.	$225.00
1703	300	6 ft. 7 in. x 6 ft. 7 in.	285.00
1707	400	6 ft. 7 in. x 6 ft. 7 in.	320.00
1709	500	8 ft. 0 in. x 8 ft. 0 in.	350.00
1711	600	8 ft. 0 in. x 8 ft. 0 in.	400.00
1713	700	8 ft. 0 in. x 8 ft. 0 in.	450.00
1715	800	8 ft. 0 in. x 8 ft. 0 in.	500.00
1717	1000	8 ft. 0 in. x 8 ft. 0 in.	600.00
1719	1200	8 ft. 0 in. x 8 ft. 0 in.	700.00

Hopper Scales for Grain

Dormant Pattern

For weighing grain in lots of 60 to 125 bushels we furnish these scales in the sizes and capacities shown below. They are well built and sensitive and are largely in use at small grain warehouses, flour mills and in floating elevators. The scales are set in floor as pictured. The prices do not include hoppers.

With Iron Pillars

No.	Capacity, Bush.	Pounds.	Platform, Inches.	Opening for Hopper.	Price.
1608	60	3,600 x ½	42 x 44	15 x 15 in.	$125.00
1612	100	6,000 x 1	48 x 48	22 x 22 in.	160.00
1616	125	7,500 x 1	48 x 48	22 x 22 in.	180.00

With Single Wood Pillar

No.	Capacity, Bush.	Pounds.	Platform, Inches.	Opening for Hopper.	Price.
1606	60	3,600 x ½	42 x 44	15 x 15 in.	$105.00
1610	100	6,000 x ½	48 x 48	22 x 22 in.	140.00
1614	125	7,500 x ½	48 x 48	22 x 22 in.	160.00

First dimensions are parallel to pillars.

Dormant Warehouse Scales

With Tall Iron Pillar Outfit and Double Beam

These scales are for use in warehouses, etc., and are equipped with tall iron pillar outfit. This is a very substantial arrangement and is much in use. For some locations the short iron pillar outfit is preferred—not being as high—and where this is desired we furnish it instead.

Price of full capacity beam, extra, $20.00.

No.	Capacity.	Platform.	Platform to Pillar.	Single Beam Iron Weights.	Single Beam Brass Weights.	Double Beam Iron Weights.	Double Beam Brass Weights.
1046	5000 x ½ lb.	48 in. x 48 in.	23 in.	$170.00	$208.85	$180.00	$218.85
1069	4000 x ½ lb.	48 in. x 48 in.	23 in.	155.00	179.15	165.00	189.15
1048	3500 x ½ lb.	42 in. x 44 in.	12 in.	125.00	151.60	133.00	159.60
1052	3500 x ½ lb.	42 in. x 44 in.	20 in.	133.60	159.60	141.60	167.60
1067	3000 x ½ lb.	46 in. x 37 in.	11 in.	115.00	132.85	123.00	140.85
1050	2500 x ½ lb.	46 in. x 37 in.	12 in.	105.00	124.25	113.00	132.25

First dimensions are parallel to pillars.

Dormant Warehouse Scales

With Short Iron Pillar Outfit

The short iron pillar outfit is often found more desirable for some locations, as the pillars are not so high and are therefore more convenient where space is a consideration. The single, double, or full capacity beam may be used and the particular kind desired should be specified. The full capacity beam does away with use of loose weights. This may be ordered at an additional price of $20.00.

			Prices,	
No.	Capacity.	Platform.	Single Beam.	Double Beam.
1035	5000 x ½ lb.	48 in. x 48 in.	$150.00	$160.00
1037	4000 x ½ lb.	48 in. x 48 in.	135.00	145.00
1039	3500 x ½ lb.	42 in. x 44 in.	110.00	118.00
1053	3500 x ½ lb.	42 in. x 44 in.	118.00	126.00
1059	3000 x ½ lb.	46 in. x 37 in.	100.00	108.00
1041	2500 x ½ lb.	46 in. x 37 in.	95.00	103.00

First dimensions are parallel to pillars.

Dormant Warehouse Scales

WITH SINGLE WOOD PILLAR

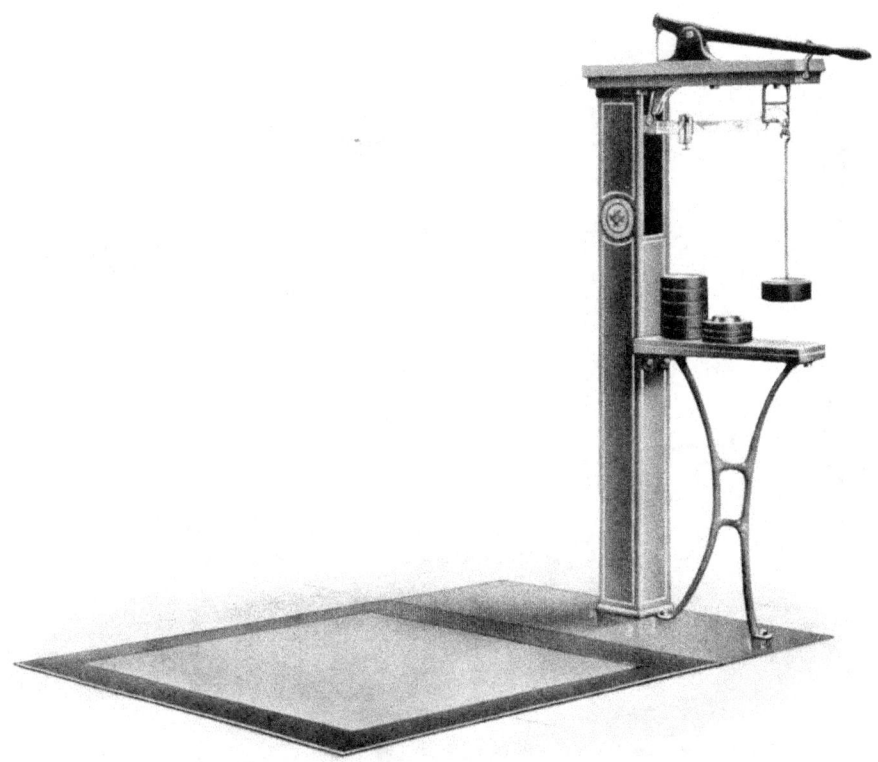

With Drop Lever or Without Drop Lever

Where there is considerable weighing to be done in one location, making it unnecessary to haul scales to different parts of building, this form of scale is extremely handy for the platform, being even with floor it does away with the necessity of lifting load up on scale—as is the case where the portable styles are used. Barrels, boxes, or trucks may thus rapidly be placed on or taken off platform, facilitating the amount of weighing greatly.

These scales may be ordered with or without drop lever.

No.	No.	Capacity	Platform	Platform to Pillar	Price
1036	1026 D. L.	5000 x ½ lb.	48 x 48	23 in.	$145.00
1038	1028 D. L.	3500 x ½ lb.	42 x 44	12 in.	105.00
1019	1023 D. L.	3000 x ½ lb.	46 x 37	11 in.	95.00
1040	1030 D. L.	2500 x ½ lb.	46 x 37	12 in.	90.00

First dimensions given are parallel to beam

Dormant Scales

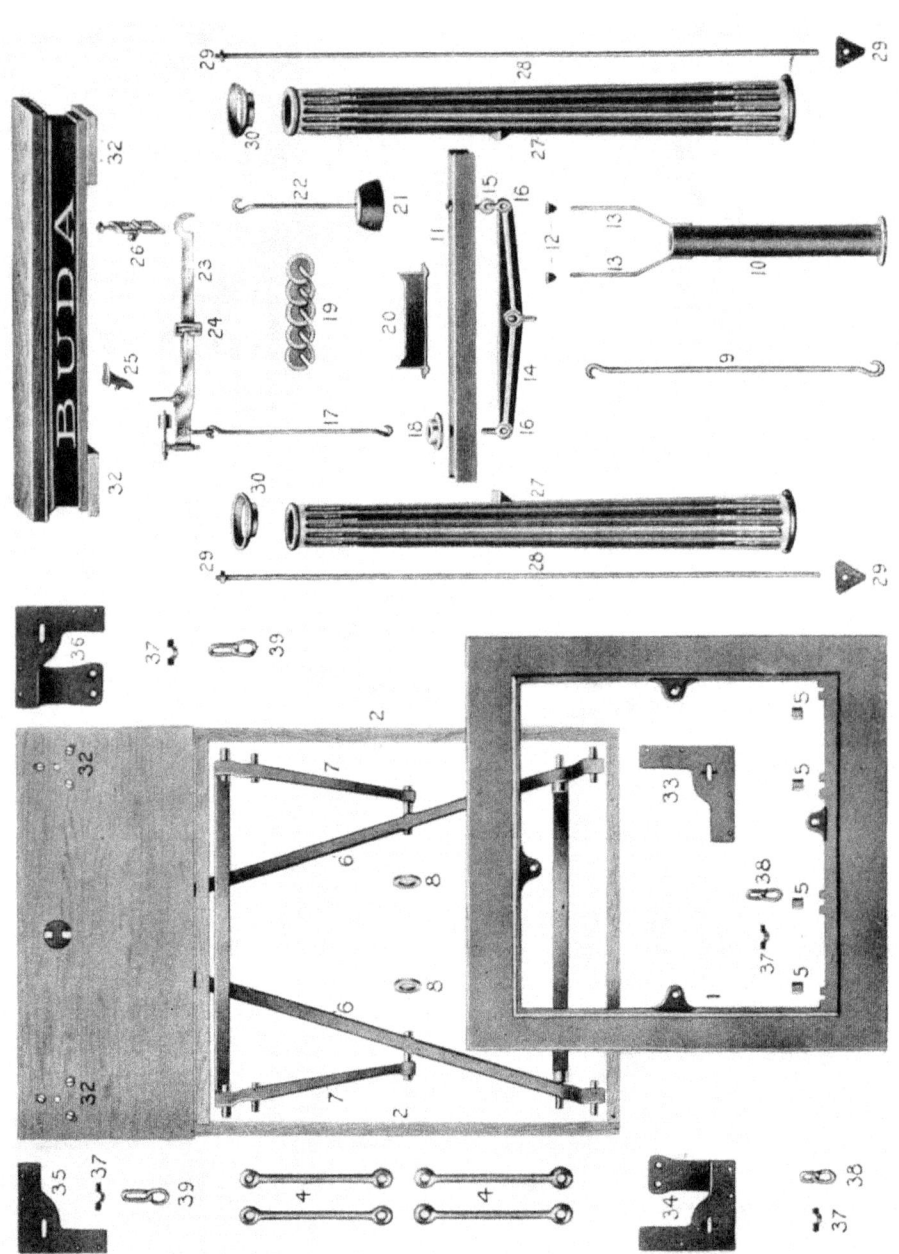

Repair Parts, Dormant Scales

Dormant Scales

LIST OF PARTS

1. Platform.
2. Box.
3. Neck board.
4. Check rods.
5. Blocks.
6. Long lever.
7. Short lever.
8. Rings.
9. Steelyard rod.
10. Tube.
11. Shelf.
12. Shelf irons.
13. Tube straps.
14. Shelf lever.
15. Shelf lever eye-bolt.
16. Shelf lever loops.
17. Beam rod.
18. Beam rod thimble.
19. Weights.
20. Weight rack.
21. Counterpoise.
22. Counterpoise stem.
23. Beam.
24. Poise.
25. Beam hook.
26. Trig loop.
27. Pillars.
28. Pillar rods.
29. Pillar rod nuts.
30. Pillar capitals.
31. Cap.
32. Buttons.
33. No. 1 Corner iron.
34. No. 2 Corner iron.
35. No. 3 Corner iron.
36. No. 4 Corner iron.
37. Pins.
38. Loop and link for long lever.
39. Loop and link for short lever.

Portable Platform Scales

Without Drop Lever

This is a good scale and is thoroughly substantial. All metal parts are well made of good material. The bearings and pivots are of tempered steel, hard wood platform, extra strong wheels and generally rugged in design.

This style is considerably used for weighing purposes within certain capacities and for such is unequalled by any similar scale.

No.	Lbs. Capacity.	Platform, Inches.	Price.
1116	2,500 x ½	26 x 34	$85.00
1118	2,000 x ½	25 x 33	75.00
1120	1,500 x ½	21 x 28	56.00
1122	1,200 x ½	20 x 28	49.00
1124	1,000 x ½	18 x 27	43.00
1126	800 x ¼	17 x 26	38.00
1128	600 x ¼	16 x 25	33.00

First dimensions given are parallel to beam

Drop Lever Portable Scales

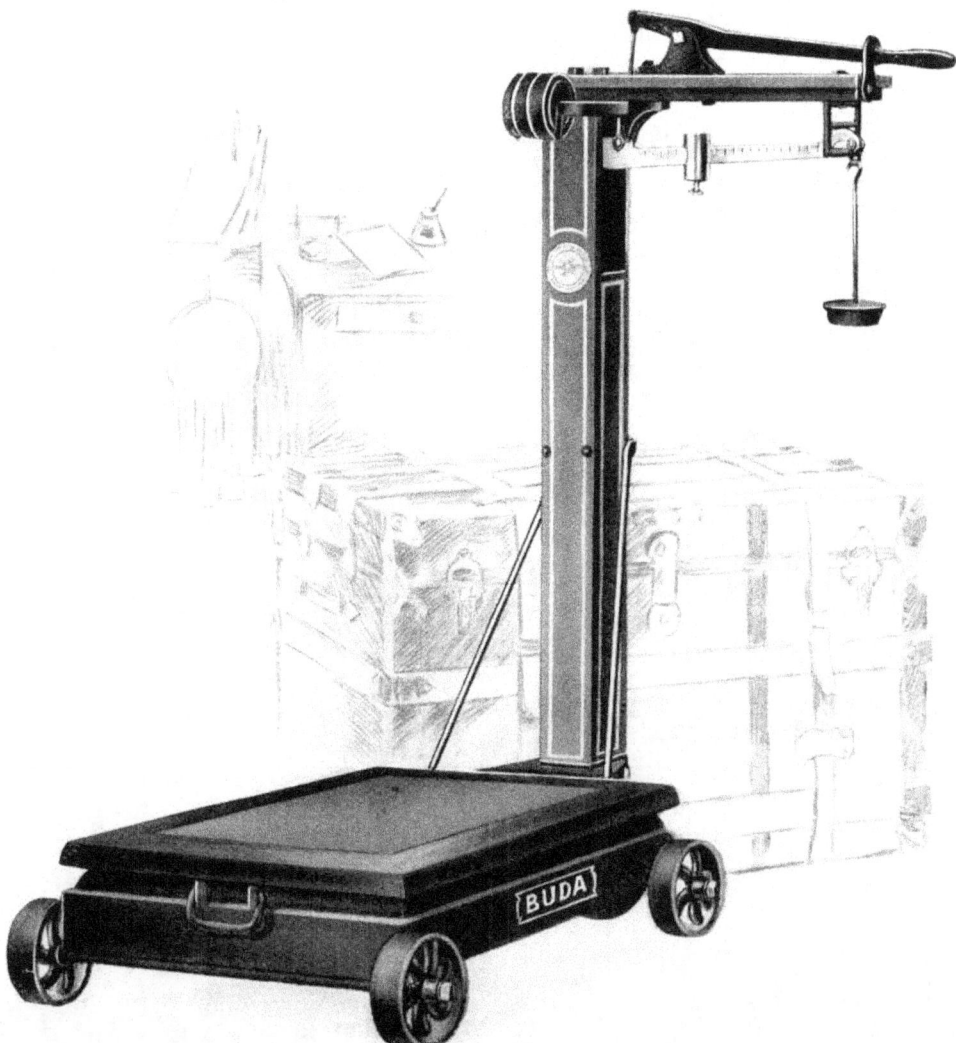

With Drop Lever

For general weighing purposes, and use in smaller freight houses, warehouses, baggage rooms, etc. This is a rugged scale, and well adapted for railroad use. It is supplied also with drop lever, by which means the levers are lowered, allowing the platform to rest upon the frame so that the bearings are relieved from all strain except during the actual process of weighing. This is a particularly desirable arrangement when heavy articles are being handled, as it prevents breakage of scale in putting them on or taking them off the platform.

The single beams have sliding poises graduated up to 100 lbs. by one-half pound divisions. The capacities of the scales are shown in the following list:

No.	Lbs. Capacity.	Platform.	Price.
1166	2,500 x ½	26 x 34 in	$94.00
1168	2,000 x ½	25 x 33 in	82.00
1170	1,500 x ½	21 x 28 in	70.00
1172	1,200 x ½	20 x 28 in	59.00
1174	1,000 x ½	18 x 27 in	51.00
1176	800 x ½	17 x 26 in	46.00

First dimensions given are parallel to beam

Portable Platform Scales

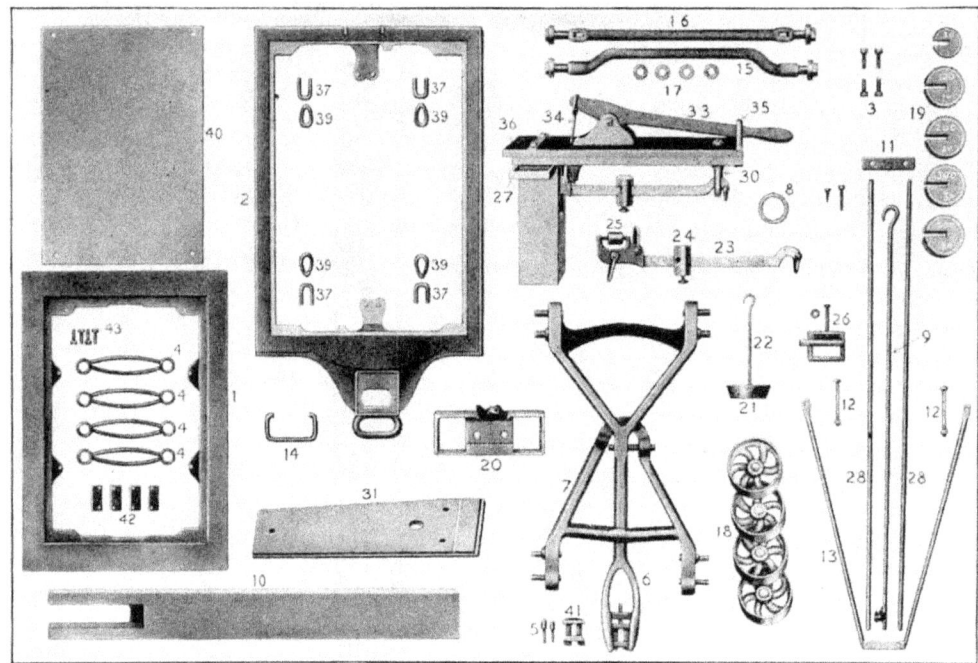

LIST OF PARTS

1. Platform.
2. Frame.
3. Axle Bolts.
4. Check Rods.
5. Nose Iron Screws.
6. Long Lever.
7. Short Lever.
8. Ring.
9. Beam Rod.
10. Pillar.
11. Strap Washer.
12. Brace Bolts.
13. Brace.
14. Handle.
15. Crooked Axle (for drop lever).
16. Straight Axle.
17. Axle nut.
18. Wheels.
19. Weights.
20. Cap.
21. Counterpoise Cup.
22. Counterpoise Stem.
23. Beam.
24. Poise.
25. Balance Ball.
26. Trig Loop.
27. Drop Lever Cap.
28. Pillar Rods.
30. Cap Loop (drop lever).
31. Cap.
32. Fulcrum Lever Stand.
33. Fulcrum Lever (DL).
34. Fulcrum Lever Beam Hook (DL).
35. Fulcrum Lever Hook (DL).
36. Drop Lever Cap.
37. Short Staples.
38. Long Staples.
39. Loops.
40. Platform Board.
41. Nose Iron.
42. Bearing Plates.
43. Bearing Plate Bolts.

U. S. Standard Test Weight

Weights, as above, 50 lbs.　.　.　$5.00

Buda Pressed Steel Wheels

SINGLE SHEET PRESSED STEEL

We early recognized the desirability of a pressed steel wheel which would be light, strong, durable, and unaffected by climatic changes. The design we perfected and patented has been unequaled at any time in the past or present.

Buda wheels are made from a single plate of steel. This originally square—is sheared into circular shape. It is then heated and partially pressed into shape beween dies. The wheel is then reheated and rolled into its completed form. The effect of this latter operation is to produce a wheel which is perfectly round; and no consequent truing-up being necessary the skin of the metal is preserved on the tread and being compressed in the spinning process its wearing qualities are unexcelled. Attention is called to the following important features of the Buda wheel:

Our flange is in accordance with M. C. B. standards. This advantage is claimed for some makes of wheels; but a sectional cut, however, shows the statement to be unwarranted and not the fact—in some instances by a considerable degree. It is important that the flange be of the M. C. B. standard to prevent the car going off the rails on curves and at switches—an unpleasant and costly contingency which can easily result expensively, to say nothing of the ever present possibilities of personal injury and all that follows.

Absolute M.C.B. Flange

Attention has already been directed to the fact that the tread of the Buda wheel requires no truing; thus preserving the skin of the metal; also to the fact that in the spinning process the steel is compressed and its hardness thereby much increased. We now desire to point out the fact that no other wheel has a reinforced tread. That this feature is a strengthening factor experience and tests have proved.

Reinforced Tread

We desire to call particular notice to this feature of our wheels. It will be observed that it is not of the "dished" type but that the load falls almost in a direct line from hub to the point where the tread rests upon the rail. The superiority of the Buda wheel in this respect needs only to be mentioned as the greater resistance to a vertical load is apparent to the glance. A dished hand car wheel is no more desirable than a dished wagon wheel. Note also that the web is strengthened by prominently pressed ribs.

Line of Vertical Load

Hubs Proof Against Loosening

A difference will be observed between the method of construction in the hub of our wheel and others which largely adds to making the Buda the safest wheel to use. Instead of the hub projecting inward—as it does on wheels of the "dished" type, the projection is outward, thus causing the load to fall in a straight line through the web to the ball of the rail. The hub is pressed on cold under a hydraulic pressure of 100,000 pounds, and as the corrugations in the plates through which the rivets are extended conform with those of the web, we guarantee the hubs to be proof against becoming loosened and shearing of the rivets is an occurrence not to be feared.

Sizes and Thickness

Buda pressed steel wheels are made in various sizes to meet the demands occasioned by preference, usage and character of the country in which they are to be used. They are made in sizes ranging from 14 to 24 inches in diameter with thicknesses from 3-16 to ⅜ of an inch.

Insulation

For roads using block systems with track circuit, we furnish insulated wheels for our hand cars, push cars and velocipedes and our method has been approved and fully endorsed by the Hall and other signal companies.

Buda Wheels Used for Refitting Other Cars

So thoroughly have our wheels fulfilled all demands, many roads order them to refit cars of other makes previously ordered. There is also a growing demand for them, on account of their lightness, durability and strength, for use on industrial cars, lumber yard cars, motor cars, mine cars, plantation and similar cars. For uses on cars other than our make we make a specialty of supplying hubs to adapt them to any make.

Strength of Buda Wheels

In order to ascertain the exact strength of our wheel and compare it with another which was considered its nearest competitor, we had made, at the University of Illinois, a test and the figures actually obtained are briefly given herewith. The vertical load at which the Buda wheel set was 6,500 lbs.;—the competitor's wheel at 4,000 lbs. In relative stiffness, taking the Buda as a unit the other wheel compressed at one-seventh. In other words, showing our wheel to be seven times stronger in stiffness. A test for axle thrust was also made and the other wheel spoken of set at 1,850 lbs., whereas the Buda wheel stood 2,300 lbs., at which point there was no apparent set and the bending of the shaft of the testing machine at this point prevented testing the full strength of our wheel. The report summarized is as follows: "The Buda wheel is of the best form, considering stiffness, side strength and general effectiveness."

Buda Pressed Steel Wheels

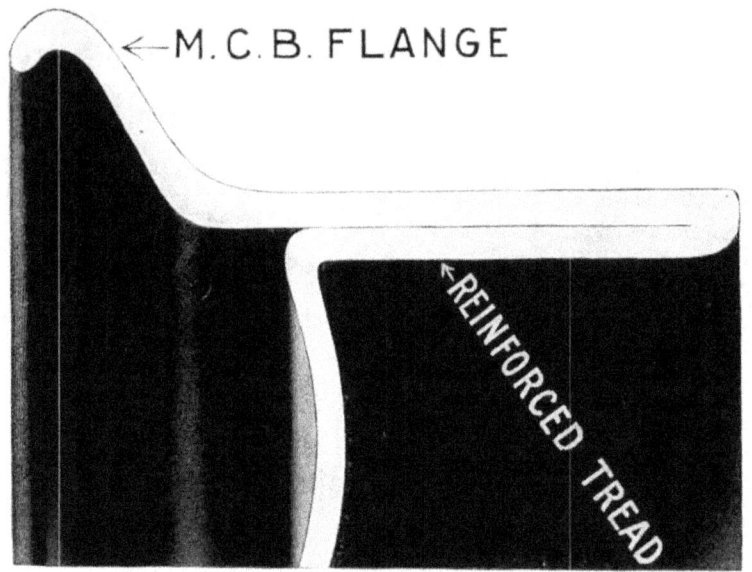

The Strength of Buda Pressed Steel Wheels is Apparent

The general design and reinforced features of the Buda pressed steel wheel is shown in this illustration. The wheel is spun into shape while hot so that it comes from the press perfectly true and requires no machine work.

We call special attention to the reinforced tread. Examination of worn out hand car wheels will show that the wear comes on that part of the tread where we have arranged our reinforcement—wheels do not wear out where the metal bends up into the flange. The quickest way to ascertain this fact is to examine the scrap heap of old wheels. Wheels which are reinforced at this latter point are not any more durable; in fact they are weakened because the extra metal is rolled out of the tread, making it thinner than it otherwise would be.

It will be readily seen that in other wheels when the metal is partly worn through on the tread they are weakened correspondingly; whereas with our style of reinforcement the tread may be worn nearly through and yet be as strong (owing to the double thickness) as other wheels are when new. Buda wheels have M. C. B. flange which prevents derailments on curves and at switches, thus avoiding annoyance and accidents.

Buda Pressed Steel Wheels

Outside View of Buda Wheel

Inside View of Buda Wheel

Sectional View of Buda Wheel

Note reinforced flange and that the web of the wheel supports the load in a nearly vertical line, being slightly arched to strengthen it against side thrust.

SIZES AND LIST PRICES OF BUDA WHEELS

Diameter.	Thickness.	Price each.
14 inches	3/16 inch	$3.25
17 "	3/16 "	3.50
17 "	1/4 "	3.75
18 "	3/16 "	3.75
18 "	1/4 "	4.00
18 "	5/16 "	4.30
18 "	3/8 "	4.70
20 "	3/16 "	4.00
20 "	1/4 "	4.30
20 "	5/16 "	4.60
20 "	3/8 "	4.90
24 "	3/16 "	4.50
24 "	1/4 "	4.85
24 "	5/16 "	5.25
24 "	3/8 "	5.60

The Buda Foundry & Manufacturing Company

Buda Wood Center Wheel

M. C. B. Flange

Where a wood center wheel is desired we furnish the one shown above.

These wheels are sometimes called for on roads having track circuits on account of the natural insulation of the wood center. Our steel wheels have insulation between the hub and the axle and are perfectly reliable, but if the wood center wheel is ordered we are glad to furnish it.

In making this style of wheel we have not in any way slighted the construction, but have made it as strong and true as any other wheel of this class. We have made the tread of high-grade stock and the flange is in accordance with the M. C. B. standards. The hub may be had with taper or straight fit, as desired, and the wheels are made in standard sizes.

Our facilities for manufacturing are such that we can offer these wheels at favorable prices to those who, for the reason stated, prefer them. Unless specified with wood center wheels our cars are fitted with Buda pressed steel wheels.

No. 1 Standard Hand Car

STANDARD GAUGE

Standard gauge; platform 6 feet long by 4 feet 5 inches wide; wheels 20 inches in diameter; axles 1½ inches in diameter; weight 525 pounds.

Fitted with Buda pressed steel wheels; diameter 20 inches. For roads having block signals with track circuit, we can furnish insulated. Our method of insulation is fully approved by the Hall and other signal companies.

No. 2 Bridge Gang Hand Car
STANDARD GAUGE

This is a popular car for bridge work, being thoroughly substantial and built especially for that purpose. It will be noted that the platform extends over the wheels, thereby adding considerably to its width. The brake foot plate is located in the center of platform at end of gallows frame.

Platform 8 feet long by 5 feet 7 inches wide. Fitted with 20-inch steel wheels; axles 1¾ inches diameter. Weight 740 pounds.

No. 3 Narrow Gauge Hand Car

STANDARD AND OTHER NARROW GAUGES

This car is shown for standard narrow gauge. It is built on the same general lines as are our other cars, and unless otherwise specified we ship it without side bearings. We can furnish with inside bearings if desired.

Platform on standard narrow gauge car is 6 feet long by 4 feet wide; wheels 20 inches in diameter; weight 540 pounds.

The Buda Foundry & Manufacturing Company

No. 4 Hand Car

WITH SEATS

This car is provided with seats to accommodate the transportation of men to and from work. We also furnish car without seats if desired.

Standard gauge; 20-inch steel wheels; platform 7 feet 6 inches long; weight 650 pounds.

All cars requiring insulation should be so specified; otherwise they are shipped for use on tracks which carry no circuit.

No. 11 Hand Car

WITH TOOL BOXES

Our No. 11 car is supplied with our 20-inch pressed steel wheels. The platform is the same size as that of our No. 1 car—6 feet long by 4 feet 5 inches wide; weight 600 pounds; standard gauge.

Tool boxes with which the car is supplied are shown in illustration.

This car insulated upon specification.

No. 12 Hand Car

WITH GUARD RAILS

Fitted with 20-inch steel wheels; can be insulated if specified. Standard gauge.

The platform is the same size as our No. 1 car—6 feet long by 4 feet 5 inches wide; weight 550 pounds.

The guard rails with which this car is supplied extend 3 inches above the deck. This feature is shown in the illustration.

No. 13 Hand Car

TEE IRON GALLOWS FRAME

This car is of special construction throughout and is in every way exceptionally durable. Special Tee iron gallows frame; all bearings made of bronze; size of platform 6 feet long by 4 feet 5 inches wide; has guard rails. Weight 575 pounds.

Like our other cars it can be furnished with insulated wheels upon specification.

The Buda Foundry & Manufacturing Company

No. 5 Inspection Car

FOR ROADMASTERS AND SUPERVISORS

Our No. 5 Inspection car has the same size platform as our No. 1 hand car—6 feet long by 4 feet 5 inches wide. Size of wheels 20 inches, furnished insulated upon specification.

The construction is somewhat lighter than our No. 1 car, the weight being about 475 pounds.

Shown in illustration with single end lever; but we furnish it with double end lever if desired. Has hand lever brake in front of seat, to be operated by passengers.

No. 5 ½ Inspection Car

FOR ROADMASTERS AND SUPERVISORS

Similar to our No. 5; the platform being the same size.

Shown with double end lever, or walking beam, and with two swivel chairs instead of seat. Foot rest projection on front end and hand lever brake.

Weight, 500 pounds.

No. 5A Inspection Car

SPRING SETTEE

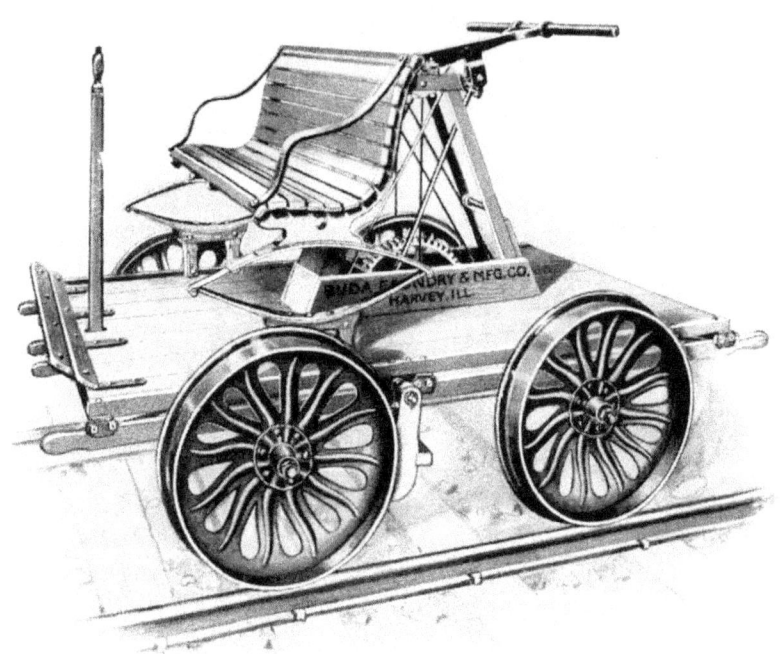

This car can be equipped with ball bearings if desired and supplied with either 20 or 24 inch wheels.

Has single end lever; hand lever brake and spring settee with foot rest. Size of platform, 6 feet long by 4 feet 5 inches wide.

Weight, 500 pounds.

A popular car for Roadmasters and Supervisors on account of compactness, ease of operation and comfortable but durable seat.

Furnished with insulated wheels upon specification.

Buda Hand and Push Cars

BEST MATERIAL. PRESSED STEEL WHEELS

The many years which we are known to have manufactured hand cars should be an argument of their merit, particularly should this appeal to those who are acquainted with our progressive policy. Despite what experience teaches, ideas often differ among users as to the desirability of various features; but we have found that the points of advantage on our cars have met with singular unanimity of acceptance from railroad users. The conclusion to be drawn from this is that Buda cars have always proven their worth in a manner to still any difference in opinion.

In the construction of Buda cars we use select material for every detail.

The Frame is of seasoned maple, especially selected by us for this use.

The Platform, or decking is of first-class kiln dried, long leaf, yellow pine, dressed both sides to a uniform thickness. Experience has shown this to be the most suitable wood.

The gears on our cars may be had either cast or machine cut. Unless specified we furnish cast gears on account of the fact that they wear much longer. They do not at first run quite as easy, but they quickly become smooth and having the tough skin of the metal preserved do not wear down and run hard after the manner of the cut gears which are necessarily made of softer material in order to be machined. One pair of cast gears will be found to outwear two pair of cut gears.

Wheel Seats

We prefer straight wheel seat and key, it being our practice to press wheels on under heavy hydraulic pressure, an additional protection being secured by means of a $\frac{3}{8}$ inch key. We guarantee Buda wheels thus attached not to come loose. We furnish taper seat, however, if desired.

Insulated

Cars perfectly insulated when specified. Our method of insulation is fully approved by the Hall and other signal companies.

We can duplicate any part and call attention to illustrations and list in following pages.

Repairs

The strength and durability of Buda cars together with the low cost of maintenance makes them without exception most economical to use even over others which may be offered at much lower prices.

No. 6 Push Car

STEEL WHEELS

Standard gauge; platform 7 feet long by 5 feet 7 inches wide; wheels, 20 inches diameter; machine steel axles, 1½ inches diameter. Weight, 500 pounds.

All our push cars may be furnished insulated, the method being exactly the same as used on our hand cars.

Our method of insulation fully approved by Hall and other signal companies.

No. 6½ Push Car

EXTRA HEAVY

This is a very strong car and is intended for heavier work than the No. 6. It is unusually durable, the sills and stringers being of extra thickness and it has the addition of heavy iron straps across each end on the platform. The axles are also heavier, being 2 inches in diameter.

Standard gauge. Platform 5 feet 7 inches wide. Has 20-inch wheels.

Weight, 700 pounds.

Furnished with insulated wheels upon specification.

No. 9A Push Car

STEEL WHEELS

General dimensions same as No 6, but without decking; car sills being covered with heavy plate iron.

Furnished with insulated wheels upon specification.

Weight, 470 pounds.

No. 7 Push Car

HEAVY PUSH CAR, WITH IRON PLATE WHEELS

Standard gauge; platform 7 feet long by 5 feet 7 inches wide; wheels 18 inches in diameter; extra heavy framing and axles. Weight, 800 pounds; capacity, 4 tons.

If desired this car can be equipped, at a slight advance in price, with our patented steel wheel, thereby reducing weight to 772 pounds.

No. 8 Push Car

IRON SPOKE WHEELS

Standard gauge; platform 7 feet long by 5 feet 7 inches wide; wheels 20 inches in diameter. Weight, 596 pounds.

No. 9 Push Car

CAST IRON CURVED SPOKE WHEELS

Standard gauge; platform 7 feet long by 5 feet 7 inches wide; wheels 18 inches in diameter; steel axles, 1½ inches in diameter. Weight, 636 pounds.

Tie Car

For tie treating plants. Cast wheels and all iron frame with chains for securing load.

No. 10 Extra Heavy Track-Laying Car

15-TON CAPACITY RAIL CAR

Our No. 10 car, illustrated, is built in an exceedingly substantial manner and is not approached by any other for strength and durability. Standard gauge. Capacity, 30,000 pounds; weight, 2,000 pounds. In size the car is 8 feet by 6 feet 6 inches wide; has 4 by 8 inch sills, the cross sills being plated heavily with iron. Large tool box as shown, and four extra size rollers on end sills. The wheels are of chilled cast iron, 16 inches in diameter, with wide tread—extra heavy and strong. This car should not be confused with similar cars of lighter construction. It is an excellent car and stands in a class by itself.

No. 11. TEN-TON TRACK-LAYING CAR.—Well built throughout but is of lighter construction than style No. 10, its weight being about 1,350 pounds; capacity, 10 tons. Standard gauge. It is 7 feet 8 inches long by 6 feet 3 inches wide; has chilled cast iron wheels, 16 inches in diameter, 5½ inch tread. The cross sills are strapped with iron and each end sill provided with two rollers. Car is also supplied with box for tools.

Repair Parts of Buda Hand Cars

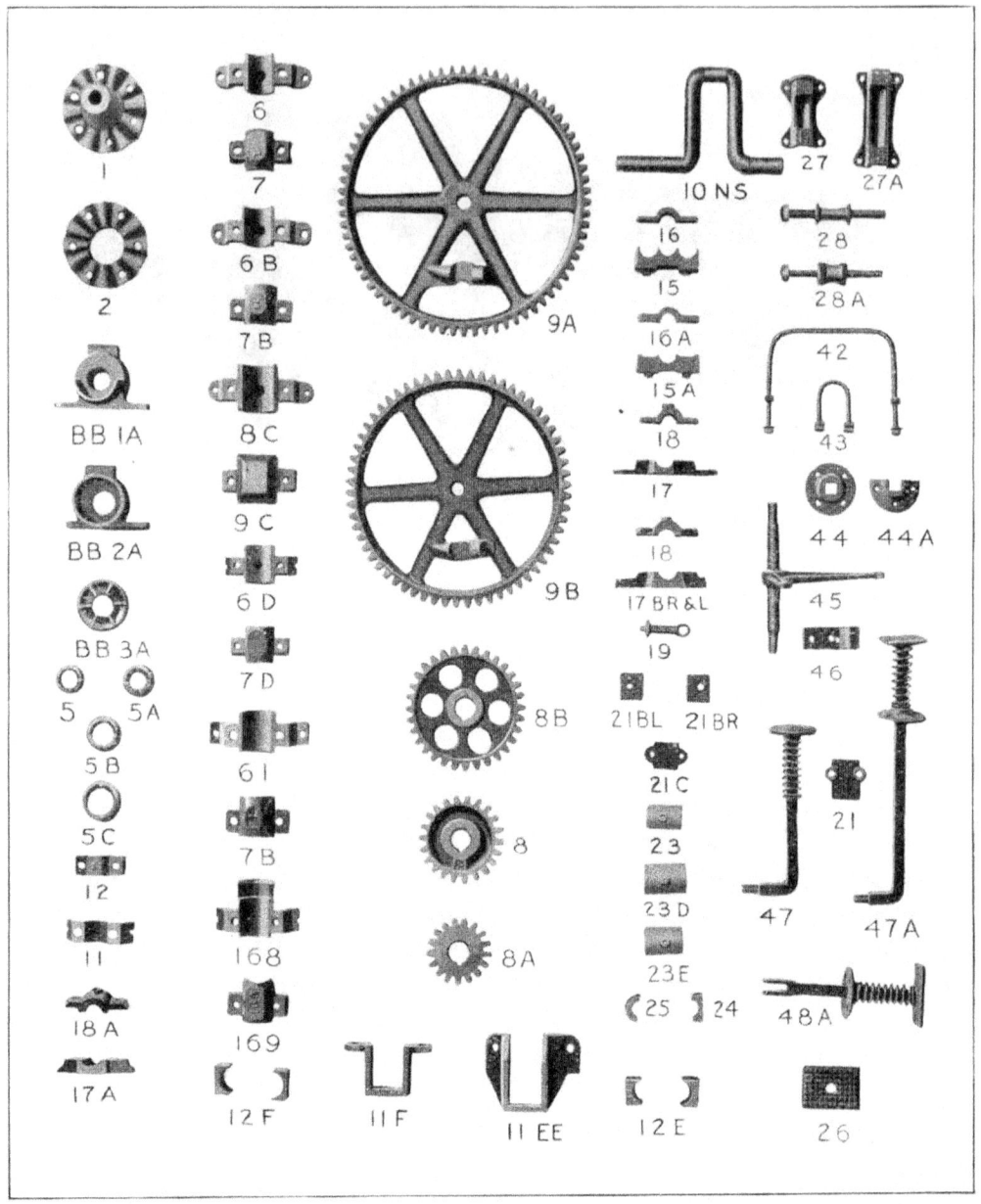

For corresponding list see opposite page

List of Repair Parts for Buda Hand Cars

No.	Description		Price
1	Hub for Steel Wheel		$ .40
2	Collar for Steel Wheel		.10
BB1A	Ball-Bearing Pedestal		1.50
BB2A	Ball-Bearing Center Bearing		1.00
BB3A	Ball-Bearing Nut for Pedestal and Center Bearing		.50
5	Collar for loose wheel, 1¼ in. Bore		.03
5A	Collar for loose wheel, 1⅛ in. Bore		.03
5B	Collar for loose wheel, 1½ in. Bore		.03
5C	Collar for loose wheel, 1⅞ in. Bore		.03
6	Pedestal for 1¼ in. Axle, for No. 3 Car	set	1.00
7	Cellar for 1¼ in. Axle, for No. 3 Car		
6B	Pedestal for 1½ in. Axle	set	1.00
7B	Cellar for 1½ in. Axle		
6D	Pedestal for 1¼ in. Axle, for Inspection Car	set	1.00
7D	Cellar for 1¼ in. Axle, for Inspection Car		
6I	Pedestal for Insulated Cars		.15
8C	Pedestal for 1¾ in. Axle, for No. 2 Car	set	1.00
9C	Cellar for 1¾ in. Axle, for No. 2 Car		
8	Pinion Wheel, 22 teeth, Cast Pinion		.75
8A	Pinion Wheel, 17 teeth, Cast Pinion		.75
8B	Pinion Wheel, 32 teeth, Cast Pinion		.75
8	Cut Teeth, 22 T		1.00
8A	Cut Teeth, 17 T		1.00
8B	Cut Teeth, 32 T		1.00
9	Drive Gear Wheel, 72 teeth, Cast Gear		1.25
9B	Drive Gear Wheel, 62 teeth, Cast Gear		1.25
9	Cut Teeth, 72 T		3.00
9A	Cut Teeth, 72 T		3.00
9B	Cut Teeth, 62 T		3.00
10N-S	Crank, New Style		1.35
11	Center Bearing Box for 1½ in. Axle, for special Cars	set	.25
12	Center Bearing Box Cap for 1½ in. Axle, for special Cars		
11EE	Center Bearing Box for 1½ in. Axle, Standard No. 1 Car		.50
11FF	Center Bearing Box for 1¾ in. Axle, for No. 2 Car		.50
12E	Center Bearing, for No. 1 Car		.50
12F	Center Bearing, for No. 2 Car		.50
15	Rock Shaft Box	set	.50
16	Rock Shaft Box Cap		
15A	Rock Shaft Box, for Inspection Car	set	.50
16A	Rock Shaft Box Cap, for Inspection Car		
17	Gear Box	set	1.00
18	Gear Box Cap		
17A	Gear Box, for Inspection Car	set	1.00
18A	Gear Box Cap, for Inspection Car		
17B R&L	Gear Box, for Bridge Gang Car		.35
19	Truss Rod Post		.10
21	Double Truss Rod Cap		.05
21B-L	Truss Rod Cap, for Inspection Car		.05
21B-R	Truss Rod Cap, for Inspection Car		.05
21C	Double Truss Rod Cap, for Inspection Car		.05
23	Axle Bearing Brass, for No. 3 Car	set	1.25
23D	Axle Bearing Brass, for No. 2 Car	set	1.50
23E	Axle Bearing Brass, for No. 1 Car	set	1.25
24	Connecting Rod Brass	set	1.00
25	Connecting Rod Brass		
26	Step for Brake		.10
27	Brake Sleeve		.10
27A	Brake Sleeve, for No. 3 Car		.15
28	Spool, Standard		.10
28A	Spool, for Inside Bearing Cars		.10
42	Pick Racks		.15
43	Stirrups		.05
44	Collar		.20
44A	Half Collar		.20
45	Bell Crank		.20
46	Bell Crank Clips		.15
47	Brake Plunger, for No. 1 Car		.25
47A	Brake Plunger, for No. 3 Car		.25
48A	Brake Plunger, for No. 2 Car		.30
168	Special Pedestal	set	1.00
169	Special Cellar		

Repair Parts of Buda Hand Cars

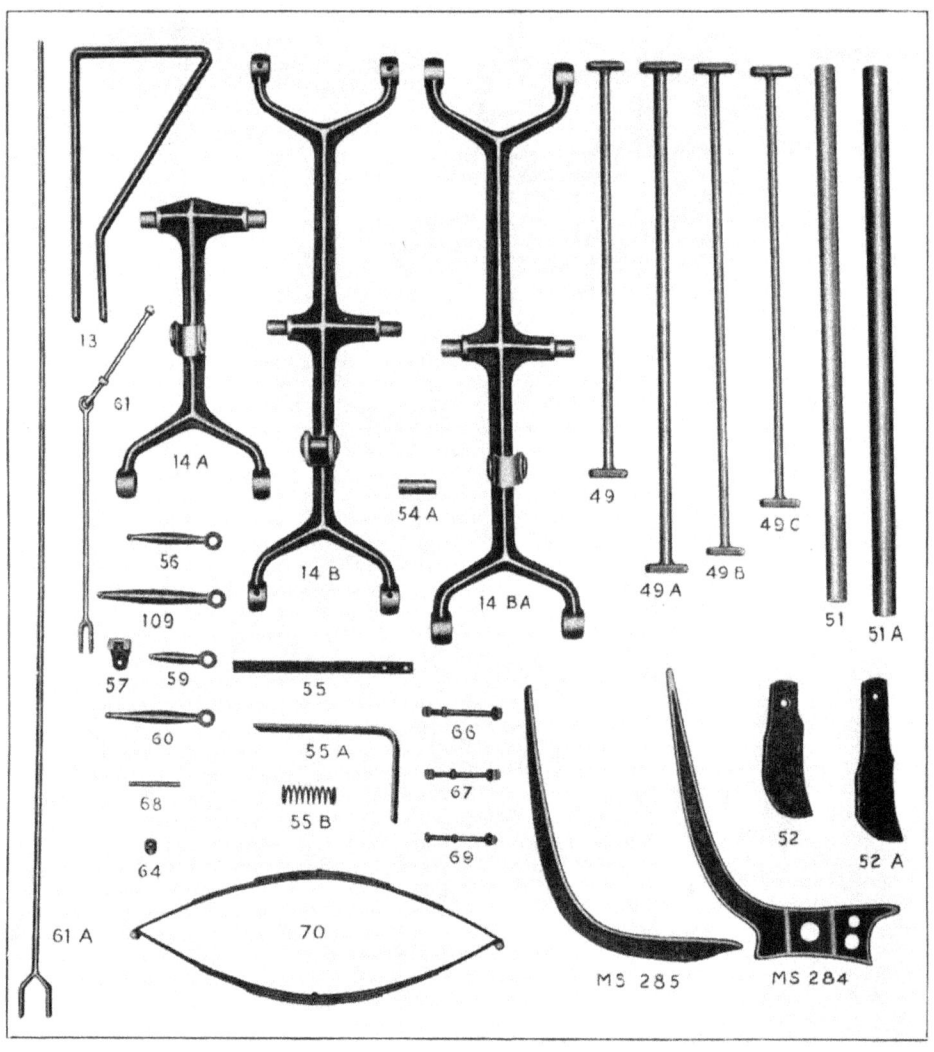

List continued on opposite page

List of Repair Parts for Buda Hand Cars—Continued

No.	Description.	Price.
13	Side Seat Arm, for No. 4 Car	$ .40
14A	Single End Walking Beam	4.50
14B	Double End Walking Beam	4.50
14BA	Heavy Double End Walking Beam	5.50
49	Connecting Rod, for No. 1 Car	.75
49A	Connecting Rod, for No. 2 Car	.75
49B	Connecting Rod, for No. 3 Car	.75
49C	Connecting Rod, for No. 4 Car	.75
51	Wood Handle	.15
51A	Gaspipe Handle	.50
52	Brake Shoe .... pair	.25
52A	Brake Shoe, for No. 2 Car .... pair	.25
54A	Wrist Pin	.30
55	Brake Spring	.25
55A	Brake Spring	.25
55B	Brake Spring	.20
56	Brake Toggle	.15
57	Toggle Clip	.05
59	Brake Toggle	.15
60	Brake Toggle	.15
61	Brake Rod	.35
61A	Brake Rod	.50
64	Bevel Washer	.03
66	Pedestal Rod	.05
67	Gear Box Rod	.05
68	Oil Tube	.05
69	Rock Shaft Box Rod	.05
70	Spring for Settee	1.75
109	Brake Toggle	.25
MS-284	Settee Arm	.75
MS-285	Settee Center Arm	.70

Repair Parts of Buda Hand Cars

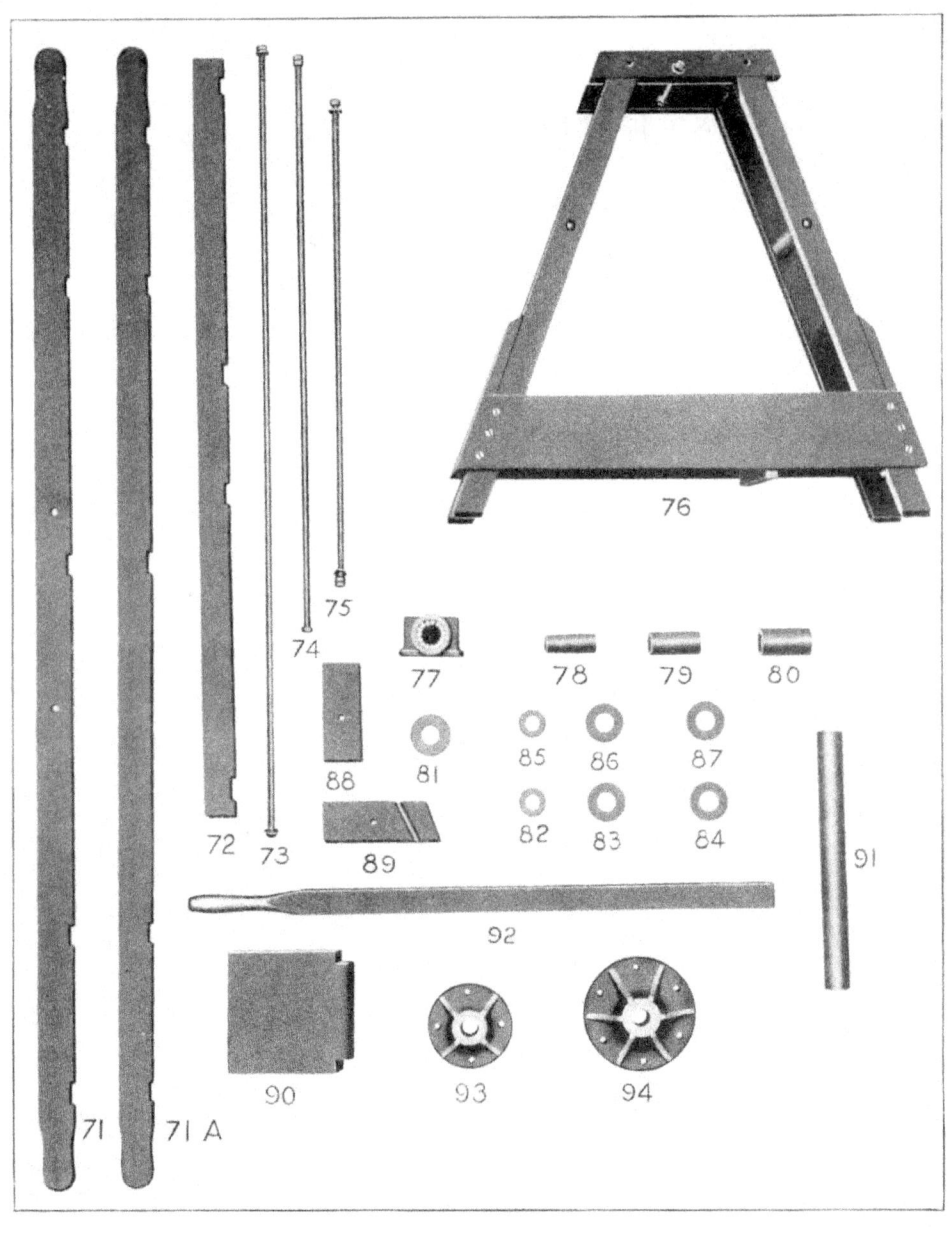

List concluded on opposite page

The Buda Foundry & Manufacturing Company

List of Repair Parts for Buda Hand Cars—Concluded

No.	Description.	Price.
71	Longitudinal Sill	$ .40
71A	Longitudinal Sill, for Brake Side	.40
72	Cross Sill	.30
73	Truss Rod, ⅜ x 4 feet 9 inches	.15
74	G. F. Rod, ⅜ x 3 feet 6 inches	.10
75	G. F. Rod, ⅜ x 35½ inches	.10
76	Gallows Frame	5.00
77	Roller Bearing Pedestal	1.25
78	Fibre Bushing, 1½-inch Axle	.50
79	Fibre Bushing, 1¾-inch Axle	.60
80	Fibre Bushing, 2-inch Axle	.66
81	Steel Washer for R. B. Pedestal	.10
82	Steel Washer for 1½-inch Axle, 1⅛ x 2-inch x ⅛-inch	.05
83	Steel Washer for 1½-inch Axle, 1¼ x 2½-inch	.05
84	Special Washer for 1½-inch Axle, 1½ x 2½-inch	.15
85	Fibre Washer for 1½-inch Axle, 1⅛ x 2 inch	.10
86	Fibre Washer for 1½-inch Axle, 1¼ x 2⅝-inch	.10
87	Special Fibre Washer for 2-inch Axle	.15
88	Tool Box Board	.10
89	Tool Box Board	.10
90	Tool Box Board	.15
91	Chair Post, for Inspection Hand Car	1.00
92	Brake Lever for Inspection Hand Car	.25
93	Top Plate, for Chair	.90
94	Bottom Plate, for Chair	1.00

Repair Parts of Push Cars

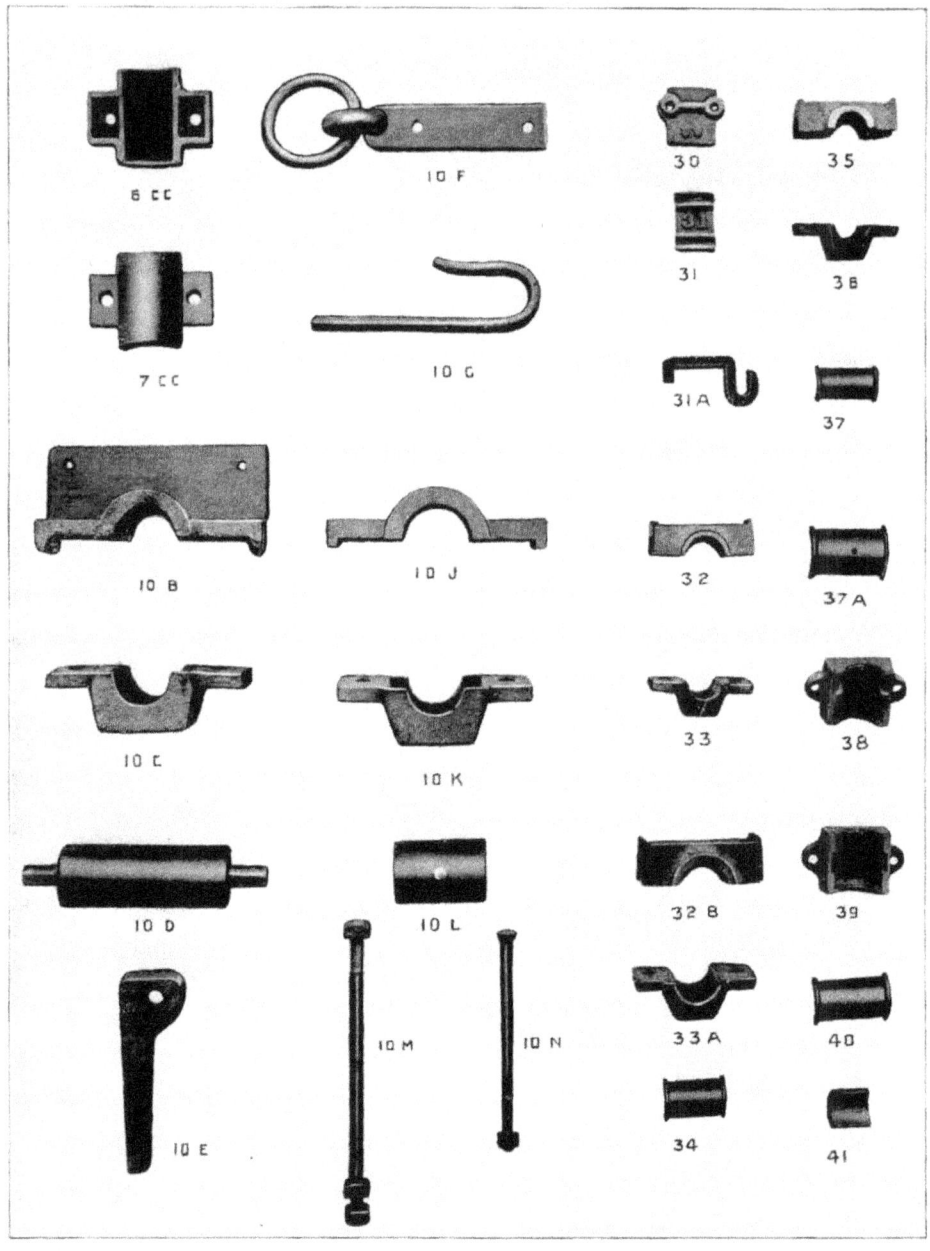

List on Opposite Page

The Buda Foundry & Manufacturing Company

List of Repair Parts for Buda Push Cars

No.	Description.	Price.
6CC	Pedestal (Babbitted).... ⎰	
7CC	Cellar .... ⎱	set $2.75
10B	Pedestal (Babbitted).... ⎰	
10C	Cellar .... ⎱	set 6.00
10D	Roller	.40
10E	Roller Bracket	.30
10F	Bull Ring	1.50
10G	Hook	.50
10J	Pedestal............... ⎫	
10K	Cellar .... ⎬	set 6.00
10L	Brass.................. ⎭	
10M	Pedestal Bolt, ¾-inch....	.15
10N	C. S. H. Strap Bolt, ⅝-inch	.10
30	Double Truss Rod Cap....	.10
31	Double Truss Rod Bearing.	.05
31A	Truss Rod Clip	.15
32	Pedestal for 1½-inch Axle ... ⎰	
33	Cellar for 1½-inch Axle..... ⎱	set 1.25
32B	Pedestal for 1¾-inch Axle... ⎰	
33A	Cellar for 1¾-inch Axle..... ⎱	set 1.35
34	Brass for 1½ inch Axle	set 1.25
35	Pedestal for N. G. Axle ..... ⎰	
36	Cellar for N. G. Axle ..... ⎱	set 1.00
37	Brass 1½-inch for N. G. Axle.	set 1.50
37A	Brass for Axle	set 1.75
38	Pedestal for 1¾-inch Axle—Special ⎰	
39	Cellar for 1¾-inch Axle—Special.. ⎱	set 1.25
40	Brass for 1¾-inch Axle.....	set 1.50
41	Brass for 1¾-inch Axle.....	set 1.25

Buda Velocipedes

BALL-BEARING

All the desirable features which go to make up a first-class velocipede will be found in these we make. They are light, easily operated, and they are durable. Our extended experience in the manufacture of hand cars enables us to produce velocipedes in every way improved in accordance with modern demands.

Construction — In the construction of our velocipedes we use ash to secure lightness, combined with toughness and durability. The wood is thoroughly seasoned and in the finished velocipede is painted a beautiful vermilion. We finish in any color, however, which may be specified to accord with standard of railroad ordering.

Metal Parts. — All the metal parts are of the best malleable gray iron.

Cut Gears — We furnish cut gears exclusively on our velocipedes in order to obtain ease of propulsion from the very start. This is done by accurate machinery provided for the purpose and the result is all that could be wished in the way of smooth running. All other metal parts are of malleable gray iron and steel castings of the highest grade.

Ball Bearings — To further in every way possible ease of operation, all our velocipedes are equipped with ball bearings after the most approved method. The balls and cones are hardened with the special intent of improving and lengthening their wearing qualities.

Wheels — We use only our special pressed steel wheels. These absolutely have the M. C. B. flange and will not climb the rails on curves or at switches—an ever-recurring annoyance with wheels which are claimed to have the M. C. B. flange, but which do not really come up to the specifications—some far from it. Buda wheels are not affected by climatic changes and their special advantages have already been spoken of in previous pages devoted exclusively to that subject.

The Nos. 1, 2 and 4 cars are equipped with 17-inch wheels and a 14-inch guide wheel. The No. 3 car is equipped with a 17-inch forward wheel, a 20-inch rear wheel and 14-inch guide wheel.

Gauge and Extras. — Our Nos. 1, 2 and 4 velocipedes are shipped with standard gauge arm. If adjustable arm is specified we furnish it without charge. This arm may be adapted to any gauge from three to five and one-half feet.

The No. 3 car is also shipped for standard gauge. If special gauge is required, the gauge should be specified, and it is better to order an additional arm and brace rod. Price, $3.00 extra.

Tools, Repairs — With each car is furnished oil can and wrench to fit any nut on the car. All repair parts are carried by us, and repairs can be made without sending car to shop. Illustrated list of repair parts will be found in pages following.

All Buda Velocipedes Insulated. — All velocipedes which we make are now insulated and may be used on roads with track circuits. The insulation is perfect in every respect.

No. 1 Velocipede

BALL-BEARING

For One Person

Our No. 1 Velocipede shown herewith is for one person. Has place for carrying packages, with small railing to retain same.

Ball-bearing; cut gears; 17-inch wheels and a 14-inch guide wheel. For standard gauge unless otherwise ordered. When so specified we can furnish it with arm adjustable to any gauge from three to five and one-half foot track. No extra charge. Our wheels positively have M. C. B. flange and will not climb track on curves or at switches.

No. 2 Velocipede

BALL-BEARING

For Two Persons

For two persons. Same style as No. 1, but with seat for passenger.

This velocipede is essentially the same as our No. 1, with the exception that the seat is arranged to carry operator and one passenger, with footboard for latter.

There are two 17-inch and a 14-inch guide wheel, same as on the No. 1 style, having also cut gears. Standard gauge, but upon specification we supply arm adjustable to any gauge from three to five and one-half feet. No extra charge.

No. 3 Velocipede

BALL-BEARING

For Three Persons

Especially adapted for the use of telegraph linemen; carrying as it does three persons and having tray for tools. Is arranged for two operators, but can easily be operated by one man. Cut gears and ball bearings. Has 17-inch forward wheel, 20-inch rear wheel and 14-inch guide wheel.

When ordered for other than standard gauge it is necessary to specify the gauge desired, as we do not furnish an adjustable arm. We also recommend ordering an additional arm and brace rod—$3.00 extra.

All wheels have M. C. B. flange and will not climb curves or switches.

No. 4 Velocipede

BALL-BEARING

For One or Two Persons

This Velocipede is similar in style to the No. 1 Velocipede, but the construction of the seat is such as to accommodate one or two persons, the seat being arranged to swing crossways when there are two passengers. When only one person is to use velocipede the seat is swung parallel with under board. Can be furnished with adjustable arm without cost same as No. 1, but unless specified otherwise is regularly shipped for standard gauge.

Buda Special Velocipede

BALL-BEARING

For Signal Work

Similar to our No. 1, but designed especially for signal departments. The tray is for carrying batteries, switch lamps or for any like purpose.

It has two 17-inch wheels and 14-inch guide wheel. Cut gears and ball bearing. A light, easy running velocipede, which can be readily handled by one man.

Repair Parts of Buda Velocipedes

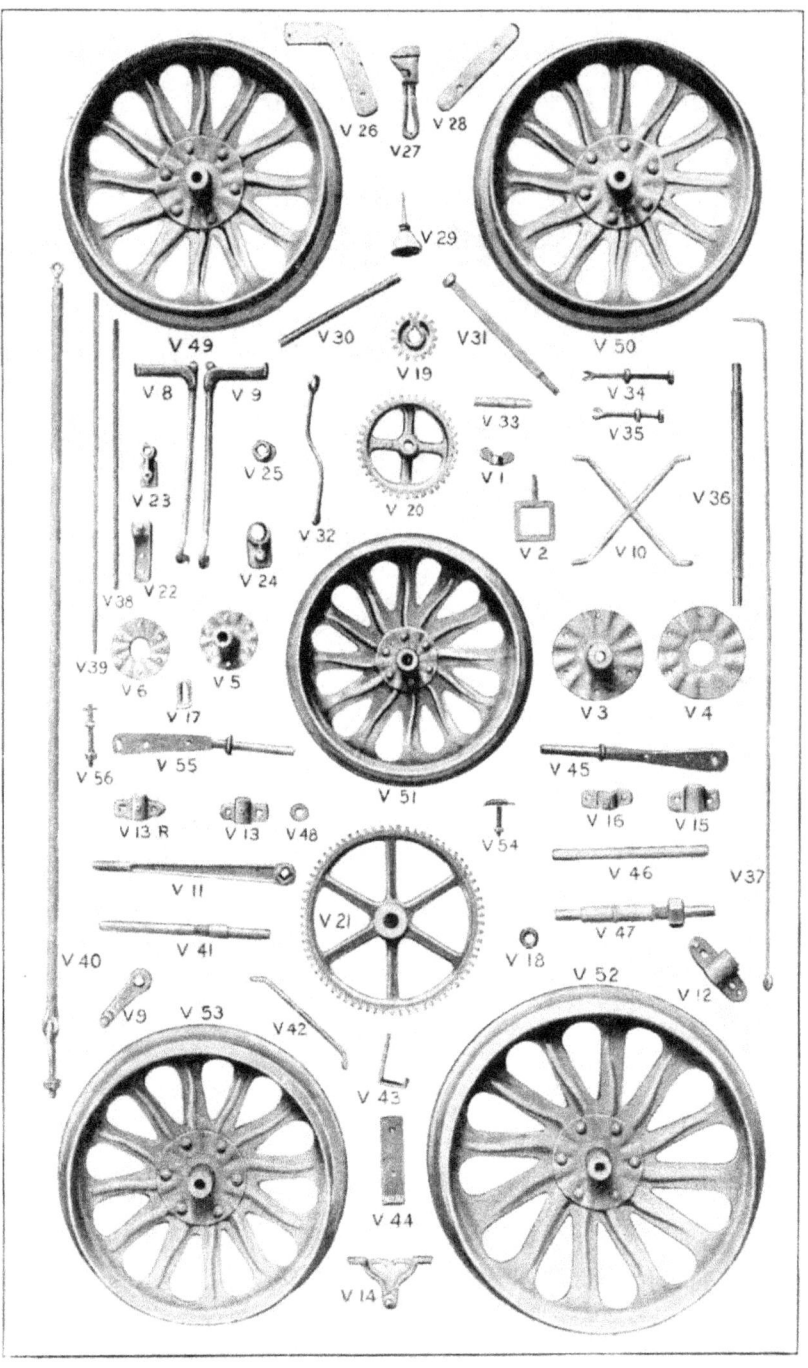

List on opposite page

The Buda Foundry & Manufacturing Company

List of Repair Parts for Velocipede Cars

No.	Description.	See Page 82.	For Use On.
V 1	Thumb Nut	"	1—2—3—4
V 2	Arm Clamp	"	1—2—3—4
V 3	Large Hub	"	1—2—3—4
V 4	Large Collar	"	1—2—3—4
V 5	Guide Wheel Hub	"	1—2—3—4
V 6	Guide Wheel Collar	"	1—2—3—4
V 7	R. H. Foot Rest	"	1—2—3
V 8	L. H. Foot Rest	"	1—2—3
V 9	Crank	"	1—2—3—4
V 10	X Brace	"	1—2—4
V 11	Brake Lever	"	1—2—3
V 12	Pedestal, Plain Bearing	"	1—2—3—4
V 13	R. & L. Hanger Box	"	1—2—3—4
V 14	Lever Bracket	"	1—2—3—4
V 15	Crank Axle Box	"	1—2—3—4
V 16	Idler Gear Box	"	1—2—3—4
V 17	Arm Stop	"	1—2—3—4
V 18	Guide Arm Collar	"	1—2—3—4
V 19	Pinion—17 Teeth	"	1—2—3—4
V 20	Idler Gear—38 Teeth	"	1—2—3—4
V 21	Driver Gear—70 Teeth	"	1—2—3—4
V 22	Brake Shoe Head	"	1—2—3
V 23	Rear Brake Bracket	"	1—2—3
V 24	Front Brake Bracket	"	1—2—3
V 25	Brake Stop	"	1—2—3
V 26	Guide Arm Hinge	"	3
V 27	Screw Wrench	"	1—2—3—4
V 28	Friction Plate	"	1—2—3—4
V 29	Oil Can	"	1—2—3—4
V 30	Rocker Shaft	"	1—2—3—4
V 31	Brake Shaft	"	1—2—3
V 32	Idler Brace	"	1—2—3—4
V 33	Idler Gear Shaft	"	1—2—3—4
V 34	Arm Strut	"	3
V 35	Arm Strut	"	1—2—4
V 36	Foot Rest Hook Shaft	"	1—2—3—4
V 37	Guide Arm Truss Rod	"	1—2—4
V 38	Lever Handle Rod	"	1—2—4
V 39	Tool Box Rod	"	3
V 40	Guide Arm Brace	"	1—2—4
V 41	Gear Shaft	"	1—2—3—4
V 42	Brace	"	3
V 43	Foot Rest Clip	"	2
V 44	Brace for Tool Box	"	3
V 45	Trailing Axle	"	3
V 46	Front Axle	"	1—2—3—4
V 47	Taper Axle and Nut for Drive Wheel	"	1—2—3—4
V 48	Washer for Cranks	"	1—2—3—4
V 49	17 in. Front Wheel	"	1—2—4
V 50	17 in. Rear Wheel	"	1—2—4
V 51	14 in. Guide Wheel	"	1—2—3—4
V 52	20 in. Rear Wheel	"	3
V 53	17 in. Front Wheel	"	3
V 54	Guide Arm T Bolt	"	1—2—3—4
V 55	Guide Wheel Axle	"	1—2—4
V 56	Brace Pin	"	1—2—4
V 57	Seat	See Page 84.	1
V 58	Seat	"	2
V 59	Seat Riser	"	1—2
V 60	Brake Shoe	"	1—2—3
V 61	Brake Handle	"	1—2
V 62	Guide Arm	"	1—2
V 63	Top Side Rail	"	1—2—3
V 64	Bottom Side Rail	"	1—2—3
V 65	Drive Rod	"	1—2—3—4
V 66	Top Cross Handle for W. B.	"	1—2—4
V 67	Lever Complete	"	1—2—4
V 68	Seat Spool	"	1
V 69	Top Lever Spool	"	1—2—4
V 70	Center Lever Spool	"	1—2—3—4

List of Repair Parts for Velocipede Cars—Continued

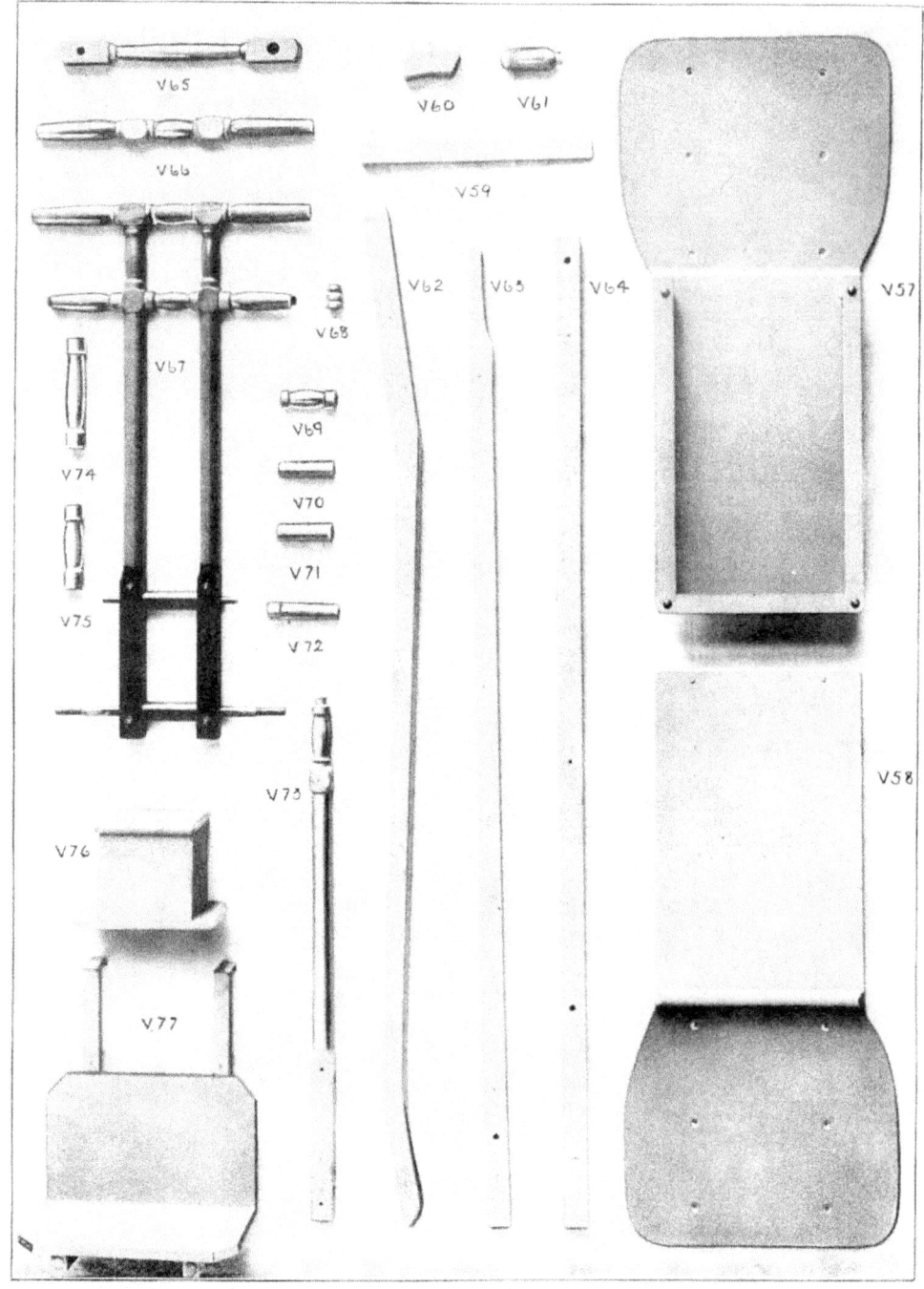

No.	Description.	See Page 84.	For Use On.
V 71	Bottom Lever Spool	"	1—2—3—4
V 72	Short Lever Handle	"	1—2—4
V 73	Combination Lever Upright	"	1—2—4
V 74	Cross Frame Spool	"	1—2—4
V 75	Upright Frame Spool	"	1—2—4
V 76	Tool Box	"	1—2—4
V 77	Foot Rest	"	2

List of Repair Parts for Velocipede Cars—Continued

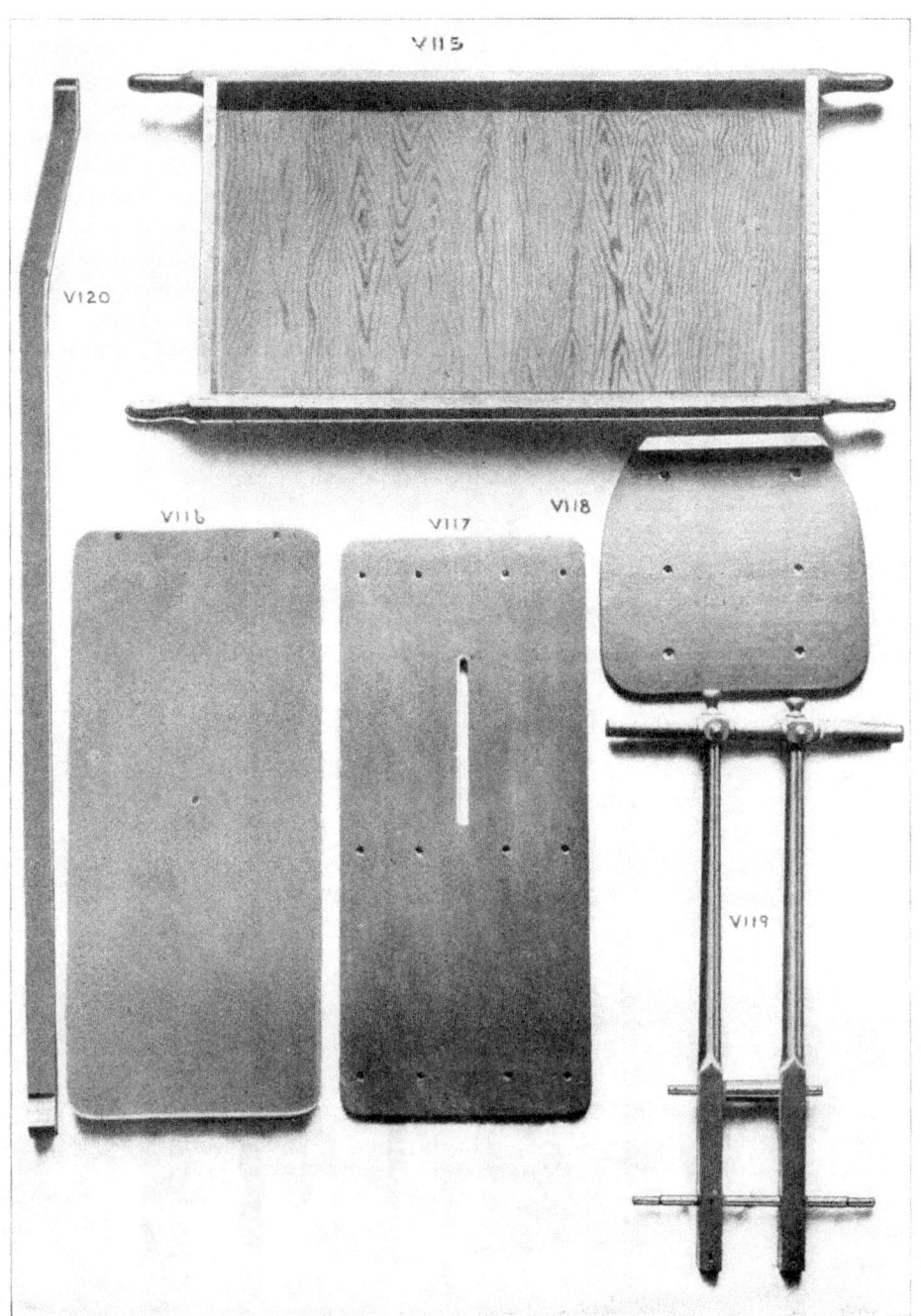

No.	Description.	See Page 85.	For Use On.
V115	Tray	"	1—3
V116	Seat Top Board	"	4
V117	Seat Bottom Board	"	4
V118	Seat	"	3
V119	Walking Beam Complete	"	3
V120	Tray Support (Special)	"	1

The Buda Foundry & Manufacturing Company

Buda Velocipedes

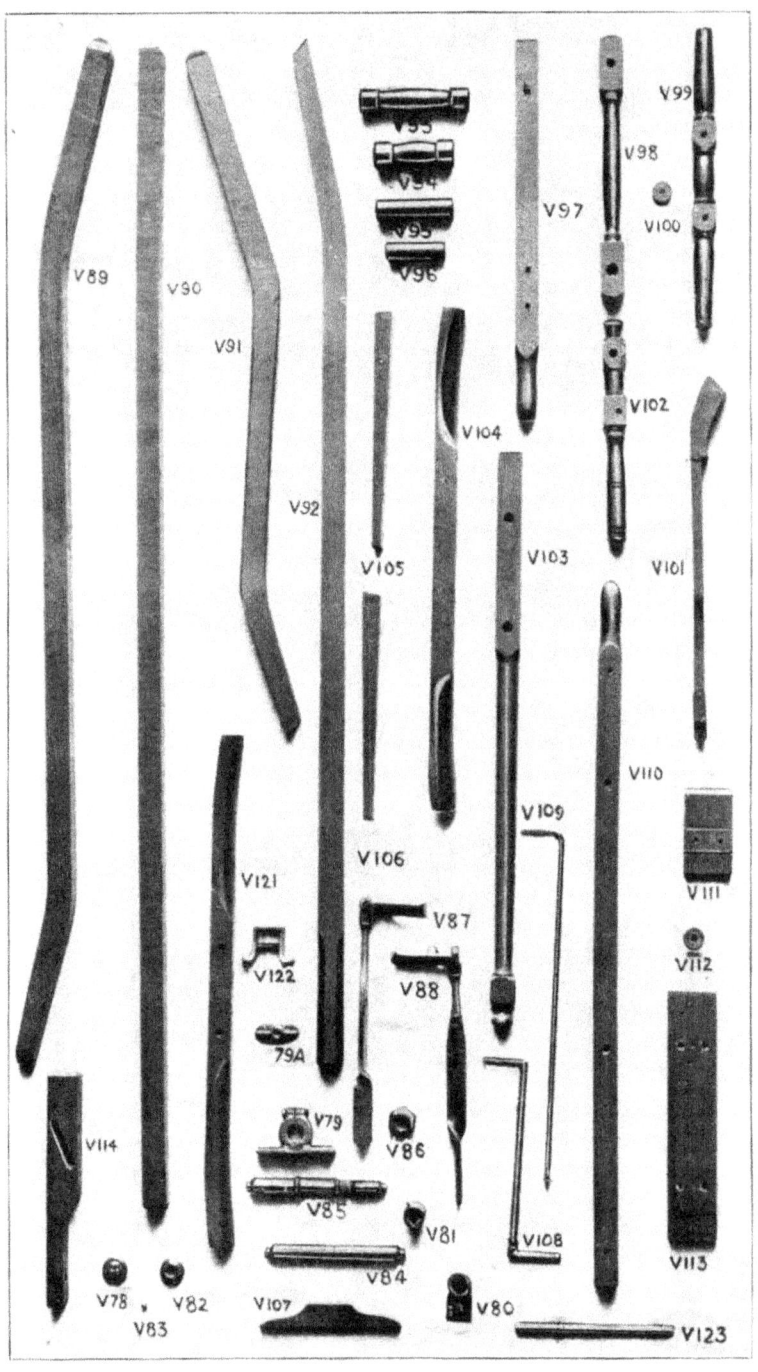

Repair Parts

The Buda Foundry & Manufacturing Company

List of Repair Parts for Velocipede Cars—Continued

No.	Description.	See Page 86.	For Use On.
V 78	Cap Nut for Ball Bearing Box	"	1—2—3—4
V 79	Pedestal for Ball Bearing	"	1—2—3—4
V 79A	Seat Clamp	"	4
V 80	L. H. Brake Stop	"	1—2—3
V 81	L. H. Brake Bracket	"	1—2—3
V 82	Ball Bearing Cup	"	1—2—3—4
V 83	Balls	"	1—2—3—4
V 84	Front Axle for Ball Bearing	"	1—2—3—4
V 85	Drive Axle for Ball Bearing	"	1—2—3—4
V 86	L. H. Nut for Gear Shaft	"	1—2—3—4
V 87	R. H. Foot Rest	"	4
V 88	L. H. Foot Rest	"	4
V 89	Guide Arm	"	3
V 90	Bottom Side Rail	"	3
V 91	Guide Arm for 3 ft. Gauge	"	1—2—4
V 92	Guide Arm Brace	"	3
V 93	Cross Frame Spool	"	3
V 94	Upright Frame Spool	"	3
V 95	Spool for Guide Arm Brace Extension	"	3
V 96	Lever Spool	"	3
V 97	Front End Top Rail	"	3
V 98	Connecting Rod	"	3
V 99	Top Handle for W. B.	"	3
V100	Handle Spreader	"	3
V101	Brake Shoe and Clip	"	4
V102	Brake Lever	"	4
V103	Lever Side Handle	"	3
V104	Foot Rest	"	3
V105	Seat Riser (Rear)	"	3
V106	Seat Riser (Front)	"	3
V107	Tray Riser	"	3
V108	Foot Rest Hanger	"	1—2—3—4
V109	Guide Arm Truss Rod for 36 in. Gauge	"	1—2—4
V110	Rear End Top Rail	"	3
V111	Seat Cleat	"	4
V112	Spreader for Brake Lever	"	4
V113	Seat Cleat	"	4
V114	Guide Arm Brace Support	"	3
V121	Lever Foot Rest	"	3
V122	Brake Shoe Guide	"	4
V123	Lever Shaft	"	3

New-Style Paulus Track Drill

BALL-BEARING THRUST

For many years the Paulus track drill has been the leading device for rail drilling and we have now greatly improved its construction, retaining all the best features of the old style and adding improvements which make the drill the most ideal track drilling machine ever placed on the market. Aside from the retention of the collapsing frame which may be instantly thrown back to permit the passage of trains, and immediately reset without disturbing the bit there will be found increased advantages.

Features of the New-Style Paulus Drill

1. Variable feed, giving three distinct feeds.
2. Dust-proof ball-bearing thrust reducing friction and promoting ease of operation.
3. Arrangement for quickly feeding bit up to and return from work.
4. Heavier construction throughout in frame.
5. Rich Spindle for using Rich flat bits, of high speed steel. Can be fitted with plain spindle for using twist bits, also.

In the illustration is shown the base of the Improved Paulus drill fitted with the Rich spindle and Rich flat bit. The advantages of using Rich flat bits are explained on pages 114-120.

We would call attention to the device for feeding the bit up to the work and returning it from same. The small crank at the rear of the frame is connected with a pinion which operates the gear wheel that actuates the feed screw. Two or three seconds will feed the bit up to the rail or return it. This does not cause the spindle to revolve nor require any movement of the operating handles.

An ingenious arrangement, which is very simple and cannot get out of order, is that which regulates the feed of the bit while drilling. The pawl, which drops into the feed gear, will be seen resting on a circular shield. As shown, the pawl catches but one gear tooth, thus giving a comparatively light feed to the revolving bit. This shield is regulated by a thumb screw seen near it on the right of the frame. When the shield is allowed to slip back the pawl, falling into the gear teeth sooner, gives a greater feed. The pawl will thus feed one, two or three teeth at a time, according to the adjustment of the circular shield.

The rocker arm, which actuates the pawl, is attached to the side of the frame and is operated by an eccentric which revolves with the spindle.

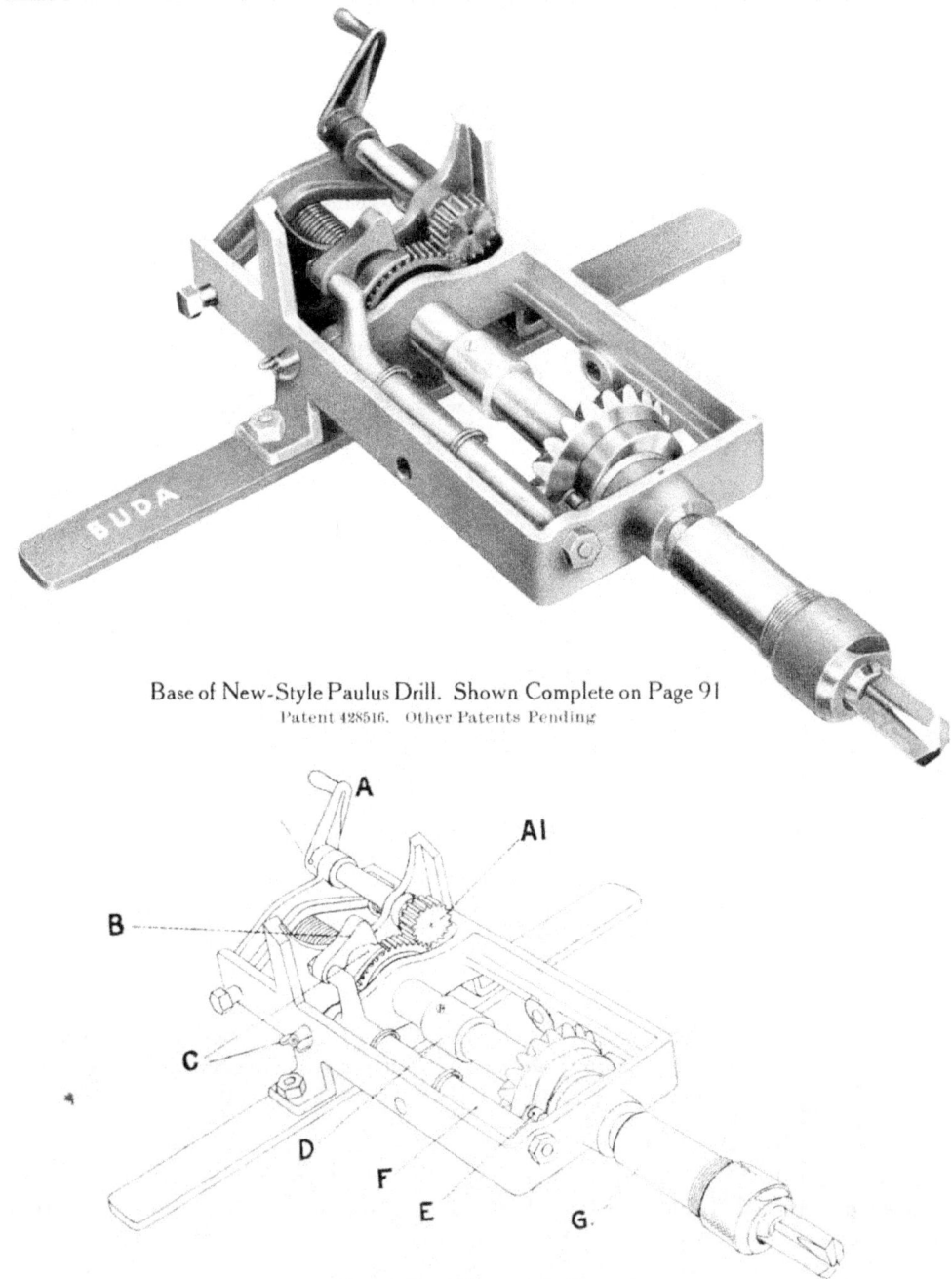

Base of New-Style Paulus Drill. Shown Complete on Page 91
Patent 428516. Other Patents Pending

Key to Parts Illustrated Above

A. Crank operating pinion A1. Used to feed bit quickly to or recede it from work.
B. Pawl which actuates feed gear.
C. Variable feed attachment and thumb screw that regulates it.
D. Dust-proof ball-bearing thrust between feed screw and spindle.
E. Eccentric which operates rocker shaft.
F. Rocker shaft on arm of which is pawl.
G. Rich spindle, chuck and Rich flat bit. Bit recedes into barrel G, where it rests on an adjustable thrust block, leaving only enough exposed to penetrate work. Torsional strength of bit thus greatly increased.

Between the feed screw and the spindle is a dust-proof ball bearing thrust. This obviates all possibility of the spindle cutting the feed screw and by lessening the friction enables the operator to apply all power directly to the action of the bit on the rail.

In the gearing of the New-Style Paulus we have paid particular attention to securing a ratio that enables the operator to perform the work more easily. In this manner more power is applied to the cutting point of the bit with a lesser expenditure of energy at the handles.

We desire to call particular attention to the frame and base of this drill. It will be noted that we have used a T section, making the drill exceptionally strong and adapting it for drilling work of any nature up to the very heaviest required.

How to Handle the New-Style Paulus Drill

Pull the handle and "break" the back braces. Throw the hooks over the rail and bring the frame to an upright position.

Run the bit up to the rail by means of the small crank at the back of the frame. The point of bit may thus be firmly set against the place where hole is to be drilled.

Stand on the foot plate when drilling.

Do not turn handles backward. To remove the bit from hole simply turn the small crank at back of drill backward and the spindle will rapidly recede.

For trains or engines to pass throw frame back as illustrated. The bit is not disturbed and the drilling may be immediately resumed.

We recommend the use of Rich flat bits, of high speed steel. Many of them drill more than 200 holes without requiring to be resharpened and have twice the usable steel found in twist bits. No water or oil is required on bit when drilling.

If twist bits are used it is well to have a strong solution of soap and water dripping on the bit when drilling. If you prefer twist bits, be sure to order those which are stamped "Buda."

New-Style Paulus Track Drill

VARIABLE FEED   BALL-BEARING THRUST

New-Style Paulus Drill in Working Position. Fully Described on Pages 88-90

Patent No. 428516. Other Patents Pending

The working parts of the New-Style Paulus are better shown on page 89. This is the latest development in track drills. Has variable feed; dust-proof ball-bearing thrust; small crank for feeding bit to and from work quickly. Frame and base are of T Section making drill firm and suitable for the heaviest work. The gears are arranged so that the operator may exert greater power with less effort than heretofore.

Weight ....95 lbs.
Price, equipped with Rich Spindle, chuck and one Rich flat bit..........$25.00
Equipped with spindle for twist bits only, one twist bit included........ 20.00

New-Style Paulus Track Drill

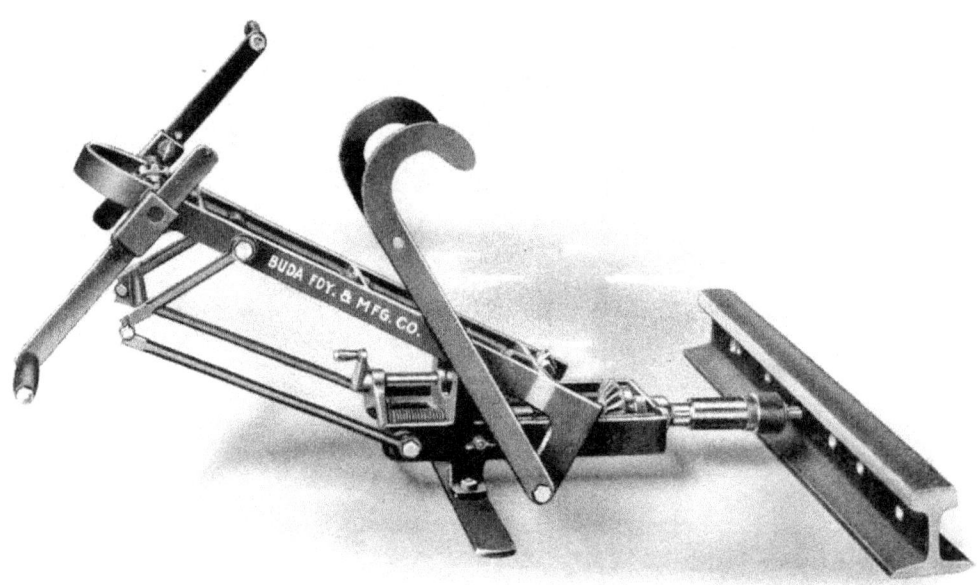

Thrown back to let train pass.   This drill shown in working position on page 91

This drill is also illustrated on preceding page, being shown in working position. To clear passing trains or engines, the drill is instantly thrown back, without disturbing the bit in the work. This is accomplished by breakng the back brace, as shown. The frame may be thrown in an upright position in a moment and work resumed. This drill is similar to our Paulus but has many advanced features, including ball bearing thrust, variable feed; arrangement for advancing the bit quickly up to, or receding it from the work. It is also ruggedly designed and is capable of rail work of any nature. Fully described on preceding pages.

Repair Parts for New-Style Paulus Track Drill

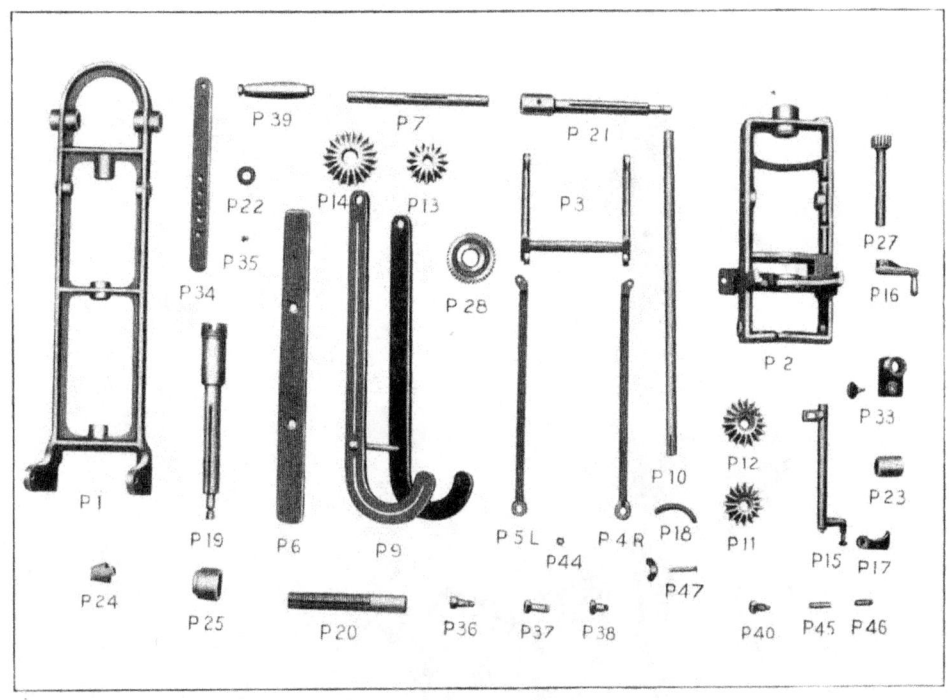

P- 1	Upper Frame $2.50	P-21	Standard Spindle 2.50
P- 2	Lower Frame 2.25	P-22	Thrust Collar .... .25
P- 3	Upper Back Bone Brace .... .75	P-23	Ball Bearing Shield .... .25
P-4R	Lower Back Bone Brace } .Pr. .75	P-24	Jaw for Rich Chuck 1.00
P-5L	" " " " }	P-25	Sleeve for Rich Chuck .... .70
P- 6	Foot Plate .... .50	P-27	Quick Return Pinion .... .75
P- 7	Crank Shaft .... .75	P-28	Ratchet Wheel 1.25
P- 9	Rail Hooks 1.00	No. 7	Cranks (not illus.), pair...... 1.00
P-10	Vertical Shaft .... .75	P-35	Set Screw .... .02
P-11	Upper Gears ..... } .Pr. 1.00	P-36	Special Shoulder Screw .... .10
P-12	" " ..... }	P-37	" " " .... .10
P-13	Lower Gears ..... } .Pr. 1.00	P-38	" " " .... .10
P-14	" " ..... }	P-39	Wood Handle .... .10
P-15	Rocker Shaft .... .75	P-40	Special Screw .... .05
P-16	Quick Return Handle .... .25	P-44	Steel Ball .... .03
P-17	Ratchet Feed Dog .... .25	P-45	Taper Pin .... .05
P-18	Thumb Nut .... .02	P-46	Key .... .03
P-19	Rich Spindle and Chuck 6.00	P-47	Belt and Wing Nut for adjusting feed .... .05
P-20	Feed Screw 1.25		

Paulus Track Drill

AUTOMATIC FEED

Equipped for Use of Twist Drill

Over Clutch

Regular style for use of twist drills.
The drill is shown in working position.

Weight	60 lbs.
Price, complete with one twist bit	$20.00
Equipped with Rich Spindle, chuck and one flat bit	25.00

Paulus Track Drill

AUTOMATIC FEED

Illustrating Position When Thrown Back to Permit Passage of Train

On opposite page the Paulus drill is shown in working position. This style has been on the market a number of years and its introduction was a distinct advance in rail drilling over other forms then in use, and has maintained the lead in this respect. Using the Paulus, an operator can drill holes in one-fifth the time required by ratchet drill.

How to Handle the Paulus Drill

To set up the drill for operation, pull handle back between braces and throw the upright part of the drill down, as shown in cut on page following.

Throw the hooks over the rail, then straighten up the brace and bring the drill to an upright position.

Screw the ratchet wheel with hand, and tighten the bit up against the rail where you wish to drill the hole.

Stand on the foot plate when drilling.

Never turn the handles backward to take out the drill bit. Throw down the upright part and remove the hooks from the rail. Pull the machine back to take the bit out of the hole.

For trains to pass when drilling, throw the upright part down and the hooks back.

Keep the screw in the end of feed screw set up tight to insure easy work.

It is well to have a strong solution of soap and water dropping on the bit when drilling.

Rich Spindle and Chuck Attachment.—New Paulus drills, or those now in use, may be equipped with the Rich spindle to permit the use of Rich flat bits, of high speed steel. The expense of the equipment is slight. The change of spindles is simple and may be made by anyone. For description of Rich flat bits, and their advantages, see pages 114 to 120.

Paulus Track Drill

AUTOMATIC FEED

Under Clutch

This style is designed for use on roads objecting to the hooks over rails. We do not send this style unless specified, as the majority desire the over clutch.

Weight .... 60 lbs.
Price, complete with one twist bit $20.00
Equipped with new Rich Spindle and one flat drill bit 25.00

The Buda Foundry & Manufacturing Company

Paulus Track Drill

REPAIR PARTS

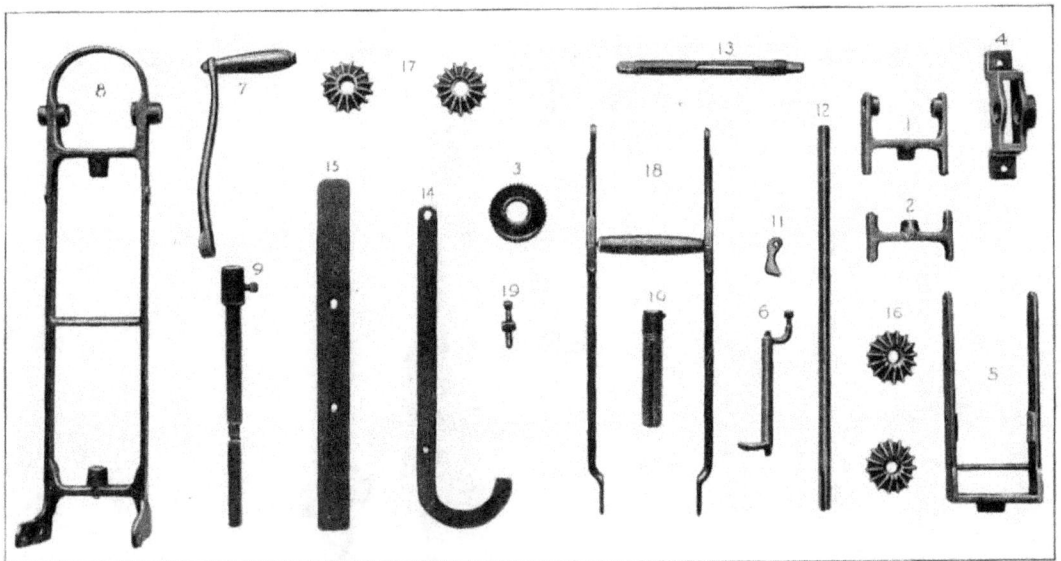

Order by Number

No.	Description.	Price.
1.	Upper Box, old style	$1.00
2.	Lower Box, old style	.75
3.	Ratchet Wheel	1.25
4.	Housing for Ratchet Wheel	1.50
5.	Lower Frame	1.50
6.	Rocker Shaft	.75
7.	Two Cranks	1.00
8.	Upper Frame, new style	2.50
9.	Spindle	2.50
10.	Feed Screw	1.25
11.	Ratchet Feed Dog	$0.25
12.	Vertical Shaft	1.00
13.	Crank Shaft	.75
14.	Rail Hooks	1.05
15.	Foot Plate	.50
16.	Two Upper Gears	1.00
17.	Two Lower Gears	1.00
18.	Back Brace	1.25
19.	Set Screw	.10

Buda-Pattern Track Drill

HEAVY BASE

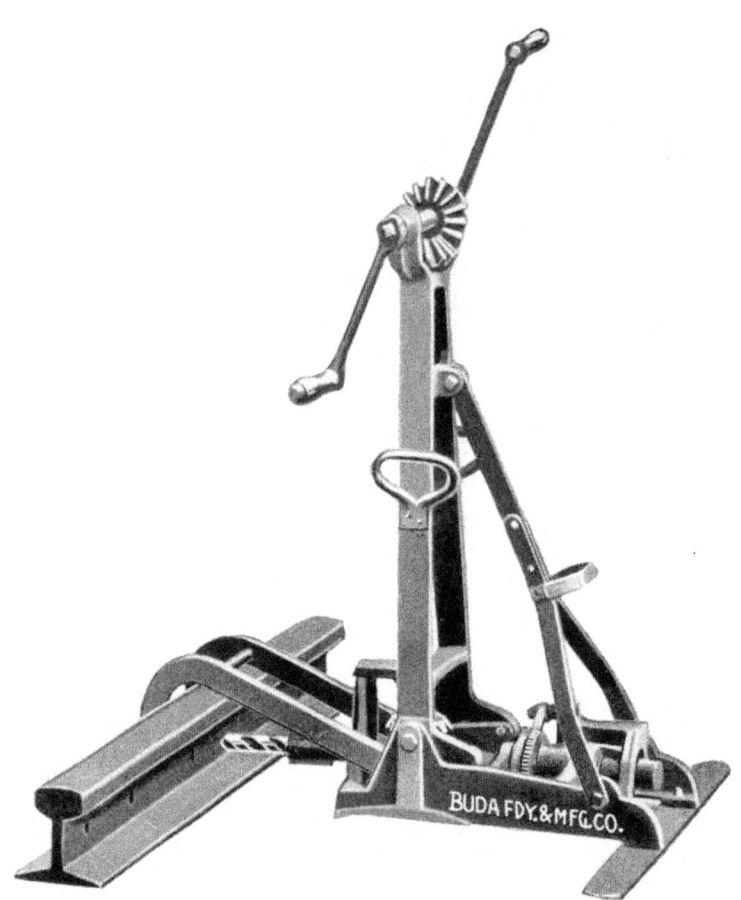

Paulus Patent

Operates practically the same as the Paulus drill. Has heavy base and is designed for more severe service.

Can be equipped with Rich Spindle and chuck; but Rich bits for use with Buda drill should be so specified.

Weight .... 90 lbs.
Price, complete for using twist drills............................... $20.00
Price, with Rich Spindle and chuck.................................. 25.00

Above prices include one bit.

Buda-Pattern Track Drill

HEAVY BASE

Paulus Patent

The heavy base drill is here shown in position for train to pass. By pulling on the handle on the back brace the top is made to collapse, bringing the hooks upward and back from the rail.

The Buda Foundry & Manufacturing Company

Buda-Pattern Track Drill

REPAIR PARTS

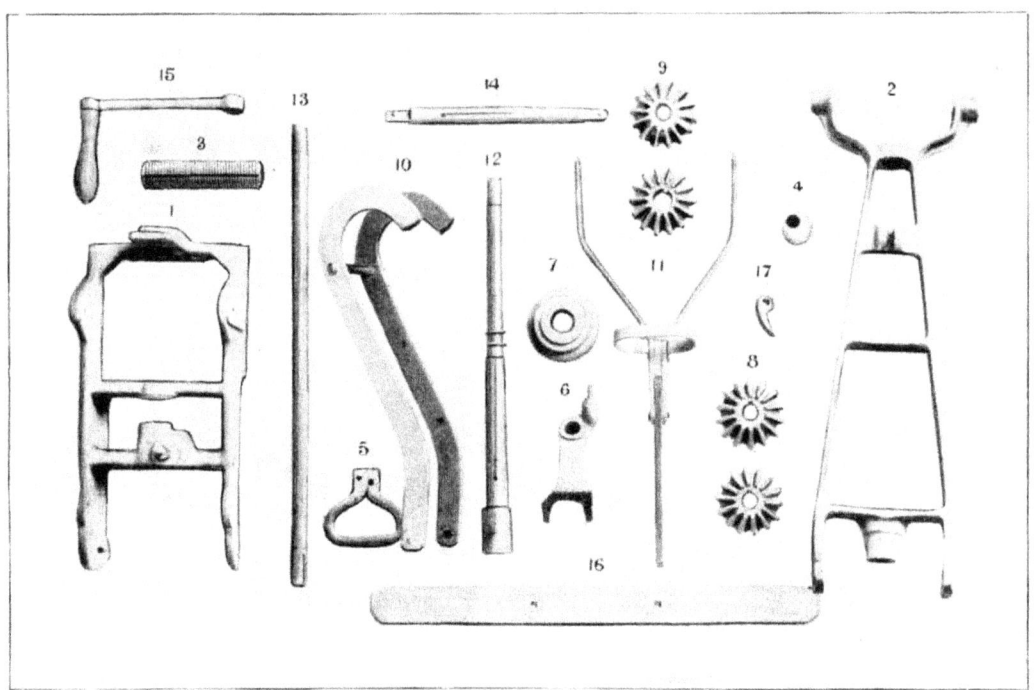

Order by Number

No.	Description.	Price.	No.	Description.	Price.
1.	Base	$2.00	10.	Rail Hooks	$1.00
2.	Upright Frame	2.50	11.	Back Brace	1.25
3.	Feed Screw	3.00	12.	Spindle	2.50
4.	Eccentric	.50	13.	Vertical Shaft	1.00
5.	Two Side Handles	.20	14.	Crank Shaft	.75
6.	Ratchet Finger	.50	15.	Two Cranks	1.00
7.	Ratchet Wheel	1.25	16.	Foot Plate	.50
8.	Two Upper Gears	1.00	17.	Ratchet Feed Dog	.25
9.	Two Lower Gears	1.00			

Paulus Girder Drill

AUTOMATIC FEED

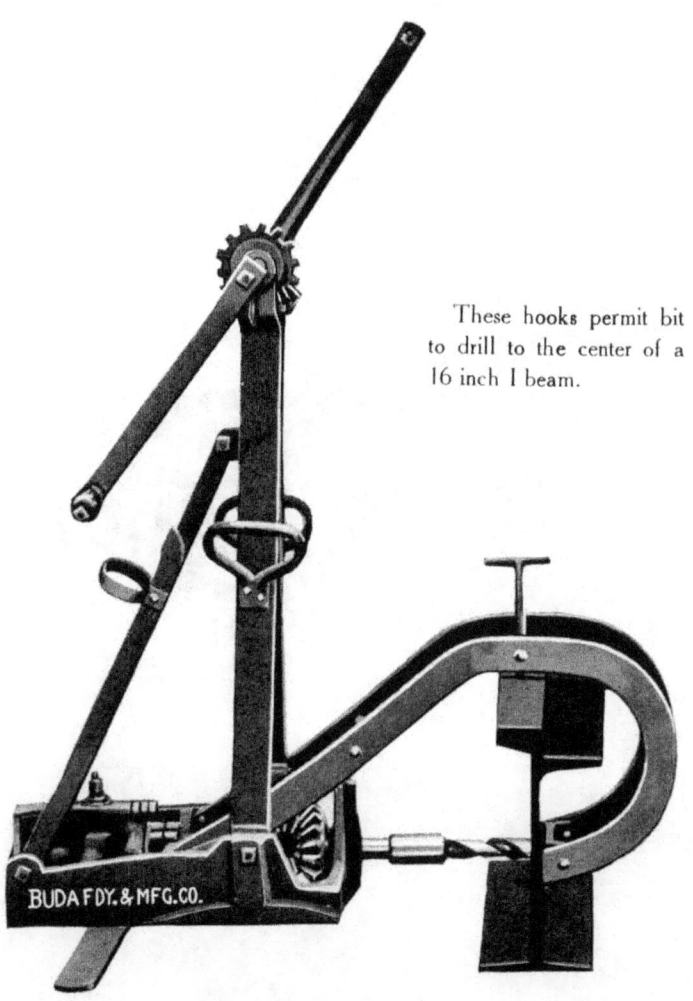

These hooks permit bit to drill to the center of a 16 inch I beam.

PAULUS GIRDER DRILL
For Drilling Girder Rails, I Beams and Channels

Will drill to the center of a 16-inch I beam, making it applicable to work on structural iron as well as on girder rails, if fitted with Rich chuck for using Rich flat bits. In ordering Rich bits name of drill should be given.

Weight ....100 lbs.
Price, complete as above with one twist bit..........................$25.00
Fitted with Rich Spindle, chuck and one ⅞-in. bit...................... 30.00

Paulus Girder Drill

AUTOMATIC FEED

Special Pattern

The method of detaching the girder drill is practically the same as that of the Paulus, except that the hooks may be lifted free of the machine and rail as shown.

The Wilson Drill

FOR BOND WIRE HOLES ON STEAM, INTERURBAN AND STREET RAILWAYS

The rail-drilling machine illustrated on following pages is the latest device for light work, and supplies a tool that is especially adapted for the use of railroad and street-car companies where it is necessary to drill holes from ¼ to ⅜ inch for bond wires.

By an ingenious arrangement the machine can be attached to and detached from the rail in a second or two. By simply throwing back a lever which is connected to a link motion, the frame slides back far enough to clear the drill point from the ball of the rail, so that the machine is entirely free and can be taken direct from the rail.

The mechanism of the automatic feed is a new departure. The driving gear is of the sprocket and chain type. On the crank shaft are two sprocket wheels; one, fastened rigidly to the shaft and revolving with it, drives the feed nut on the drill spindle; the other is placed loosely on the shaft and revolves with it only when engaged by a pawl on the end of the shaft. This wheel, when engaged by the pawl, drives the drill spindle; thus the drill spindle and the feed nut both revolve in the same direction, but so geared that the feed nut travels a little faster than the drill spindle, and so imparts to it an even and continuous feed, either forward or back, as the crank is turned.

Another excellent feature is that by disengaging the pawl the sprocket wheel which drives the drill spindle is made stationary while the feed nut revolves, imparting a quick forward or back movement to the drill spindle. This pawl is disengaged when the machine is placed on the rail, and by a few forward turns of the crank the drill is moved quickly forward until it comes in contact with the rail; then, by simply engaging the pawl, the quick feed is cut out and the slow automatic feed is brought into action until the hole is drilled. The pawl can then be instantly disengaged, thus cutting out the slow feed, and a few backward turns of the crank will retract the drill bit.

The machine is simple, being composed of few parts, and is light. The feed nut is mounted on ball bearings to reduce the friction of the thrust to a minimum.

Can be fitted with Rich Spindle for using Rich flat bits. The economy of these bits is explained on pages 114-120.

Wilson Drill

HOOK OVER TOP OF RAIL

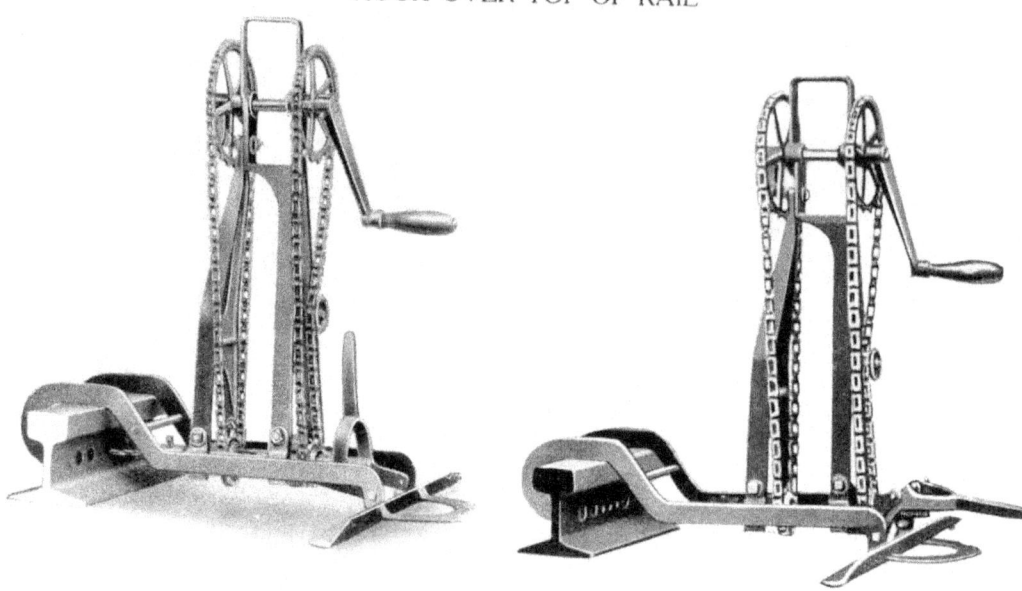

In Position for Work — Thrown Back to Detach from Rail

Quick acting for light work. Specially designed for bond wire holes for track circuit signal work.

Weight .... 25 lbs.
Price, complete for using twist bits $25.00
Price, complete with Rich Spindle and one flat bit 28.50

Prices of Bits for Use in Wilson Drills

TWIST BITS

Diameter Inches	Price each	Length
$\frac{15}{64}$	26c	4
$\frac{1}{4}$	28c	4
$\frac{9}{32}$	32c	4

RICH FLAT BITS

Diameter Inches	Price each	Length
$\frac{15}{64}$	65c	4
$\frac{1}{4}$	65c	4
$\frac{9}{32}$	65c	4

Wilson Drill

UNDER CLUTCH

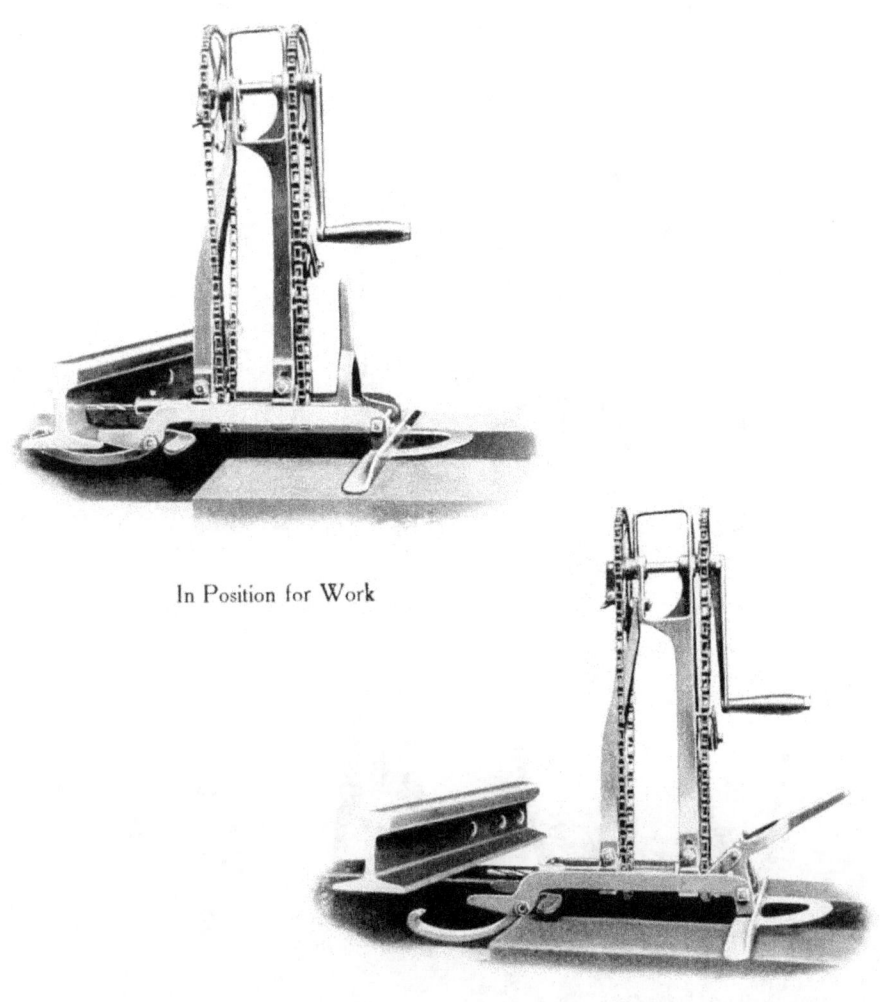

In Position for Work

Thrown Back to Detach from Rail

Same as drill on preceding page, except that the clutch is under base of the rails. Price same as over clutch style.

Wilson Drill

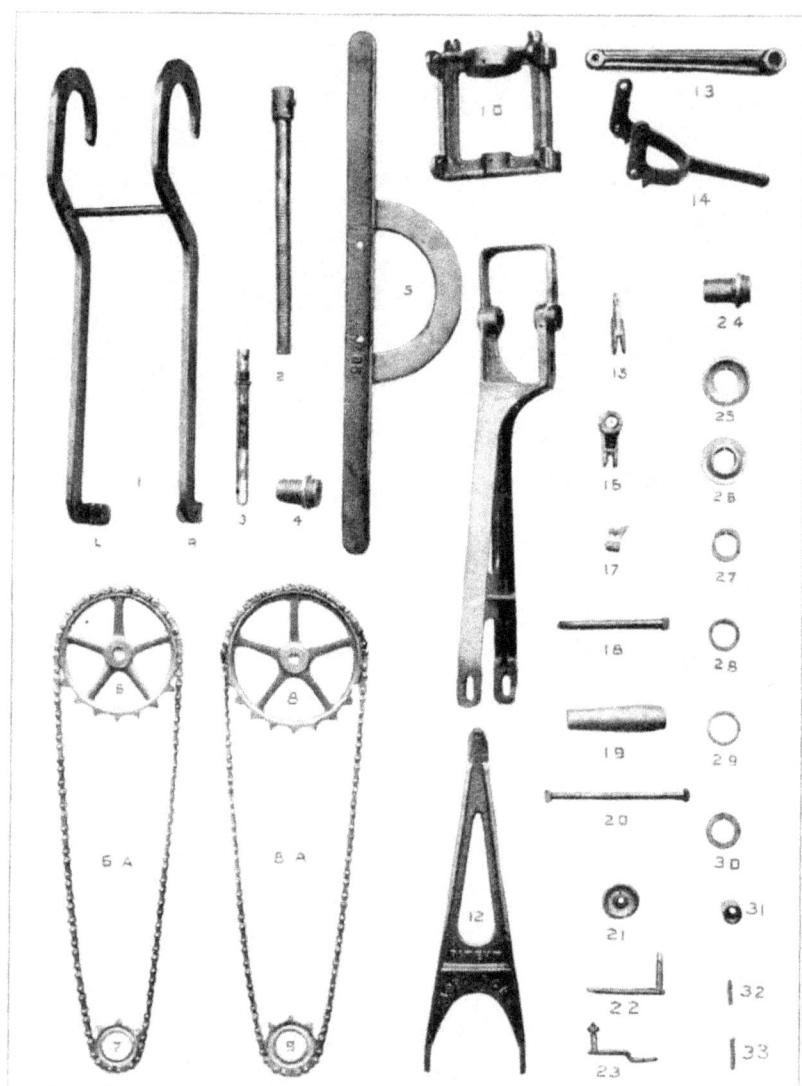

Repair Parts for Wilson Drill

No.	Description.	Price.
1.	Rail Hooks	$1.00
2.	Spindle	1.25
3.	Crank shaft	.60
4.	Drive Sleeve	1.80
5.	Foot Plate	.75
6.	Feed Sprocket, 19 Teeth	1.25
6A.	Feed Chain, 47 links	.85
7.	Feed Nut Sprocket, 7 Teeth	1.20
8.	Drive Sprocket, 21 Teeth	1.50
8A.	Drive Chain, 48 Links	.85
9.	Drive Sleeve Sprocket, 8 Teeth	1.20
10.	Sliding Frame	1.75
11.	Upright Frame	1.50
12.	Upright Frame Brace	.75
13.	Crank	.50
14.	Toggle Lever	.60
15.	Toggle 2	.30
16.	Arm	.45
17.	Pawl	.45
18.	Bolt for Handle doz.	.40
19.	Wood Handle	.10
20.	Toggle Lever Bolt	.40
21.	Idler Wheel	.10
22.	Idler Adjusting Plate	.20
23.	Idler Bracket	.20
24.	Feed Nut	1.80
25.	Cup for Ball Bearing	.75
26.	Cone for Ball Bearing	.75
27.	Adjusting Nut	.45
28.	Washer for Adjusting Nut	.08
29.	Lock Nut	.25
30.	Collar for Drive Sleeve	.15
31.	Bushing for Crank Shaft 2	.30
32.	Pawl Spring and Pin	.30
33.	Crank Shaft Pins	.07
—	20 ½-inch Steel Balls	.30

1. To permit train to pass, the small eccentric is thrown. This enables the back brace to be detached.
2. The upper part of frame is then removed as shown.
3. It is then placed to clear the train; to replace, the process is reversed. Very simple, and quickly done.

The Harvey Drill

FOR HEAVY OR LIGHT WORK

Variable Feed for Using Large or Small Bits with Soft or Hard Rail.
Made in Two Sizes

An important and desirable feature in this drill is an automatic and variable feed combined. When using large bits, coarser feeds may be employed than would be possible with the use of smaller bits, which latter would be snapped off—not being of sufficient diameter to stand the torsional strain imposed upon them.

The Harvey drill is capable of adjustment, so that large or small drills may be used and proper allowance made for hard or soft rail, the feed being regulated to suit the conditions. As all twist drills furnished by us have a uniform shank, no change is necessary in the spindle to enable the operator to use any large size bit.

Attention is called to the adjustable hook which goes over the top of the rail. This is so arranged that it may be made to fit special conditions. It sometimes happens where there is a guard rail it becomes necessary to use a longer over clutch. This is readily accomplished by removing the center bolt in the neck and replacing same after the hook has been pulled out to a suitable length.

The Harvey Drill

In Position for Drilling

This drill is equipped for use of our regular twist drill bits. The illustration shows style with hook over rail. Made in two sizes:

No. 1 Weighs 60 lbs.; price, complete for using twist bits...............$20.00
No. 1 Fitted with Rich Spindle and chuck.................................. 25.00
No. 2 Weighs 100 lbs.; price, complete for using twist bits............... 25.00
No. 2 Fitted with Rich Spindle and chuck.................................. 31.00

Above prices include one ⅞ bit.

There is also an arrangement whereby the feed may be operated independent of the spindle. This is accomplished by throwing a lever which releases a clutch between the spindle and feed, after which, by turning the handles, the spindle is driven directly to or from the work in a rapid manner.

The top frame is quickly removed to permit passing of trains by releasing the eccentric on the back bone and lifting clear and away from the base.

This simple procedure is shown in the small illustrations.

By the addition of a few parts the Harvey drill may be used for drilling holes in the base of the rail. When so specified, we forward an underclutch instead of the hook going over the top of the rail.

Harvey Drill Made in Two Sizes

The Harvey drill is made in two sizes. The No. 1, weighing 60 lbs., is for all ordinary work.

The No. 2 Harvey drill weighs 100 lbs. and is designed for the heaviest work. The construction is somewhat better than the smaller size. The bevel gears at the top and bottom of the upright frame, instead of being cast, are machine cut, which promotes easier operation and imparts a steadier action to the bit.

Friction is also reduced by means of a ball-bearing thrust. The No. 2 Harvey drill may be used for all-around work if desired, from the heaviest to the lightest. As before stated, the size of all shanks on our twist drills are uniform, so that no change in spindle is made necessary when using the smallest or largest bits.

Special Rich Spindle

The advantage of using Rich high-speed steel flat drills is mentioned elsewhere. A special spindle and chuck are required. These are furnished upon specification.

Harvey Drill

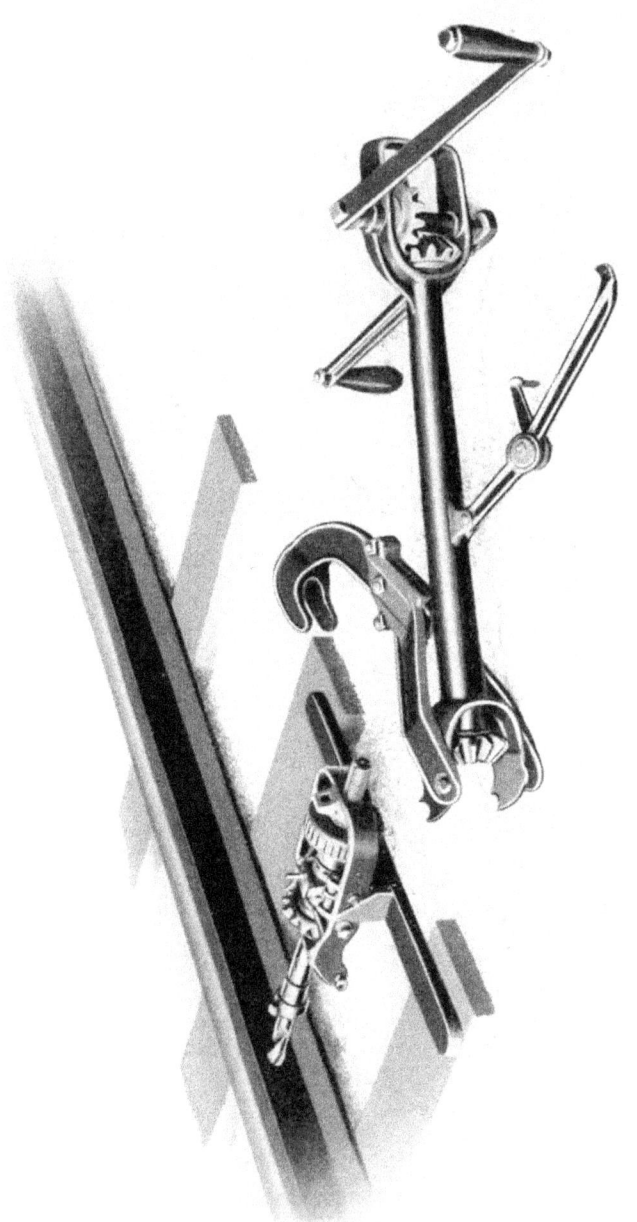

Over Clutch

The illustration shows upper part removed for passing train. The detachment can be done instantly. No delay taking off or putting on.

Harvey Drill

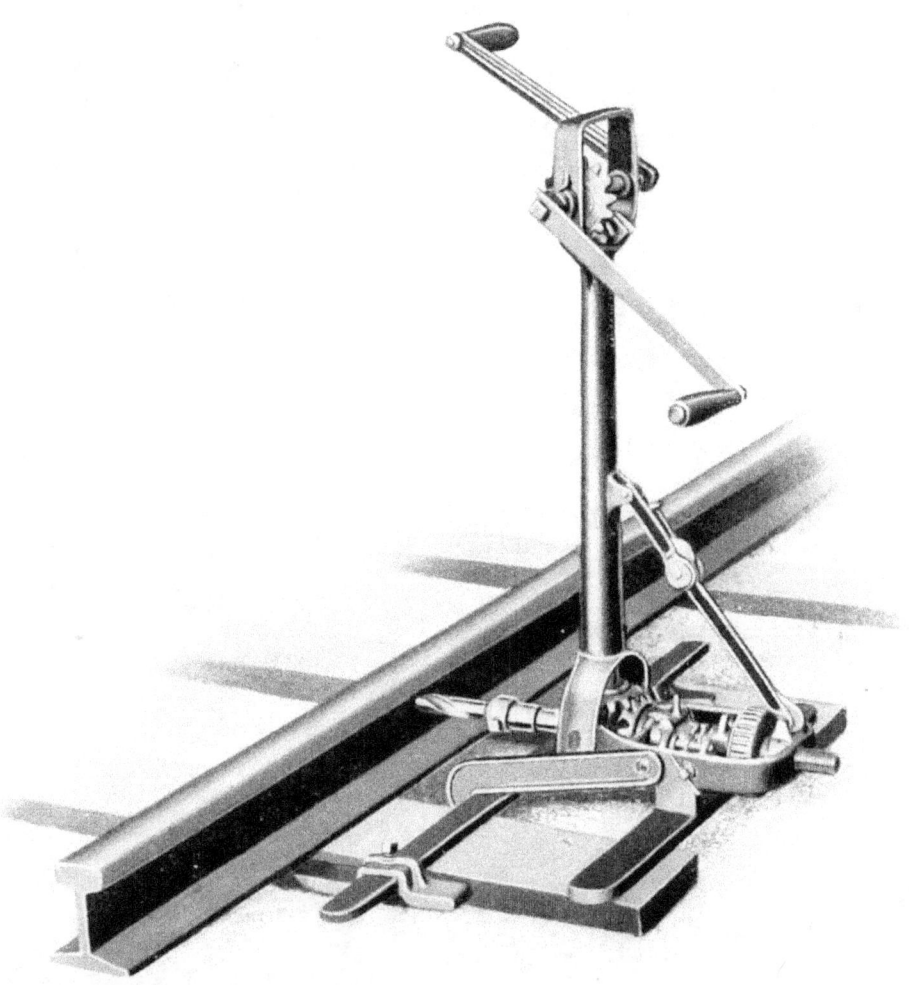

Under Clutch

Where an under clutch is desired we furnish the arrangement above shown. Can be had in No. 1 and 2 sizes and fitted either for twist bits or for Rich flat bits. Weights and prices same as with hook over rail shown on a preceding page.

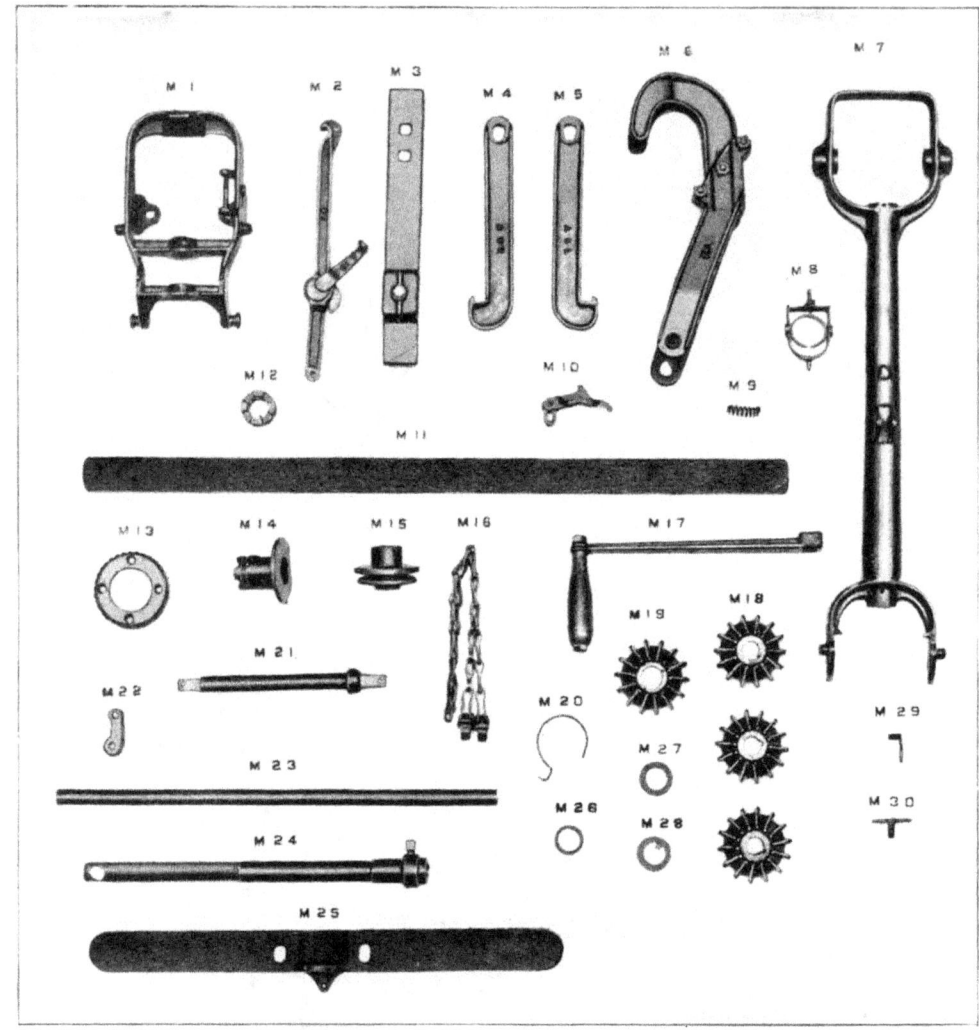

Repair Parts. No. 1 Harvey Drill

No.	Description.	Price.
M-1	Base	$2.50
M-2	Back Bone Brace	1.25
M-3	Two Underclutch Eye Bars	1.40
M-4	Underclutch Hook R. H.	.25
M-5	Underclutch Hook L. H.	.25
M-6	Rail Hook	1.30
M-7	Upright Frame	3.00
M-8	Shifting Lever	1.25
M-9	Clutch Spring (Coil)	.10
M-10	Feed Lever and Link	.50
M-11	Underclutch Cross Bar	.50
M-12	Clutch Collar	.50
M-13	Feed Nut Case	.75
M-14	Clutch Flange	1.00
M-15	Feed Nut	1.25
M-16	Two Underclutch Lugs with Chain	.30
M-17	Two Cranks, Wood Handles	$1.00
M-18	Three Gears (1 for Crank Shaft, 2 for Vertical)	1.50
M-19	One Gear for Spindle	.50
M-20	Feed Dog Spring	.10
M-21	Crank Shaft	.75
M-22	Feed Bracket and Roll	.30
M-23	Vertical Shaft	1.00
M-24	Spindle and Set Screw	2.50
M-25	Foot Plate	.50
M-26	One Steel Collar for Spindle Gear	.15
M-27	Two Wood Fibre Washers	.15
M-28	One Steel Collar Hardened, with Key	.45
M-29	Feed Dog Hardened	.25
M-30	Feed Adjusting Screw	.25

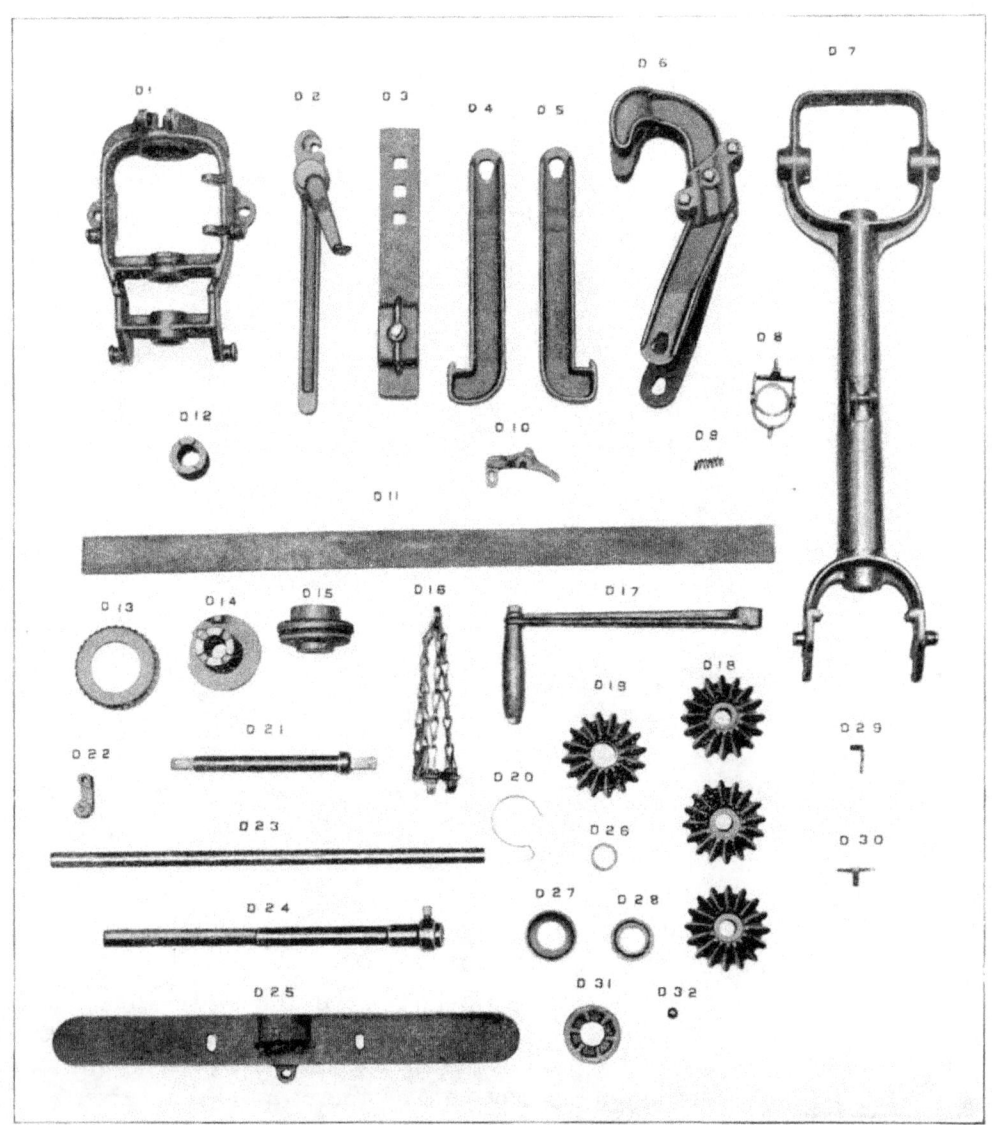

Repair Parts. No. 2 Harvey Drill

No.	Description.	Price.
D- 1	Base	$4.00
D- 2	Back Bone Brace	2.00
D- 3	Two Underclutch Eye Bars	2.00
D- 4	Underclutch Hook R. H.	.40
D- 5	Underclutch Hook L. H.	.40
D- 6	Rail Hook	2.35
D- 7	Upright Frame	5.00
D- 8	Shifting Lever	2.25
D- 9	Clutch Spring (Coil)	.10
D-10	Feed Lever and Link	.90
D-11	Underclutch Cross Bar	.90
D-12	Clutch Collar	.90
D-13	Feed Nut Case	1.30
D-14	Clutch Flange	1.80
D-15	Feed Nut	2.25
D-16	Two Underclutch Lugs with Chain	.50
D-17	Two Cranks, Wood Handles	$1.80
D-18	Three Cut Gears (1 for Crank Shaft, 2 for Vertical Shaft)	3.75
D-19	One Cut Gear for Spindle	1.25
D-20	Feed Dog Spring	.10
D-21	Crank Shaft	1.20
D-22	Feed Bracket and Roll	.55
D-23	Vertical Shaft	1.50
D-24	Spindle and Set Screw	4.00
D-25	Foot Plate	.90
D-26	Steel Collar for Spindle Gear	.15
D-27	Ball Bearing Cup	.75
D-28	Ball Bearing Cone	.75
D-29	Feed Dog Hardened	.25
D-30	Feed Adjusting Screw	.30
D-31	Ball Bearing Adjusting Nut	1.00
D-32	⅜-in. Steel Ball (16 per set)	.50

High Speed Steel

THE ADVANTAGES OF RICH FLAT BITS OF HIGH SPEED STEEL OVER ORDINARY TWIST BITS OF "CARBON" STEEL

High speed steel—also called air hardening steel—has found extensive use in machine shop practice. It is used to make cutting tools on lathes, planers and boring mills and is called high speed steel because it is so superior to ordinary "carbon" steel cutting tools that the lathes and similar machine tools can be speeded up to run three times as fast enabling the shop to turn out more than double the work formerly.

Up to a few years ago, carbon steel was the highest type used for cutting purposes. Carbon is a high form of coal and, roughly speaking, when combined with iron went to make steel; the greater the amount of carbon the finer the quality of steel; though what is called low carbon steel is better for some purposes. But all steel contained carbon. The fact is well known that if steel is heated to a considerable degree it loses its temper, becomes soft and fails to hold its cutting edge. The reason of this is that the carbon in the steel is affected by heat just as coal is.

High speed steel made its appearance with the discovery of how to make steel without carbon, other elements of a mineral nature being introduced into its composition which are not affected by heat as is carbon; and, because of this, cutting tools on a lathe are not affected even though they become red hot.

Practically the only important branch where high speed steel has not until now found greater use has been in that of drilling. This was due to the fact that bits in use were largely of the twist type. Twist drills break easily, and there is also much useless metal in the shank of the drill. High speed steel being more expensive than the ordinary tool steel, its use for drilling purposes was therefore discouraged.

What was required was a simple form of bit less expensive to manufacture, one form that would not break easily, and one where more of the metal could be used. The development of the Rich Flat Bit, illustrated on page 118 solved this problem. It is used in connection with the Rich Spindle and Chuck. For rail drilling this special attachment and bit are sold for use with our drilling machines only. The utility of the Rich Flat Bit, of high speed steel, can be readily understood when it is stated that many of these bits have drilled more than 200 holes before requiring to be resharpened. Contrasted with the usual average of 10 holes accomplished by the use of the ordinary twist drill, the great saving can be seen in cost of grinding, and also in the advantage of having more than twice the usable steel. These features are explained on pages devoted to the Rich Flat Bit and Rich Spindle and Chuck for use on track drills made by the Buda company.

Rich Flat Bit

MADE OF HIGH SPEED STEEL

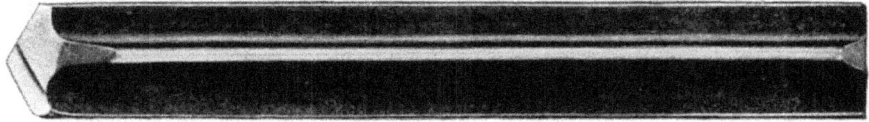

The Rich flat bit, of high speed steel, is illustrated above. It is simple in form and has none of the disadvantages of twist bits, either in construction or material. These bits are rolled into shape and cut off in suitable lengths after which they are sharpened. The bit is flat, as may be seen, but has a rib extending its length on both sides. This rib serves to strengthen it and also acts as a guide to keep it in the center of the jaws of the chuck. These jaws are made with a bead into which the rib fits.

Being straight the Rich bit is allowed to extend into the chuck until only enough projects to penetrate the work. This increases the torsional strength. As the bit is gradually worn down by sharpening it can be brought forward until five inches of the metal have been used. As only about two inches of steel can be used in the twist bit the available steel is more than double. Again there are no fluted edges to become nicked by careless handling. When this happens in a twist drill, the nick must be ground past in sharpening and this is likely to take off a quarter inch or more of the steel. Another point obviated is the tendency of bit to taper toward the cutting edge and thus stick in the rail and twist off or work very hard. Then there is no difficulty in taking the bit from the chuck. Twist bits frequently, on account of being improperly inserted, become "burred" by the retaining screw and it is almost impossible to release them for grinding.

The drilling capacity of these bits is exceedingly greater than that of twist drills. Many of them grind over 200 holes without resharpening, compared with the average of 10 holes by twist drills.

The fact that all steel mills now use these flat bits exclusively for rail drilling, may be accepted as conclusive evidence of their superiority. It should be remembered that aside from having more than twice the usable steel in Rich flat bits, they do not require one tenth, or one fifteenth, the sharpening, therefore there is a double economy which can be readily estimated.

Tests Made With Rich Flat Bits

Comparative tests between twist bits and Rich flat bits of high speed steel, which have been made in various kinds of drilling, have always resulted in a substantially economical showing in favor of the latter.

In some of the large manufacturing concerns, such as in steel mills, navy yards, shipbuilding companies and similar companies, rigid tests are conducted along all lines of manufacture with a view of adopting whatever has the slightest advantage over former methods. So exhaustive are the tests, and being in charge of men of highest technical experience, that the results may unquestionably be accepted.

It should be understood that the Rich form of high speed steel bit is superior to forged bits from the same material, and that in comparison with twist bits they are far superior. The following figures and tests are briefly given as a basis of comparison for the benefit of those not familiar with their merits.

One of the prominent steel mills of the country, having discarded twist bits for forged bits of high speed steel tested the latter with Rich flat bits. It was found that the cost alone of Rich drills was slightly more than one fourth that of the forged drills, and in addition this enabled a saving of two drill presses, and labor to the extent of $39.93 per 25-hour turn. As has been stated, twist bits had previously been discarded for the forged bit over which the Rich form of high speed steel bit made this showing.

Other tests heretofore conducted with Rich flat bits have been at the Navy Yard, New York. Ten 1¼-inch holes drilled by Rich bit in armor plate turrets after eight twist bits had been dulled finishing one hole.

At Fore River Shipbuilding Company, Quincy, Mass., fifty-two 1-inch holes drilled in armor of battleship Vermont without regrinding Rich flat bit.

At Newport News Shipbuilding Company, competitive test between twist bits, forged flat bits and Rich flat bits, all being 1⅛-inch holes. The twist bit and seven forged flat bits were used without completing one hole. Rich flat bit was used to complete hole and drilled ten similar holes without being reground.

In another test a ⅞-inch Rich flat bit at 400 revolutions per minute was fed at a rate of ten inches per minute through several thicknesses of bridge plate.

These government tests were official in character, the report being on file in the Navy Department (C. & R. Dept.) where it is available for inspection. The result was the adoption of Rich flat bits of high speed steel.

These tests, while not in the nature of track drilling are given on account of the rigid and severe conditions surrounding them, and from the fact that they were made under official inspection. Also it is to be concluded that their superiority for track drilling purposes is equally as great, in comparison with twist bits. In fact where the average of twist bits is claimed by trackmen to be about ten holes, that of Rich flat bits is much greater. Reports have reached us where Rich flat bits have drilled more than 200 holes before requiring to be reground. Considering this and the fact that there is double the usable steel, the economy of Rich flat bits of high speed steel may be conceived.

Rich Chuck

Only enough of the drill to penetrate work is projected. The increased torsional strength is apparent

How the Rich flat bit is held in the chuck is shown in the above illustration. Only enough of the bit projects to penetrate the work. The torsional strength which is already greater is enhanced by this arrangement. The bit is permitted to recede into the barrel and rests against an adjustable thrust block. As the point is ground away the bit is brought forward to compensate for the wear. The thrust block in the barrel is adjusted by using the butt of the bit as a screw-driver after the jaws have been opened sufficiently to allow the bit to be turned. In this way the entire length of the bit may be used up to within about two inches of the butt. A great economy is again manifested, for with twist bits only about two inches of the bit can be used, the other four inches being thrown away. About five inches of steel are usable in the Rich flat bit.

No trouble is experienced with Rich bits sticking in the chuck as is often the case with twist bits which have become burred on the shank by careless setting of the retaining screw, involving much lost time and annoyance.

We call attention to the advantages of high speed steel mentioned on page 114.

The Rich Spindle, Chuck and Flat Drill Bit

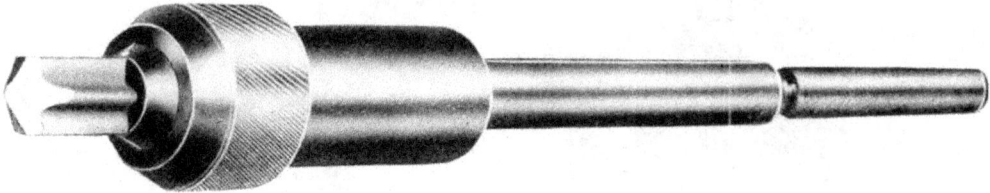

For Use on Drills of Our Manufacture Only

The Rich Spindle, Chuck and Flat Bit are shown here. This spindle may be used in connection with any of our drilling machines in place of that which is intended for use with twist bits. The spindle being interchangeable, old Paulus drills can be re-equipped by anyone, as the change is simple.

In ordering be sure to state for which of our drilling machines it is wanted.

In purchasing new machines we recommend that they be ordered fitted with the Rich attachment; for, by the use of these flat bits a great economy can be effected, not only in the time required in resharpening bits, but there is twice the usable steel in the flat bits. Flat bits have also the advantage of being free of any chance of damage by nicked flutes.

This attachment is sold for and applicable to only drilling machines of our manufacture.

Prices of Rich Spindle, Chuck and Bit for New-Style Paulus, Paulus, Buda, Girder and No. 1 Harvey Drills

Spindle and chuck complete..$6.00
Spindle, chuck and one ⅞-in. flat drill bit.. 7.40
    Repair parts: Spindle, $4.00; Jaws, $1.00; Sleeve, 70c; Thrust Block, 30c.

Prices of Rich Spindle, Chuck and Bit for No. 2 Harvey Drill

Spindle and chuck complete..$7.00
Spindle, chuck and one ⅞-in. drill bit... 8.40
    Repair parts: Spindle, $5.00; Jaws, $1.00; Sleeve, 70c; Thrust Block, 30c.

Note.—Rich chucks come fitted with jaws having No. 2 bead for using bits ¾ in. and larger. For using bits smaller than ¾ in., an extra set of jaws with No. 1 bead is required. Extra set, $1.00.

Price of Rich Spindle, Chuck and Bit for Wilson Drill

Spindle and chuck complete..$3.25
Spindle, chuck and one bit... 3.90

Paulus Drill

FITTED WITH RICH SPINDLE CHUCK AND BIT

This is the regular Paulus drill; but is especially fitted with the Rich spindle and chuck to permit the use of Rich flat, high-speed steel bits. The spindles being interchangeable, Paulus drills now in use may be thus equipped by anyone.

Price of drill complete with Rich spindle, chuck and one ⅞-in. flat drill bit.$25.00

Prices of Twist Drill Bits

FOR USE IN NEW-STYLE PAULUS, PAULUS, BUDA, GIRDER, AND HARVEY DRILLS

The twist bits are exceptionally high grade, and are made especially for us for use on our drills. To insure the best results see that our name is on the bit.

Diameter Inches	Price Each	Length Inches	Diameter Inches	Price Each	Length Inches
13-32	$0.90	6	13-16	$1.35	6
7-16	.90	6	27-32	1.40	6
15-32	.95	6	7/8	1.45	6
1/2	.95	6	29-32	1.55	6
17-32	1.00	6	15-16	1.60	6
9-16	1.00	6	31-32	1.70	6
19-32	1.05	6	1	1.80	6
5/8	1.05	6	1 1-16	2.00	6
21-32	1.10	6	1 1/8	2.20	6
11-16	1.15	6	1 3-16	2.30	6
23-32	1.20	6	1 1/4	2.40	6
3/4	1.25	6	1 3/8	2.80	6
25-32	1.30	6	1 1/2	3.20	6

Prices of Twist Bits for Wilson Drills given on page 104

Prices of Rich High Speed Steel Flat Drill Bits

FOR USE IN NEW-STYLE PAULUS, PAULUS, BUDA, GIRDER, AND HARVEY DRILLS WITH RICH CHUCK

NOTE: Drill bits 1/2 in. to 23/32 in., inclusive, require jaws for the No. 1 bead. Drill bits 3/4 in. to 1 1/4 in., inclusive, require jaws for the No. 2 bead.

Diameter, Inches.	Price, Each.	Diameter, Inches.	Price, Each.
1/2	$0.95	29/32	$1.45
17/32	.95	15/16	1.50
9/16	1.00	31/32	1.52
19/32	1.00	1	1.55
5/8	1.05	1—1/32	1.60
21/32	1.10	1—1/16	1.65
11/16	1.10	1—3/32	1.70
23/32	1.15	1 1/8	1.75
3/4	1.20	1—5/32	1.80
25/32	1.25	1—3/16	1.85
13/16	1.30	1—7/32	1.90
27/32	1.35	1 1/4	1.95
7/8	1.40		

Prices of Rich Bits for Wilson Drills given on page 104

No. 1 Grinder　　　　　　　　　　No. 2 Grinder

Buda Tool Grinders

Do work equal to power machines. Fitted with carborundum wheels, the hardest, sharpest abrasive known. Non-heating to steel. One Buda grinder will outdo twenty grindstones

The Buda portable grinders illustrated herein are a great advance over anything heretofore offered. They cut rapidly, never become "dull," and, what is one of the most important features is the fact that by their use the temper is not taken from the tool.

The use of grindstones is no longer considered economy, in fact they are an extravagance. They cut in a very slow manner and it is usually impossible to keep the wheel true in order to grind with any accuracy at all. Aside from the sandstone, there is also employed emery and corundum, both of which are more rapid cutters and very much harder. The principal objection to their use is, however, that they glaze over, leaving a smooth surface and the tool rubbing against the smooth surface causes friction which produces heat, thereby destroying the temper.

Buda Tool Grinders Have Carborundum Wheels

Carborundum is the ideal abrasive. It is by far the hardest substance ever produced. It was first discovered in the Edison laboratories and was the result of an attempt to artificially produce diamonds. It is now produced in electric furnaces at Niagara Falls, being made under the enormous heat of 7000 degrees. The substance is diamond in character, rivaling that stone in hardness, and when broken and formed into wheels it gives a sharp cutting surface that never wears smooth. When we say "cutting," we make a distinction between that process and grinding, and it is this difference that enables the user to sharpen his tools without heating the steel and destroying the temper.

To properly use our carborundum grinders a high speed should be attained and then only the lightest touch of the metal is required to properly perform the work. In fact it is essential that the work be done in this manner; for a slow speed and heavy pressure would be injurious to the long life of the wheel, the heavy pressure tending to break away the grains from the wheel. Properly used, carborundum wheels will do the work of from six to ten emery wheels, carborundum itself being about eight times as hard as emery.

Temper Not Destroyed When Buda Tool Grinders Are Used

As has been stated, the principle involved is that of cutting and not grinding. Carborundum cuts; emery grinds. A sharp tool will cut faster than a dull one, therefore carborundum wheels cut faster, last longer and **do not heat the steel;** also they never get dull like wheels made of other substances.

Tools Always Dull Where Grindstones Are Used

Dull tools are a poor investment, and where grindstones are used dull tools will usually be found. The reason for this is plain. Grindstones require considerable time to do the work, therefore the men try to get along with as little grinding as possible. Then, again, the work is usually unsatisfactorily done. Working with dull, or with poorly sharpened tools, more time is required, thus it is a loss all around, and the importance of having proper grinding facilities becomes all the more apparent.

One man with a Buda grinder can do the work of twenty men using the ordinary sand grindstone. Only a few seconds is required to perform grinding of almost any character and when it is no longer an arduous duty the workmen keep their tools in proper working order and do a correspondingly greater amount of work.

When the tools are sent in to some shop to be kept ground the results are always the same; they are never sent in until too dull for use, thus the work is done with dull tools much of the time. The plan is also expensive, as it requires a double outfit, one being in use while the dull outfit is away being sharpened.

Tools Always Sharp Where Buda Grinders Are Used

The advantage of having sharp tools always on hand will be admitted by anybody. With a Buda Tool Grinder on hand there is no excuse for tools being dull. A few moments' time is all that is required for drills, shovels, picks or any other implement used on a railroad section.

These grinders are an economical investment that will pay for themselves many times over every year.

They are fully as efficient as any power machine and may be taken out on the line and fastened to the platform on a hand car. The shop advantages of grinding may thus be had at any time and at any point on the line.

Drill Grinding Attachment

The proper grinding of drills is a simple matter with our attachments. In the illustration will be noticed a removable bracket into which twist bits may be placed. The bit is placed as shown and then grasped by one hand and the bracket swung back and forth as far as it will go. This arrangement gives proper clearance, doing the work as well as a high priced device and far better than even the most expert mechanic could expect to do it without mechanical aid.

For sharpening Rich High Speed Flat Bits—which we furnish exclusively for use with track drilling machines of our make, the small table is made to tilt a certain angle and a groove provided for the bit to rest in. This does the most important part of the work, the rest being accomplished in the manner illustrated.

No extra charge is made for these drill-grinding attachments. We make them a part of the outfit.

General Construction

These grinders are built in a very strong manner, being designed for railroad work, and will do any work required.

All bearings are exceptionally wide and this one feature alone adds years of service to the grinder.

A dust-proof arrangement prevents dust from getting in the bearings, thus reducing wear to the minimum.

Oil holes for every bearing permit proper lubrication.

The chain is of the Locke Steel Belt type, oil tempered. The use of over 500,000 feet of this chain in connection with this type of grinder has resulted in perfect satisfaction.

A simple arrangement provides for taking up slack in the chain and there is no possibility of its getting out of adjustment.

These grinders are geared up for high speed and 3500 revolutions of the grinding wheel is easily attained. Remember that high speed is a vital necessity; it insures long life to the carborundum wheel and assists in rapid cutting.

The operation is extremely easy and involves no hard work at all.

REMEMBER THAT ANYTHING TO BE GROUND SHOULD HAVE NO PRESSURE AT ALL EXERTED ON IT. THE MERE TOUCHING OF THE STEEL TO THE WHEEL IS SUFFICIENT. NOT ONLY IS IT SUFFICIENT, BUT IT IS THE ABSOLUTELY CORRECT WAY TO GET RESULTS.

The hand power grinders are fitted with an adjustable malleable iron clamp fitting over hand car, bench or timber up to four inches in width.

Made in Two Styles

Our grinders are made in two styles, known as Nos. 1 and 2.

General description of each style follows:

Buda Grinder No. 1

Substantially constructed, being intended for all around service for shop, section house or out on track. The bearings are exceptionally wide and all parts are described under "General Construction." The illustrations of hand power grinder shown herein were photographed from our No. 1 style.

Each grinder is complete with the following:

1 Ideal attachment for use in sharpening twist bits.

1 attachment for sharpening Rich flat bits of high speed steel, which we sell for use only in track drills of our manufacture.

1 6x1⅜ No. 60 grit carborundum wheel for general work such as sharpening drill bits, axes, shovels, chisels, etc.

1 5x1⅜ No. 90 grit for scythes and fine tools.

1 5x1⅜ No. 24 grit for pick axes, grub hoes castings, bolt heads and all other work where a rapid cutter is required.

The main gear is 8 inches in diameter and teeth have ⅝ inch face. The shafts are ⅝ inch in diameter and have 5½ inch bearings. The crank has a 17 inch sweep so that ample leverage is obtained to do the heaviest grinding.

The cutting wheels are easily slipped on and off and as they are accurately fitted no further adjustment is required, as they will be found to run perfectly true.

Price, complete, as above..$20.00

Buda Grinder No. 2

The Buda No. 2 grinder is constructed along the same lines as the No. 1, but is of lighter general build and sells for a lower price. It will be found just as satisfactory, but it is intended for lighter work.

Each No. 2 grinder is complete as follows:

1 Ideal attachment for sharpening twist bits.

1 attachment for sharpening Rich flat high speed steel bits.

1 5x1⅜ No. 60J grit carborundum wheel for sharpening drill bits and for general work.

1 5x1⅜ No. 90 grit carborundum wheel for scythes and fine tools.

1 5x1⅜ No. 24 grit carborundum wheel for rapid cutting where a coarser wheel is preferable, such as for sharpening pick axes, grinding castings, bolt heads, etc.

The main gear is 6¾ inches in diameter and the teeth have ½ inch face. The shafts are ½ inch in diameter and have 3½ and 4 inch bearings. The crank sweep is 14 inches.

The wheels may be put on and taken off in the same manner as on the No. 1 grinder.

Price, complete, as above..$16.00

Price List of Carborundum Wheels for Buda Grinders

No. 70.	6x1⅜, 60 Grit, for general work	each $4.00
No. 51.	5x1⅜, 60J Grit, for general work	" 2.60
No. 52.	5x1⅜, 90J Grit, for finer tools	" 2.60
No. 50.	5x1⅜, 24 Grit, for pick axes, etc.	" 2.60

All above wheels are bushed on iron centers.

For Grinding Rich Flat Drill Bits

First Operation

First Operation. The drill should be laid flat on the wheel, as shown in the illustration, and the taper thus preserved. The proper angle may be easily retained by following the original contour. This part of the sharpening process is very simple. The lightest touch should be used and the wheel made to run at high speed.

Second Operation

Second Operation. This part of the grinding is important and we have provided a special holder which is given just the right angle to obtain the proper clearance. The Rich flat bit has a rib extending its length on both sides. The attachment has a groove into which this rib fits, thus acting as a guide so sure that no trouble need be experienced in obtaining accurate results. Remember that only the slightest touch is required. Care should be taken not to grind one side more than the other. This results in throwing the point out of "center" and the bit would then cut only on one edge and the hole drilled would be increased in size. The attachment includes a gauge into which the point of bit is fitted so that any inaccuracy in this respect may be readily discovered.

Third Operation

Third Operation. A small lip should be ground at the point of the bit which is made to taper away entirely as it approaches the outer cutting edge. Care should be used not to grind away too much of the metal. Just a touch. It is best to steady the point of the bit and lay it on the motionless stone, in order to get the "position," and then, having obtained a high speed, lightly touch the bit to the wheel. Only about one second is all that is required under ordinary circumstances.

A few minutes' study will make the entire operation clear, after which drills may be sharpened in less than one minute. By following these instructions and by the aid of the attachment there is no chance to go astray.

Ideal Attachment for Grinding Twist Bits

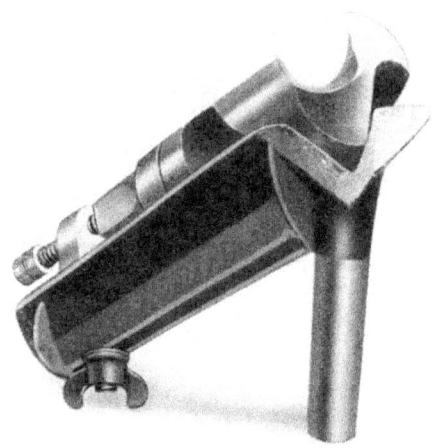

Swinging Bracket Detached from Frame

Swinging Bracket Attached to Frame and Twist Bit in Position for Sharpening

The Ideal attachment for use in sharpening twist bits is illustrated herewith. It is in the form of a bracket which fits into the frame of the grinder and may be removed at will by simply lifting it out of the socket. The twist bit is placed in the holder and by the means of an adjusting screw is brought up to the side of the wheel.

The large illustration shows how the bit should be placed in the holder. The fluted edge should be made to fit against the edge of the V-shaped opening.

The bracket swings backward and forward and when the bit is properly set, as shown, and the speed attained on the wheel the bit and bracket are grasped by the left hand and moved to and fro to the extreme limit in each direction.

After one side has been sharpened the bit is turned so that the opposite fluted edge assumes the position of that just sharpened. And the grinding operation repeated.

By the aid of this attachment twist bits are correctly sharpened, the backing or "clearance" being perfectly accomplished by the swinging motion of the attachment.

Twist bits may thus be sharpened in less than a minute each; for the cutting speed of these wheels is far greater than any other abrasive.

But remember that high speed should always be used and very light pressure
These grinders may be made to attain a speed of 3,500 revolutions a minute

Track Gauges and Levels

NEW AND OLD TYPES WITH AND WITHOUT INSULATION

To those styles manufactured formerly by us we have added other forms of gauges and levels, all of which are illustrated and described in the pages that follow.

A few years ago one or two styles alone found almost exclusive use. These same levels and gauges are still in demand, and doubtless will be for a long time, as they fulfill all the requirements in many instances. Some of the large railroads have seen advantages, however, in certain modifications, improvements and occasionally in entirely new devices for the gauging and leveling of tracks wherein it was desired to meet new conditions or special plans.

The introduction of block signals with track circuits has also made necessary proper insulation of the various forms of gauges and levels to be used on roads employing these safeguards.

Quality may vary in the manufacture of gauges and levels, and it is as important that it should exist here as elsewhere. We call particular attention to the fact that the styles we offer are all made by us of carefully selected material, both as to the metal and wood parts, and that they are put together with care and accuracy, the intention being to make them serviceable for as long a time as possible and provide against the ravages of weather and the results of the rough handling to which they are naturally subjected.

We desire particularly to mention the fact that our methods of insulation will be found perfectly satisfactory in any of the types we make and will be found to last as long as the life of the level or gauge.

Our manufacturing facilities are exceedingly favorable to our offering a better quality at lower prices than may be secured elsewhere, and we invite a comparison not alone of prices but of our levels and gauges alongside of those of other makes.

Huntington Standard Track Gauge

With and Without Insulation

This is the ordinary pattern Huntington Gauge. The construction is less expensive than our best grade; the heads simply being riveted on and the ends are not milled. Made in insulated and non-insulated styles. Unless specified we ship without insulation.

Price, without insulation................................per doz., $10.00
Price, with weather-proof insulation ....per doz., 15.00

Buda Huntington Track Gauge

Our Best Grade

This is our best grade. The method of attaching heads is shown above. The sockets are extra length, being 3½ inches; openings machined; pipe smooth finished to secure exact fit, and the threaded part being 2½ inches from the opening, a double bearing on the pipe is secured, giving heads no chance to work loose. The ends fitting against the rail are carefully milled, making the gauge absolutely accurate. Very high grade in every respect.

Price, without insulation ....per doz., $12.00
Price, with weather-proof insulation ....per doz., 17.00

Caffrey-Huntington Gauge with Guard Rail Attachment

With and Without Insulation

Same grade as above, having riveted heads, etc., but shows distance at which to set guard rail.

Price, without insulation ....per doz., $15.00
Price, with weather-proof insulation ....per doz., 20.00

McManus Gauge and Level

The gauge glass has rubber packing which protects it and greatly lessens the likelihood of levels being broken by rough and careless handling.

Price ....Per doz., $30.00

McManus Insulated Gauge

This gauge has no level, but is insulated.

Price ....Per doz., $18.00

Insulated Gauge with Adjustable Level and Graduated Elevation Slide

This is an exceptionally high grade gauge and level. It is made of the best and most thoroughly seasoned white ash. The elevation slide is made of brass to prevent rusting, and the heads carefully and accurately adjusted. The level glass is arranged in a brass tilting frame operated by a thumb-screw so it may be adjusted. This gauge is standard on the Union Pacific Railroad.

Price ....per doz., $45.00

Buda Wooden Track Level

With and Without Insulation

Made of white pine with three coats of paint, thus overcoming the tendency to warp and twist shown in common maple levels. It is thoroughly bound in steel. Shows proper distance to set guard rails.
Price, without insulation .... per doz., $15.00
Price, insulated .... per doz., 15.00

Insulated Circular Track Gauge

This gauge has radical ends and is furnished with and without guard rail attachment.
Price, with guard rail attachment .... per doz., $20.00
Price, without guard rail attachment .... per doz., 18.00

Combined Level and Spot Board

Painted white with black stripe, as shown. The ends at bottom have metal plates to prevent wear and retain accuracy. At one end the metal forms a plate to keep board from tipping. Elevation slide is made of maple, being graduated and position maintained by thumb-screw. Level glass well protected. This spot board is standard on the Baltimore and Ohio R. R.
Price .... per doz., $25.00

Level Glasses

Level glasses often become broken by accident. These we furnish fit all levels of our make.
Price .... each, $0.15

Jim Crow Rail Benders

With Cross Bar

No.	Will bend rail.	Weight complete as illustrated.	List Price.
1	80 to 100 lbs.	220 lbs.	$21.00
2	60 " 75 "	200 "	19.00
3	30 " 55 "	140 "	17.00
4	12 " 30 "	65 "	12.00

Jim Crow Rail Benders

WITHOUT CROSS BAR

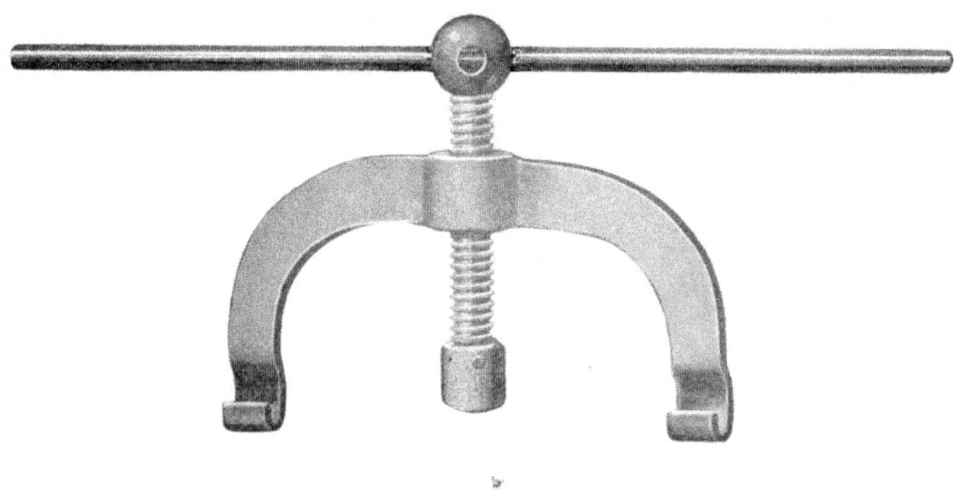

Special Note: Owing to some confusion heretofore existing, on account of there being Jim Crow benders without cross bar, carrying Numbers 1 and 2; also Jim Crow benders with cross bar having the same numbers, we have given a new series to the bender shown.

Please use the new Jim Crow style-numbers when ordering Jim Crow benders without cross bar.

Old No.	New No.	Will bend rail.	Weight complete as illustrated.	List Price.
00	5	16 lbs.	35 lbs.	$ 7.00
0	6	20 "	50 "	9.00
1	7	25 "	65 "	10.00
2	8	50 "	95 "	13.00

Roller Rail Benders

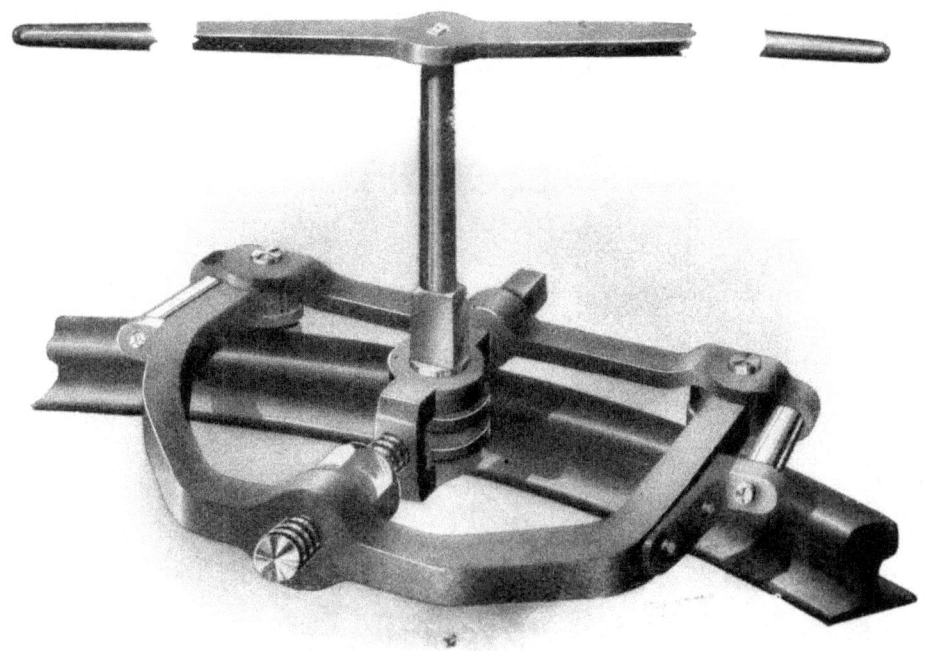

In ordering this rail bender give section and make of rail.

DIRECTIONS: Place bender over rail as shown in cut; turn up nut on center screw until set for desired curve, then place socket wrench on pin in center roller, put long lever on top of socket, and then one or more men can turn center roller, which causes the bender to move forward on rail, bending same as it moves. To straighten rails, place bender on OPPOSITE side of curve and then operate as above.

No.	Will bend rail.	Weight complete, as illustrated.	List price.	Extra rollers per set.
3	61 to 70 lbs.	400 lbs.	$140.00	$25.00
4	71 " 80 "	470 "	180.00	25.00
5	81 " 90 "	520 "	230.00	25.00
6	91 " 100 "	830 "	400.00	25.00

SPECIAL NOTE: We do not recommend this bender for use on girder rails. Rails of this description may be bent as desired in our own shops where we have also every facility for handling all classes of frog, crossing and switch work and lay-outs of the most intricate nature.

Tie Plate Beetle

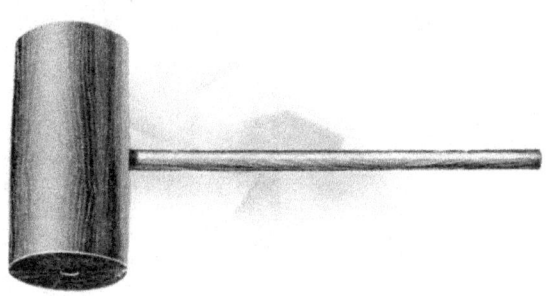

Timber Dollies

| Style No. 1 | Style No. 2 | Style No. 3 |

No.	Diam. of roll.	Size of frame.
1	7 (concave)	18 x18
2	6 (straight)	19½x26
3	6 "	16 x18
4	6 "	18 x18

The frames are of elm, strongly made. The rolls are hollow and of cast iron.

Buda Ball-Bearing Jacks

DESIGN AND CONSTRUCTION

As the arrangement of the ball-bearings is an important feature of ball-bearing jacks, we desire, in describing the general construction of our styles, to first call particular attention to the method used by us in their manufacture.

Ball Bearing Thrust between Screw and Sleeve

Top Plate Removed

Ball Cage of Phosphor Bronze to Reduce Friction

In similar makes where the balls are allowed to rub together, the general complaint is heard on every side that they wear flat and do not give satisfaction.

In our construction, the balls are held in place by a *phosphor bronze* cage designed to reduce friction to the minimum, and, being thus prevented from rubbing together, no difficulty of the kind mentioned is experienced. The result is reduction of friction, ease of operation and lower cost of repairs. Again, the openings in the case are not exactly in line, thus giving more than double the wearing surface on the thrust plates. That this arrangement is far more satisfactory than that where the balls are allowed to rub together is proved by comparative tests which we have made, as well as the experience of others. These conclusions are also borne out in a report of the American Society of Engineers, vol. 22, page 738, to the effect that where balls are enclosed in individual openings a higher efficiency is thereby obtained.

In purchasing ball-bearing jacks, the user will do well to keep these results in mind.

The general design of our ball-bearing jacks is shown in the sectional view. A standard is enveloped by a sliding sleeve which fits closely, thereby keeping out dust and dirt and also preventing side strains on the screw. The sleeve is supported by the ball-bearing thrust which

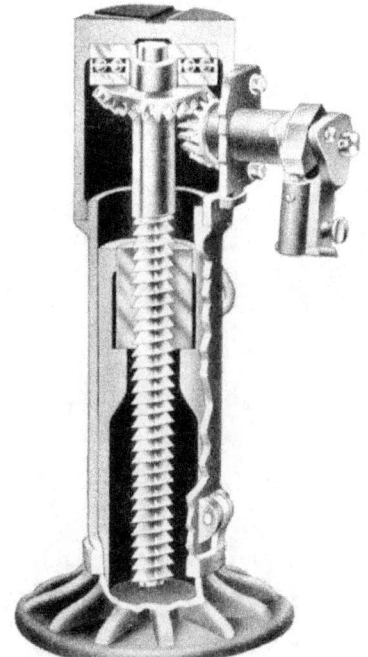

Sectional view of Buda Ball-Bearing Jack

rests on the gear near top of screw. The screw passes down through a phosphor bronze nut, as shown, and is made to revolve by means of a ratchet, the direction being reversed by changing the tilt of the pawl. A crank handle facilitates running the jack up to the load, when if the lift be heavy a bar is inserted in its place and worked in an up-and-down manner after the method of operating a ratchet jack. A pawl in the sleeve at a certain height drops into a notch in the upper part of standard, which prevents the screw running out, safeguarding against accidents of that nature.

For raising heavy loads, these jacks are unexcelled for speed, safety and convenience, as compared with hydraulic and other heavy duty jacks. They will not trip or run down, so that loads may be left standing on them with perfect safety.

Being proof against dirt and weather, they are peculiarly adapted to railroad service and for use on and around locomotives. They will be found ready, at all times, to perform any duty within their respective rated capacities.

The material used in these jacks is of high grade. The gears are accurately cut by new, automatic machine tools. The screw is cut uniform and true, being handled only by experienced workmen. Throughout, these jacks will be found fine examples of the machinists' art, and we offer them as being superior in material, improved in design and more satisfactory than those of similar makes.

Our Jacks are Tested

Realizing the importance of giving our customers jacks that are safe and free from defects, in order that property, or life, may not be unnecessarily jeopardized, before shipping we carefully test, in our hydraulic machines, all ball-bearing jacks and tag them with a certificate of inspection and test. It is our practice to submit them to a generous overload—often up to 20 per cent; so the purchaser may buy our jacks with every assurance that they will do all that is claimed for them.

BUDA
FDR'Y & MF'G CO.

INSPECTOR'S REPORT

Jack No. 116

Tested to 56 Tons

By *J V Smith*

Inspected 12/14/06

W. O. Brand.
Inspector

The cost of maintenance is small compared with hydraulic jacks, the renewal of fluid alone in the latter probably equaling any repairs that might be required on our styles. All parts are interchangeable and may be had from us.

Buda Cone-Bearing Jacks

The operating principle and construction of these jacks may be seen by the sectional view presented. It principally consists of an inverted cone resting upon a hardened steel bearing which is kept well lubricated with the oil constantly retained by the enclosed nature of the parts. We call especial attention to the superiority of these jacks. The gears, **instead of being rough castings,** like similar jacks, are of **solid forgings, machine cut.** This feature adds much to the value of the jack in the way of ease of operation, length of service and strength, and while it adds considerable to our cost of production it is along the line of our policy to increase the demand for our goods by the greater value given the user, for the same money he would pay for inferior quality.

Sectional view of Buda Cone-Bearing Journal Jack

Special Note

Reference is made in the preceding paragraph to the fact that some manufacturers make a practice of using gears of practically unfinished steel castings. It is also their practice to use a cast steel main gear on ball-bearing jacks of 50 tons capacity upward.

All gears used in Buda ball-bearing and cone-bearing jacks, regardless of size or capacity are of solid steel forgings, machine cut.

Jacks for the Engineering Department

This department of a railroad covers a broad field, and its requirements in the way of jacks are extensive, using, as it does, a large number of styles and sizes.

The jacks mentioned in the following list are designed for special and general lifting purposes, including bridge work; for use by extra gangs; general construction; track and maintenance of way.

In quality, these jacks represent the best there is to be had in material, design and workmanship. In purchasing these our customers may do so with the assurance that they are receiving jacks that are unsurpassed, or unequaled, and being carefully tested before shipment they carry our unconditional guarantee of safety up to their respective rated capacities.

Ball-Bearing Jacks

Page	No.	Capacity Tons	Height Inches	Rise Inches	Dia. Base Inches	Weight Lbs.	List Price	Hook Extra	Code Word
156	103	15	20	9	10	80	$ 60.00	$5.00	Durance
150	104F	15	22	10	7x9	80	60.00	Foot	Domain
150	105F	15	26	13	7x9	110	70.00	Foot	Dorsal
148	115	25	26	13	8x9	157	96 00	Foot	Dipper
147	115A	25	20	9	10	125	90 00	Foot	Drum
146	118	35	26	13	12	175	130.00	Foot	Diverge
146	119	35	32	19	12	195	138 00	Foot	Duty
144	116	50	24	9	14	270	150.00	Foot	Dish
144	117	50	27	13	14	292	150.00	Foot	Dispel
144	125	60	26	12	14	323	175.00	Foot	Dismiss
164	B60	25	10	4½	7	68	56.00	......	Dragon

Ratchet Jacks

Page	No.	Capacity Tons	Height Bar Down Inches	Rise of Bar Inches	Height Bar Raised Inches	Size of Bar Inches	Weight Lbs.	List Price	Code Word
168	1B	10	24	13½	37½	1½ x 1½	62	$18.00	Dale
170	2B	10	21	10	31	1⅝ x 1½	65	25.00	Dame
172	3B	12	26½	15	41½	1¾ x 1⅞	85	30.00	Damp
174	4B	15	22	10	32	2 x 2	100	35.00	Dare
176	5B	15	28	15	43	2 x 2	115	40.00	Dash
178	6B	15	31	19	50	1⅞ x 1⅝	105	32.00	Dean
180	7B	15	35	24½	59½	2 x 2	122	42.00	Dusky
184	12B	10	17¾	8	25¾	1½ x 1½	50	17.00	Deery
186	17B	10	24	13¾	37¾	1½ x 1½	63	18.00	Dandy
188	18B	10	21	10	31	1½ x 1⅝	68	25.00	Decoy
190	19B	15	28	17½	45½	2 x 2	102	35.00	Defer
192	20B	15	31	19	50	1⅝ x 1⅞	106	32 00	Decide
194	25B	12	24½	12½	37	1½ x 1½	105	50.00	Dove
196	50B	5	16	8	24	1¼ x 1¼	38	17 00	Debar
196	51B	5	20	12	32	1¼ x 1¼	42	18.00	Deck

Friction Jacks

Page	No.	Capacity Tons	Height Bar Down Inches	Rise of Bar Inches	Height Bar Raised Inches	Size of Bar Inches	Weight Lbs.	List Price	Code Word
198	1J	5	29	12	41	1½ diam.	62	$20.00	Delta
198	2J	10	33	15	48	1¾ diam.	85	24.00	Dent

Numbers 1B, 6B, 12B, 17B and 25B are trip jacks, which are particularly adapted to, and we recommend them for, track work only. Attention is called to the 25B for lining up purposes. The 1J and 2J are also essentially track jacks.

Jacks for the Motive Power Department

For use in and around locomotive repair shops, roundhouses, and on locomotives we give below a list of jacks usually called for on account of their suitableness for this class of service.

The ball-bearing and cone-bearing jacks not being affected by dirt or weather, besides having large capacities and being easy to operate, are finding large use in the motive power departments. The improved construction used by us in the manufacture of these jacks has made them great favorites and is widening their demand.

Ball-Bearing Jacks

Page	No.	Capacity Tons	Height Inches	Rise Inches	Dia. Base Inches	Weight Lbs.	List Price	Hook Extra	Code Word
156	103	15	20	9	10	80	$ 60 00	$5.00	Durance
156	104	15	22	10	10	80	60.00	6.00	Dogma
156	105	15	26	13	10	92	70.00	6 00	Divert
154	109	25	20	9	10	106	80.00	6.00	Donor
154	110	25	24	11	13	149	85.00	6.00	Dial
154	111	25	26	13	12	164	90.00	6 00	Demon
152	O	35	26	13	12	165	125.00	8.00	Digit
152	OX	35	31	18	12	190	135.00	8 00	Dike
151	LX	50	27	13	14	282	150 00	....	Ditto
12	116	50	24	9	14	270	150.00	...	Dish
12	117	50	27	13	14	292	150.00	....	Dispel
141	125	60	26	12	14	323	175.00	....	Dismiss
164	B60	25	10	4½	7	68	56 00	....	Dragon

Cone-Bearing Journal Jacks

| 162 | 120 | 15 | 9¾ | 4 | 7 | 43 | $22.00 | .... | Dissent |
| 162 | 122 | 15 | 11 | 4 | 7 | 45 | 22.00 | .... | Divan |

Ratchet Journal Jacks

Page	Style	Capacity Tons	Height Bar Down Inches	Rise of Bar Inches	Height Bar Raised Inches	Size of Bar Inches	Weight Lbs.	List Price	Code Word
182	8 B	10	11	5	16	1⅝ x 1½	48	$22.00	Debit
182	48 B	15	11	5	16	1¾ x 1⅞	60	25.00	Deploy

Additional jacks for use in car repair shops are shown on another page.

Jacks for the Car Department

For use in and around car shops, there will be found in the list following jacks which we recommend, and are popularly demanded for work of this class.

As the equipment of cabooses and locomotives is arranged for by this department on some roads we have included, in this list, those jacks suitable for these purposes, including journal-box jacks for use in replacing brasses.

Illustrations of the jacks mentioned will be found on other pages, with fuller descriptions.

Ball-Bearing Jacks

Page	No.	Capacity Tons	Height Inches	Rise Inches	Dia. Base Inches	Weight Lbs.	List Price	Hook Extra	Code Word
160	101	25	33	20	12	154	$95.00	$6.00	Deny
160	102	15	34	20	12	154	75.00	6.00	Despot
154	109	25	20	9	10	106	80.00	6.00	Donor
154	110	25	24	11	13	149	85.00	6.00	Dial
154	111	25	26	13	12	164	90.00	6.00	Demon
152	O	35	26	13	12	165	125.00	8.00	Digit
152	OX	35	31	18	12	190	135.00	8.00	Dike
151	LX	50	27	13	14	282	150.00	....	Ditto
164	B60	25	10	4½	7	68	56.00	....	Dragon

Cone-Bearing Jacks

Page	No.	Capacity Tons	Height Inches	Rise Inches	Dia. Base Inches	Weight Lbs.	List Price	Hook Extra	Code Word
162	120	15	9¾	4	7	43	$22.00	....	Dissent
162	122	15	11	4	7	45	22.00	....	Divan

Ratchet Jacks

Page	No.	Capacity Tons	Height Bar Down Inches	Rise of Bar Inches	Height Bar Raised Inches	Size of Bar Inches	Weight Lbs.	List Price	Code Word
172	3 B	12	26½	15	41½	1¾ x 1⅞	85	$30.00	Damp
176	5 B	15	28	15	43	2 x 2	115	40.00	Dash
180	7 B	15	35	24½	59½	2 x 2	122	42.00	Dusky
182	8 B	10	11	5	16	1⅝ x 1½	48	22.00	Debit
188	18 B	10	21	10	31	1½ x 1⅝	68	25.00	Decoy
190	19 B	15	28	17½	45½	2 x 2	102	35.00	Defer
182	48 B	15	11	5	16	1¾ x 1⅞	60	25.00	Deploy
196	50 B	5	16	8	24	1¼ x 1¼	38	17.00	Debar
196	51 B	5	20	12	32	1¼ x 1¼	42	18.00	Deck

Geared Ratchet Jacks

Page	No.	Capacity Tons	Height Bar Down Inches	Rise of Bar Inches	Height Bar Raised Inches	Size of Bar Inches	Weight Lbs.	List Price	Code Word
166	130 B	35	28	17	45	2½ x 3	225	$120.00	Deforce
166	500 B	30	27	17	44	2½ x 3	237	120.00	Douse

Jacks for the Operating Department

For the equipment of freight and passenger trains, for wrecking and tool car outfits, and for use at division points, the jacks listed below will be found to cover all that is demanded for these purposes.

Every year sees a decided advance in the way of utilities furnished train and wrecking crews. Competent men contending with disaster and battling against minutes cannot be expected to adequately perform their work and with the same dispatch as when provided with reliable appliances and tools designed to meet all exigencies. The spreading realization of this is rapidly doing away with slow-working and inefficient jacks and their places are being taken by strong, reliable, handy, easy-working styles.

We call attention also to our traversing base, page 157, and to car replacing jacks on pages 158-159.

Ball-Bearing Jacks

Page	No.	Capacity Tons	Height Inches	Rise Inches	Dia. Base Inches	Weight Inches	List Price	Hook Extra	Code Word
160	109	25	20	9	10	103	$80.00	$6.00	Donor
160	110	25	24	11	13	149	85.00	6.00	Dial
160	111	25	26	13	12	164	90.00	6.00	Demon
148	115	25	26	13	8 x 9	157	96.00	Foot	Dipper
152	O	35	26	13	12	165	125.00	8.00	Digit
152	OX	35	31	18	12	190	135.00	8.00	Dike
144	116	50	24	9	14	270	150.90	Foot	Dish
144	117	50	27	13	14	292	150.00	Foot	Dispel
144	125	60	26	12	14	323	175.00	Foot	Dismiss
164	B60	25	10	4½	7	68	56.00	......	Dragon

Cone-Bearing Jacks

Page	No.	Capacity Tons	Height Inches	Rise Inches	Dia. Base Inches	Weight Inches	List Price	Hook Extra	Code Word
162	120	15	9¾	4	7	43	$22.00	....	Dissent
162	122	15	11	4	7	45	22.00	....	Divan

Geared Ratchet Jacks

Page	No.	Capacity Tons	Height Bar Down Inches	Rise of Bar Inches	Height Bar Raised Inches	Size of Bar Inches	Weight Lbs.	List Price	Code Word
166	500B	30	27	17	44	2½ x 3	237	$120.00	Douse
166	130B	35	28	17	45	2½ x 3	225	120.00	Deforce

Ratchet Jacks

Page	No.	Capacity Tons	Height Bar Down Inches	Rise of Bar Inches	Height Bar Raised Inches	Size of Bar Inches	Weight Lbs.	List Price	Code Word
172	3B	12	26½	15	41½	1¾ x 1⅞	85	$30.00	Damp
176	5B	15	28	15	43	2 x 2	115	40.00	Dash
180	7B	15	35	24½	59½	2 x 2	122	42.00	Dusky
182	8B	10	11	5	16	1⅝ x 1½	48	22.00	Debit
188	18B	10	21	10	31	1½ x 1⅝	68	25.00	Decoy
190	19B	15	28	17½	45½	2 x 2	102	35.00	Defer
182	48B	15	11	5	16	1¾ x 1⅞	60	25.00	Deploy
196	50B	5	16	8	24	1¼ x 1¼	38	17.00	Debar
196	51B	5	20	12	32	1¼ x 1¼	42	18.00	Deck

Buda Extra Heavy Bridge Jack

NO. 127. CAPACITY 75 TONS

The mechanism of the No. 127 differs considerably from that of our other ball-bearing jacks. Near the top of the screw, and supporting the ball-bearing thrust, in place of the bevel gear used in our jacks of lower capacity, is a spur gear which meshes with a pinion also horizontally maintained by a vertical, stationary shaft in the gear box. The pinion is keyed to a bevel gear which lies beneath it and through which the shaft also passes, the bevel gear resting on a shoulder which rises, to a proper height, about the shaft. This latter gear is actuated by a smaller bevel gear vertically maintained and made integral with a horizontal shaft and ratchet. In this construction all gears are positively supported, the design having many advantages over smilar arrangements which will appeal, without argument, to mechanical minds.

Unlike the rough steel castings usually found in heavy capacity ball-bearing jacks of other makes, these used by us are machine cut from solid steel forgings and are consequently accurate and as much superior as would naturally be expected.

The screw used in the No. 127 is cut with a double pitch which not only increases the efficiency but gives greater speed, and this, combined with the special gear mechanism, enables the operator to handle heavy loads without the loss of speed that ordinarily occurs.

By use of a crank handle the jack is quickly run up to the load when the bar is inserted to accomplish the lift.

The general rugged design may be seen from the illustration. The head and gear box, it will be noted, are reinforced against vertical and side strains by strong ribs.

The material used is carefully selected with the view of obtaining only that of the highest order and worthy of a jack of great capacity. All parts are fitted with extreme accuracy, so as to reduce friction and wear to the lowest degree and promote ease of operation.

All Buda ball-bearing jacks are tested in our hydraulic testing machines and have attached to them certificates of inspection. This is worthy of note, for it is an insurance against accidents to property and life.

No. 127 Buda Ball-Bearing Bridge Jack

CAPACITY 75 TONS

PATENTS APPLIED FOR.

Extra Strong — Easy Working

The jack illustrated is one of unusually heavy build, the head being reinforced by strong ribs connecting with the barrel. The gear and journal box are also ribbed. The side ribs have holes through which bars may be inserted for carrying purposes.

The mechanism of this jack is somewhat different from that used in our other ball-bearing jacks, enabling the operator to exert great power. The gears are heavy, accurately fitted, and the No. 127 is without doubt the safest, strongest and best-made on the market.

Not more than one-half the rated capacity should be lifted on the foot.

Style	Capacity Tons	Height Inches	Rise Inches	Diameter of Base	Diameter of Head	Weight Lbs.	List Price	Code Word
127	75	26	12	14 in.	12 in.	385	$200.00	Din

Buda Extra Heavy Bridge Jacks

BALL-BEARING

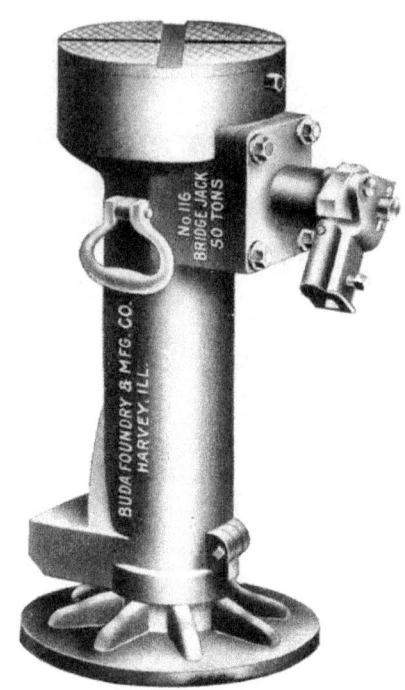

PATENTS APPLIED FOR.

No. 116, 50 tons
No. 117, 50 tons
No. 125, 60 tons

When extra heavy bridge work is being handled, these jacks will be found equal to any emergency up to their rated capacity. Made with great care, and of choice material; full reliance may be placed on their operation, both from a standpoint of power and safety.

It should be noted that the rated capacity refers to the head. The foot will lift about one-half of the rated capacity.

Style	Capacity Tons	Height Inches	Rise Inches	Diameter of Base	Diameter of Head	Weight Lbs.	List Price	Code Word
116	50	24	9	14 in.	10½ in.	270	$150.00	Dish
117	50	27	13	14 in.	10½ in.	292	150.00	Dispel
125	60	26	12	14 in.	10½ in.	323	175.00	Dismiss

Buda Extra Heavy Bridge Jacks

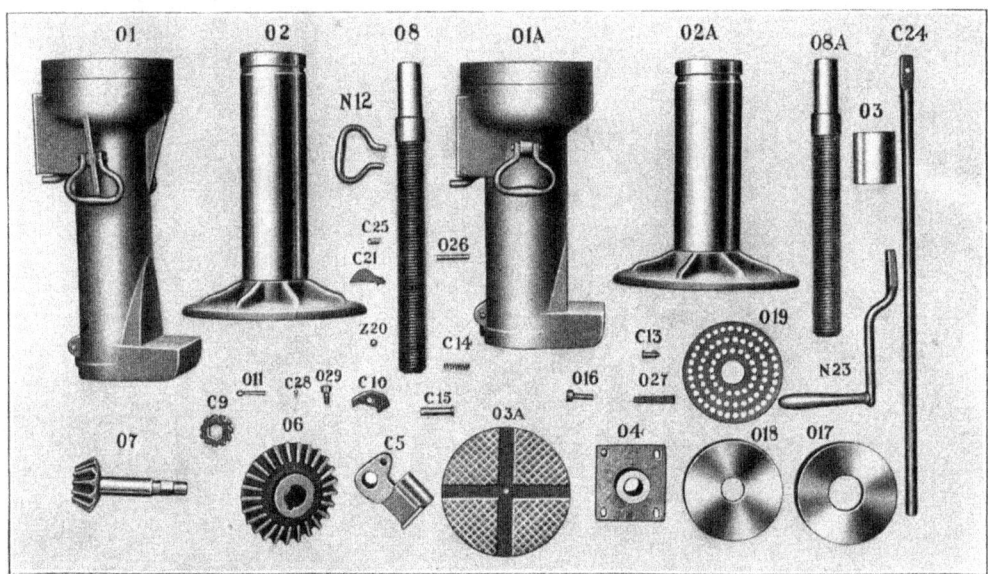

Repair Parts for Nos. 116 and 117

Repair Parts for No. 117 Jack

Shell	O. 1
Standard	O. 2
Brass Nut	O. 3
Top of Shell	O. 3A
Cap	O. 4
Lever Socket	C. 5
Gear with Hub	O. 6
Gear with Shaft	O. 7
Screw	O. 8
Ratchet	C. 9
Pawl	C.10
Cotter	O.11
Handles	N.12
Reversing Pin	C.13
Spring for Reversing Pin	C.14
Pawl Bolt	C.15
Stud and Nut	O.16
Bottom Bearing Plate	O.17
Top Bearing Plate	O.18
Ball Retainer	O.19
Steel Ball	Z.20
Stop Dog	C.21
Crank	N.23
Steel Bar	C.24
Spring for Stop Dog	C.25
Pin for Gear	O.26
Key for Gear	O.27
Reversing Pin Screw	C.28
Cap Screw for Cap	O.29

Repair Parts for No. 116 Jack

Shell	O. 1A
Standard	O. 2A
Screw	O. 8A

NOTE—The remainder of repair parts for the No. 116 Jack are the same as for the No. 117.

Buda Ball-Bearing Bridge Jacks

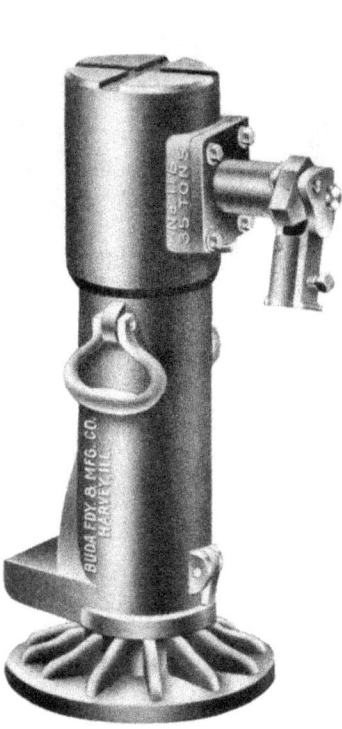

PATENTS APPLIED FOR.
No. 118

PATENTS APPLIED FOR.
No. 119

Very substantial and useful jacks, both of the same capacity but differing in height and lift as indicated in the following table.

They are easily handled and can be used for all-around purposes.

While the capacity of each is 35 tons, only about one-half this should be attempted on the foot.

Style	Capacity Tons	Height Inches	Rise Inches	Diameter of Base	Weight Lbs.	List Price	Code Word
118	35	26	13	12 in.	175	$130.00	Diverge
119	35	32	19	12 in.	185	138.00	Duty

Buda Ball-Bearing Bridge Jack

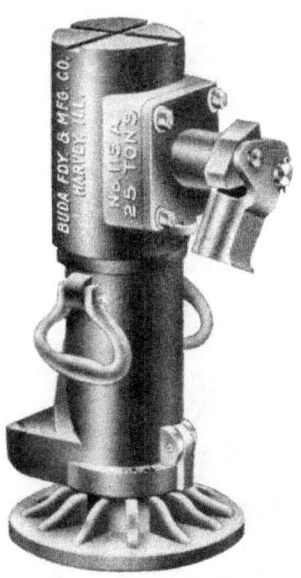

PATENTS APPLIED FOR.

No. 115 A

The No. 115A is particularly suited for certain kinds of bridge building and other work. It is a sturdy little jack that can be used in places where other jacks are inapplicable.

Do not use foot for lifting more than one-half the capacity.

Style	Capacity Tons	Height Inches	Rise Inches	Diameter at Base	Weight lbs.	List Price	Code Word
115 A	25	20	9	10 in.	125	$90.00	Drum

No. 115 Buda Ball-Bearing Bridge Jack

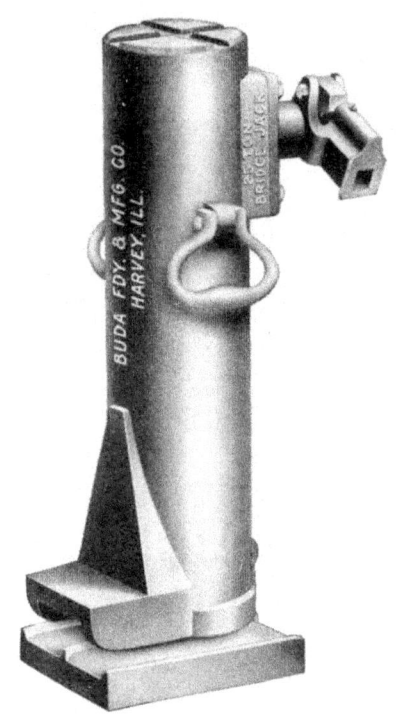

PATENTS APPLIED FOR.

For Bridge Work

Designed and built for extra heavy bridge and other work.

This Jack is built to stand a strain of 25 tons, and being—like the others of our make—carefully made of chosen material, may be thoroughly relied on.

NOTE.—Foot of jack is intended to lift only one-half full capacity.

Style	Capacity Tons	Height Inches	Rise Inches	Size of Base	Diameter of Head	Weight Lbs.	Price	Code Word
113	35	22	10	8 x 9 in.	5½ in.	190	$130.00	Depict
114	25	22	10	8 x 9 in.	5½ in.	136	90.00	Dagmar
115	25	26	13	8 x 9 in.	5½ in.	157	96.00	Dipper

No. 115 Buda Ball-Bearing Bridge Jack

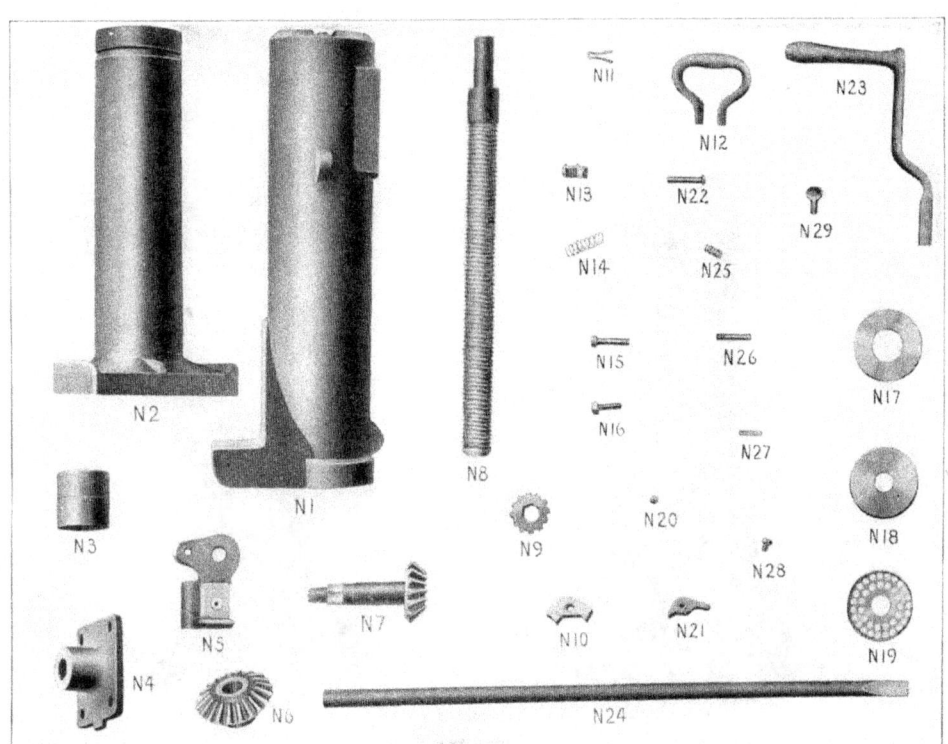

Repair Parts

Shell	N-1	Stud and Nut	N-16
Standard	N-2	Bottom Bearing Plate	N-17
Nut	N-3	Top Bearing Plate	N-18
Cap	N-4	Ball Retainer	N-19
Lever Socket	N-5	Steel Ball	N-20
Gear with Hub	N-6	Stop Dog	N-21
Gear with Shaft	N-7	Stop Dog Bolt	N-22
Screw	N-8	Crank	N-23
Ratchet	N-9	Steel Bar	N-24
Pawl	N-10	Spring for Stop Dog	N-25
Cotter	N-11	Taper Pin for Gear	N-26
Handle	N-12	Key for Gear	N-27
Reversing Pin	N-13	Reversing Pin Screw	N-28
Spring	N-14	Thumb Screw	N-29
Pawl Bolt	N-15		

Buda Ball-Bearing Bridge Jacks

No. 104 F

No. 105 F

It will be noted that these two jacks have square bases, which facilitates their use for some kinds of work and enables the base to be placed in closely in corner and sustain load in vertical manner.

The jacks can be easily handled by one man and are a convenient addition to the equipment of a bridge or building gang.

Only one-half the capacity should be lifted on foot.

Style	Capacity Tons	Height Inches	Rise Inches	Size of Base	Weight Lbs.	Price List	Code Word
104 F	15	22	10	7x9	80	$60.00	Domain
105 F	15	26	13	7x9	110	70.00	Dorsal

Buda Ball-Bearing Locomotive and Car Jack

STYLE LX. EXTRA HEAVY

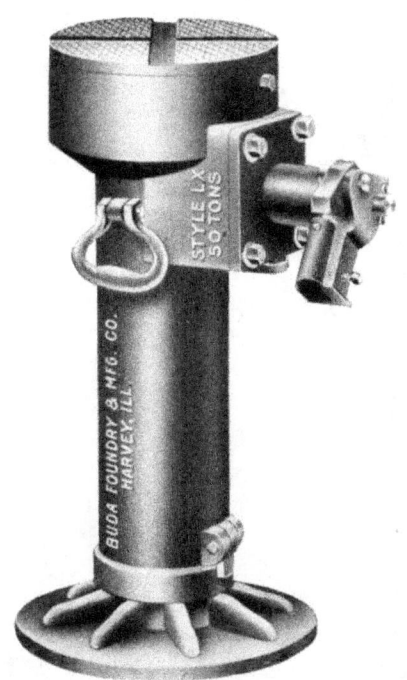

PATENTS APPLIED FOR.

Capacity 50 Tons

For use in motive power and car departments this is an excellent jack. It is strong, well built and intended for heavy work. The diameter of head is 10½ inches and that of base 14 inches with capacity of 50 tons. It is particularly adapted for raising and sustaining heavy loads, and, as with all our ball-bearing jacks there is no danger of running down, it is a desirable addition to the shop equipment.

Note: Jacks 116, 117 and 127 have foot which is convenient. For illustration see page 144.

Style	Capacity Tons	Height Inches	Rise Inches	Diameter of Base	Diameter of Head	Weight Lbs.	List Price	Code Word
LX	50	27	13	14½	10½	282	$150.00	Ditto
116	50	24	9	14	10½	270	150.00	Dish
117	50	27	13	14	10½	292	150.00	Dispel
127	60	26	12	14	10½	323	175.00	Dismiss

Styles O and OX Ball-Bearing Jacks

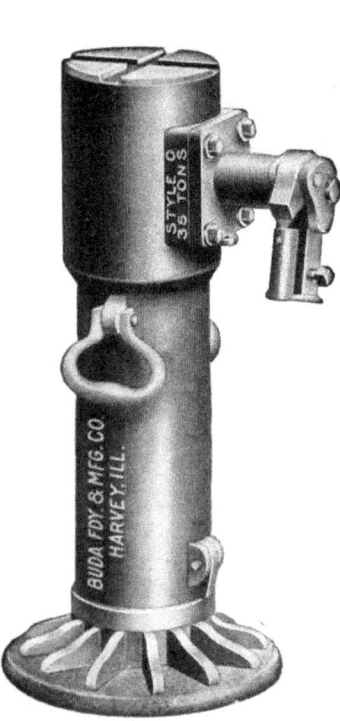

PATENTS APPLIED FOR.
O

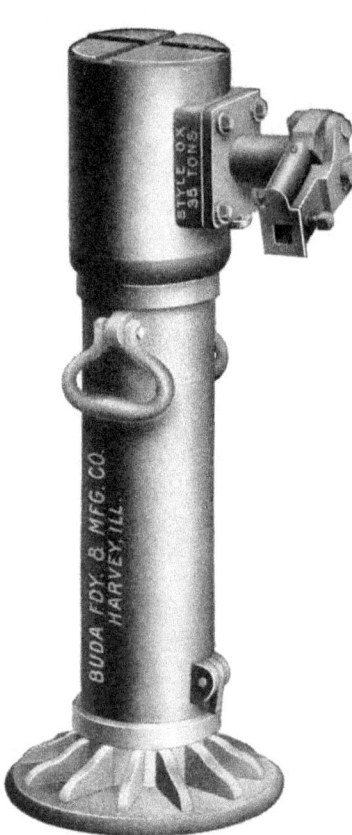

PATENTS APPLIED FOR.
OX

These jacks are designed for heavy work. They are used generally on heavy cars, locomotives and form a part of wrecking-car equipments. They are exceedingly popular and much in demand. Both of the same capacity but different height and lift as shown by the following list.

Style	Capacity Tons	Height Inches	Rise Inches	Diameter of Base	Weight Lbs.	List Price	Hook Extra	Code Word
O	35	26	13	12 in.	165	$125.00	$8.00	Digit
OX	35	31	18	12 in.	190	135.00	8.00	Dike

Styles O and OX Ball-Bearing Jacks

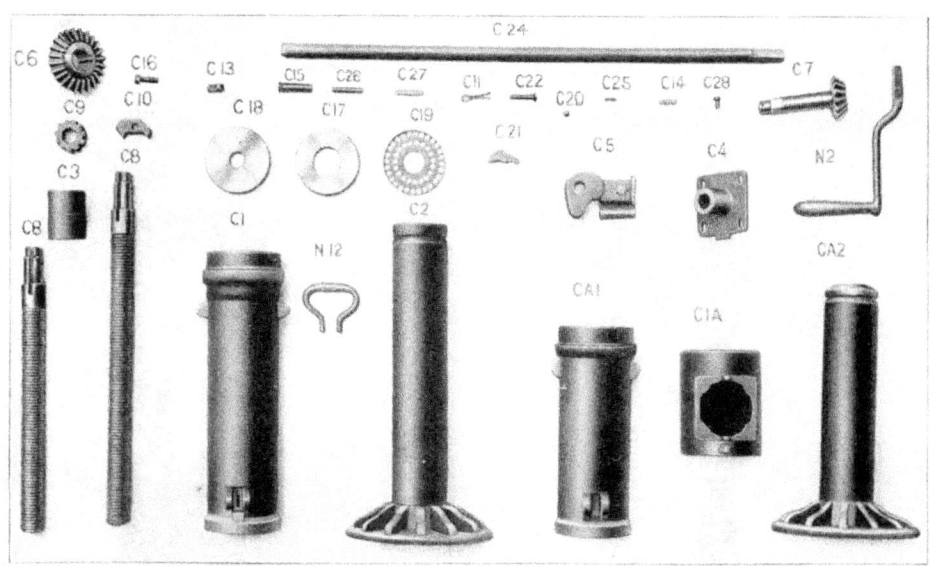

REPAIR PARTS STYLE OX.

Top of Shell	C-1-A
Shell	C-1
Standard	C-2
Nut	C-3
Cap	C-4
Lever Socket	C-5
Gear with Hub	C-6
Gear with Shaft	C-7
Screw	C-8
Ratchet	C-9
Ratchet Pawl	C-10
Cotter	C-11
Handle	N-12
Reversing Pin	C-13
Spring for Reversing Pin	C-14
Pawl Bolt	C-15
Stud and Nut	C-16
Bottom Bearing Plate	C-17
Top Bearing Plate	C-18
Ball Retainer	C-19
Steel Ball	C-20
Stop Dog	C-21
Stop Dog Bolt	C-22
Crank	N-23
Steel Bar	N-24
Spring for Stop Dog	C-25
Pin for Gear	C-26
Key for Gear	C-27
Reversing Pin Screw	C-28

REPAIR PARTS FOR STYLE O.

Top of Shell	C-1-A
Shell	C-A-1
Standard	C-A-2
Screw	C-8-A

NOTE.—The balance of the repair parts for this jack are the same as for style OX.

Buda Ball-Bearing Locomotive Jacks

No. 109

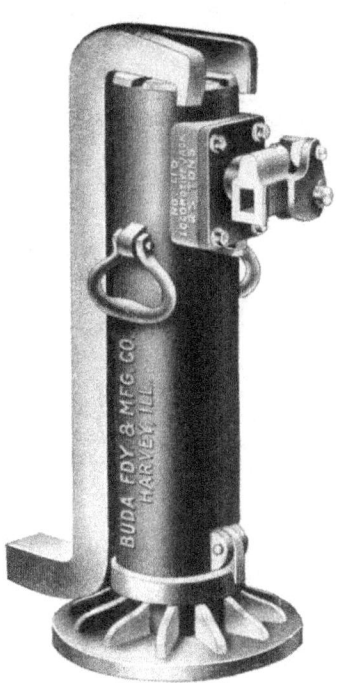

No. 110
Showing Hook for Low Set Loads

Equipped with hook for ground lift.

These jacks are especially adapted to locomotive service. Not affected by exposure to coal, dirt or weather. No chance of being out of order when needed. Always ready for service

Style	Capacity Tons	Height Inches	Rise Inches	Diameter at Base	Weight Lbs.	List Price	Hook Extra	Code Word
109	25	20	9	10	106	$80.00	$6.00	Donor
110	25	24	11	13	149	85.00	6.00	Dial
111	25	26	13	12	164	90.00	6.00	Demon

Buda Ball-Bearing Locomotive Jack

Repair Parts. No. 110 Jack

Shell N-A-1	Stud and Nut....................N-16
Standard N-A-2	Bottom Bearing Plate..........N-17
Nut N-3	Top Bearing Plate N-18
Cap N-4	Ball Retainer N-19
Lever Socket N-5	Steel Ball N-20
Gear with Hub N-6	Stop Dog N-21
Gear with Shaft..................N-7	Stop Dog Bolt...................N-22
Screw N-8	Crank N-23
Ratchet N-9	Steel Bar N-24
Pawl N-10	Spring for Stop Dog............N-25
Cotter N-11	Taper Pin for Gear.............N-26
Handle N-12	Key for Gear...................N-27
Reversing Pin N-13	Reversing Pin Screw N-28
Spring for Reversing Pin.........N-14	Thumb Screw N-29
Pawl Bolt N-15	

Nos. 104 and 105 Buda Ball-Bearing Jacks

No. 104

No. 105

PATENTS APPLIED FOR.

For Car Shops and General Lifting Purposes

These two jacks are very handy and useful. Either may be readily handled by one man, the weight of the No. 104 being only 80 pounds and that of the No. 105, 92 pounds. For general use they are very popular.

Jack No. 103 is same style, but only 20 inches in height. See list below.

Hook can be used for low set loads. This comes extra, as is shown in list.

Style	Capacity Tons	Height Inches	Rise Inches	Diameter of Base	Weight Lbs.	List Price	Hook Extra	Code Word
103	15	20	9	12	80	$60.00	$5.00	Durance
104	15	22	10	10	80	60.00	6.00	Dogma
105	15	26	13	10	92	70.00	6.00	Divert

Buda Traversing Base

May be used with any size Jack

We call special attention to the traversing base shown above; for it is a valuable accessory in moving loads horizontally. For replacing derailed cars the base is so useful that it ought to be included in every wrecking-car equipment, where it will save its cost in a short time.

The base is made of best malleable iron and steel and comes in two capacities.

Style	Capacity Tons	Traverse Inches	Height Inches	Weight Lbs.	List Price	Code Word
1	25	15	4	60	$35.00	Ding
2	50	20	4	124	40.00	Dong

Buda Car Replacing Jacks

The efficiency of wrecking car and tool car outfits is so increased by the addition of ball-bearing traversing jack that it should command the attention of all railroad officers having this work under their supervision.

Aside from the time-saving features, there is to be considered, as well, the eliminating of possible damage to equipment.

Capable workmen are often handicapped by lack of proper facilities, and the ever pressing necessity of rapid action often compels expedients which enlarge a cost that might otherwise have been minimized.

Anything that promotes quick work and does away with rough handling of equipment is a desirable addition which ought to be favorably recognized by those departments that are obliged to make a showing through the saving of cost.

The traversing base illustrated comes in two capacities, one for duty up to 25 tons; the other up to 50 tons. Any of our ball-bearing jacks may be fitted and by removing the bolts which secure the base of jack to the table, the jack can, of course, be used separately.

These bases are made of best malleable iron and steel throughout and are in every way reliable.

Not being an expensive accessory, and being so useful an adjunct, a traversing base should find a place in the equipment of every tool car or wrecking outfit. They are a saving investment that may be put to frequent use and are really indispensable when badly wanted.

Buda Car Replacing Jacks

BALL-BEARING JACK WITH TRAVERSING BASE

PATENTS APPLIED FOR.

Style OT 20-Inch Traverse

A useful addition to tool and wrecking car outfits. Jacks can be unbolted from table and used separately. Any jack may be used in connection with base. The list below shows prices of jacks and bases complete.

Style	Capacity Tons	Height Over All Inches	Rise Inches	Traverse	List Price	Code Word
105T	15	30	13	15	$105.00	Best
103T	15	24	9	15	95.00	Banner
109T	25	24	9	15	115.00	Blanket
110T	25	28	11	20	125.00	Bitter
111T	25	30	13	20	130.00	Bought
OT	35	30	13	20	165.00	Band
LXT	50	31	13	20	190.00	Bluster
125T	60	30	12	20	215.00	Blow

The Buda Foundry & Manufacturing Company

No. 101 Buda Ball-Bearing Car Jack

PATENTS APPLIED FOR.

In Two Sizes

Style 102 is same pattern as 101, but has larger gear on shaft, doubling the speed.

The long lift on these jacks adapts them particularly for car work. With empty or light loaded cars, crank can be used, giving greater speed. Cars can also be left standing on jacks while changing trucks, thus obviating the ordinary delay of blocking.

Style	Capacity Tons	Height Inches	Rise Inches	Diameter of Base	Weight Lbs.	Price	Hook Extra	Code Word
101	25	33	20	12	154	$95.00	$6.00	Deny
102	15	34	20	12	154	75.00	6.00	Despot

Nos. 101 and 102 Buda Ball-Bearing Car Jacks

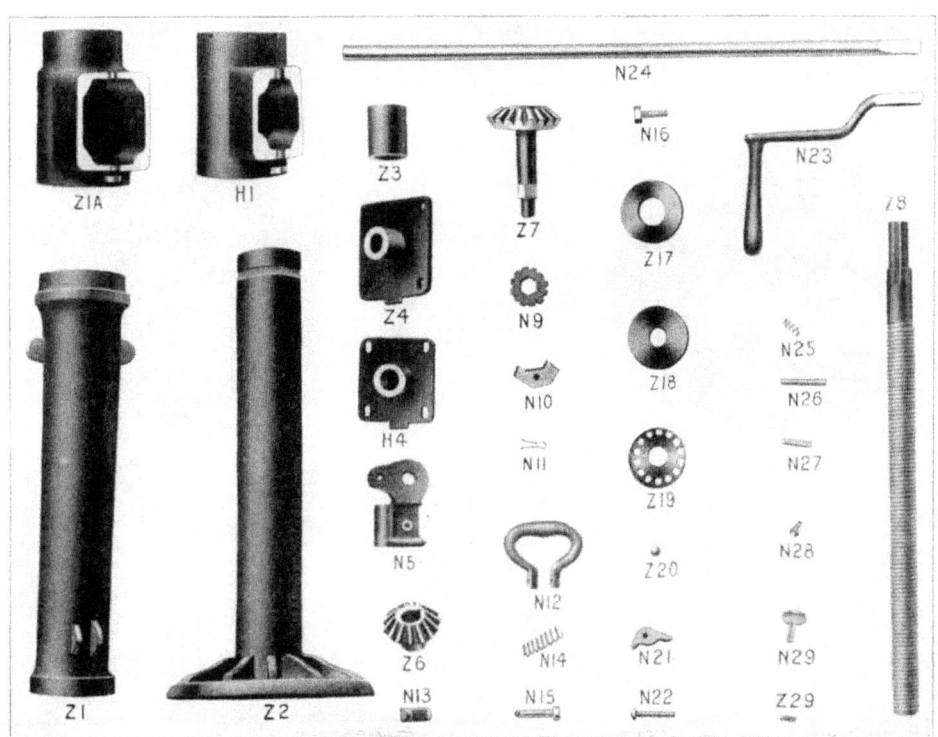

Repair Parts for No. 102, Fifteen-Ton Jack

Shell Z-1	Pawl Bolt N-15
Top of Shell Z-1-A	Stud and Nut N-16
Standard Z-2	Bottom Bearing Plate Z-17
Nut Z-3	Top Bearing Plate Z-18
Cap Z-4	Ball Retainer Z-19
Lever Socket N-5	Steel Ball Z-20
Gear with Hub Z-6	Stop Dog N-21
Gear with Shaft Z-7	Stop Dog Bolt N-22
Screw Z-8	Crank N-23
Ratchet N-9	Steel Bar N-24
Pawl N-10	Spring for Stop Dog N-25
Cotter N-11	Taper Pin for Gear N-26
Handles N-12	Key for Gear N-27
Reversing Pin N-13	Reversing Pin Screw N-28
Spring for Reversing Pin N-14	Headless Set Screw Top of Shell Z-29

Repair Parts for No. 101, Twenty-five Ton Jack

Top of Shell H-1	Top Bearing Plate N-18
Cap H-4	Ball Retainer N-19
Bottom Bearing Plate N-17	Steel Ball N-20

Parts N-17 to N-20 inclusive are on page 155.

Note.—The remainder of the repair parts for this jack are the same as for the No. 102, 15-ton, Ball-bearing Car Jack shown above.

Buda Cone-Bearing Jacks

WITH WHEEL HOLDING DEVICE

PATENTS APPLIED FOR.

No. 120

PATENTS APPLIED FOR.

No. 122

For Car Inspectors

These jacks are especially built for car inspectors. They have a short lift and are very powerful and quick acting. The time they save makes them a particularly economical investment.

All our journal jacks are now equipped with the wheel holding device shown on the No. 122. This is a valuable though simple means of overcoming the difficulty often experienced in removing brasses. When not in use the projecting arm is slid upward and off the rack and is vertically sheathed in the recess provided, where a spring prevents it from dropping out.

The Nos. 120 and 122 cone-bearing jacks are superior in durability and ease of operation to similar jacks. The gears, instead of being of unfinished steel castings are made of machine cut solid steel forgings.

Style	Capacity Tons	Height Inches	Rise Inches	Weight Lbs.	Price	Code Word
120	15	9¾	4	43	$22.00	Dissent
122	15	11	5	45	22.00	Divan

Buda Cone-Bearing Jack

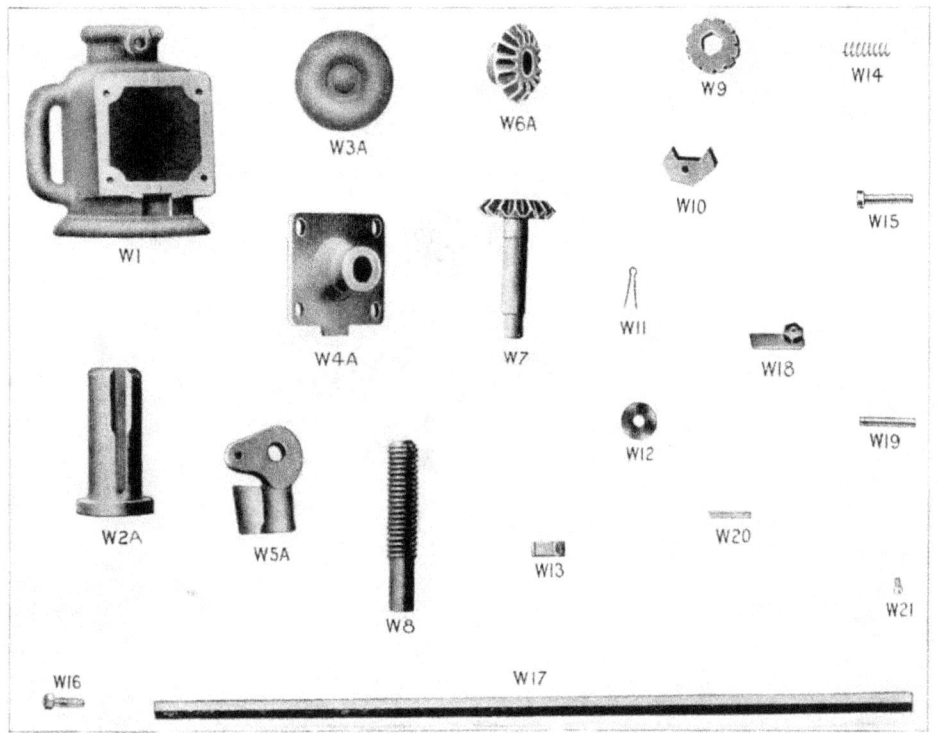

Repair Parts. No. 120 Cone-Bearing Jack

Shell .... W- 1	Cotter W-11
Standard .... W- 2-A	Steel Bushing W-12
Base Plate .... W- 3-A	Reversing Pin W-13
Cap .... W- 4-A	Reversing Pin Spring W-14
Lever Socket .... W- 5-A	Pawl Bolt W-15
Gear with Hub .... W- 6-A	Stud and Nut W-16
Gear with Shaft .... W- 7	Lever W-17
Screw .... W- 8	Key for Standard W-18
Ratchet .... W- 9	Taper Pin for Gear W-19
Pawl W-10	Key for Gear W-20
	Reversing Pin Screw W-21

The Buda Foundry & Manufacturing Company

No. B60 Buda Ball-Bearing Journal Jack

WITH WHEEL HOLDING DEVICE

PATENTS APPLIED FOR.

25-Ton Car Inspector's Jack

This journal jack differs somewhat from those of the cone-bearing type. It is fitted with ball-bearings and is made to handle heaviest equipment, being very powerful and easy working.

The B60 is supplied with the wheel holding device shown on the No. 122 cone-bearing jack. This arrangement effectively accomplishes the purpose and is a handy and valuable addition to the jack.

Style	Capacity	Height	Rise	Weight	List Price	Code Word
B 60	25 tons	10 inches	4½ inches	68 pounds	$56.00	Dragon

Buda Geared Ratchet Jacks

The two styles of geared ratchet jacks which we manufacture, and which are illustrated on the following page, are of improved design and construction. They are thoroughly dependable jacks and may be relied on to withstand full capacity. This is a very essential point for experience with jacks of similar design shows a too light general construction which fails to hold up under the load. All parts of both jacks are high grade.

No. 130B. The strongest and most powerful jack of this type on the market. Will surely lift full rated load without injury to any of its working parts. The rack, pinion, pawls, socket lever, pins and bearings are of case hardened high carbon steel. All small parts subject to wear are case hardened. The large gear is of open hearth steel. The rack and gears are cut from the solid. The direction of lifting bar is changed by eccentric at the side. Both pawls are positively operated on both the raising and lowering movements, and are of very heavy, substantial drop forgings. The main castings and gear covers are of malleable iron. An adjustable steel plate is provided at the back of the rack, so that any wear between the rack and pinion may be taken up and these parts maintained in proper relative position. The metal in all the parts is distributed to give the greatest strength consistent with weight. The jack is simple, strong and efficient, and the mechanism is arranged to prevent possibility of load dropping.

No. 500B. The rack, pinion and gear of this jack are cut from solid steel. Rack, pinion, socket lever, pins and bearings are of case hardened high carbon steel. In order to compensate for any wear, an adjustable steel plate is provided at back of rack so that rack and pinion are always in proper mesh. A small crank at side of jack changes direction of the lifting bar. This jack is equipped with safety pawl which positively prevents jack from dropping load. This safety pawl is thrown out in lowering load, and is so arranged that when lever is raised to the extreme upper position safety pawl engages with teeth of gear and defeats any accidental dropping of load when lowering. The main castings and those of gear cover are of malleable iron.

It will be noted that these jacks are both high grade in every respect, and we do not hesitate to offer them as much superior to any other jacks of similar construction heretofore offered.

Buda Geared Ratchet Jacks

WITH SAFETY CATCH

PATENTS APPLIED FOR.
No. 130 B

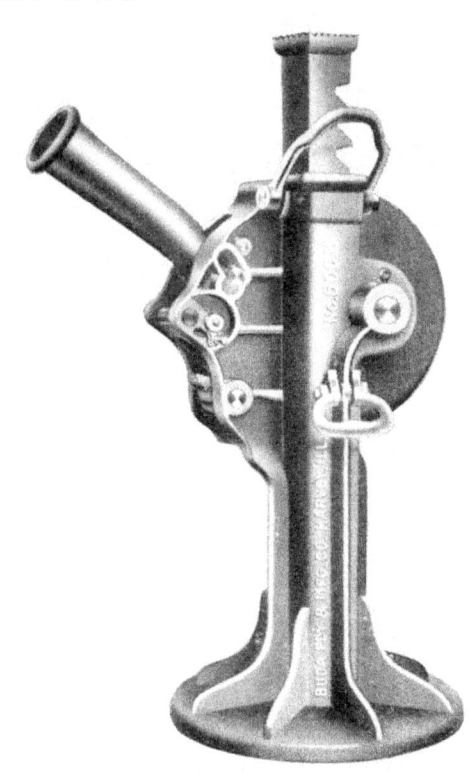

PATENTS APPLIED FOR.
No. 500 B

These jacks are much improved in construction, all working parts being unusually heavy and the general design much stronger than found in similar styles. They work easily and rapidly and are much favored by some for use in handling passenger equipment, etc.

The No. 130B has an eccentric at side by which direction of lifting bar is changed.

The No. 500B has a similar arrangement in the way of a small crank which when upright causes load to be lifted, and when down, as in illustration, causes load to lower. Each stroke of lever lifts load ¼ inch.

Both jacks have safety dog which safeguards against load falling.

Style	Capacity Tons	Height Bar Down	Rise Inches	Size of Bar	Weight Lbs.	List Price	Code Word
130 B	35	28 in.	17	3 x 2½ in.	225	$120.00	Deforce
500 B	30	27 in.	17	3 x 2½ in.	237	120 00	Douse

Buda Ratchet Jacks

Ratchet jacks have a wide field of use and up to certain capacities they are very desirable because they are simple, inexpensive, are comparatively light and easy to handle and are quick operating. They have the following general characteristics:

Single acting—in which the jack operates on the downward stroke of lever only.

Double acting—in which the jack operates on upward and downward strokes of lever.

Automatic lowering—where the load is lowered by the same movement by which it is raised, the direction of the lifting bar, or rack, being reversed by an eccentric at side of jack.

Trip jacks—where the load is raised and allowed to fall by releasing the pawls. These last styles of jacks should not be used for heavy loads, for they are likely to be carelessly tripped with accidental results. They are recommended only for track work where the load may be instantly discharged and jack quickly withdrawn in cases of approaching trains.

Many varieties of ratchet jacks are shown in following pages and attention directed to their substantial construction reinforced by strong ribs. Made of refined material, they are subjected to careful inspection throughout their process of manufacture, and they come to the user perfectly fitted and capable of fulfilling all requirements up to their respective capacities. We guarantee them to render satisfactory and safe service and to be unsurpassed or even equaled by any similar make.

Buda ratchet jacks are composed of the following materials:

Frame or Base—Malleable iron.

Rack—Forged steel, machine-cut teeth.

Pawls—Drop forged, open hearth, high carbon steel.

Fulcrum Pin—High carbon rolled steel, machined.

Bearings—Hardened steel.

In the manufacture of our jacks we are using new and latest improved machine tools which results in accuracy and ease of operation and reduces friction wear and cost of maintenance. We do not hesitate to invite comparison and are pleased to co-operate to this end.

No. 1B Ratchet Jack

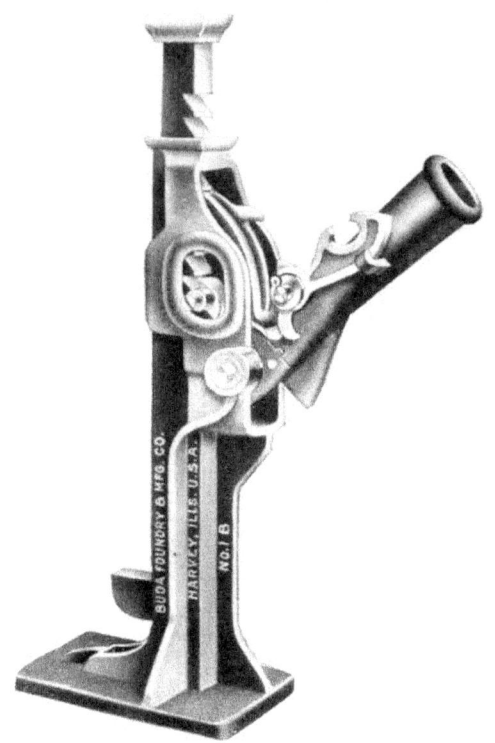

Double Acting Trip Jack.   For Track Work

One of the important considerations regarding a track jack is that it should have the advantage of being able to quickly discharge its load to permit its immediate withdrawal. This safety factor is apparent. For this reason we recommend for track work, our trip ratchet jacks. Our No. 1 B shown above has a capacity of 10 tons and is constructed to meet the requirements of the Roadmasters' Association. It lifts load on upward and downward strokes. Other trip jacks are Nos. 6 B, 12 B, 17 B, 20 B and 25 B.

We recommend trip jacks for track work only.

We call attention to jack No. 25 B for lining up purposes.

Capacity in Tons	Height Bar Down Inches	Rise of Bar Inches	Height Bar Raised Inches	Size of Bar Inches	Weight Lbs.	Code Word	List Price
10	24	13½	37½	1½x1½	62	Dale	$18.00

No. 1B Trip Ratchet Jack

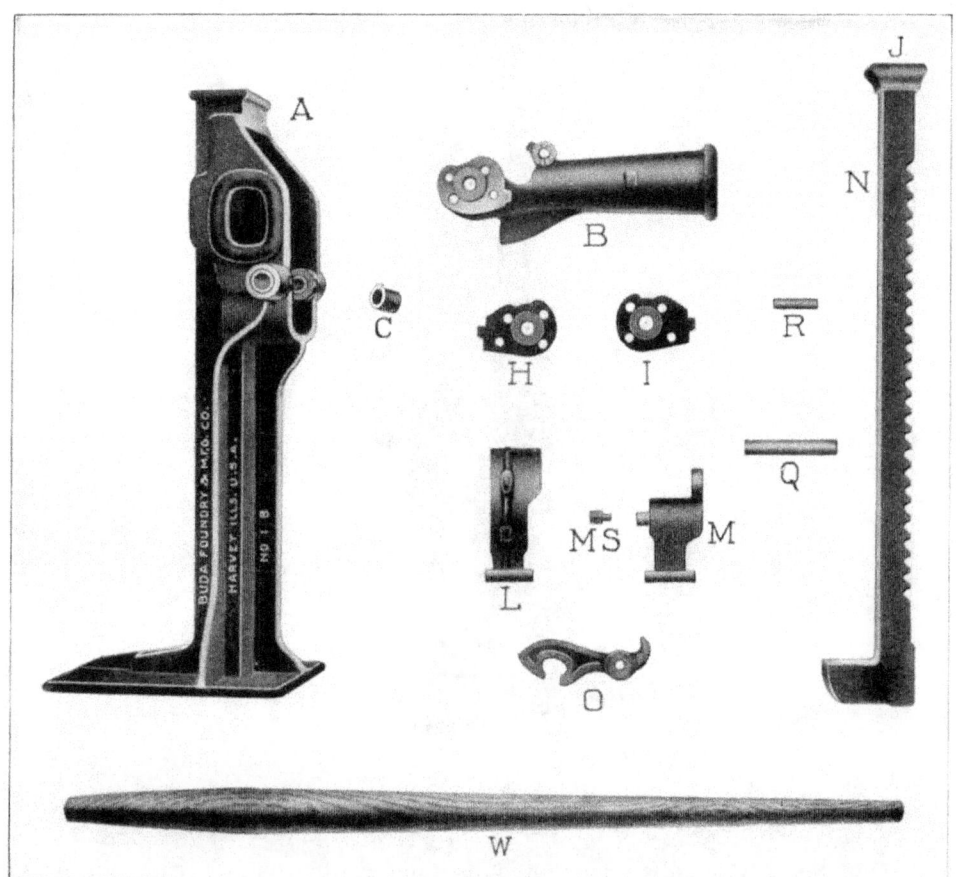

Repair Parts

Symbol.	Name of Part.	Price.
A	Base with Bushings	$7.50
B	Socket Lever with Side Plates	3.00
C	Bushing (2) each	.20
H	Right Hand Side Plate	.30
I	Left Hand Side Plate	.30
J	Top of Rack	.30
L	Long Pawl	1.50
M	Short Pawl	$1.50
N	Steel Rack	4.50
O	Trip	.50
Q	Fulcrum Pin	.30
R	Side Plate Rivet (2) each	.05
MS	Short Pawl Screw	.10

No. 2B Ratchet Jack

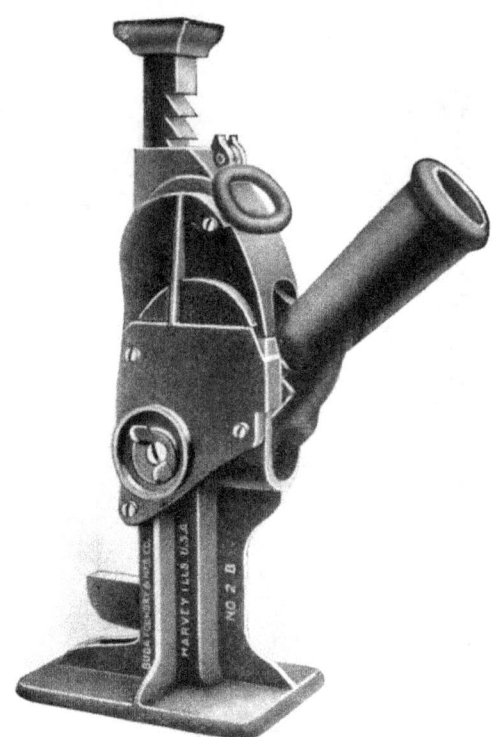

Double Acting. Automatic Lowering

Our No. 2 B jack will be found useful for all-around lifting purposes. It lifts and lowers load on both the upward and downward strokes—one-half notch to each stroke. It is automatic lowering, the direction being changed at the will of operator by turning the eccentric at the side. It has been extensively used in traction line construction and as a traction car jack in cases of derailments, etc. Having no trip by which the load may be carelessly thrown, it is a jack well calculated to fulfill such requirements. It will operate at any angle.

Capacity in Tons	Height Bar Down Inches	Rise of Bar Inches	Height Bar Raised Inches	Size of Bar Inches	Weight Lbs.	Code Word	List Price
10	21	10	31	1⅝x1½	65	Dame	$25.00

No. 2B Ratchet Jack

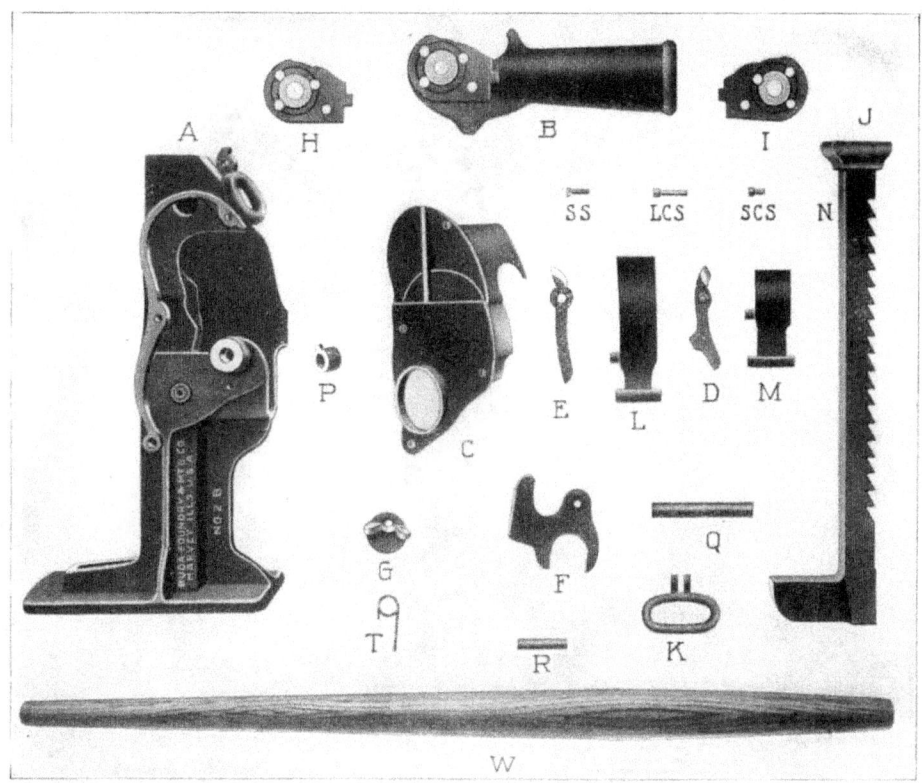

Repair Parts

Symbol.	Name of Part.	Price.
A	Base with Bushings and Handle	$10.00
B	Socket Lever with Side Plates	3.50
C	Shield	.90
D	Short Pawl Spring Lever	.30
E	Long Pawl Spring Lever	.30
F	Lowering Block	.80
G	Eccentric	.30
H	Right Hand Side Plate	.30
I	Left Hand Side Plate	.30
J	Top of Rack	.30
K	Carrying Handle	$0.20
L	Long Pawl	1.60
M	Short Pawl	1.60
N	Steel Rack	5.00
P	Bushing (2) each	.20
Q	Fulcrum Pin	.30
R	Side Plate Rivet (2) each	.05
T	Spring (2) each	.10
SS	Shoulder Screw (4) each	.10
SCS	Short Shield Screw (3) each	.08
LCS	Long Shield Screw	.10

No. 3B Ratchet Jack

Double Acting.   Automatic Lowering

This jack operates in the same manner as the No. 2, but it is heavier and stronger. It has a capacity of twelve tons and raise of bar of 15 inches. Adapted to general work on railroads and in moving machinery. It will take low-set loads and raise same to full range of lift.

This jack will operate at any angle.

Capacity in Tons	Height Bar Down Inches	Rise of Bar Inches	Height Bar Raised Inches	Size of Bar Inches	Weight Lbs.	Code Word	List Price
12	26½	15	41½	1¾ x 1⅞	85	Damp	$30.00

No. 3B Ratchet Jack

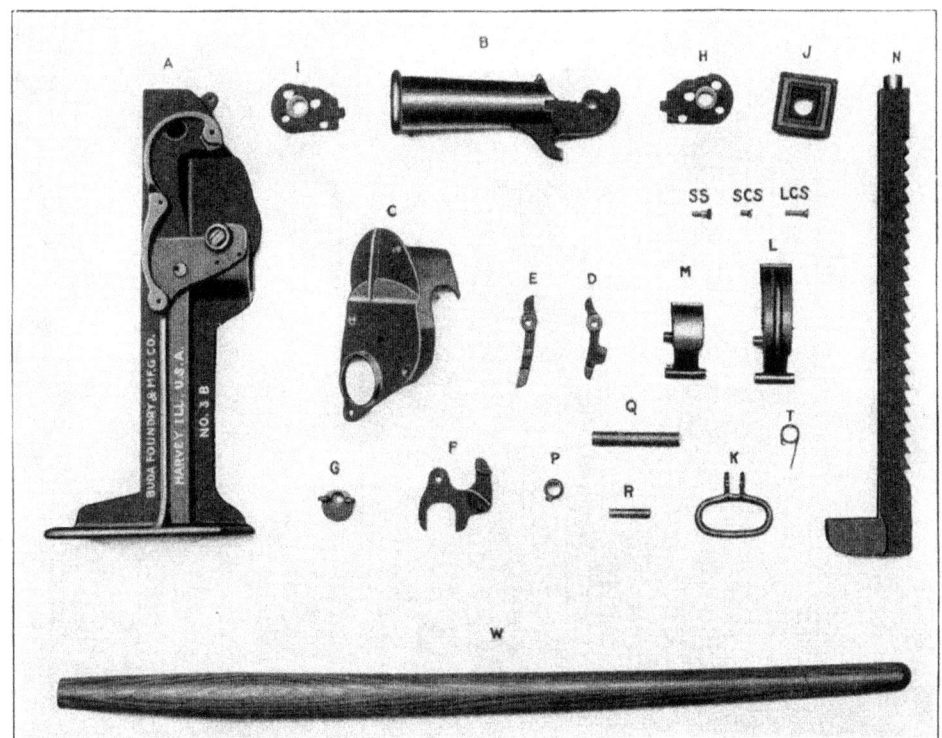

Repair Parts

Symbol.	Name of Part.	Price.
A	Base with Bushings and Handle	$12.50
B	Socket Lever with Side Plates	3.50
C	Shield	.90
D	Short Pawl Spring Lever	.30
E	Long Pawl Spring Lever	.30
F	Lowering Block	.80
G	Eccentric	.30
H	Right Hand Side Plate	.30
I	Left Hand Side Plate	.30
J	Top of Rack	.40
K	Carrying Handle	.20
L	Long Pawl	$2.00
M	Short Pawl	1.70
N	Steel Rack	8.50
P	Bushing (2) each	.20
Q	Fulcrum Pin	.30
R	Side Plate Rivet (2) each	.05
T	Spring (2) each	.10
SS	Shoulder Screw (4) each	.10
SCS	Short Shield Screw (3) each	.08
LCS	Long Shield Screw	.10

No. 4B Ratchet Jack

Double Acting.   Automatic Lowering

It will be seen from the cut that the frame and lifting bar of this jack are unusually heavy. It raises 15 tons ten inches. The load is raised and lowered half a notch on both upward and downward strokes, the direction being controlled by the eccentric at side of frame. Jack operates at any angle.

Capacity in Tons	Height Bar Down Inches	Rise of Bar Inches	Height Bar Raised Inches	Size of Bar Inches	Weight Lbs.	Code Word	List Price
15	22	10	32	2x2	100	Dare	$35.00

No. 4B Ratchet Jack

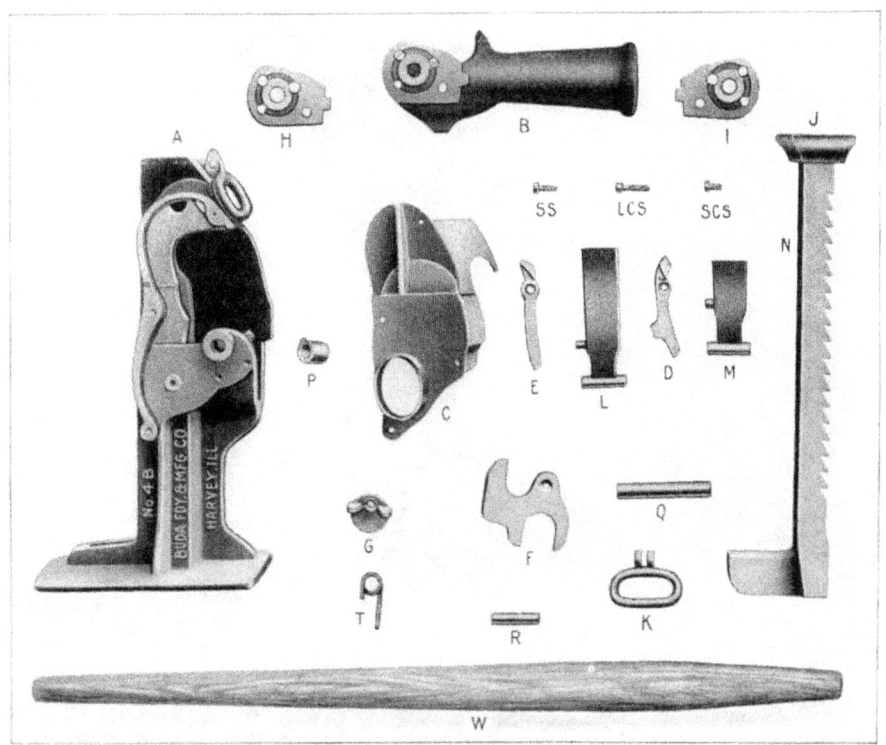

Repair Parts

Symbol.	Name of Part.	Price.	Symbol.	Name of Part.	Price.
A	Base with Bushings and Handle.	$13.50	K	Carrying Handle	$0.20
B	Socket Lever with Side Plates	4.50	L	Long Pawl	2.00
C	Shield	1.00	M	Short Pawl	1.80
D	Short Pawl Spring Lever	.30	N	Steel Rack	9.00
E	Long Pawl Spring Lever	.30	P	Bushing (2) each	.20
F	Lowering Block	.90	Q	Fulcrum Pin	.35
G	Eccentric	.20	R	Side Plate Rivet (2) each	.05
H	Right Hand Side Plate	.30	T	Spring (2) each	.10
I	Left Hand Side Plate	.30	SS	Shoulder Screw	.10
J	Top of Rack	.70	SCS	Short Shield Screw (3) each	.08
			LCS	Long Shield Screw	.10

No. 5B Ratchet Jack

Double Acting.   Automatic Lowering

This is a heavier jack, with a greater range than others in this class. It raises 15 tons to a height of 15 inches.

The illustration shows strong construction. It is substantially ribbed and has a well-broadened base—a feature of considerable advantage in handling high set loads.

The load is moved half a notch up or down on upward and downward movements of lever, direction being changed by eccentric.

Jack has two handles. Operates at any angle.

Capacity in Tons	Height Bar Down Inches	Rise of Bar Inches	Height Bar Raised Inches	Size of Bar Inches	Weight Lbs.	Code Word	List Price
15	28	15	43	2x2	115	Dash	$40.00

No. 5B Ratchet Jack

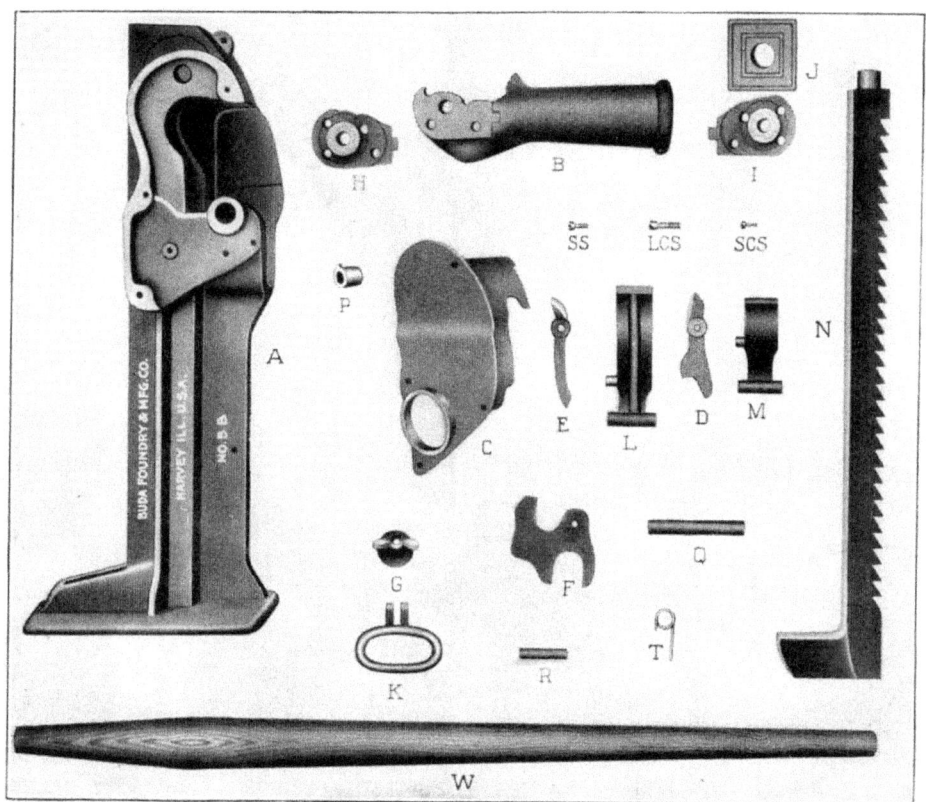

Repair Parts

Symbol.	Name of Part.	Price.
A	Base with Bushings and Handles	$16.00
B	Socket Lever with Side Plates	4.50
C	Shield	1.00
D	Short Pawl Spring Lever	.30
E	Long Pawl Spring Lever	.30
F	Lowering Block	.90
G	Eccentric	.20
H	Right Hand Side Plate	.30
I	Left Hand Side Plate	.30
J	Top of Rack	.70
K	Carrying Handle (2) each	.20
L	Long Pawl	$ 2.00
M	Short Pawl	1.80
N	Steel Rack	10.00
P	Bushing (2) each	.20
Q	Fulcrum Pin	.35
R	Side Plate Rivet (2) each	.05
T	Spring (2) each	.10
SS	Short Screw (4) each	.10
SCS	Short Shield Screw (3) each	.08
LCS	Long Shield Screw	.10

No. 6B Ratchet Ballast Gang Jack

Double Acting Trip Jack. For Track Work

This is the most powerful and has the greatest raise of any of the double-acting trip jacks. It raises a 15-ton load 19 inches. It is used widely in construction and in road ballast work.

It raises the load one-half a notch at each stroke, up or down. A "trip" is attached by means of which the load can be instantly dropped.

Other trip jacks are Nos. 1B, 12B, 17B, 20B and 25B.

Capacity in Tons	Height Bar Down Inches	Rise of Bar Inches	Height Bar Raised Inches	Size of Bar Inches	Weight Lbs.	Code Word	List Price
15	31	19	50	1⅞ x 1¾	105	Dean	$32.00

No. 6B Ratchet Ballast Gang Jack

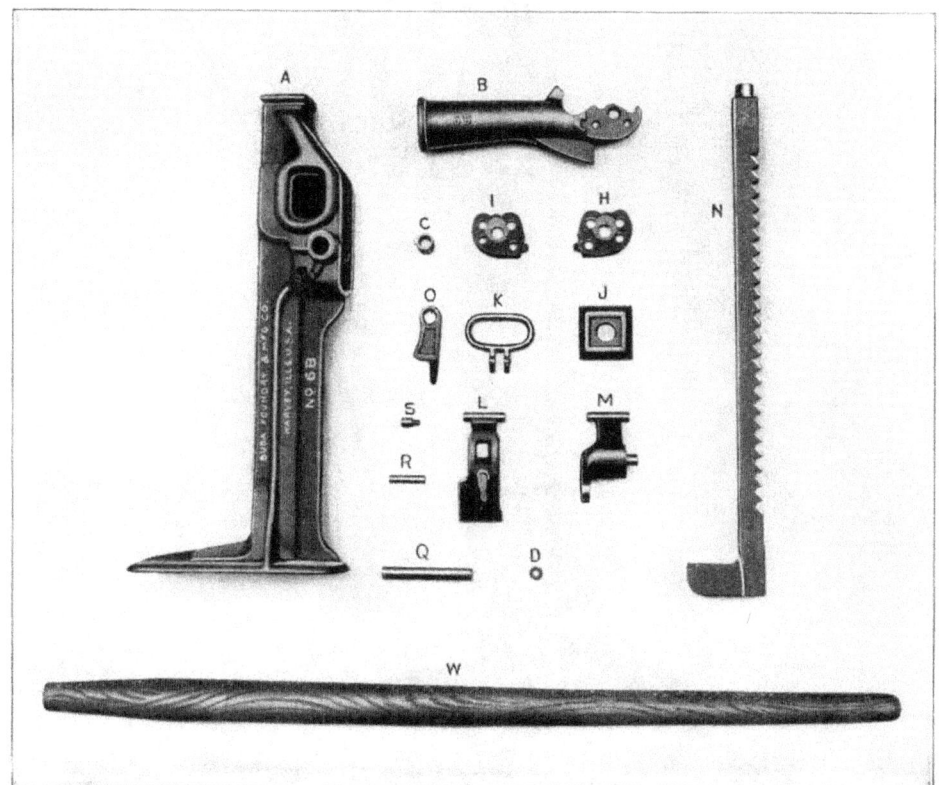

Repair Parts

Symbol.	Name of Part.	Price.
A	Base with Bushings and Handles	$16.00
B	Socket Lever with Side Plates	3.75
C	Bushing (2) each	.20
H	Right Hand Side Plate	.30
I	Left Hand Side Plate	.30
J	Top of Rack	.60
K	Carrying Handle (2) each	.30
L	Long Pawl	$2.00
M	Short Pawl	2.00
N	Steel Rack	9.00
O	Trip	.45
Q	Fulcrum Pin	.40
R	Side Plate Rivet (2) each	.05
S	Short Pawl Screw	.10

No. 7B Ratchet Jack

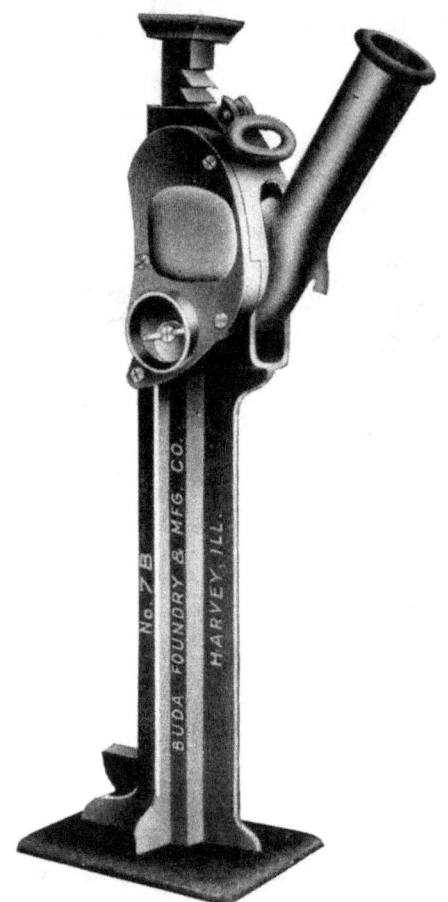

Single Acting.   Automatic Lowering

This is an exceptionally tall jack, being 35 inches high. It is particularly adapted for general car service, and for use where cars are empty or only lightly loaded it occupies a place that no other jack can fill. It is single acting—the load being raised or lowered on the downward stroke of the lever. The lifting bar is made to work in either direction by means of the eccentric at side. It will operate at any angle. It is similar to the No. 19 jack, but is taller and has a correspondingly greater lift.

Capacity in Tons	Height Bar Down Inches	Rise of Bar Inches	Height Bar Raised Inches	Size of Bar Inches	Weight Lbs.	Code Word	List Price
15	35	24½	59½	2x2	122	Dusky	$42.00

No. 04B Automobile Jack

Double Acting.   Automatic Lowering

This jack, though small, is suitable for general lifting purposes, being useful for light loads. It is double acting, raising load on the downward and upward stroke of the lever. Direction is changed at will of operator by eccentric at the side. The jack is very quick acting and easily handled. This jack operates at any angle.

Capacity in Tons	Height Bar Down Inches	Rise of Bar Inches	Height Bar Raised Inches	Size of Bar Inches	Weight Lbs.	Code Word	List Price
1	11½	6	17½	¾ x 1¾	9½	Defy	$5.00

No. 8B and 48B Ratchet Jacks

No. 8 B

Double Acting. Automatic Lowering

No. 48 B

Single Acting. Automatic Lowering

No. 8B. The load is raised and lowered half a notch on the downward and upward strokes of the lever. The direction of the lifting bar is changed by the eccentric shown on left side. It is essentially a journal jack but it can be adapted to a variety of uses. It is not heavy and is easily carried and handled. It is a capital jack for use on electric roads. It operates at any angle.

The No. 48B is 15 tons capacity and is single acting—raising and lowering load on downward stroke. An extra long rack can be used for special lifting purposes.

Style	Capacity Tons	Height Bar down Inches	Rise of Bar Inches	Height Bar Raised Inches	Size of Bar Inches	Weight Lbs.	Code Word	List Price
8B	10	11	5	16	1 5/8 x 1 1/2	48	Debit	$22.00
48B	15	11	5	16	1 3/4 x 1 7/8	60	Deploy	25.00

No. 8B Jack

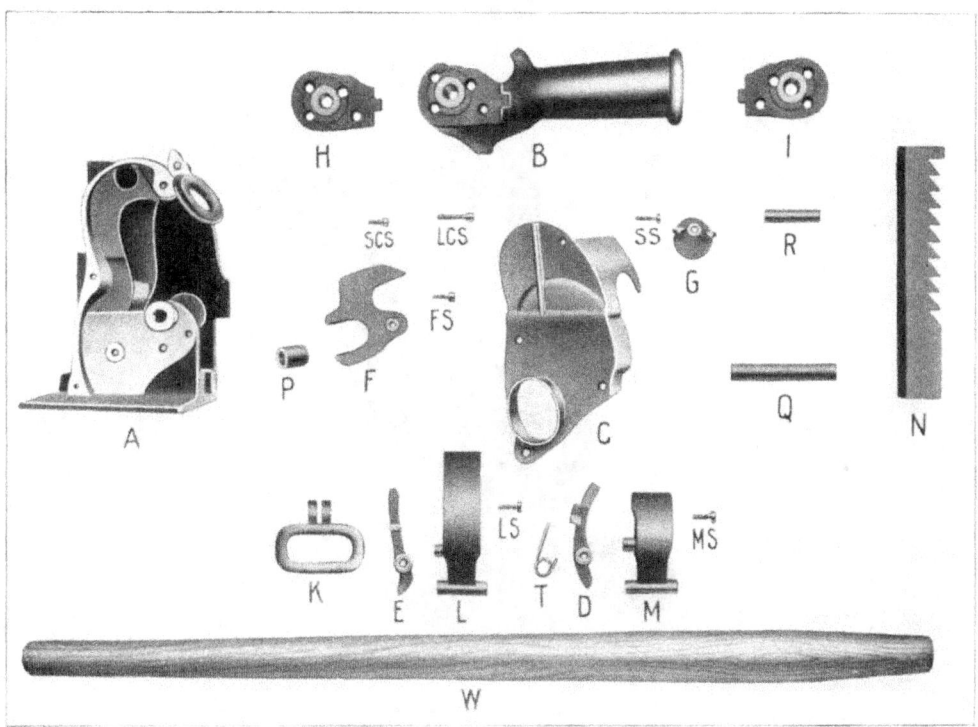

Repair Parts

Symbol.	Name of Part.	Price.
A	Base with bushings and handle.	$9.00
B	Socket Lever with Slide Plates.	3.50
C	Shield	.90
D	Short Pawl Spring Lever	.30
E	Long Pawl Spring Lever	.30
F	Lowering Block	.80
G	Eccentric	.20
H	Right Hand Side Plate	.30
I	Left Hand Side Plate	.30
L	Long Pawl	1.60
M	Short Pawl	$1.60
N	Steel Rack	2.00
K	Carrying Handle	.20
P	Bushing (2), each	.20
Q	Fulcrum Pin	.30
R	Side Plate Rivet (2), each	.05
T	Spring (2), each	.10
SS-FS-LS-MS	Shoulder Screw, each	.10
SCS	Short Shield Screw (3), each	.08
LCS	Long Shield Screw	.10

The Buda Foundry & Manufacturing Company

No. 12B Ratchet Jack

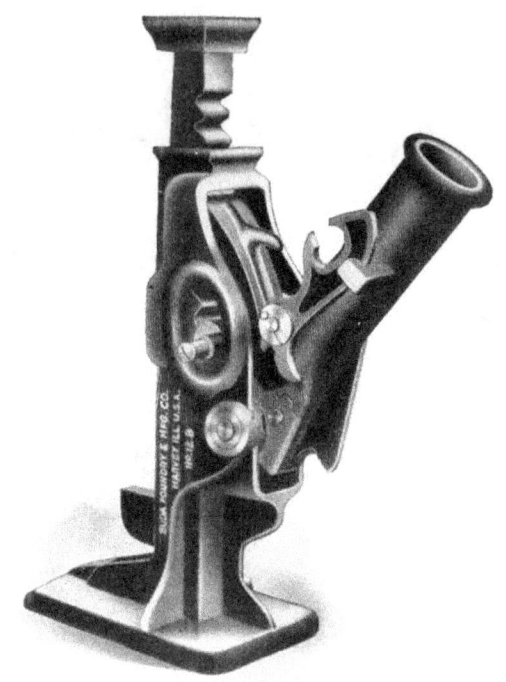

Double Acting Trip Jack.   For Track Work

This jack is a double-acting compound lever jack, raising the load half a notch on both up and down strokes. It is similar to No. 1, but shorter. It has the same capacity, and was designed to meet the requirements for a small jack with limited raise.

Other trip jacks are Nos. 1B, 6B, 17B, 20B and 25B.

We recommend trip jacks for track work only.

Capacity in Tons	Height Bar Down Inches	Rise of Bar Inches	Height Bar Raised Inches	Size of Bar Inches	Weight Lbs.	Code Word	List Price
10	17¾	8	25¾	1½ x 1½	50	Decry	$17.00

No. 12B Ratchet Jack

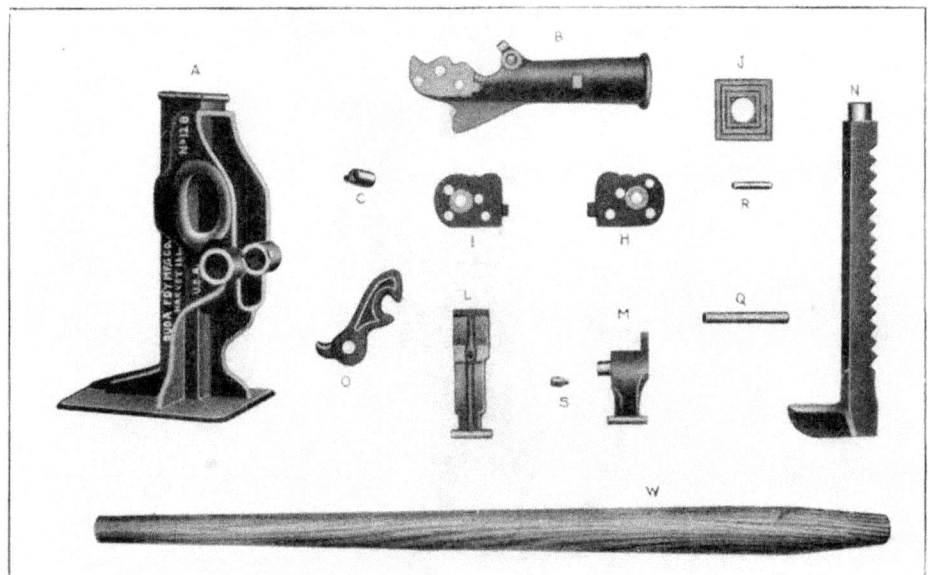

Repair Parts

Symbol.	Name of Part.	Price.	Symbol.	Name of Part.	Price.
A	Base with Bushings	$6.75	M	Short Pawl	$1.50
B	Socket Lever with Side Plates	3.00	N	Steel Rack	4.00
C	Bushing (2) each	.20	O	Trip	.50
H	Right Hand Side Plate	.30	Q	Fulcrum Pin	.30
I	Left Hand Side Plate	.30	R	Side Plate Rivet (2) each	.05
J	Top of Rack	.30	S	Short Pawl Screw	.10
L	Long Pawl	1.50			

No. 17B Ratchet Jack

Single Acting Trip Jack. For Track Work

This is like the No. 1 jack, but it raises the load a full notch on the downward stroke only; while the No. 1 raises one-half notch on downward and upward strokes of lever. The load can be dropped from any height instantly, thus providing for quick removal of jack if necessary.

We recommend trip jacks for track work only. For general lifting purposes they are not desirable, as accidental tripping would precipitate the load with perhaps disastrous consequences.

Other trip jacks are Nos. 1B, 6B, 12B, 20B and 25B.

Capacity Tons	Height Bar Down Inches	Rise of Bar Inches	Height Bar Raised Inches	Size of Bar Inches	Weight Pounds	Code Word	List Price
10	24	13¾	37¾	1½x1½	63	Dandy	$18 00

No. 17B Ratchet Jack

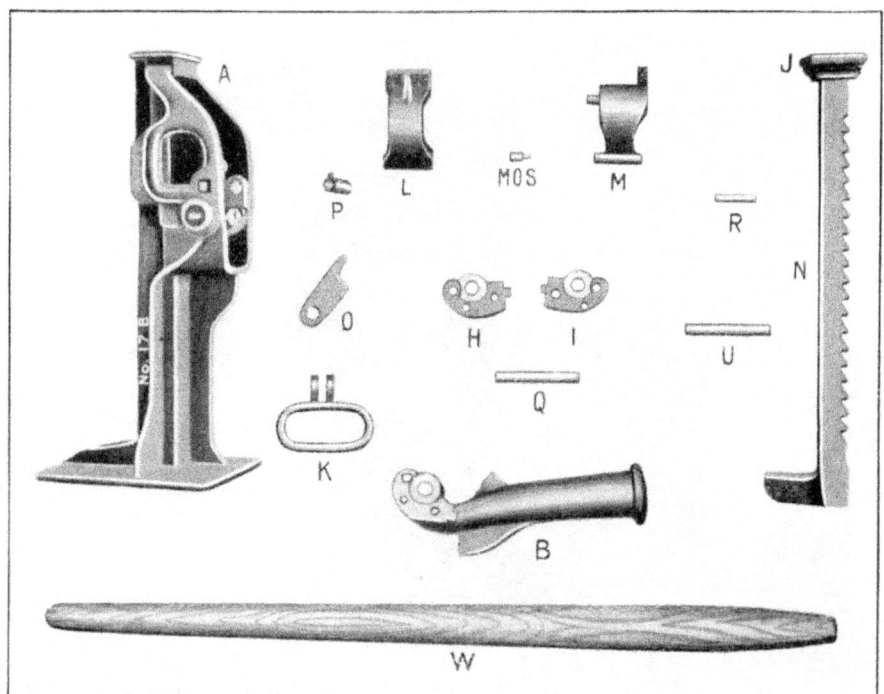

Repair Parts

Symbol.	Name of Part.	Price.
A	Base with Bushings and Handle	$7.50
B	Socket Lever with Side Plates	3.00
H	Right Hand Side Plate	.30
I	Left Hand Side Plate	.30
J	Top of Rack	.30
L	Long Pawl	1.50
M	Short Pawl	1.50
N	Steel Rack	$4.50
O	Trip	.45
P	Bushing (2) each	.20
Q	Fulcrum	.30
R	Side Plate Rivet (2) each	.05
U	Long Pawl Pin	.25
W	Wood Handle	.55
MS	Short Pawl Screw	.10

The Buda Foundry & Manufacturing Company

No. 18B Ratchet Jack

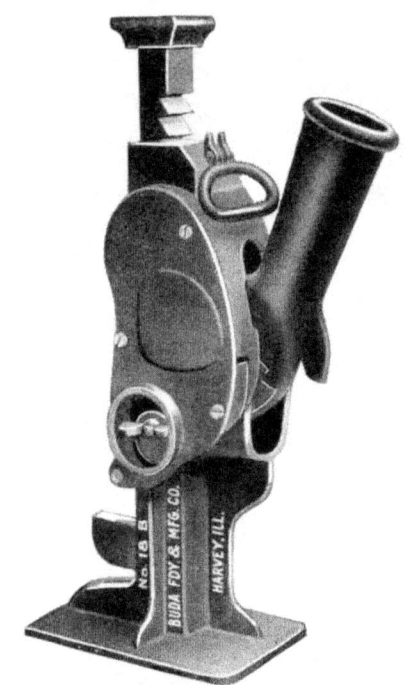

Single Acting.   Automatic Lowering

This jack is similar to our No. 2, the difference being that it raises or lowers the load on the downward stroke only, whereas the No. 2 is double-acting, raising and lowering load on downward and upward stroke.

Can be used for bridge work and track work as well as for general lifting purposes.

Operates at any angle.

Capacity Tons	Height Bar Down Inches	Rise of Bar Inches	Height Bar Raised Inches	Size of Bar Inches	Weight Lbs.	Code Word	List Price
10	21	10	31	1½ x 1⅝	68	Decoy	$25.00

No. 18B Ratchet Jack

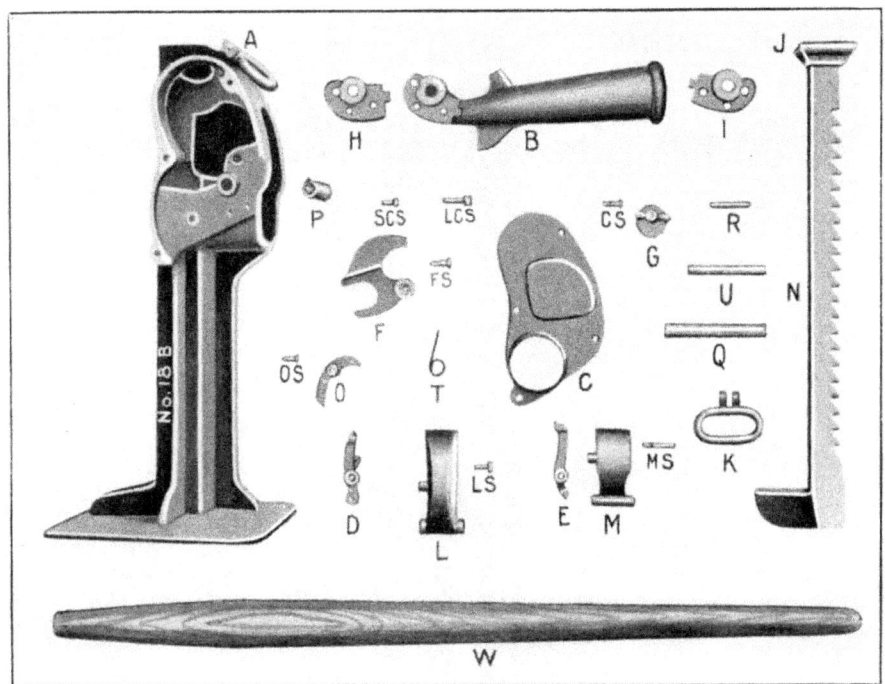

Repair Parts

Symbol.	Name of Part.	Price.
A	Base with Bushings and Handle	$10.00
B	Socket Lever with Side Plates	3.50
C	Shield	1.00
D	Short Pawl Spring Lever	.30
E	Long Pawl Spring Lever	.30
F	Lowering Block	.80
G	Eccentric	.20
H	Right Hand Side Plate	.30
I	Left Hand Side Plate	.30
J	Top of Rack	.30
K	Carrying Handle	.20
L	Long Pawl	1.80
M	Short Pawl	1.60
N	Steel Rack	5.00
O	Auxiliary Lever	$0.20
P	Bushing (2) each	.20
Q	Fulcrum Pin	.30
R	Side Plate Rivet (2) each	.05
T	Spring (2) each	.10
U	Pawl Pin	.25
W	Wood Handle	.55
OS	Auxiliary Lever Screw	.10
SCS	Short Shield Screw (2) each	.08
LCS	Long Shield Screw	.10
LS	Long Pawl Screw	.10
MS	Short Pawl Screw	.10
GS	Eccentric Screw	.10
FS	Lowering Block Screw	.10

No. 19B Ratchet Jack

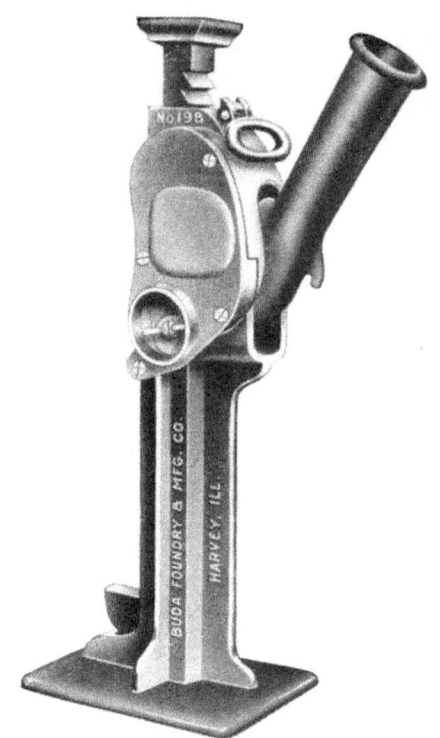

Single Acting.   Automatic Lowering

The lifting capacity of the jack is 15 tons. On account of its strength and height, it is carried in many cabooses and engines. It is conveniently carried and, operating as it does at any angle, it is easily applied where some styles of jacks would be nearly useless. It is largely used for car repairing where cars are empty or lightly loaded.

This jack lifts and lowers on the down stroke only, the direction being controlled at will of operator by simply turning the eccentric.

Capacity in Tons	Height Bar Down Inches	Rise of Bar Inches	Height Bar Raised Inches	Size of Bar Inches	Weight Lbs.	Code Word	List Price
15	28	17½	45½	2 x 2	102	Defer	$35.00

No. 19B Ratchet Jack

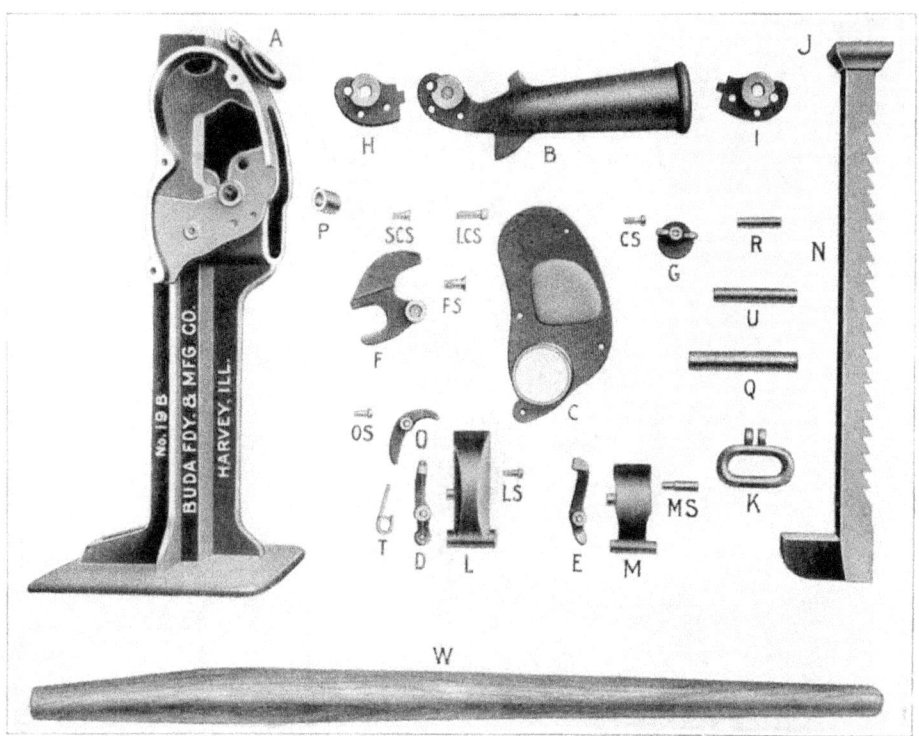

Repair Parts

Symbol.	Name of Part.	Price.
A	Base with Bushings & Handle.	$15.00
B	Socket Lever with Side Plates.	3.50
C	Shield	1.00
D	Short Pawl Spring Lever	.30
E	Long Pawl Spring Lever	.30
F	Lowering Block	.80
G	Eccentric	.20
H	Right Hand Side Plate	.30
I	Left Hand Side Plate	.30
J	Top of Rack	.70
K	Carrying Handle	.20
L	Long Pawl	1.80
M	Short Pawl	1.65
N	Steel Rack	9.25
O	Auxiliary Lever	$0.20
P	Bushing (2) each	.20
Q	Fulcrum Pin	.35
R	Side Plate Rivet (2) each	.05
T	Spring (2) each	.10
U	Pawl Pin	.30
OS	Auxiliary Lever Screw	.10
SCS	Short Shield Screw (3) each	.08
LS	Long Pawl Screw	.10
LCS	Long Shield Screw	.10
MS	Short Pawl Screw	.10
GS	Eccentric Screw	.10
FS	Lowering Block Screw	.10

No. 20B Ratchet Jack

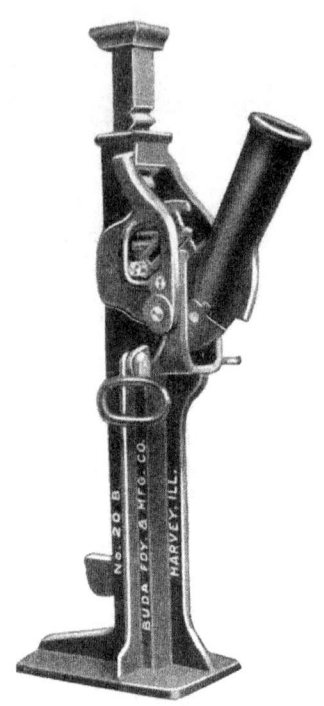

Single Acting Trip Jack.   For Track Work

For ballast-gang track work. A very strong and well-built jack. The capacity is 15 tons. It is single-acting—that is, it raises and lowers the load on the downward stroke only.

Trip jacks we recommend for track work only.

Other trip jacks are Nos. 1B, 6B, 12B, 17B and 25B.

Capacity Tons	Height Bar Down Inches	Rise of Bar Inches	Height Bar Raised Inches	Size of Bar Inches	Weight Pounds	Code Word	List Price
15	31	19	50	1⅝ x 1⅞	106	Decide	$32.00

The Buda Foundry & Manufacturing Company

No. 20B Ratchet Jack

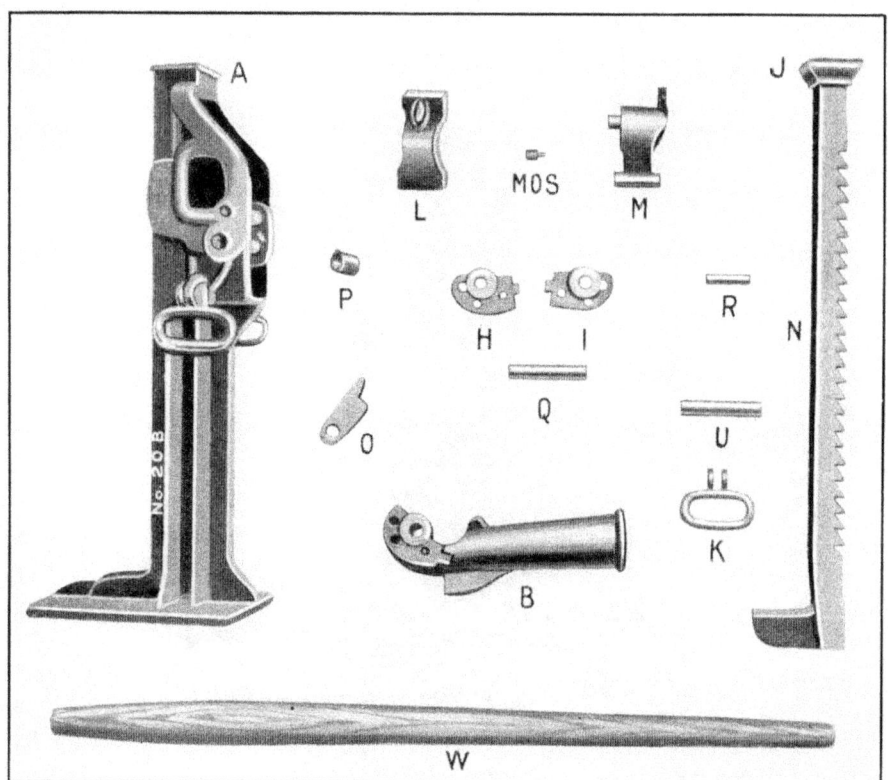

Repair Parts

Symbol.	Name of Part.	Price.	Symbol.	Name of Part.	Price.
A	Base with Bushings & Handles.	$15.00	N	Steel Rack	$9.00
B	Socket Lever with Side Plates.	3.50	O	Trip	.40
H	Right Hand Side Plate	.30	P	Bushing (2) each	.20
I	Left Hand Side Plate	.30	Q	Fulcrum Pin	.40
J	Top of Rack	.60	R	Side Plate Rivet (2) each	.05
K	Carrying Handle (2) each	.30	U	Pawl Pin	.30
L	Long Pawl	2.00	W	Wood Handle	.80
M	Short Pawl	2.00	MS	Short Pawl Screw	.10

No. 25B Buda Lining-up Jack

In Lifting Position

This is a new jack designed for lining-up purposes which combines lifting and traversing features and is operated by one interchangeable lever. The jacks are used in pairs, one outside and one inside the track, but where railroads object to use of jack inside both can be used on outside, and after track is loosened the forcing can be done by one and the other used as a simple carrier.

Two men can do the work of eight men using lining bars, thus these jacks are doubly valuable at seasons when force is reduced and on small divisions where it is always too small to give this work attention.

When load is raised enough to barely loosen ties the lift is maintained by a dog until track is thrown when load is tripped. The jack can be slid

No. 25B Lining-up Jack

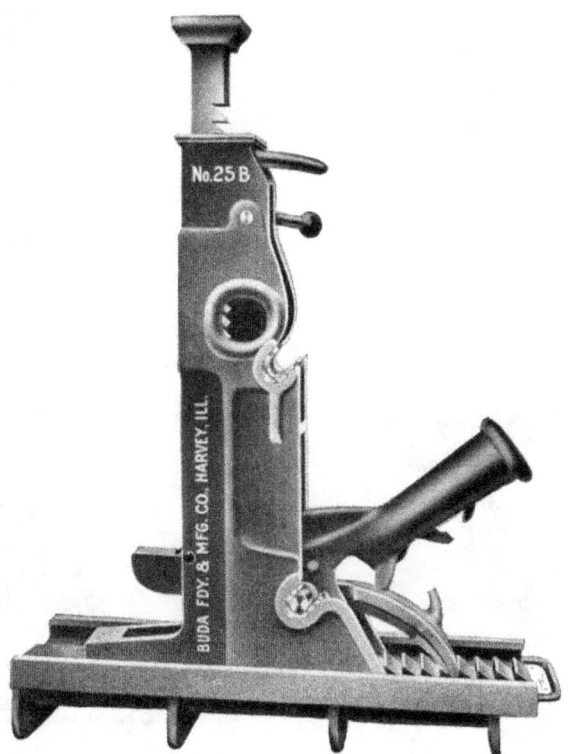

Position for Throwing Track in Line

out of base and used exactly as our No. 1 trip track jack, as it conforms to specifications of Roadmasters' Association.

The capacity of 12 tons, the safety catch dog and the traverse features make it useful for many purposes and a pair should be on every section.

Capacity in Tons	Height Bar Down Inches	Rise of Bar Inches	Height Bar Raised Inches	Size of Bar Inches	Weight Lbs.	Code Word	List Price
12	24½	12½	37	1½ x 1½	105	Dove	$50.00

Nos. 50B and 51B Ratchet Jacks

No. 50B

No. 51B

Single Acting. Automatic Lowering

The 50B jack is a very useful addition to the tool equipment of street cars for use in emergency cases, such as derailments, where it is necessary to lift the car up to be replaced, or for raising oil boxes for the purpose of renewing journal bearings. Lifts and lowers load on the down stroke only. Direction changed by eccentric at side. Operates at any angle.

The 51B jack is similar to our 50B, but it has higher frame and greater lift. Capacity 5 tons.

Style	Capacity Tons	Height Bar Down Inches	Rise of Bar Inches	Height Bar Raised Inches	Size of Bar Inches	Weight Lbs.	Code Word	List Price
50B	5	16	8	24	1¼ x 1¼	38	Debar	$17.00
51B	5	20	12	32	1¼ x 1¼	42	Deck	18 00

No. 50B and 51B Ratchet Jacks

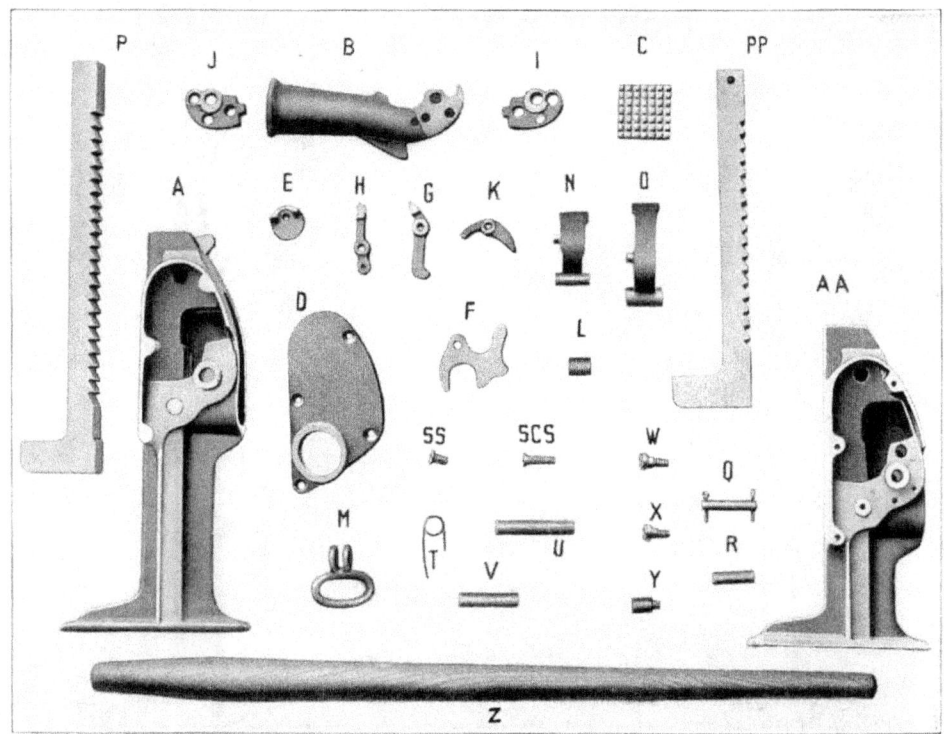

Repair Parts

REPAIR PARTS FOR 51 B JACK.

A	Base with Bushings	$7.50
B	Socket Lever with Side Plates	4.50
C	Top of Rack	.50
D	Shield	.90
E	Eccentric	.50
F	Lowering Blocks	.85
G	Long Lever Pawls	.75
H	Short Lever Pawls	.75
I	R. H. Side Plates	.50
J	L. H. Side Plates	.50
K	Spring Lever Dog	.75
L	Bushing (2) each	.50
M	Handles	.25
N	Short Pawl	2.00
O	Long Pawl	2.00
P	Rack	$4.75
Q	Pin for Rack Top	.15
R	Side Plate Rivet (2) each	.05
SS	Shield Screw, Short (3)	.12
SCS	Shield Screw, Long	.15
T	Spring for Pawl (2)	.15
U	Fulcrum Pin for Lever	.30
V	Fulcrum Pin for Long Pawl	.15
W	Shoulder Screw for Lever Block	.15
X	Shoulder Screw for Eccentric	.15
Y	Shoulder Screw for Spring Lever Dog	.15

REPAIR PARTS FOR 50 B JACK.

AA	Base with Bushings	$6.75
PP	Rack	4.50

NOTE:—The remainder of repair parts for the "50B" jack same as for "51B" jack listed above.

Friction Jacks

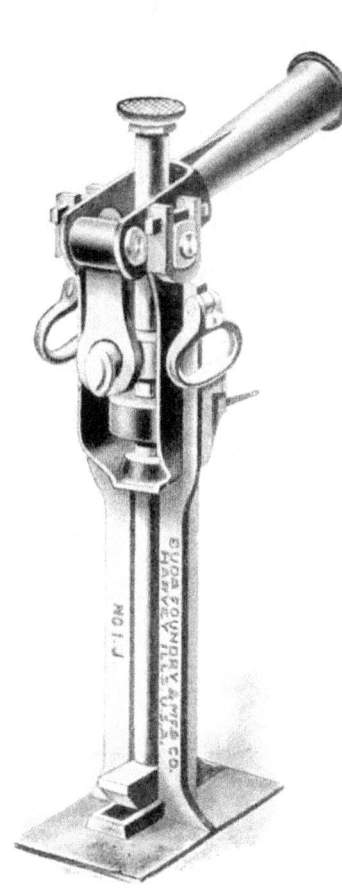
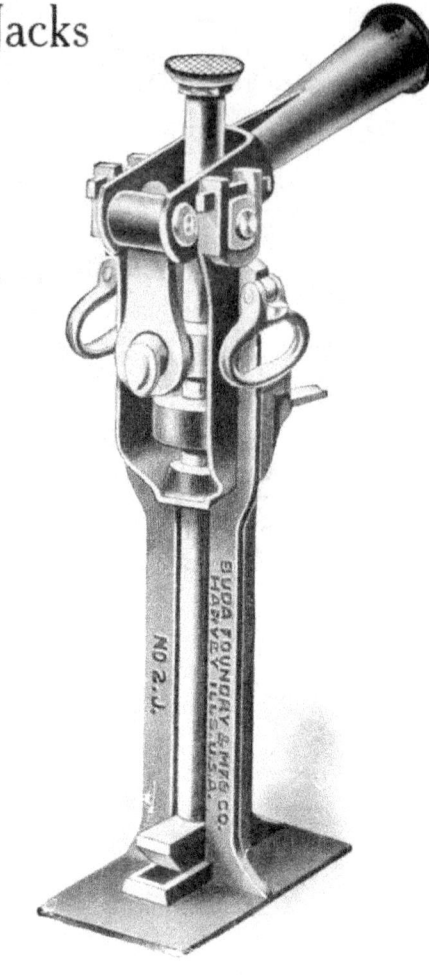

No. 1 J
For Surfacing and Track Repairs

No. 2 J
For Heavy Ballasting, Surfacing and General Repairs

No. 1 J.

Twelve-inch lift; capacity, 5 tons; weight, 62 pounds; 29 inches high, with bar down. Frame and lever socket made of best air furnace malleable iron; round lifting bar, 1½ inches diameter; steel pivots; bronze boxes; rings, hanger and lifting bar made of best refined wrought iron.

With wooden lever, complete, each..$20.00

Code word—Delta.

No. 2 J.

Fifteen-inch lift; capacity, 10 tons; weight, 85 pounds; 33 inches high, with bar down. Frame and lever socket made of best air furnace malleable iron; round lifting bar, 1¾ inches diameter; steel pivots; bronze boxes; rings, hanger and lifting bar made of best refined wrought iron.

With wooden lever, complete, each..$24.00

Code word—Dent.

All bars and rings should have **oil and grease burned off** from them before putting the Jack together. **This is important.**

The Buda Foundry & Manufacturing Company

Friction Jacks

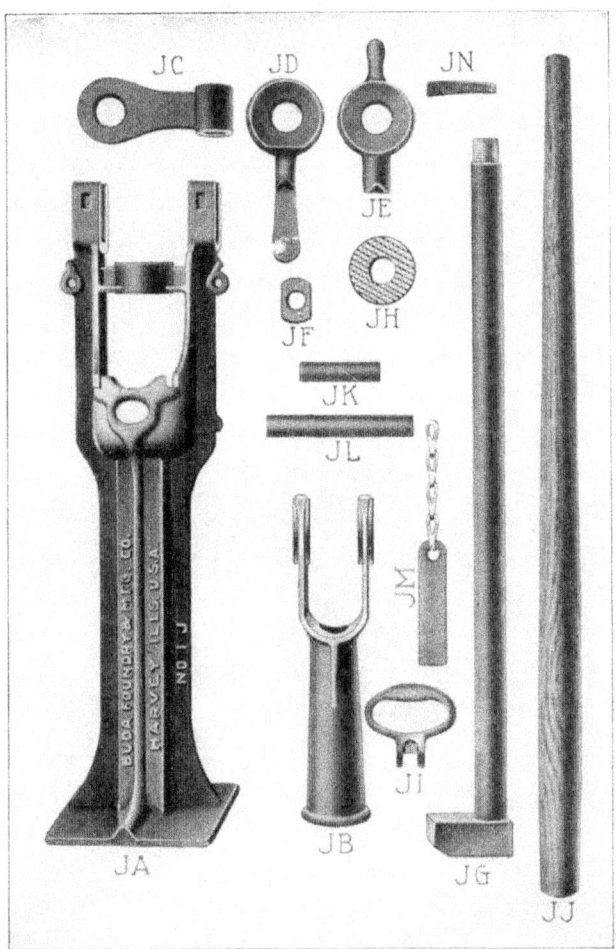

Repair Parts. Nos. 1J and 2J

Symbol.	Description.	Size of Jack. No. 1	No. 2	Symbol.	Description.	Size of Jack No. 1	No. 2
JA	Base or Stand	$7.00	$10.00	JF	Bronze Boxes, per pair	$0.90	$1.00
JG	Lifting Bar	1.50	2.00	JH	Lifting Bar Cap	.40	.50
JB	Lever Socket with Hanger and Steel Pivot	2.00	2.50	JL	Steel Fulcrum Pin	.40	.50
				JK	Hanger Pin	.30	.40
JE	Upper Lifting Ring	1.00	1.25	JM	Trip Latch with Chain	.40	.50
JD	Lower Lifting Ring	1.00	1.25	JN	Split Keys, per pair	.30	.40
JC	Hanger	.75	1.00	JI	Malleable Handle	.40	.50

This jack, although very strong and durable, will wear out in time. All parts that wear can be easily replaced without sending to shop. At the reduced prices, money can be saved by buying repairs from us, and then the parts will be perfect and repairs can be properly made, making old jacks as good as new.

Buda Lightning Jack

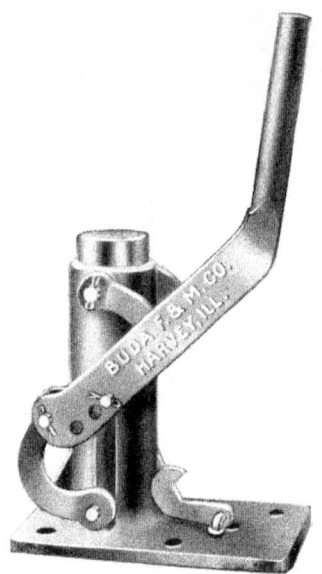

Quick Lift

This jack is of 5 tons capacity and is designed for quick work. The rise is limited, being 2½ inches, but it is accomplished at a single stroke. The frame is of malleable iron and the links are of steel. It is intended for use in removing journal brasses and similar uses where rapidity and short lift is required. Price, $25.00; code word, Donkey.

Sizes, Dimensions and Prices of Buda Jacks

Buda Ball-Bearing Jacks

Page	No.	Capacity Tons	Height Inches	Rise Inches	Dia. Base Inches	Weight Lbs.	List Price	Hook Extra	Code Word
160	101	25	33	20	12	154	$ 95.00	$6.00	Deny
160	102	15	34	20	12	154	75.00	6.00	Despot
154	109	25	20	9	10	106	80.00	6.00	Donor
154	110	25	24	11	13	149	85.00	6.00	Dial
154	111	25	26	13	12	164	90.00	6.00	Demon
152	O	35	26	13	12	165	125.00	8.00	Digit
152	OX	35	31	18	12	190	135.00	8.00	Dike
148	115	25	26	13	8 x 9	157	96.00	Foot	Dipper
144	116	50	24	9	14	270	150.00	Foot	Dish
144	117	50	27	13	14	292	150.00	Foot	Dispel
156	104	15	22	10	10	80	60.00	6.00	Dogma
156	105	15	26	13	10	92	70.00	6.00	Divert
156	103	15	20	9	10	80	60.00	5.00	Durance
164	B60	25	10	4½	7	68	56.00	......	Dragon
143	127	75	26	12	14	385	200.00	Foot	Din
144	125	60	26	12	14	323	175.00	Foot	Dismiss
146	118	35	26	13	12	175	130.00	Foot	Diverge
146	119	35	32	19	12	195	138.00	Foot	Duty
147	115A	25	20	9	10	125	90.00	Foot	Drum
151	LX	50	27	13	14	282	150.00	......	Ditto
148	114	25	22	10	8 x 9	136	90.00	Foot	Dagmar
148	113	35	22	10	8 x 10	190	130.00	Foot	Depict
150	104F	15	22	10	7 x 9	80	60.00	Foot	Domain
150	105F	15	26	13	7 x 9	110	70.00	Foot	Dorsal

Buda Cone-Bearing Jacks

162	120	15	9¾	4	7	43	$22.00	......	Dissent
162	122	15	11	4	7	45	22.00	......	Divan

Buda Ratchet Jacks

Page	No.	Capacity Tons	Height Bar Down Inches	Rise of Bar Inches	Height Bar Raised Inches	Size of Bar Inches	Weight Lbs.	List Price	Code Word
168	1B	10	24	13½	37½	1½ x 1½	62	$18.00	Dale
170	2B	10	21	10	31	1⅝ x 1½	65	25.00	Dame
172	3B	12	26½	15	41½	1¾ x 1⅞	85	30.00	Damp
181	04B	1	11½	6	17½	¾ x 13/16	9½	5.00	Defy
174	4B	15	22	10	32	2 x 2	100	35.00	Dare
176	5B	15	28	15	43	2 x 2	115	40.00	Dash
178	6B	15	31	19	50	1⅞ x 1⅝	105	32.00	Dean
180	7B	15	35	24½	59½	2 x 2	122	42.00	Dusky
182	8B	10	11	5	16	1⅝ x 1½	48	22.00	Debit
184	12B	10	17¾	8	25¾	1½ x 1½	50	17.00	Decry
186	17B	10	24	13¾	37¾	1½ x 1½	63	18.00	Dandy
188	18B	10	21	10	31	1½ x 1⅝	68	25.00	Decoy
190	19B	15	28	17½	45½	2 x 2	102	35.00	Defer
192	20B	15	31	19	50	1⅝ x 1⅞	106	32.00	Decide
194	25B	12	24½	12½	37	1½ x 1½	105	50.00	Dove
182	48B	15	11	5	16	1¾ x 1⅞	60	25.00	Deploy
196	50B	5	16	8	24	1¼ x 1¼	38	17.00	Debar
196	51B	5	20	12	32	1¼ x 1¼	42	18.00	Deck

Buda Geared-Ratchet Jacks

166	130B	35	28	17	45	2½ x 3	225	$120.00	Deforce
166	500B	30	27	17	44	2½ x 3	237	120.00	Douse

Buda Friction Jacks

198	1J	5	29	12	41	1½ diam.	62	$20.00	Delta
198	2J	10	33	15	48	1¾ diam.	85	24.00	Dent

Buda Switch Stands

We manufacture over thirty different styles of switch stands in the following general classes:

> RAMAPO AUTOMATIC SAFETY STANDS
> SEMAPHORE STANDS
> OPEN BASE STANDS
> COLUMN STANDS
> STANDS WITH TRIPOD
> YARD STANDS
> GROUND THROW
> CONNECTING RODS

General Specifications

In the manufacture of Buda switch stands we use only first class gray and malleable iron castings. The crank shafts are forged from one piece of wrought iron without weld. All bearings are bored and the journals turned to insure good fit and reduce lost motion as much as possible.

Unless otherwise ordered, all stands have five-inch throw. The taper of mast provides for a lamp fit of dimensions shown on page 237, unless otherwise specified.

Any form of target may be specified.

We furnish with each stand, unless otherwise specified, machine forged connecting rod. This rod is made without weld. Our standard jaw fits a ¾-inch head-rod, either vertical or horizontal according to order, and is drilled for ¾-inch pin. We can, however, furnish special jaw to fit any head-rod.

Directions for Ordering

In ordering switch stands please give the following information:

(a) Throw of switch measured at the point of attachment.
(b) The size of the head rod.
(c) The size of the bolt hole.
(d) Is switch rod vertical or horizontal?
(e) Length and diameter of connecting rod.
(f) Height of top of target above tie.
(g) Form and color of targets.
(h) Dimensions of lantern tip.

If figures are desired on any special modifications, furnish sketch or blue print.

Ramapo Safety Switch Stands

The Ramapo Automatic Safety Switch Stand, which has been on the market for over twenty years, and which is now much improved over the earlier forms, was designed to secure the advantages and overcome the undesirable features of the Lorenze, or spring switch.

One of the objections to the spring switch, for use on steam roads, was that a slight obstruction prevented the switch points coming up against the stock rail. Another undesirable feature was that a train having trailed part of its length through the switch would meet with an accident if an attempt was made to back down, for the reason that the points being made to return to original position after the passage of each pair of wheels would cause one end of train to take the main track while the other was on the siding. This is avoided by the use of Ramapo Automatic Safety Switch Stands.

The Ramapo Automatic Safety Switch Stands Nos. 7, 8, 9 and 14

are so designed that the first pair of wheels trailing a switch throw the points entirely over, in which position they remain, the target definitely indicating the new position. The rod, mast and handle of these stands being positively connected there is no possibility of the target not at all times showing the exact position of the switch points. The No. 14 stand, recently brought out, has all the features of the 7, 8 and 9, but the throw is parallel instead of rotary. The parallel throw is one which is much favored by some officials because it can be operated by practically a single movement of the hand. This is particularly useful in yards, because about half the time the handle being toward the approaching operator he can throw switch without stopping and almost without diminishing his speed as he runs along.

Ramapo Automatic Return Stand

The automatic return style of Ramapo stand finds considerable use on electric interurban roads. The Nos. 11, 12 and 13 in size, appearance and general construction correspond with Nos. 7, 8 and 9. The return feature is accomplished by the substitution, in the base, of a differently designed cam, illustrated on page 7. Instead of the trailing wheels throwing switch points entirely over, they automatically return to original position. In this connection it should be noted that as the throw on spring switches is usually made as small as practicable—3 in. to 3½ in.—a slight movement of the switch points gives a decided angle to the target so that any obstruction would be unmistakably communicated to the approaching car.

General Design of Ramapo Stands

The lever handle for throwing the switch stand is attached rigidly to the spindle, and consequently to the switch points. To throw the switch the operator in lifting the lever handle raises a square block from a square hole in the top of the stand, and cannot lower the handle again until a quarter turn has been made, that is, a complete throw of the switch. If there was any obstruction in the switch preventing the points closing tight against the stock rail the operator could not make the quarter turn or lower or lock the lever handle, and consequently would look for the obstruction. When the stand is thrown and locked it is a sure indication that the switch has been completely thrown and locked.

The safety cams shown on pages 6 and 7 are held in position by a roller in an equalizing bar; the latter being held by two springs. The roller eliminates friction and the safety cam is so shaped as to give the same effective pull on the switch throughout an entire automatic movement.

The safety block is attached rigidly to the spindle by a square block fitting in the top of it below the lever handle; but when the lever handle is raised the square block is raised and the spindle is then free for operation of the stand by hand. The springs can be tightened or loosened to give greater or less-effective strain on the switch points according to their length, weight of rail section, etc. This insures the switch points always being held snugly against the stock rail, and does not increase the strain on the points when they are thrown wide open automatically by trailing car.

Each stand is furnished, unless otherwise specified, with an adjustable throw to fit any switch. The connection of the switch moving rod to the switch stand spindle is through a large eye-bolt; a half turn of the eye-bolt will affect the throw of the stand about 1-16 in., and any desired throw can be obtained. As a switch wears under service the throw slightly increases, but with these stands the throw can always be readily adjusted.

The foregoing description of general design refers to stands 7, 8 and 9, and 11, 12 and 13. The No. 14 stand has the same action as the 7, 8 and 9 and all the mechanical advantages, but working parts are differently arranged to permit the vertical instead of horizontal throw of lever.

In the newer forms, all the best ideas in the older styles 1, 2, 3, 4 and 5 have been preserved, including the positive throw and adjustable crank. The former types were always satisfactory, but these later styles are intended for use in connection with the heavier rail construction now in use and represent a mechanical advancement in design.

Directions for Ordering

In ordering switch stands please give the following information:
- (a) Throw of switch measured at the point of attachment.
- (b) The size of the head rod.
- (c) The size of the bolt hole.
- (d) Is switch rod vertical or horizontal?
- (e) Length and diameter of connecting rod.
- (f) Height of top of target above tie.
- (g) Form and color of targets.
- (h) Dimensions of lantern tip.

If figures are desired on any special modifications, furnish sketch or blue print.

Other Switch Stands

We manufacture also over thirty styles and sizes of other switch stands, including open base and column stands, yard and ground throw stands and semaphore stands operating with revolving lamp or with stationary lamp and spectacles. Our manufacturing facilities are such that we are able to take care of large orders and make prompt deliveries. We are also prepared to follow any specifications and comply with every detail.

Ramapo Automatic Safety Switch Stands

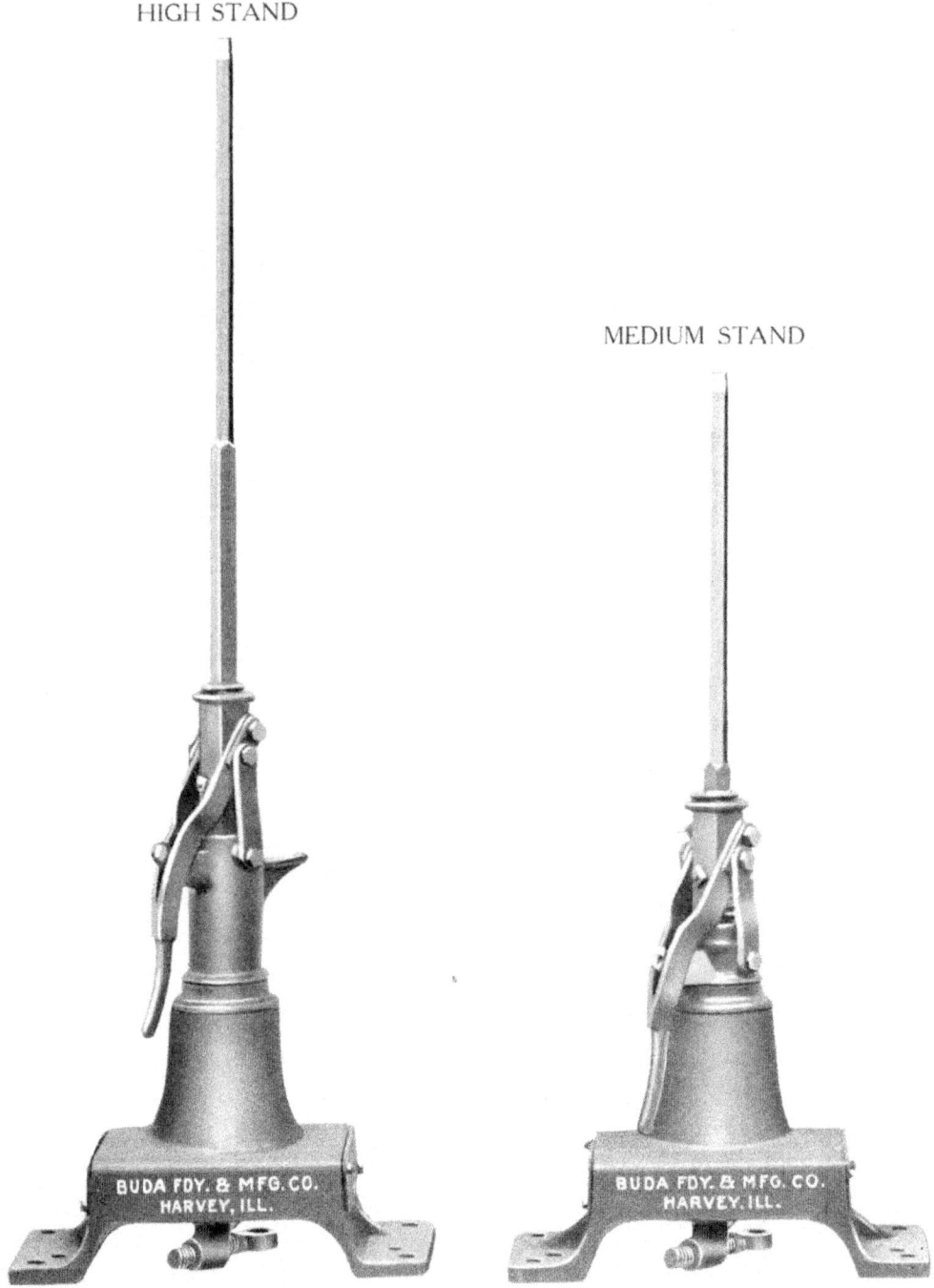

HIGH STAND

MEDIUM STAND

Automatic Safety, No. 7
Automatic Return, No. 11

Automatic Safety, No. 8
Automatic Return, No. 12

These stands may be supplied with any style target

Ramapo Automatic Safety Switch Stands

LOW STAND

LOW STAND
Parallel Throw

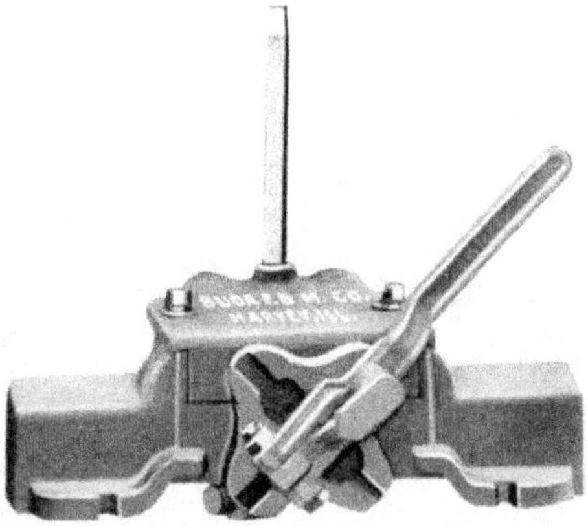

Automatic Safety, No. 9
Automatic Return, No. 13

Automatic Safety, No. 14

These stands may be supplied with any style target

No. 14. The No. 14 stand recently designed is intended to fulfill the demand for stand with parallel throw. Some prefer the parallel throw because it is more quickly operated by hand.

In yards considerable time may be saved in switching for the lever is part of the time at least in the direction of the approaching switchman enabling him to throw switch without stopping. The stand is condensed in form making it especially favorable for use in some locations. Another desirable feature of the parallel throw is that operator does not have to swing in toward cars thus avoiding chance of being struck. While differently arranged, the mechanical features are the same as the Nos. 7, 8 and 9.

The Buda Foundry & Manufacturing Company

Ramapo Automatic Safety Switch Stand

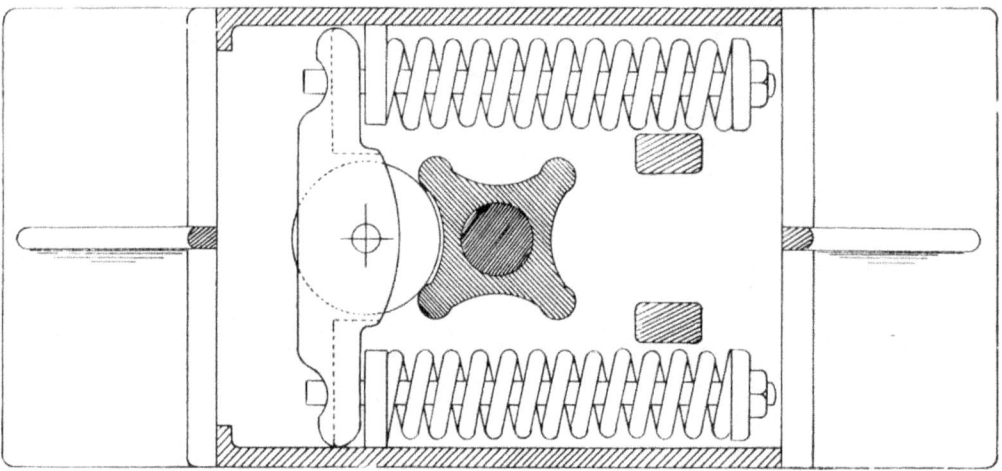

Plan View of Base
Nos. 7, 8 and 9

The improvement in the newer Ramapo Automatic Safety Switch Stands wiil be noted, by those familiar with the older types. The former styles gave excellent satisfaction but heavier rail construction was the cause of bringing out the present improved style. A train trailing through switch causes the star shaped cam to turn against the revolving roll held in the equalizer and the springs complete the throw. This action at the same time turning the mast causes the target to show the new position of the switch.

The action is positive and may be thoroughly depended upon.

Ramapo Automatic Return Stand

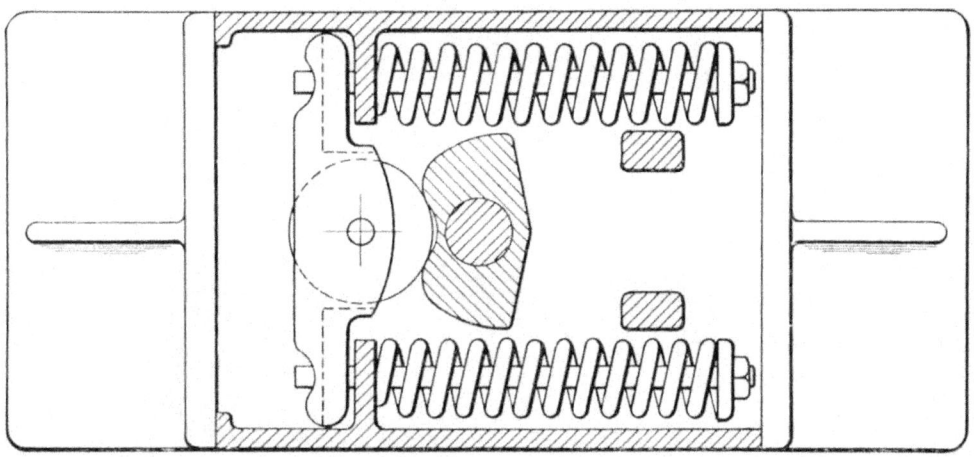

Plan View of
Nos. 11, 12 and 13

This class of stand has a different automatic action than that of the 7, 8, 9 and 14.

Instead of switch points being entirely thrown over by trailing wheels, they return to original position after the passage of each truck and the rod, mast, handle and target all being positively connected, the exact position of switch points is always shown.

Many electric interurban railways are adopting this stand in connection with right-hand or left-hand systems, for they work without any attention. They also may be used as a regular switch stand to be thrown by hand if desired.

Ramapo Automatic Safety Switch Stands

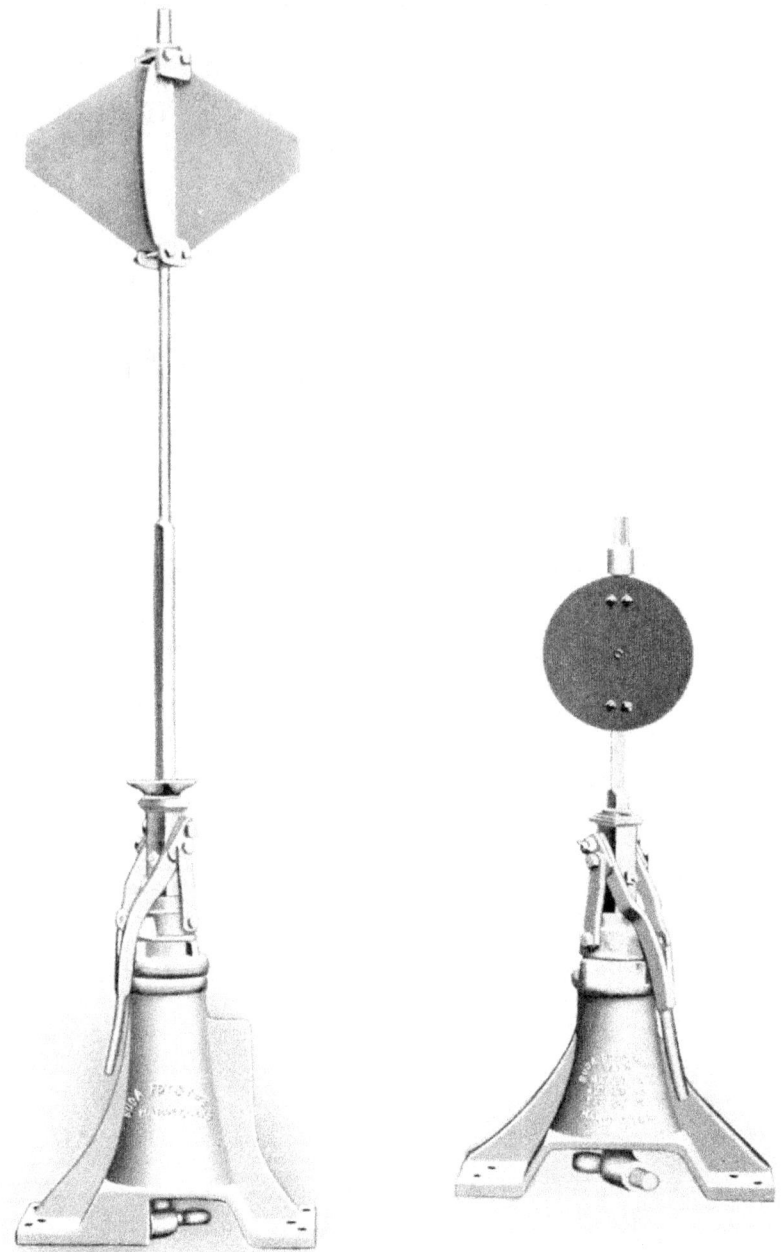

Ramapo No. 1   Ramapo No. 2

All Ramapo stands equipped with adjustable crank, unless rigid crank is specified.

We manufacture the stand in seven different styles, adapted to varying conditions of service and individual requirements, and supply any target desired.

Ramapo Automatic Safety Switch Stand

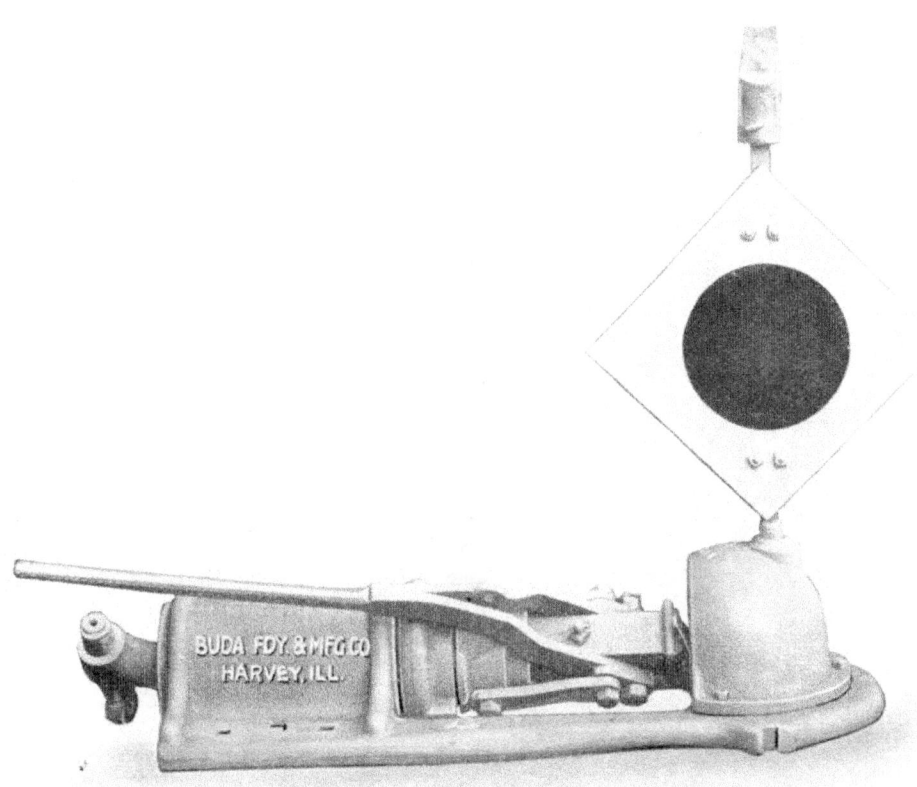

Ramapo No. 4

Patterns for Yards. Can be equipped with adjustable crank, as shown, or rigid, if so ordered.

Any target desired.

Ramapo Automatic Safety Switch Stand

Ramapo No. 5

Pattern for Yards. This stand shown with rigid crank. Can be equipped with adjustable crank, if desired

Any target furnished to comply with standard of road purchasing.

Ramapo Automatic Safety Switch Stands

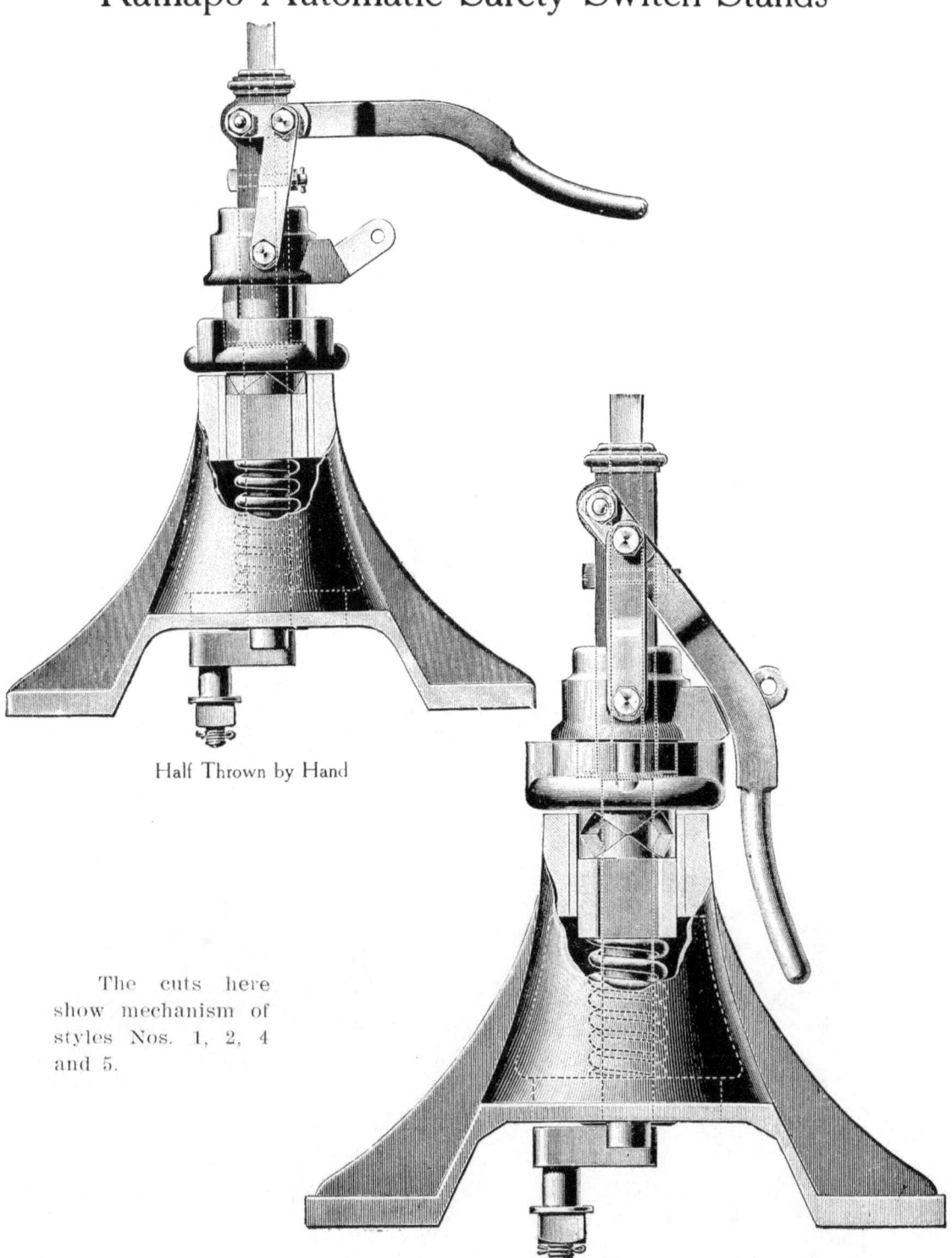

Half Thrown by Hand

The cuts here show mechanism of styles Nos. 1, 2, 4 and 5.

Half Thrown by Wheels Trailing Through Switch

Semaphore Stand

Main Line Stand with Signal Blade and Revolving Lamp

In this stand the ordinary color and shape target has been replaced by a position signal in the form of a semaphore blade, in conjunction with revolving lamp.

By day the semaphore is seen farther than the target and its indications are positive and unmistakable, and it is a step toward unification of signal standards.

This signal can be applied to any stand having revolving mast. Can also be had with stationary lamp and spectacles if desired.

The Buda Foundry & Manufacturing Company

This Stand is Illustrated also on Preceding Page. Semaphore Stands are Unmistakable and may be Seen at a Long Distance

Semaphore Stand

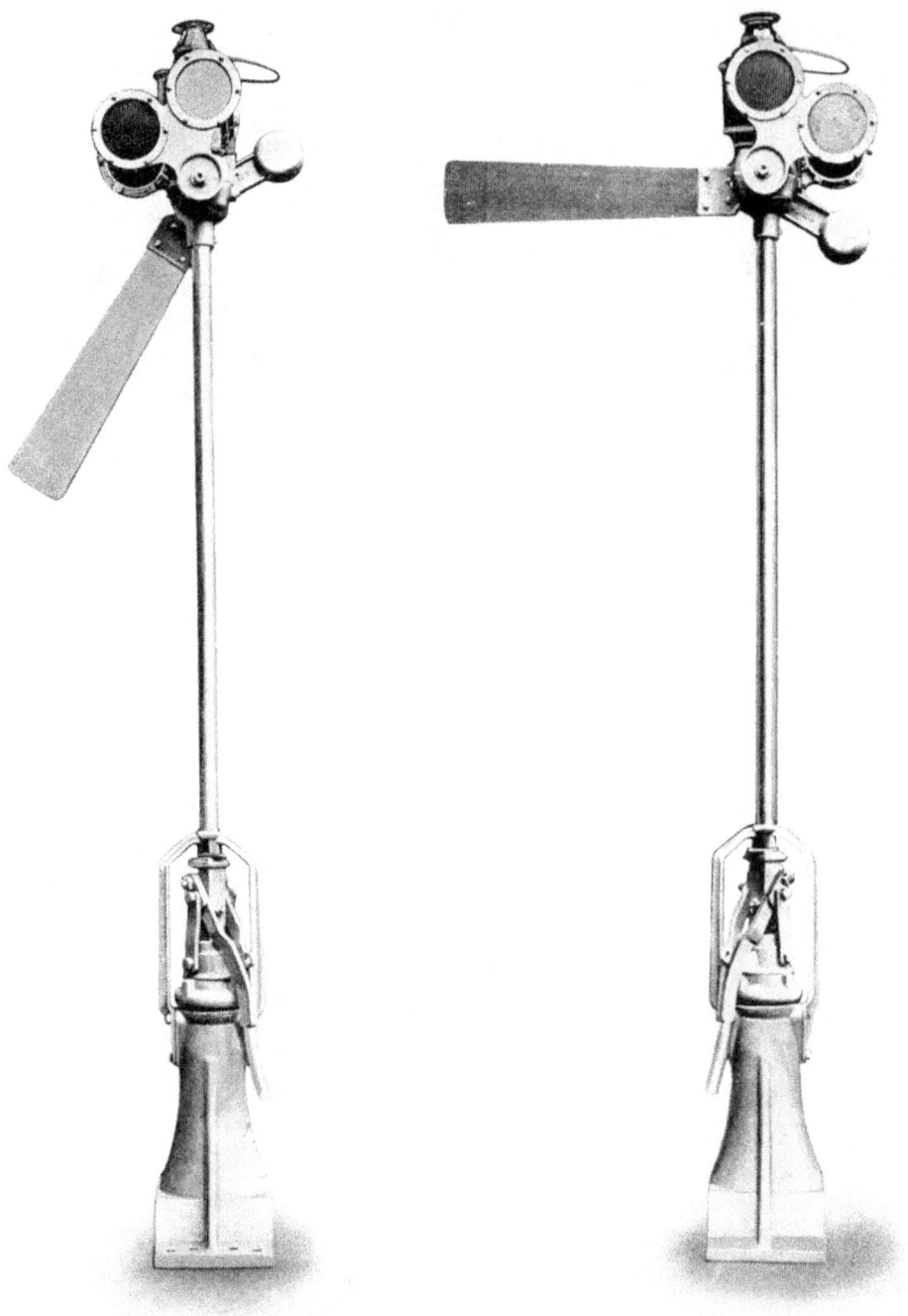

No. 1. Ramapo Stand

With semaphore attachment. Stationary lamp with spectacles.

Semaphore Stand

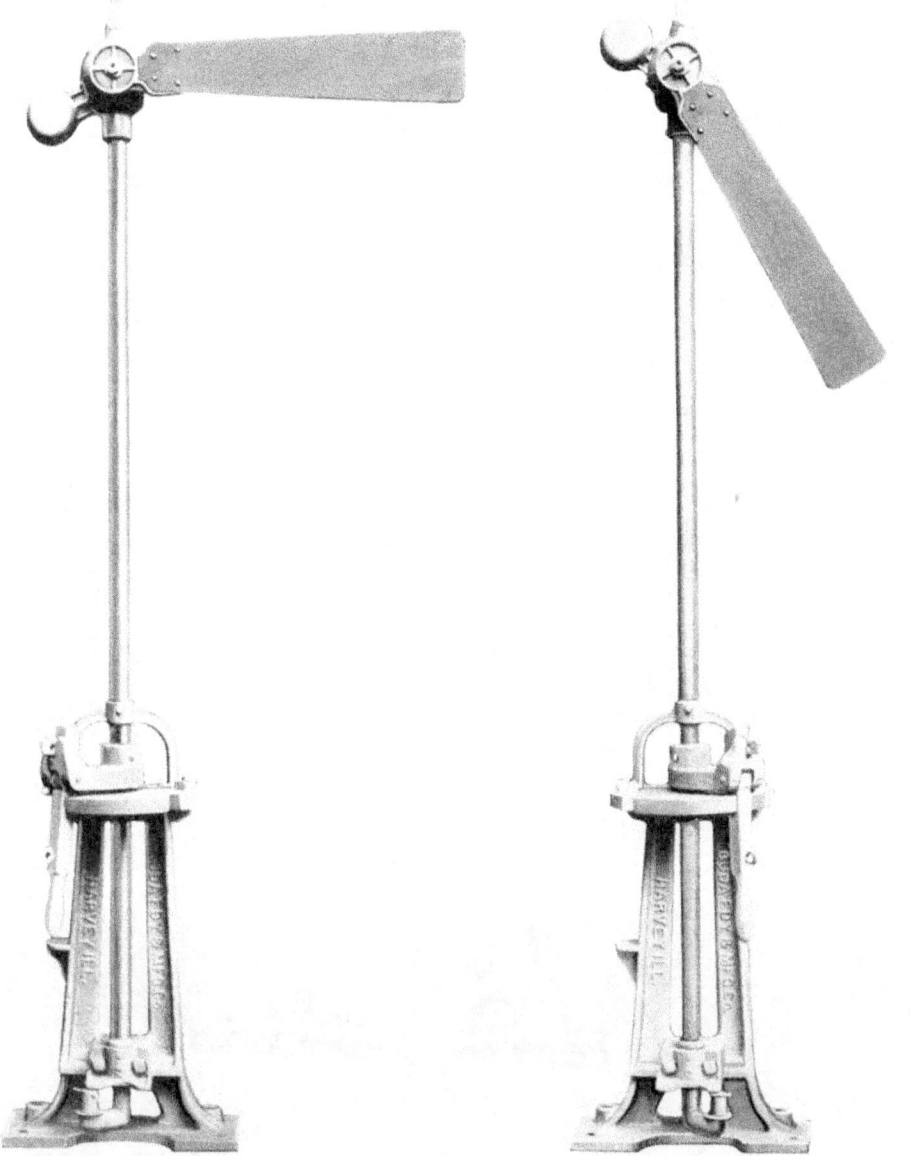

No. 10 A. Stand

Equipped with semaphore blade and revolving lamp. Can be furnished with stationary lamp and spectacles, if preferred. One tie.

Shows adaptation of semaphore device to ordinary standard type of stand.

High Signal With Tripod

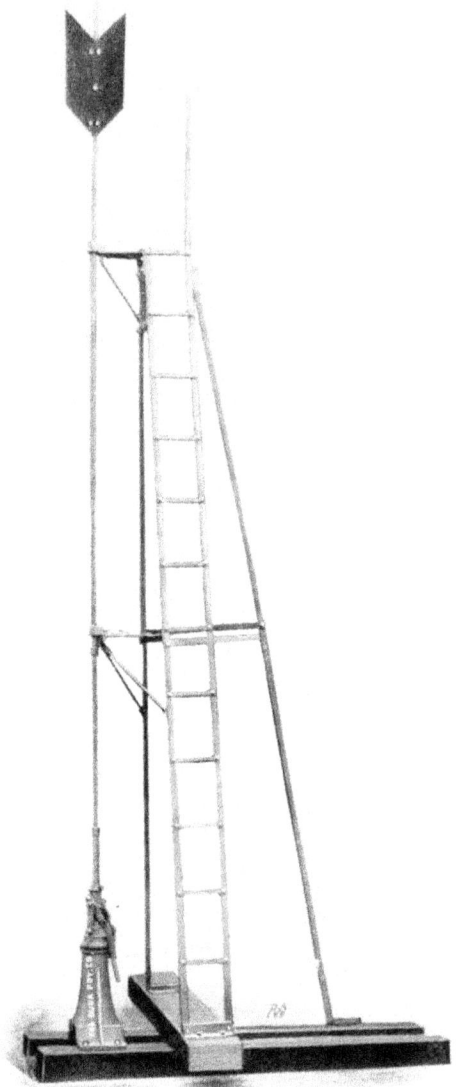

Style B

With Ramapo automatic safety switch stand, and target. Distance from rail to lamp, 18 to 20 feet.

Can be supplied with semaphore blade and revolving lamp; or, with semaphore and spectacles and stationary lamp.

Adaptable to any style of switch stand.

High Signal With Tripod

Style C

With rigid stand. Distance from rail to lamp, 18 to 20 feet.

Instead of target, can be suppled with semaphore and revolving lamp; or, semaphore and spectacles and stationary lamp.

Adaptable to any style of switch stand.

Open Base Stands

HIGH AND LOW

No. 11. Low Stand   No. 10. High Stand

Buda standard. Yard pattern.   Buda standard. Main line.
Three positions of lever. One tie.
Any target.

Open Base Stands

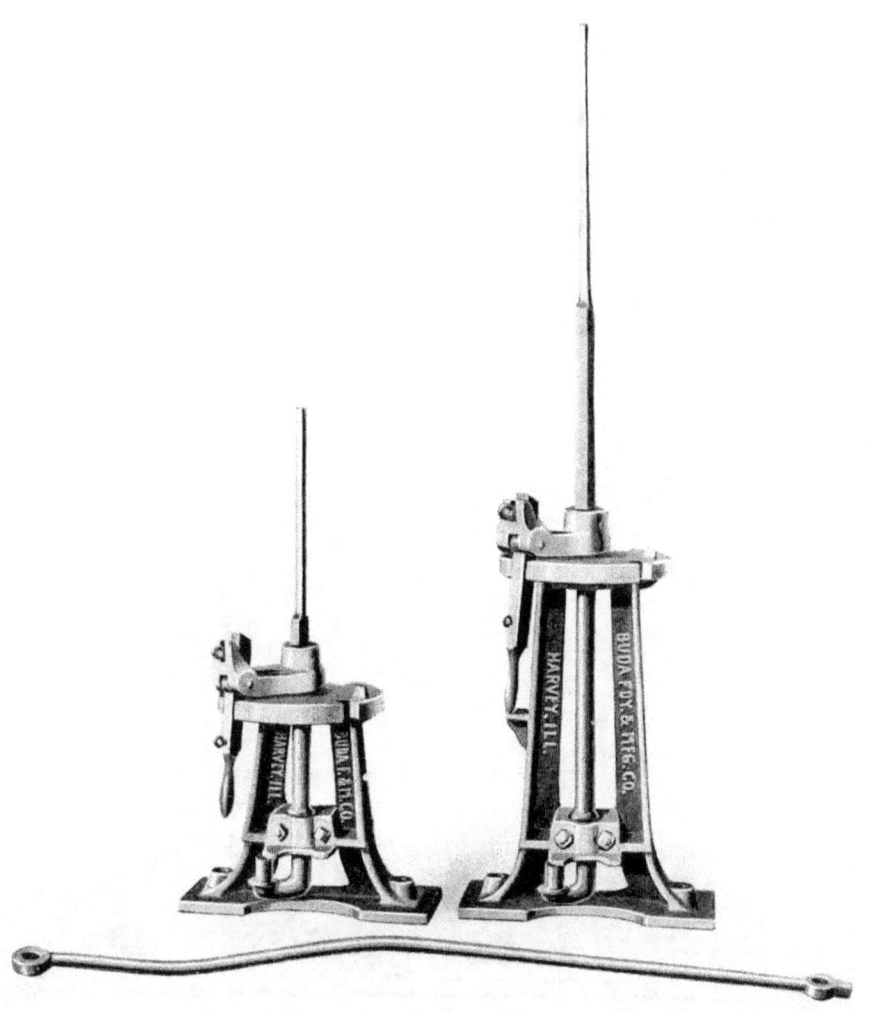

No. 11 A. Low Stand   No. 10 A. High Stand
Yard pattern.   Main line pattern.

Same as Nos. 10 and 11, except single throw, but has two positions of lever. One tie. Supplied with any target desired.

Open Base Stands

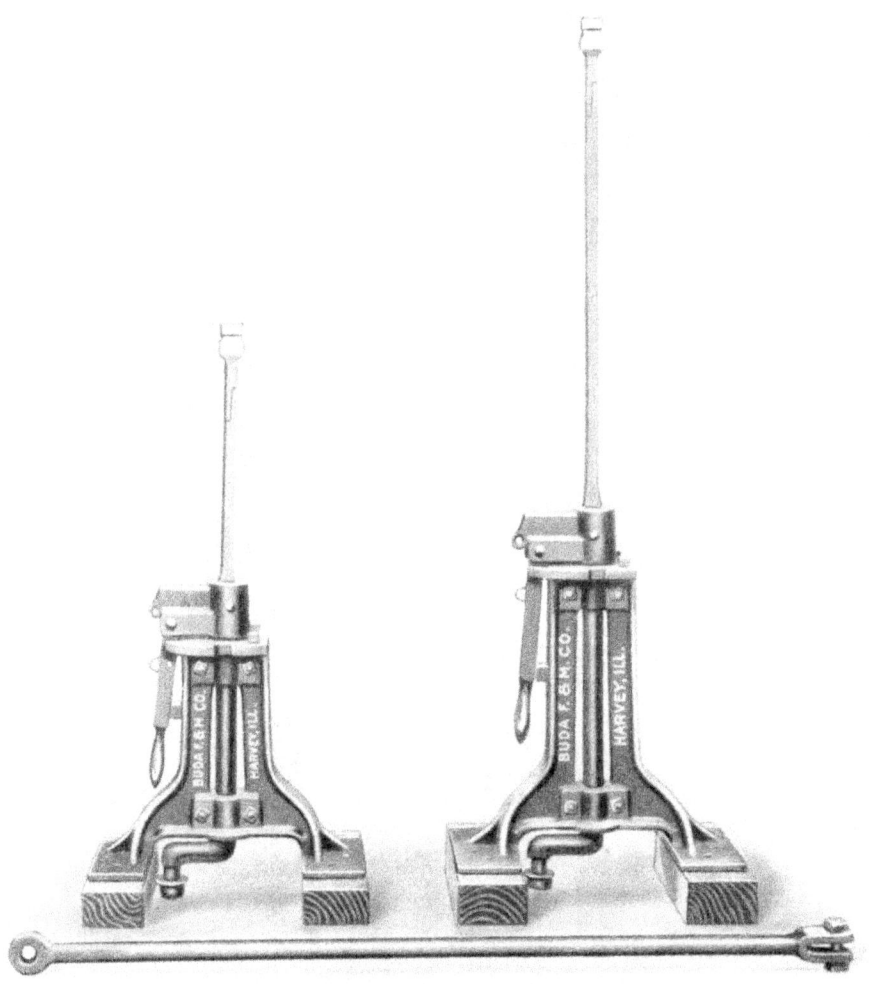

No. 22 A. Low Stand   No. 22. High Stand

Yard pattern. Two ties.   Main line pattern. Two ties.
Any target desired.

Open Base Stands

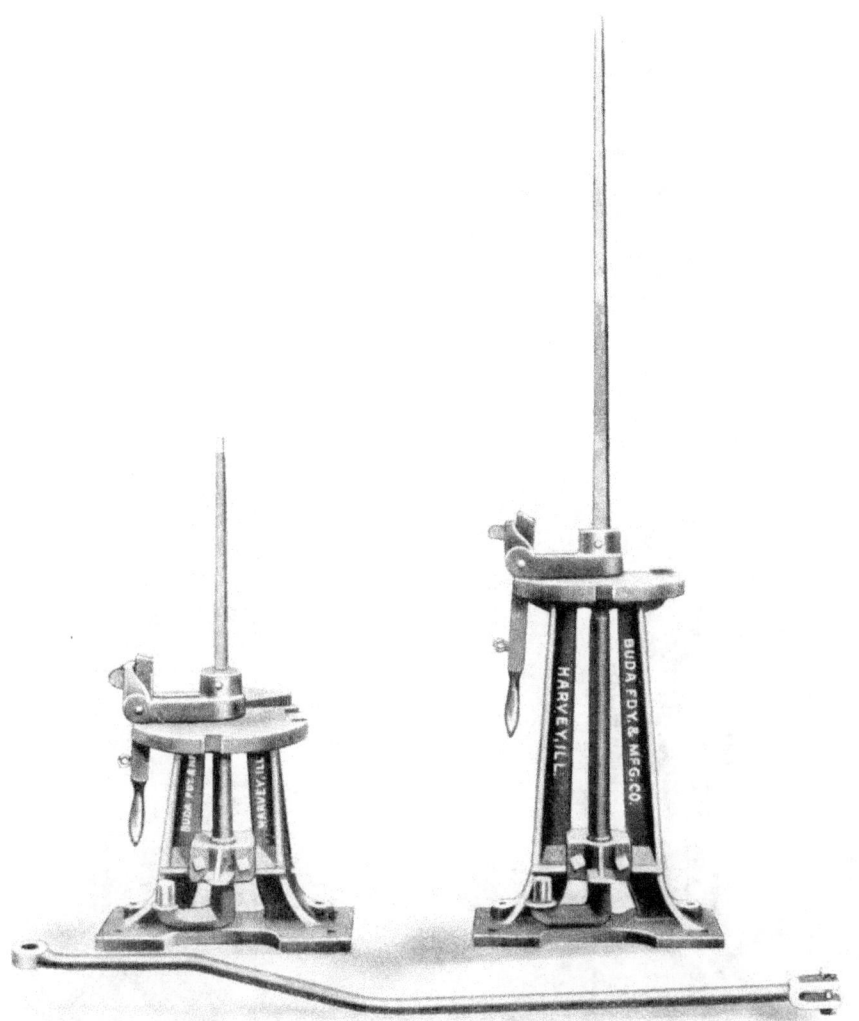

No. 15½. Low Stand   No. 15. High Stand

Yard pattern. One tie.   Main line pattern. One tie.
Any target.

Open Base Stands

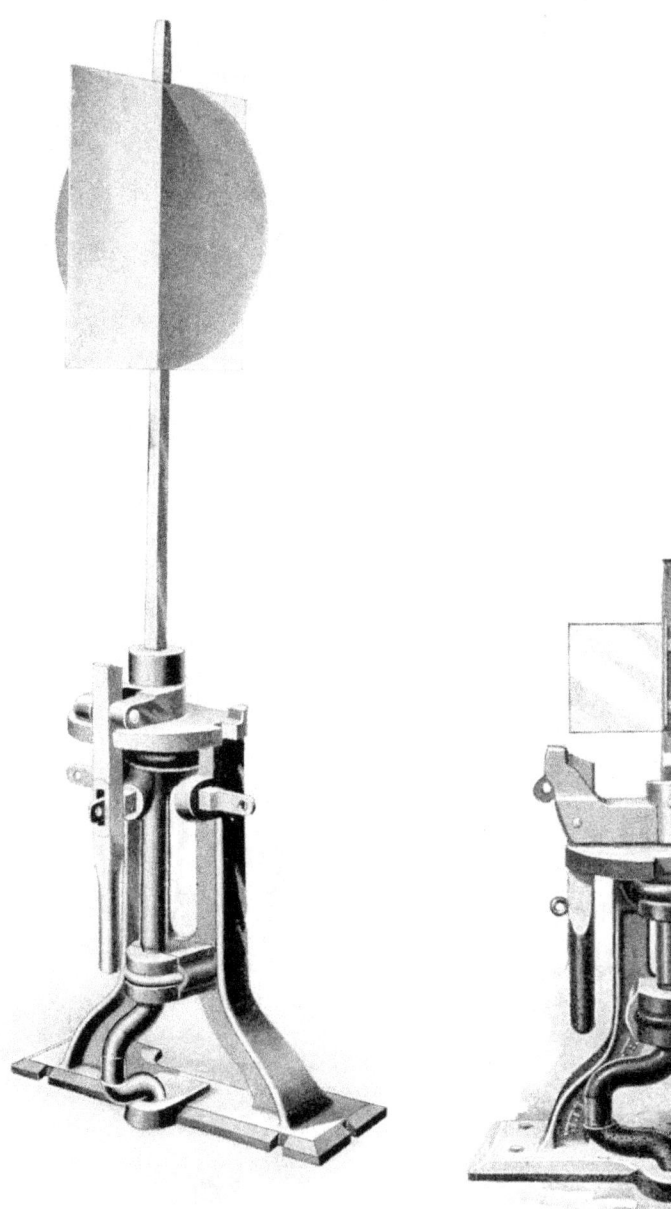
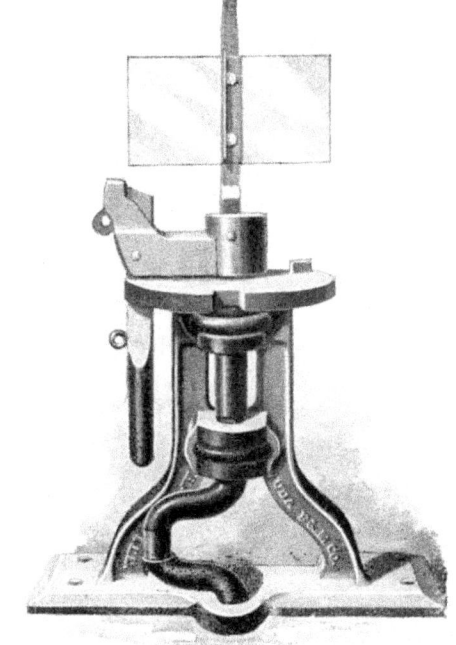

No. 17. High Stand   No. 17A. Low Stand

Main line pattern. One tie.   Yard pattern. One tie.
Any target desired.

Open Base Stands

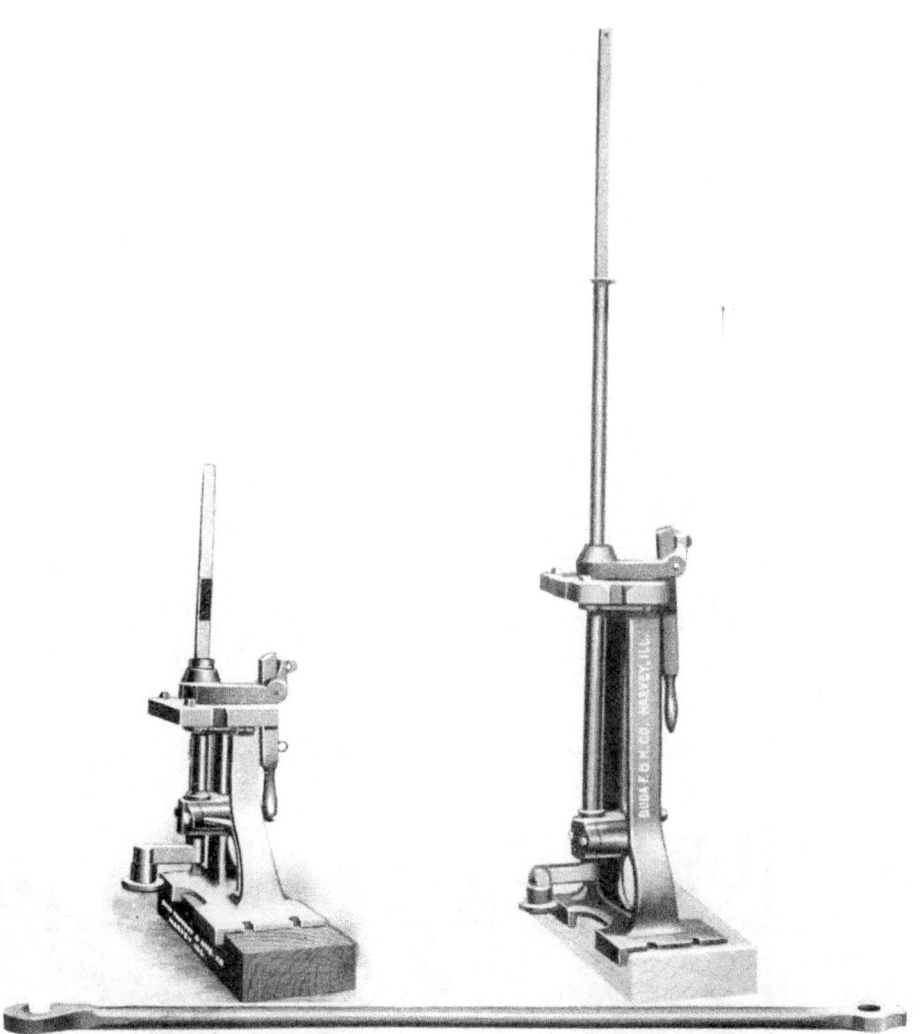

No. 21. Robinson Patent
Low Stand

No. 20. Robinson Patent
High Stand

Yard pattern. One tie.   Main line pattern. One tie.
Any target desired.

Open Base Stands

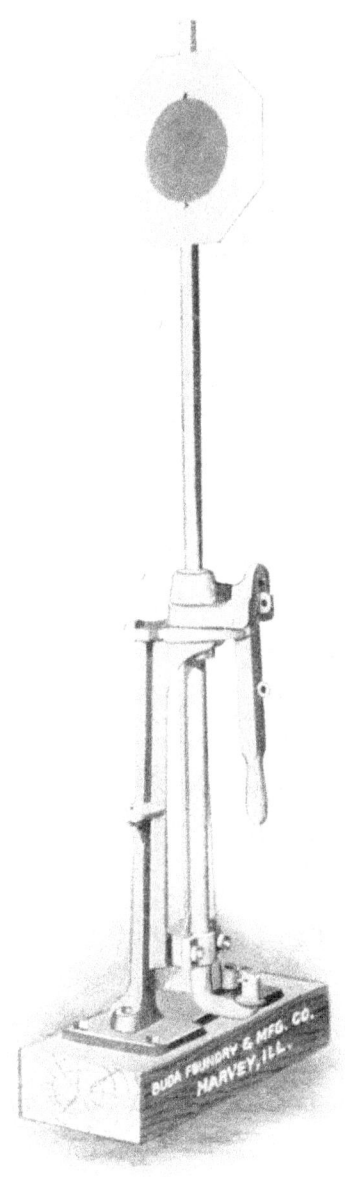
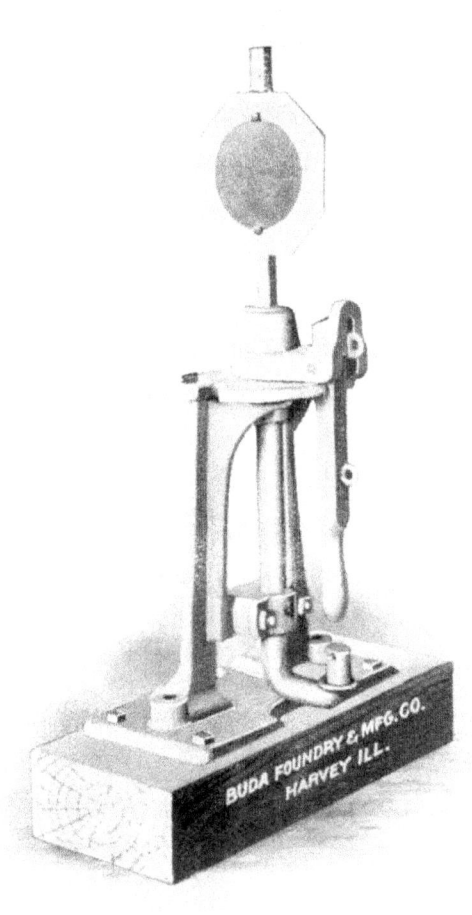

No. P 1. High Stand
Main line pattern.

No. P 2. Low Stand
Yard pattern.

One tie. Any target.

Column Stands

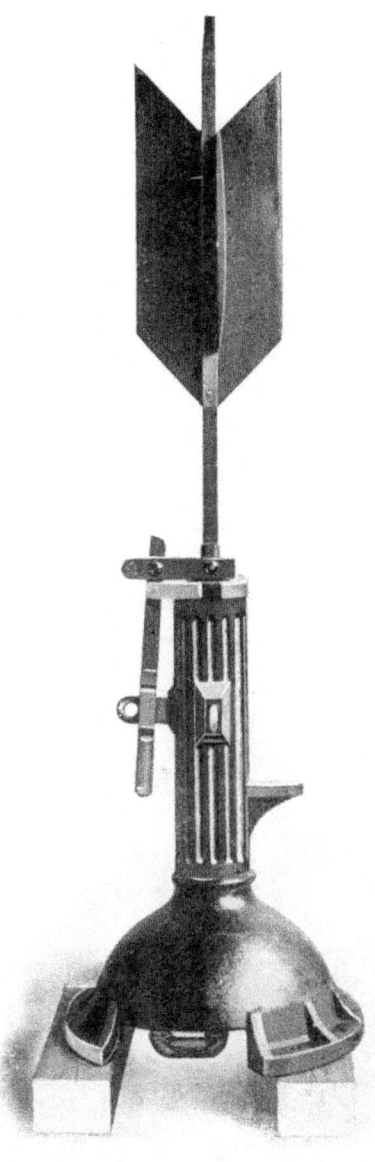

No. 16. High Stand   No. 16 A. Low Stand

Extra heavy, main line pattern.   Extra heavy, yard pattern.
Two ties. Any target.

Column Stand

No. 28. High Stand

Main line column stand. Two ties. Any target.

No. 29. Pony stand. Same as No. 28 illustrated, but is a lower stand, for yard use.

Malleable Iron Stands

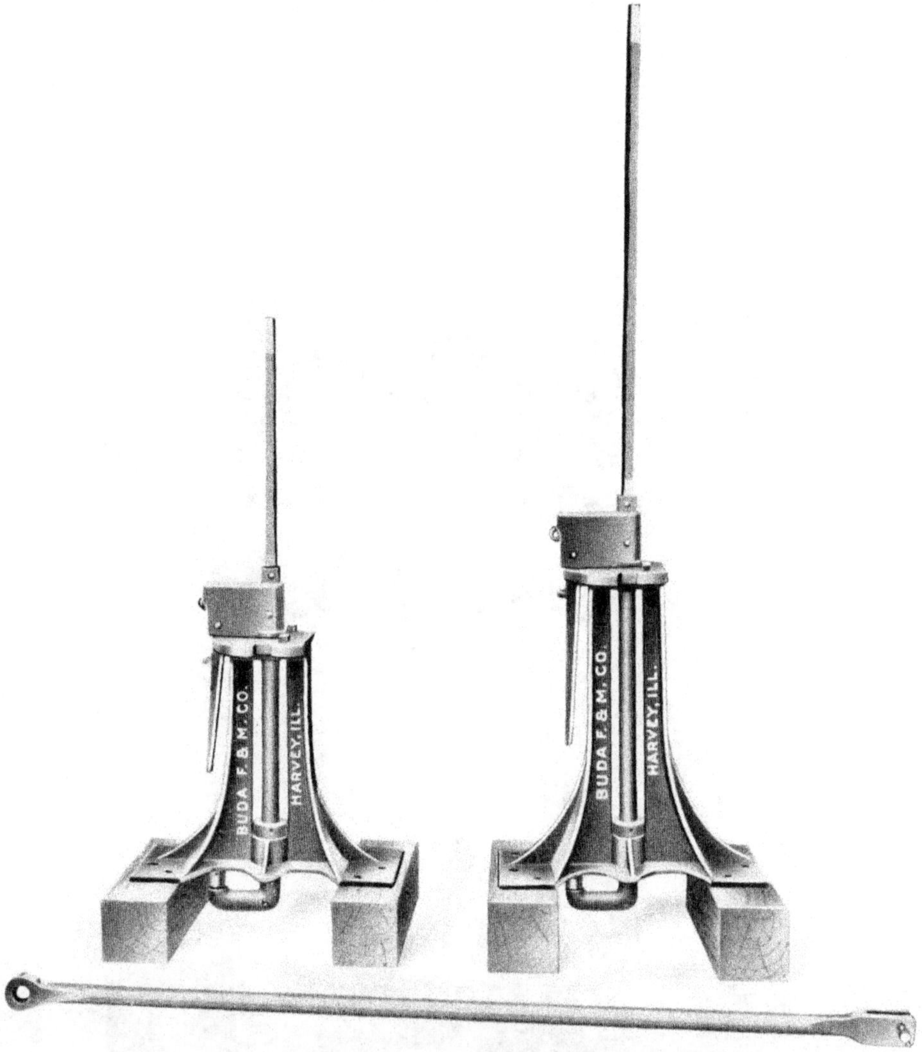

No. 31   No. 30

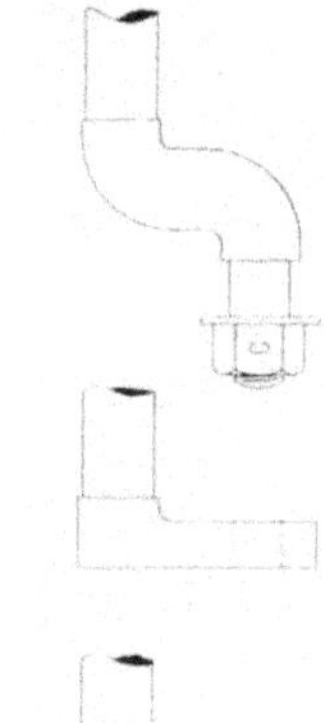

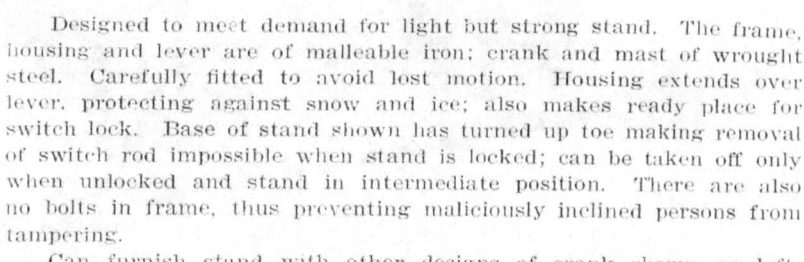

Designed to meet demand for light but strong stand. The frame, housing and lever are of malleable iron; crank and mast of wrought steel. Carefully fitted to avoid lost motion. Housing extends over lever, protecting against snow and ice; also makes ready place for switch lock. Base of stand shown has turned up toe making removal of switch rod impossible when stand is locked; can be taken off only when unlocked and stand in intermediate position. There are also no bolts in frame, thus preventing maliciously inclined persons from tampering.

Can furnish stand with other designs of crank shown on left. With turned up or turned down toe switch rod illustrated is used. If stand is desired with horizontal rigid crank, or with adjustable crank shown, connecting rod will have jaw at each end. By extending crank below base we are able to use straight rod, which is considered quite an advantage.

Stands furnished in two way or three way. Any target.

Yard Stands

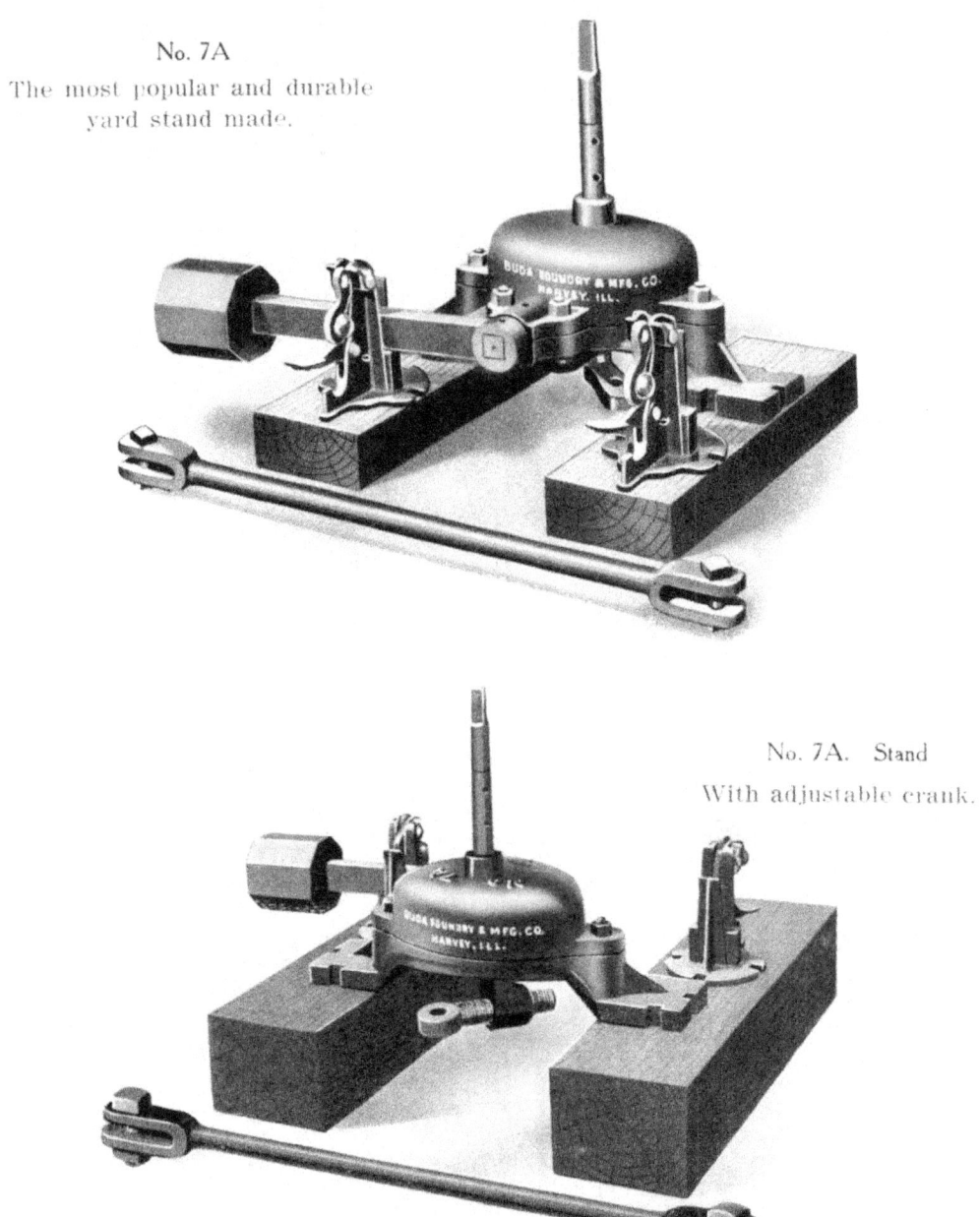

No. 7A

The most popular and durable yard stand made.

No. 7A. Stand

With adjustable crank.

Especially designed with lever throw parallel with the rail for rapid operation and safety to operate. Can be used as an automatic stand, if desired. Is used also as main line stand, and is then equipped with two locking latches. Any target.

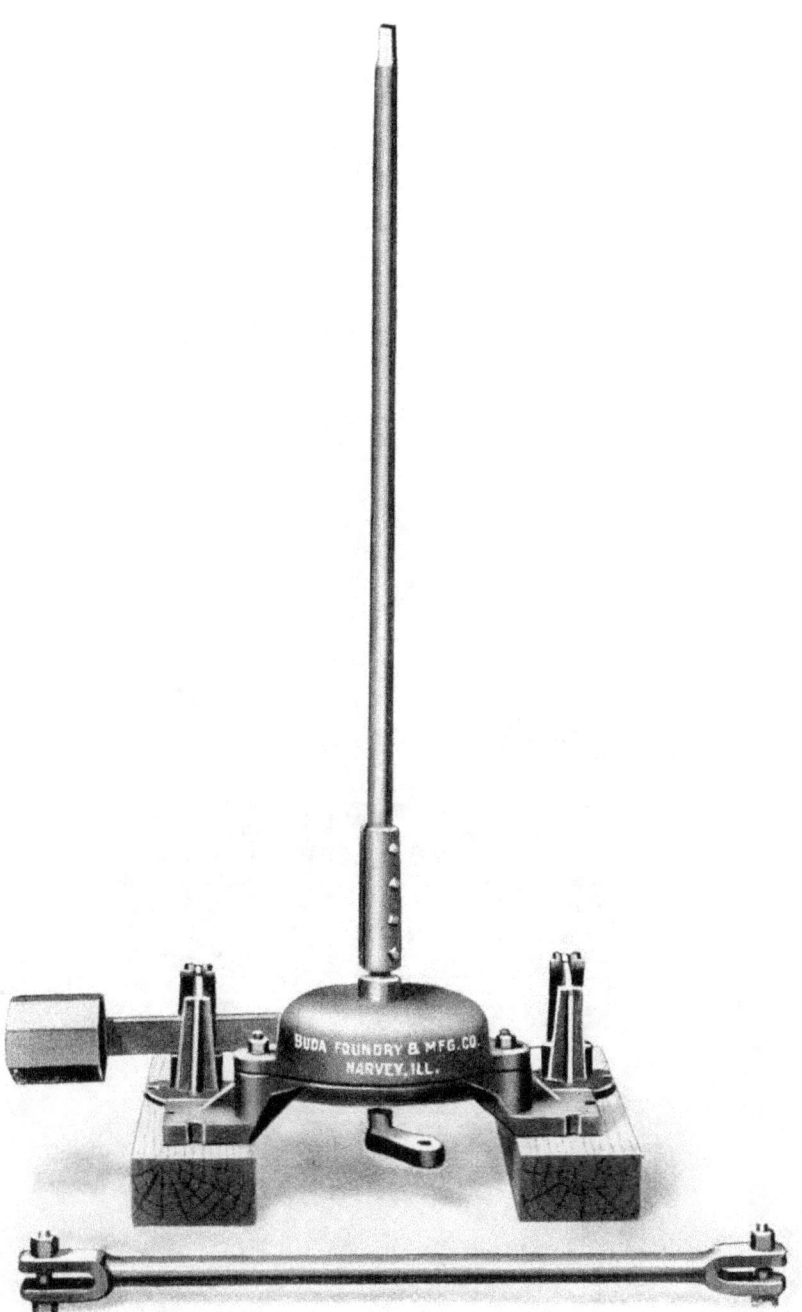

No. 7 A. High Mast

With target showing construction when employed as a main line stand. Any target.

Yard Stand

No. 7B. Yard Stand

Two ties. Target as desired.

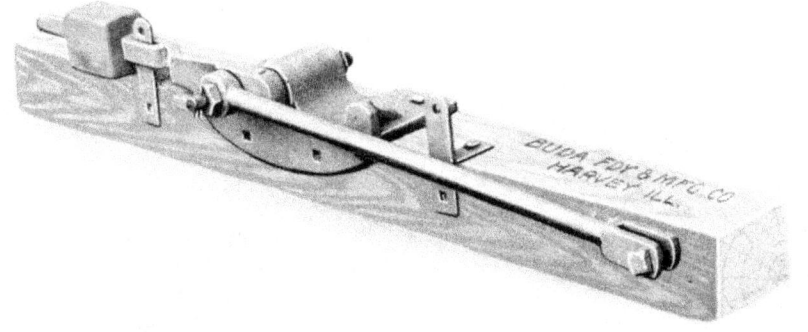

Ground Throw Stand. No. 1
With Weight and Locking Attachments.

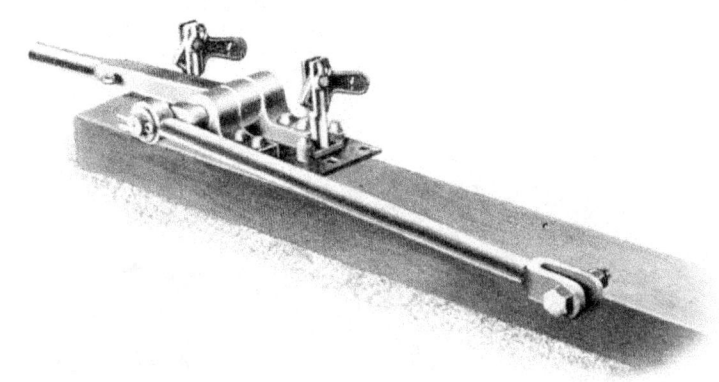

Ground Throw Stand. No. 2
Wrought Iron, with Locking Attachments.

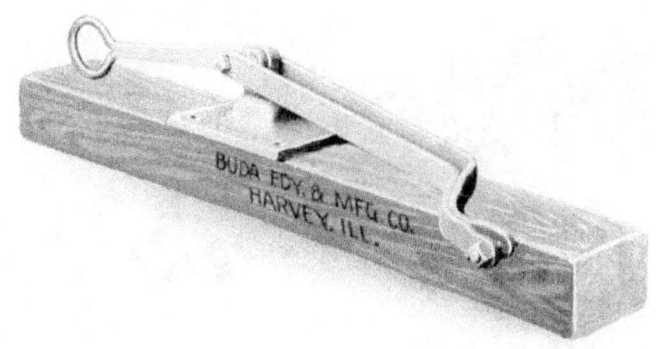

Ground Throw Stand. No. 3
Jack Knife. Two Way.

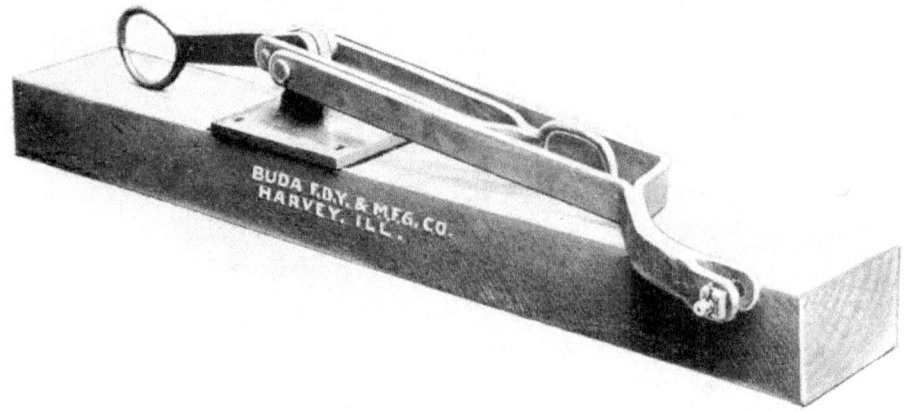

Ground Throw Stand. No. 3
Jack Knife. Three Way.

Ground Throw Stand. No. P 4

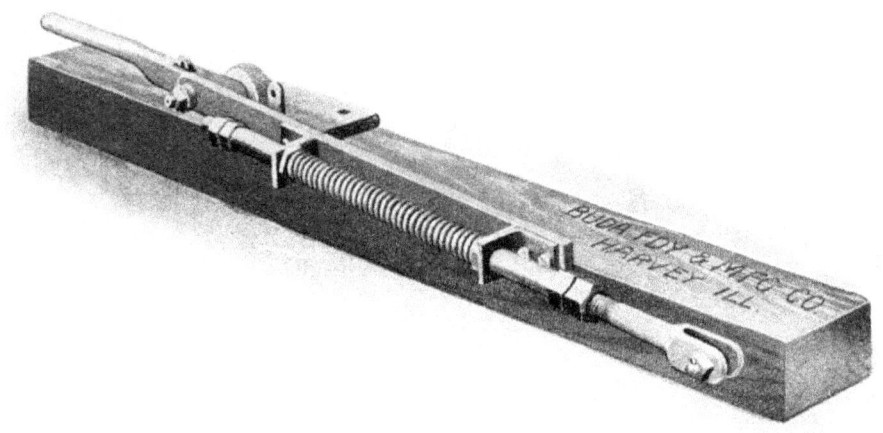

Ground Throw Stand. No. P 5
With Spring Connecting Rod.

The Buda Foundry & Manufacturing Company

Ground Throw Stand. No. P 9
Two Way.

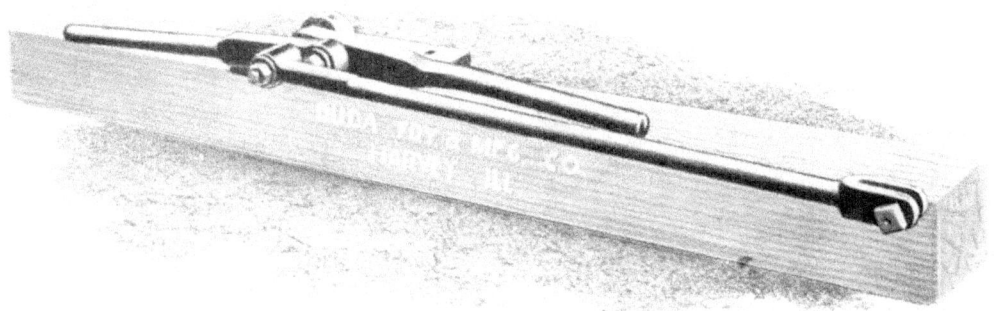

Ground Throw Stand. No. P 10
Three Way.

Ground Throw Signal Stand

Ground Throw Stands With Targets

No. 4½. Stand

Designed to supply need for light ground throw with target, as shown or as specified.

No. 5. Stand

Lever throws at right angle to track. Target as desired.

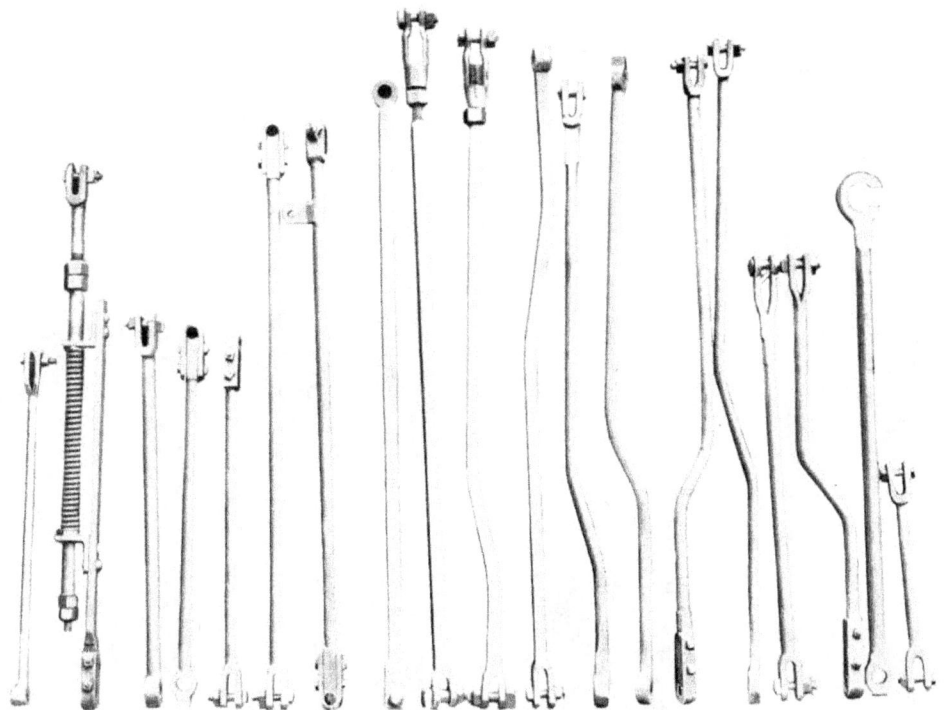

Connecting Rods

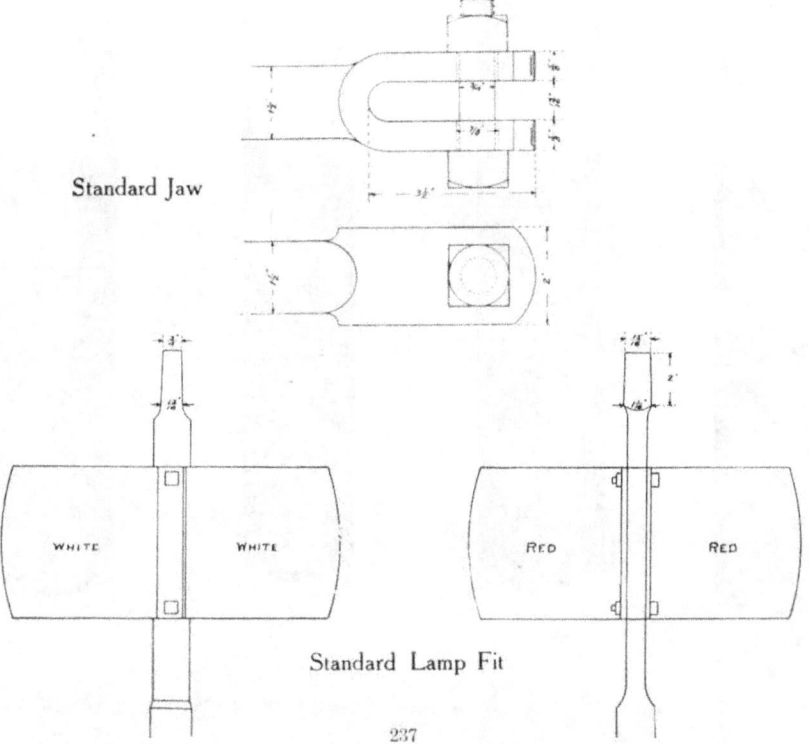

Standard Jaw

Standard Lamp Fit

Battery Chutes

No. 1　　　No. 2　　　No. 3　　　No. 4

Made of cast iron. For signal service batteries.

Safety Crossing Gates

DIAPHRAGM AND CYLINDER PNEUMATIC STYLES
MECHANICAL GATES

Regarding them a step toward economy, many railroads are voluntarily installing crossing gates, thus avoiding accident risks and forestalling civic demands which, if left to work out their own requirements are found to be frequently of unnecessary severeness and embodying perpetual expense much greater than would have been arranged for by railroad, and accepted as satisfactory by the town or city.

We make gates suitable for all locations which, aside from the familiar street gates, include swinging gates, for station entrances; folding fence gates for draw bridges, where pedestrian travel is heavy; folding arm gates, for clearing trolley wires; and we can arrange adaptations for use where the conditions are unusual.

Our pneumatically operated gates may be had in the diaphragm or of the cylinder and piston types.

The mechanically operated gates are of the lever and of the crank types.

Bogue & Mills System of Pneumatic Gates

We have for many years manufactured this style of pneumatic gates. They are operated by means of compressed air, supplied by a pump, which operates a diaphragm. The gates are locked when in an upright and in a horizontal position and can be released only by the operator. They are made with underground connections; also with overhead tie. This latter is preferred by some as it does not necessitate tearing up street to install or repair. Where trolley wires interfere, the underground connection can be used; one working equally as well as the other. No trouble from climatic conditions is experienced and they are so constructed as to be under control of the operator at all times.

Where a high-pressure air system is available, we can furnish pressure-reducing valves for enabling the operation of the gates and thus doing away with the usual hand air pump. Where right and left hand gates are required to be operated individually we arrange this by making special connections.

Buda Improved Pneumatic Cylinder Gates

The chief objection to cylinder gates heretofore on the market has been the complicated number of working parts, which cause endless trouble and annoyance by the numerous repairs necessary. In the Buda Improved Pneumatic Cylinder Gates we have obviated all such objectionable features and provided a simply constructed post which has the advantage of few parts and, at the same time, enables perfect control of gate arms by operator. This style of gate is illustrated on pages 266 and 267. Instead of the compressed air being forced against diaphragms it is let into cylinders where it works against a piston rod that operates the arms. The method of applying the air to the cylinders is simultaneous, which differs somewhat from the arrangement used in diaphragm gates where the air is applied first to one side of the street to lower the gates, and to the other side to raise them; the diaphragm to which air is applied reacting upon that in the opposite post.

The arrangements for supplying air are identical with those of the diaphragm styles, that is, hand air pump, or by means of high pressure air system reduced by special valves.

Mechanical Gates

The designs we manufacture for mechanical operation are of the patterns known as lever and of crank gates. While this class is more limited in their possibilities they are still in demand for certain locations where they serve all purposes. We furnish them in two and four post patterns, illustrated later on, and which are equipped with either underground or overhead connections.

Repair Parts

Following the illustrated descriptions of the numerous styles of gates will be found a complete list of repair parts illustrated, numbered and described, together with accompanying prices.

We call attention to the fact that we have recently adopted a new system of pattern numbers which have the advantage of sequence, the idea being to promote ready reference and avoid confusion. In the future, our gate parts will carry the new numbers. For the purpose of identifying the parts of gates now in use, we continue to show in the description a list of old numbers corresponding with those now adopted. In calling for new parts, give figures or numbers shown on parts in your possession.

When Asking for Quotations

In ordering gates or requesting prices, it is essential that blue prints or engineers' drawings should be sent us. These should show the crossings, distance across road-bed from curb to curb; width of sidewalks; distance from gate post to gate post across tracks; and location of tower or house.

Concrete Foundations

Railroads are now adopting concrete foundations for all permanent structures. This has been applied successfully to foundations for gate posts as well as for towers. Concrete foundations can be built in place with little additional expense and the permanency of the structure adds greatly to the proper working of the gates, holding them firmly in line. This style of post foundation is illustrated on gates No. 13 and 14.

The use of concrete may also be carried out in the laying of the piping. It provides a permanent and even foundation for the pipe, prevents it from coming into contact with moisture and from rusting and has other apparent advantages. It is considered well worth anything additional it may cost.

Single Steel-Post Towers

The advantage of steel construction is thoroughly recognized where permanency is desired. The cost is more than for wood but the economy is such as to fully justify any expenditures of this nature. Our single steel post tower is illustrated on page 268, where is also shown the adaptation of concrete as a foundation.

Wooden-Post Towers

Our standard wooden post tower is shown on page 269. As illustrated it is meant for dirt foundation. Where intended for erection in concrete it is not necessary to furnish the footing or base. In ordering towers with wooden posts please state whether they are to be erected in concrete or dirt.

When Desired We Erect Gates for Purchaser

While our gates are simple in construction and require only ordinary mechanical skill to erect them, when desired we are prepared to erect them at a nominal cost; or, we can send a competent mechanic to superintend the work and instruct operators; the expense to the purchaser being a per diem charge.

No. 1. Two-Post Pneumatic Gate

See Pages 246 and 247

No. 1. Having no underground connections except air pipes from tower.

Two cast iron posts.
Two bifurcated wooden main arms.
Two bifurcated sidewalk arms.
Two shafts and locking connections.
Two pairs steel bowls with rubber diaphragms.
One air pump and valves.
Half-inch iron pipe sufficient for runs from tower to posts.
One bell for tower.
Automatic bells on arms, extra.

No. 2. Four-Post Pneumatic Gate

See Pages 248 and 249

No. 2. Having air pipes from tower to post and underground chain and rod connections between posts across the street.

Four cast iron posts.
Four bifurcated wooden main arms.
Four bifurcated wooden sidewalk arms.
Four shafts and automatic locking connections.
Four pairs steel bowls with rubber diaphragms.
One air pump and valves.
Half-inch iron pipe sufficient for runs from tower to posts.
One bell for tower.
Automatic bells on arms, extra.

No. 3. Four-Post Lever Gate

See Pages 250 and 251

No. 3. Having double chain and rod connections underground between posts and from posts to tower.

Four cast iron posts.
Four bifurcated wooden main arms.
Four bifurcated wooden sidewalk arms.
One lever stand with two levers.
One bell for tower.
Automatic bells on arms, extra.

No. 4. Overhead Tie Four-Post Lever Gate

See Pages 252 and 253

No. 4. Having double chain and rod connections underground between tower and adjacent post, and overhead tie between posts across the street.

Four cast iron posts.
Four wooden main arms.
Four wooden sidewalk arms.
Four wooden posts for supporting overhead tie connections.
Four cast iron cross arms.
Four pairs cast iron headers.
One bell for tower.
Automatic bells on arms, extra.

No. 5. Four-Post Pneumatic Gate with Overhead Tie

See Pages 254 and 255

No. 5. Having no underground connections except air pipes from tower to posts.

Four cast iron posts.
Four wooden main arms.
Four wooden sidewalk arms.
Four shafts and automatic locking connections.
Two pairs steel bowls with rubber diaphragms.
One air pump and valves.
Four wooden posts for supporting overhead tie connections.
Four cast iron cross arms.
Four pairs cast iron headers.
Half-inch pipe sufficient for runs from tower to posts on tower side of street.
One bell for tower.
Automatic bells on arms, extra.

No. 6. Overhead Tie Double Pipe Connection Gate

See Page 256

No. 6. Same as No. 5, except that air is applied to all posts.

Four cast iron posts.
Four wooden main arms.
Four wooden sidewalk arms.
Four shafts and automatic locking connections.
Four pair steel bowls with rubber diaphragms.
One air pump and valves.
Four wooden posts for supporting overhead tie connections.

No. 6. Overhead Tie Double Pipe Connection Gate

(Continued)

Four cast iron cross arms.
Four pairs cast iron headers.
Half-inch pipe sufficient for runs from tower to all posts.
One bell for tower.
Automatic bells on arms, extra.

No. 7. Four-Post Pneumatic Gate

See Page 257

No. 7. Same as No. 2 except that it has double underground chain and rod connections between posts across the street.

Four cast iron posts.
Four bifurcated wooden main arms.
Four bifurcated wooden sidewalk arms.
Four shafts and automatic locking connections.
Four pair steel bowls with rubber diaphragms.
One air pump and valves.
Half-inch iron pipe sufficient for runs from tower to all posts.
One bell for tower.
Automatic bells on arms, extra.

No. 8. Two-Post Crank Gate

See Page 258

No. 8. One cast iron power or crank post.
One cast iron dead post.
Two bifurcated wooden main arms.
Two bifurcated wooden sidewalk arms.
Two shafts.
One-inch pipe sufficient to enclose rod connections between posts across the tracks.
Automatic bells for gate arms, extra.

No. 9. Four-Post Crank Gate

See Page 259

No. 9. One cast iron power or crank post.
Three cast iron dead posts.
Four bifurcated wooden main arms.
Four bifurcated wooden sidewalk arms.
Four shafts.
One-inch pipe sufficient to enclose rod connections between all posts.
Automatic bells for gate arms, extra.

No. 10. Two-Post Gate

No. 10. Having double chain and rod connections between posts and tower only.

Two cast iron posts.
Two bifurcated wooden main arms.
Two bifurcated wooden sidewalk arms.
One lever stand with two levers.
One bell for tower.
Automatic bells for arms, extra.

No. 12. Four-Post Pneumatic Gate

See Page 265

No. 12. Four-post pneumatic gate having double chain and rod connections same as the No. 7, except there are only two live posts.

Two cast iron posts with pneumatic attachments.
Two cast iron posts without pneumatic attachments.
Four bifurcated wooden main arms.
Four bifurcated wooden sidewalk arms.
Four shafts and automatic locking.
Two pair steel bowls with rubber diaphragms.
One air pump and valve.
One bell for tower.
Automatic bells for arms, extra.

No. 13. Two-Post Buda Improved Pneumatic Cylinder Gate

See Page 266

No. 13. Two-Post Buda Improved Pneumatic Cylinder Gate.

Two cast iron posts with cylinder and automatic locking connections.
Two bifurcated wooden main arms.
Two bifurcated wooden sidewalk arms.
One air pump and valves.
One bell for tower.
Automatic bells for arms, extra.

No. 14. Four-Post Buda Improved Pneumatic Cylinder Gate

See Page 267

No. 14. Four post cylinder gate having no mechanical connections.

Four cast iron posts with cylinders and automatic locking connections.
Four bifurcated wooden main arms.
Four bifurcated wooden sidewalk arms.
One air pump and valves.
Automatic bells on arms, extra.

The Buda Foundry & Manufacturing Company

No. 1. Two-Post Pneumatic Gate

The Buda Foundry & Manufacturing Company

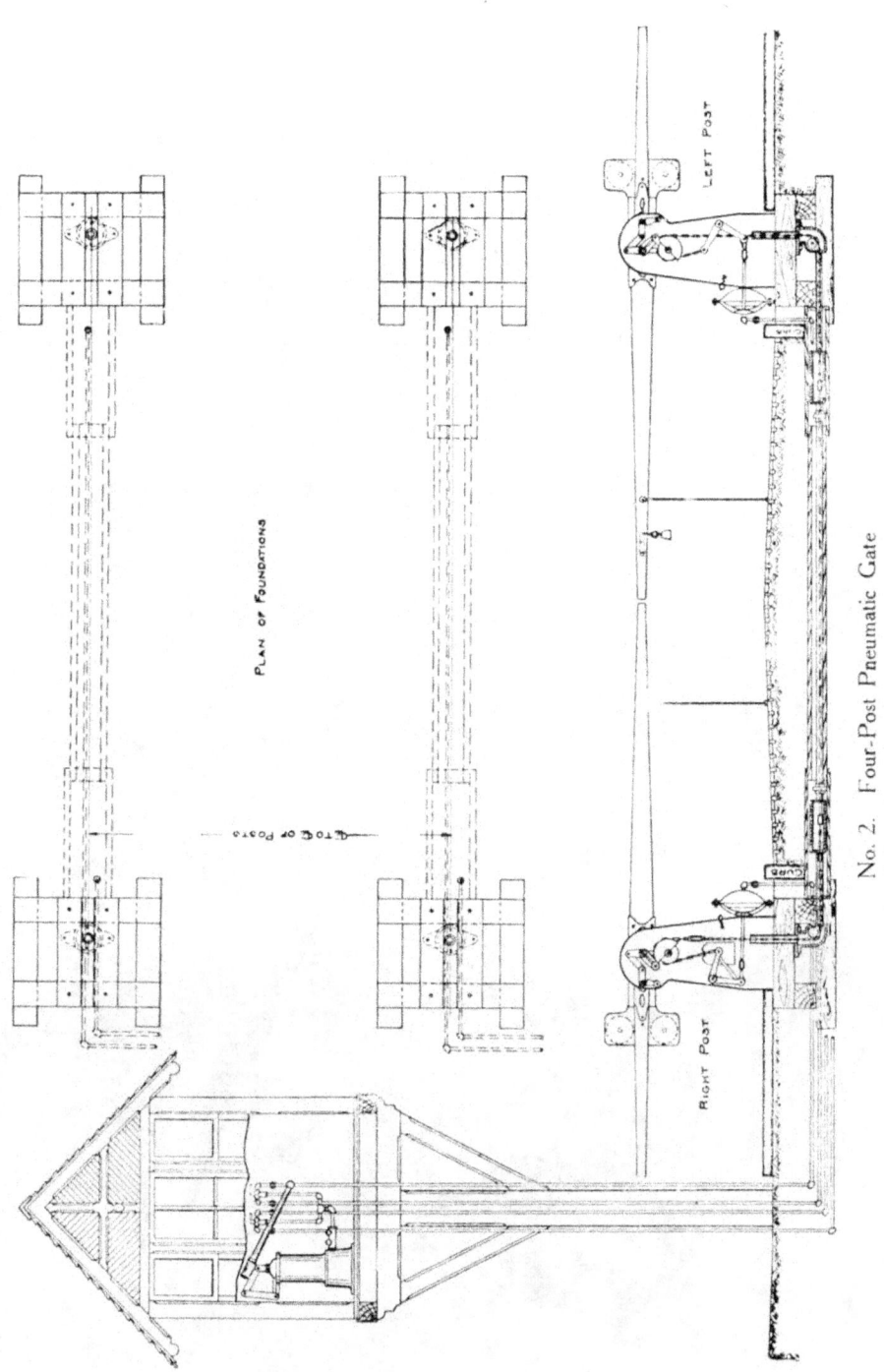

No. 2. Four-Post Pneumatic Gate

The Buda Foundry & Manufacturing Company

No. 3. Four-Post Lever Gate

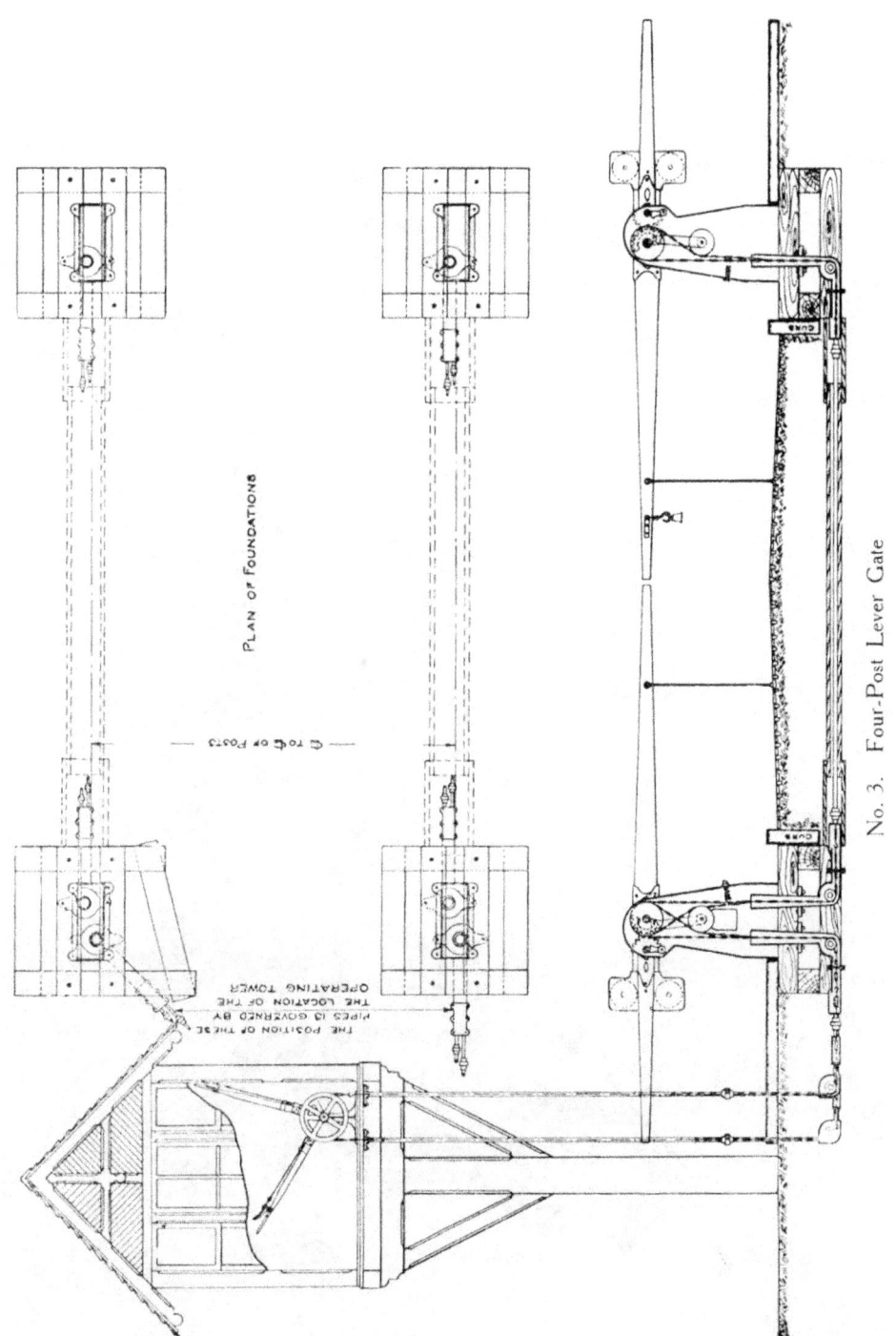

No. 3. Four-Post Lever Gate

The Buda Foundry & Manufacturing Company

No. 4. Overhead Tie, Four-Post Lever Gate

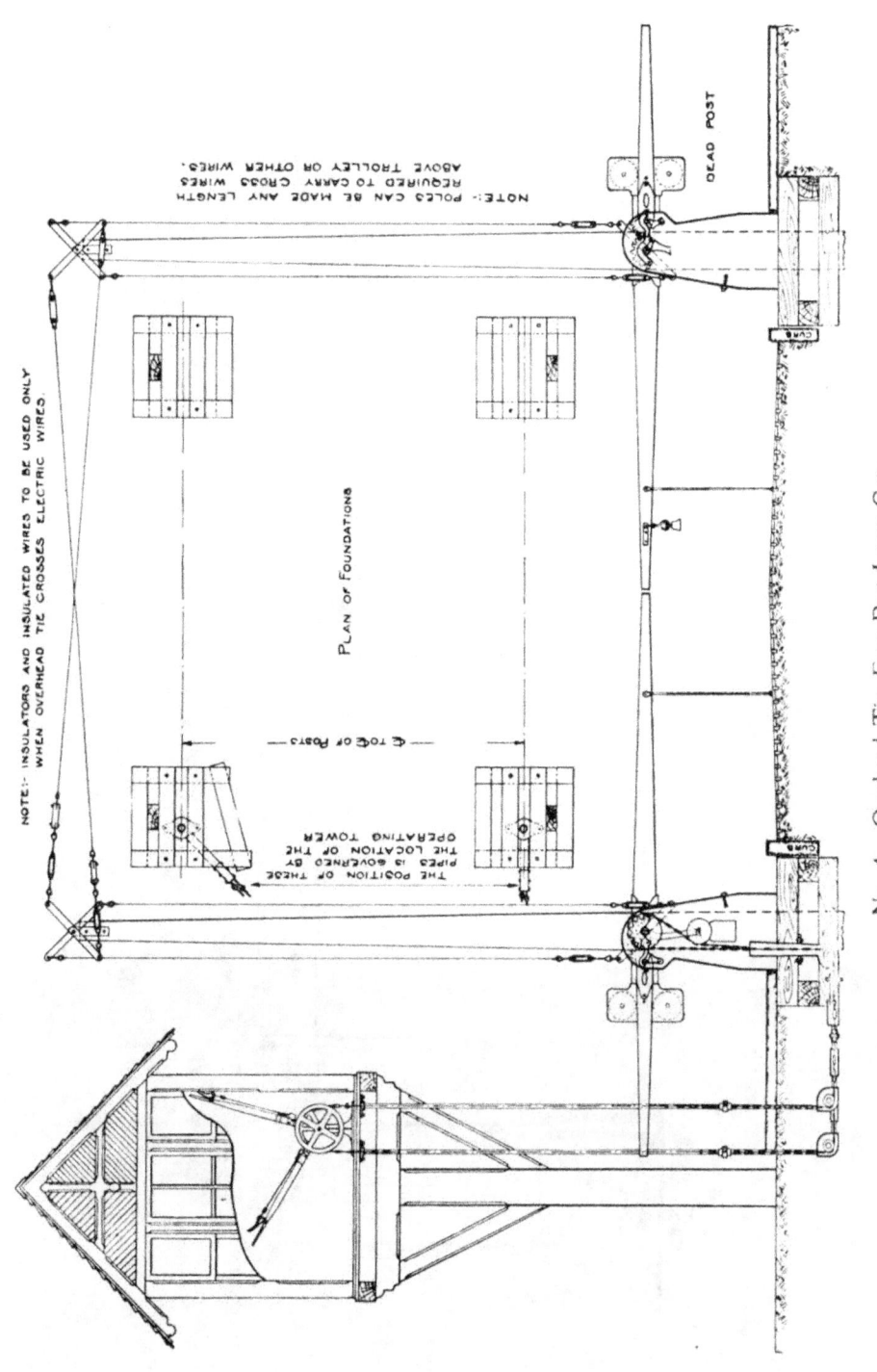

No. 4. Overhead Tie, Four-Post Lever Gate

The Buda Foundry & Manufacturing Company

No. 5. Overhead Tie, Four-Post Pneumatic Gate

The Buda Foundry & Manufacturing Company

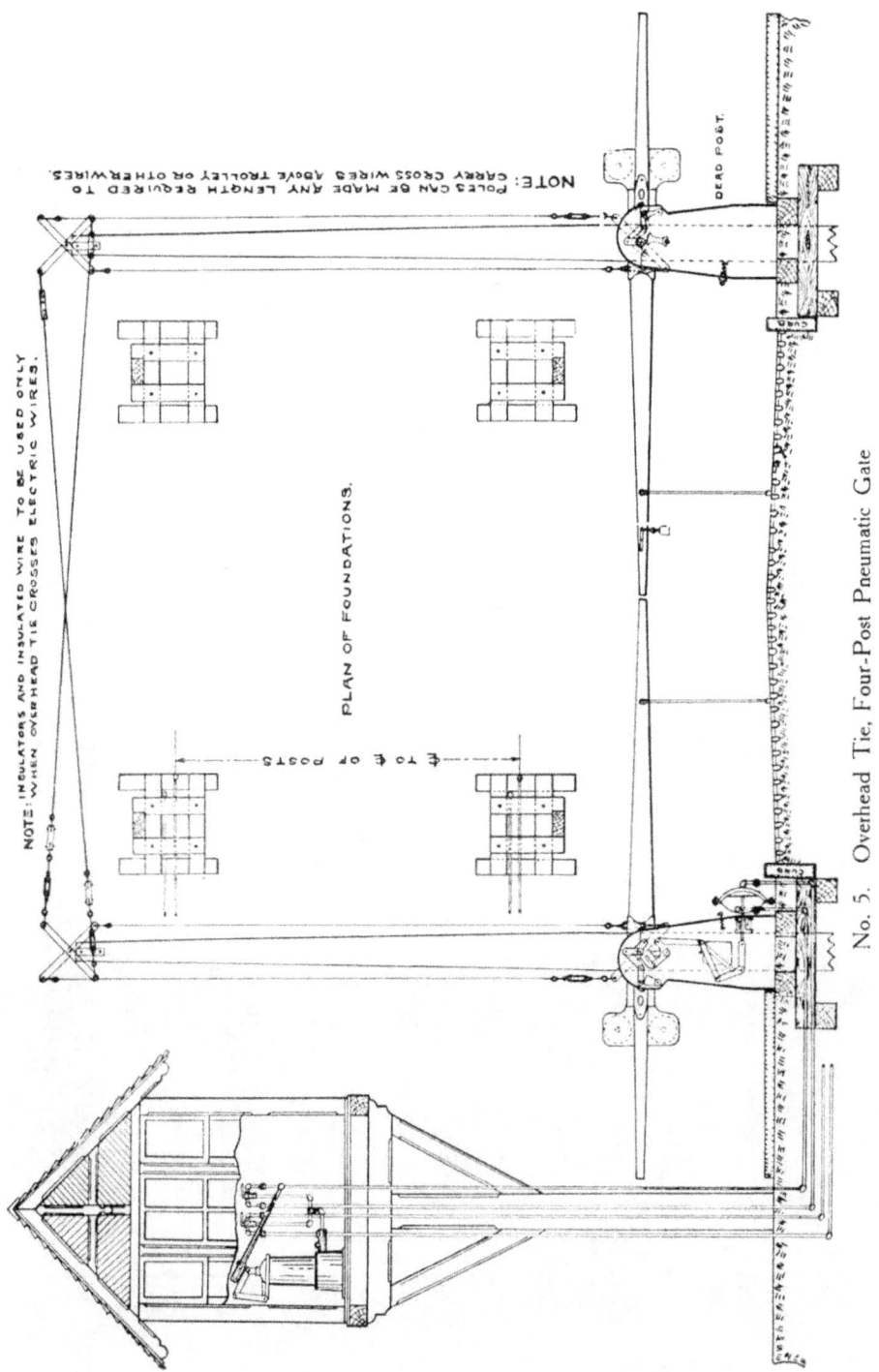

No. 5. Overhead Tie, Four-Post Pneumatic Gate

The Buda Foundry & Manufacturing Company

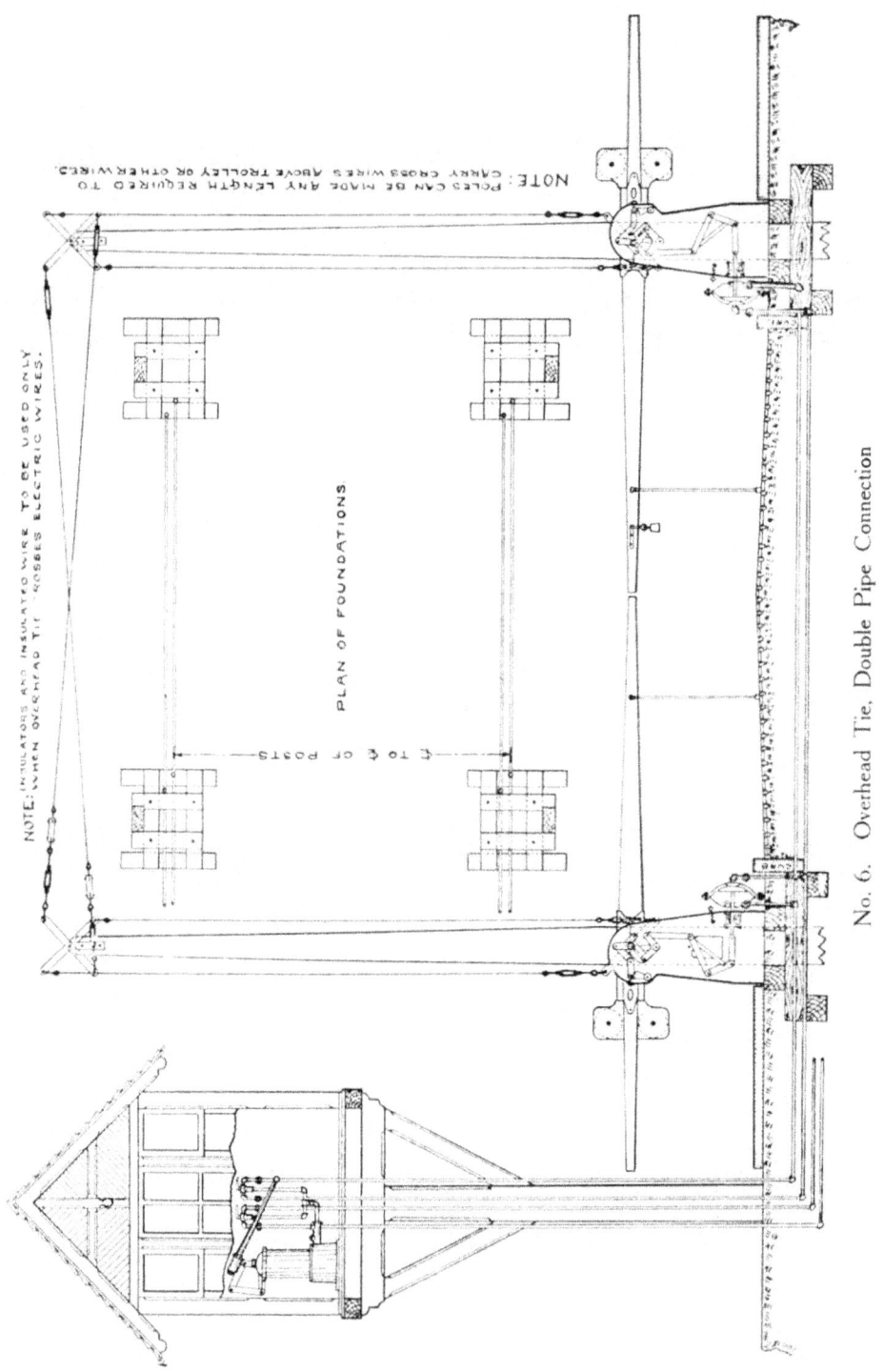

No. 6. Overhead Tie, Double Pipe Connection

The Buda Foundry & Manufacturing Company

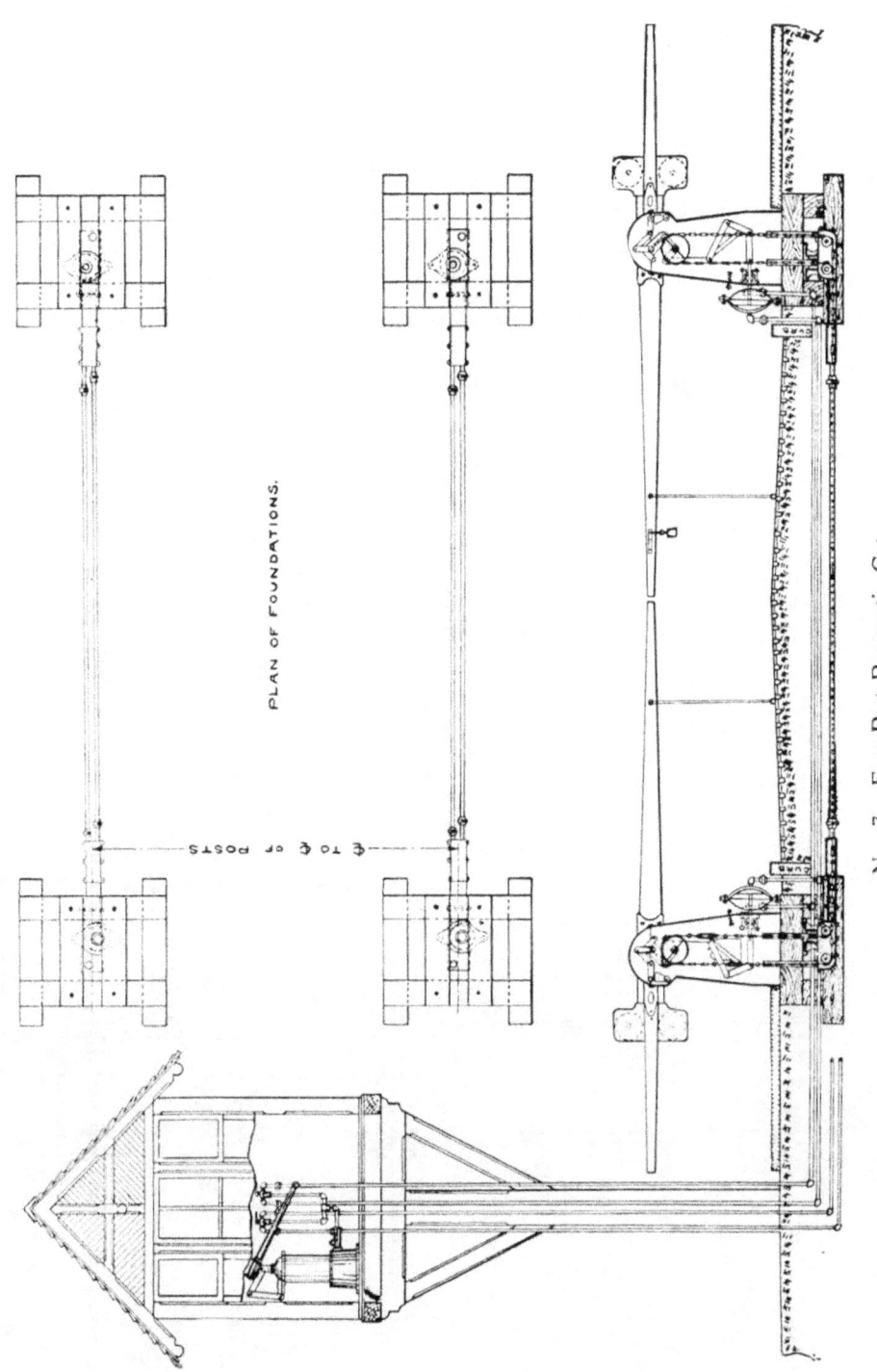

No. 7. Four-Post Pneumatic Gate

257

The Buda Foundry & Manufacturing Company

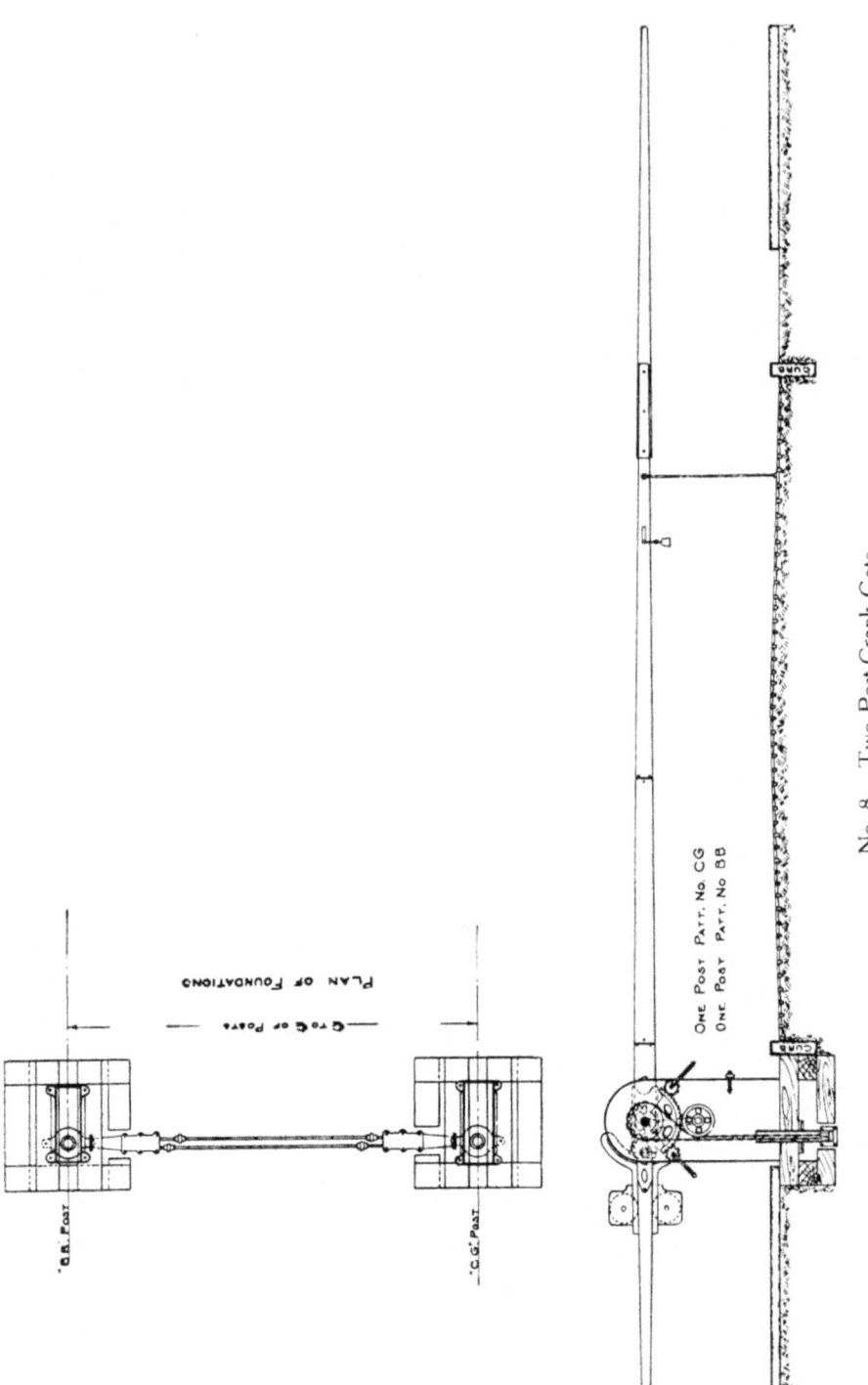

No. 8. Two-Post Crank Gate

The Buda Foundry & Manufacturing Company

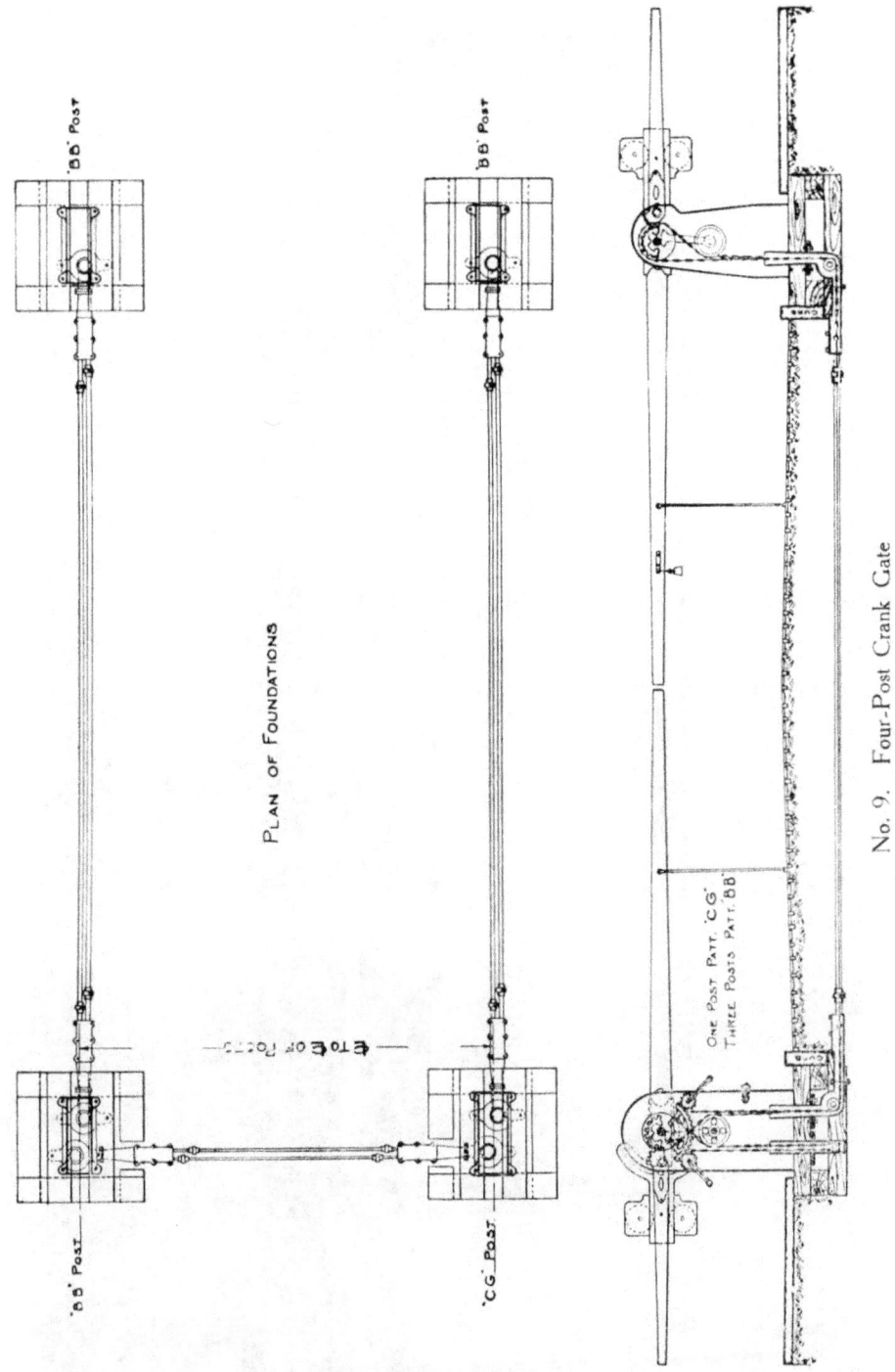

No. 9. Four-Post Crank Gate

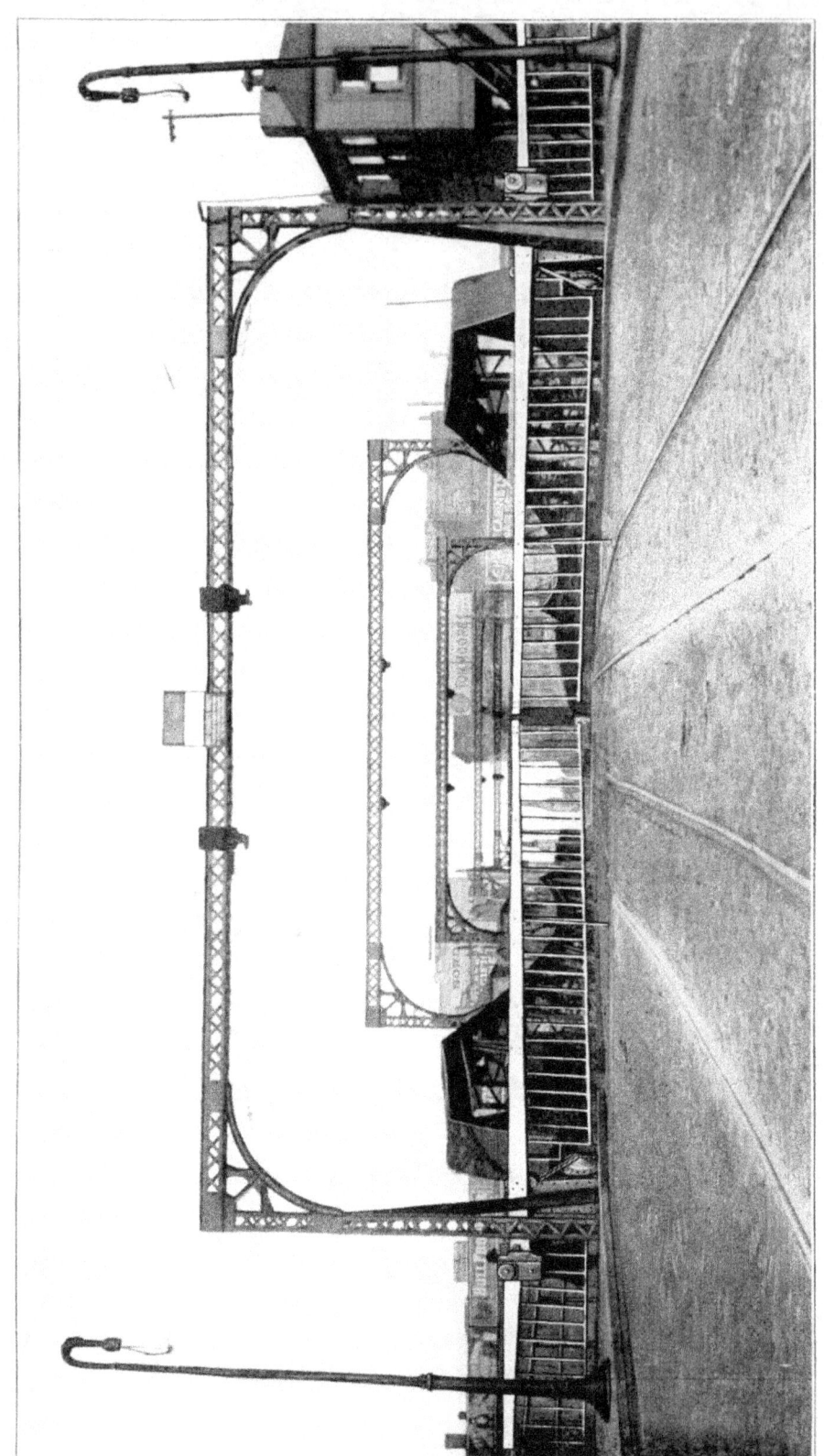

Folding Fence Gates at State Street Bascule Bridge over Chicago River

The Buda Foundry & Manufacturing Company

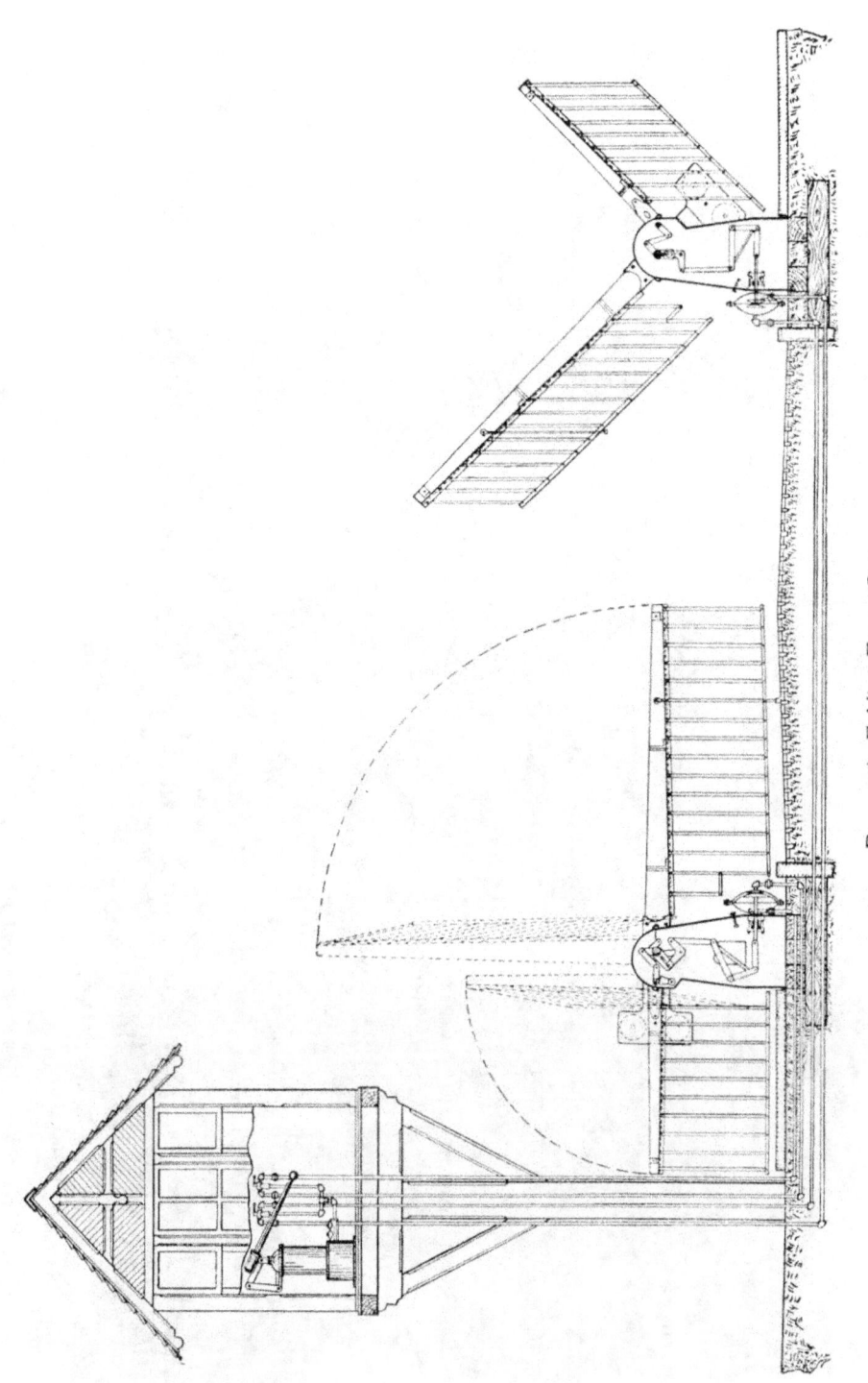

Pneumatic Folding Fence Gate

The Buda Foundry & Manufacturing Company

Folding Fence Gate at Indianapolis Train Shed of Indianapolis Traction and Terminal Co. These gates can be operated simultaneously or singly

The Buda Foundry & Manufacturing Company

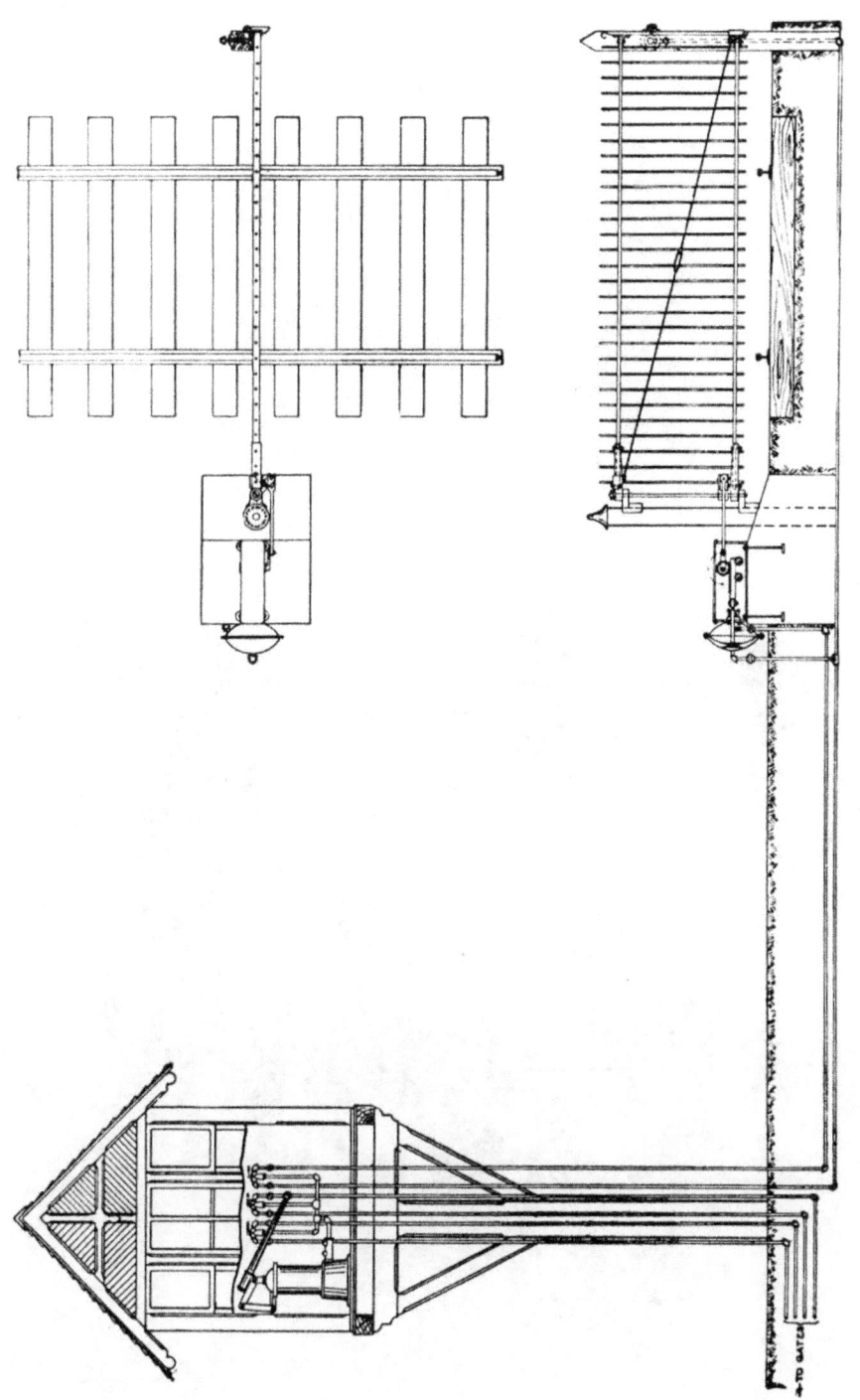

Pneumatic Swinging Gate, with Stop

The Buda Foundry & Manufacturing Company

Interlocked Pneumatic Railroad Crossing Gate

The Buda Foundry & Manufacturing Company

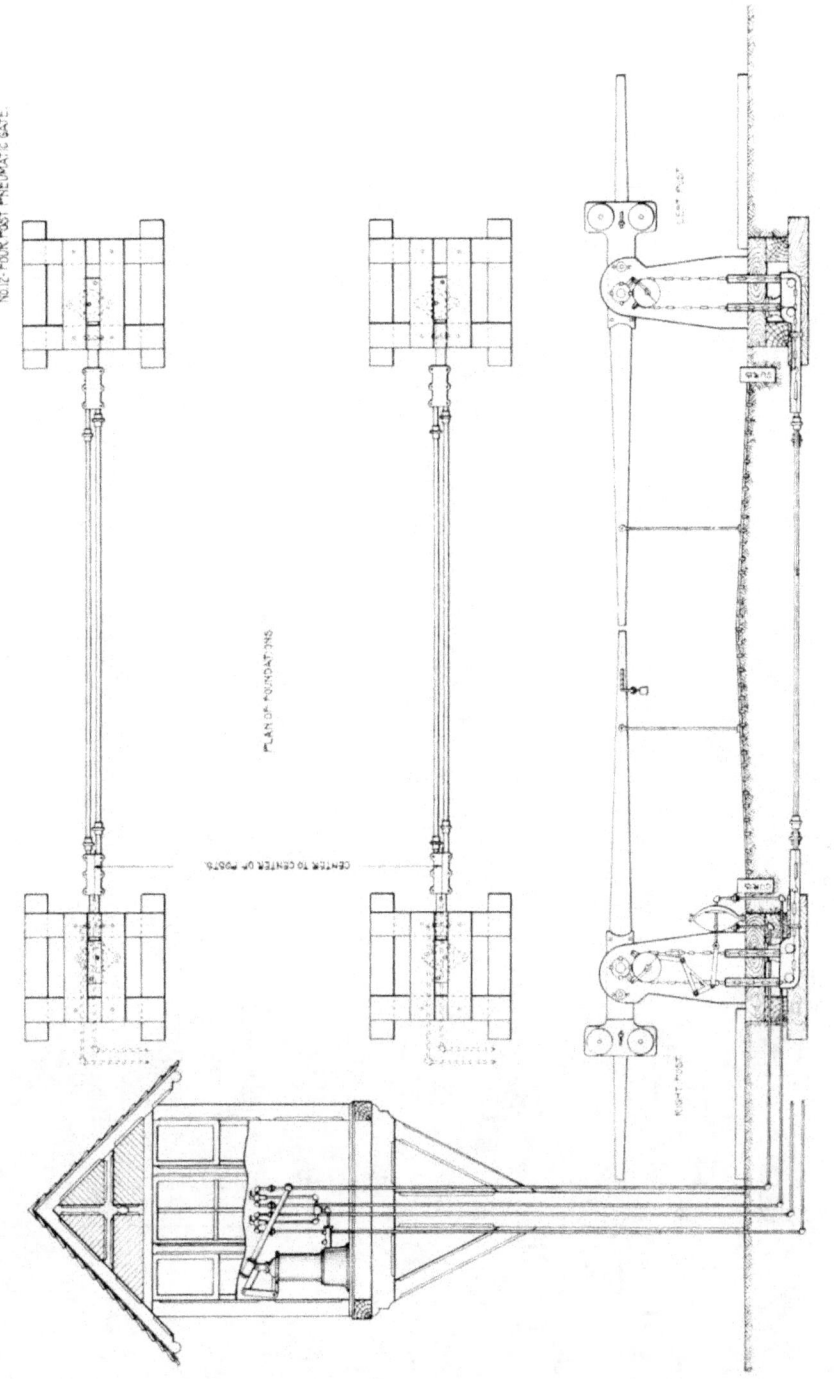

No. 12. Four-Post Pneumatic Gate

The Buda Foundry & Manufacturing Company

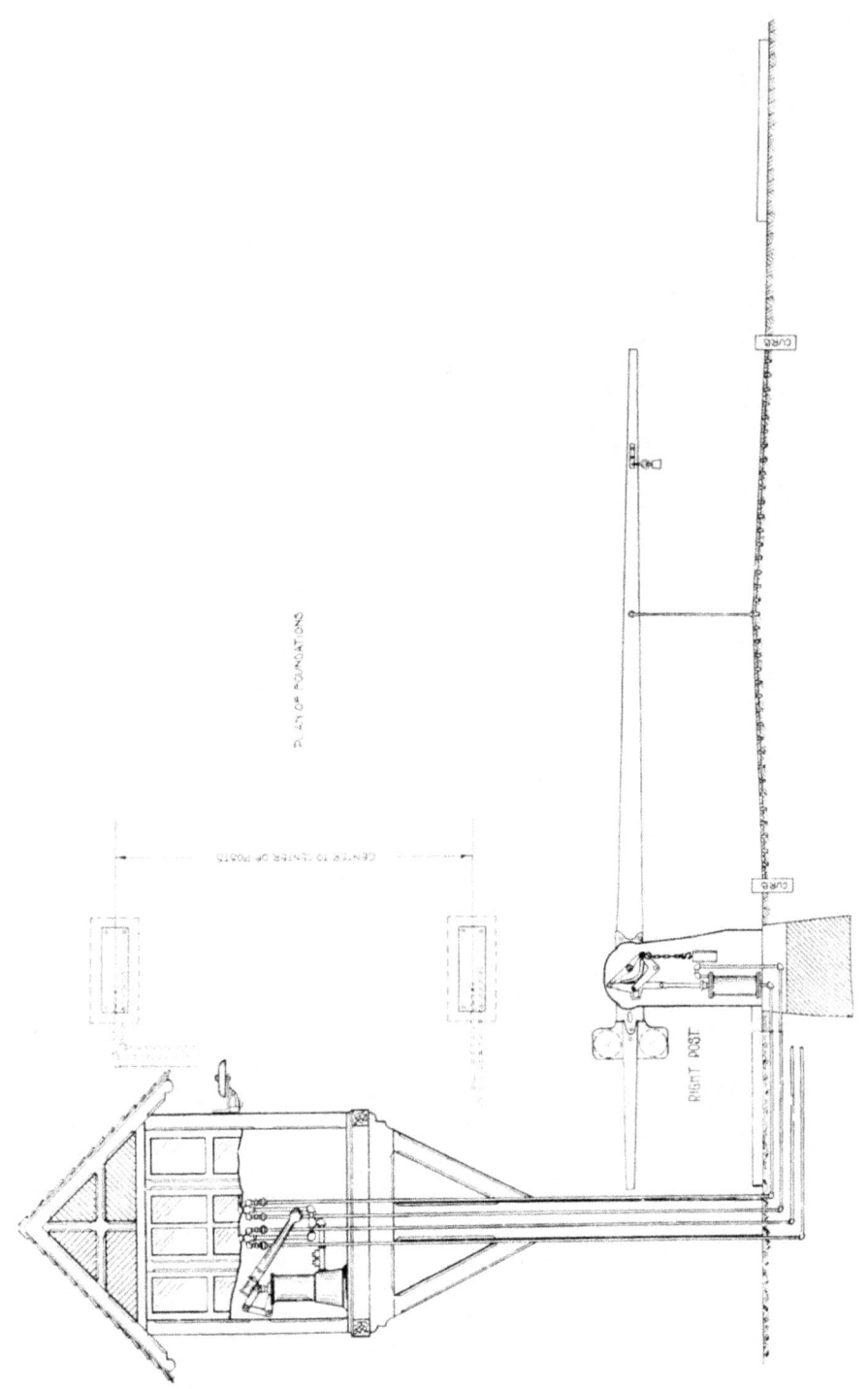

No. 13. Two-Post Buda Improved Pneumatic Cylinder Gate

The Buda Foundry & Manufacturing Company

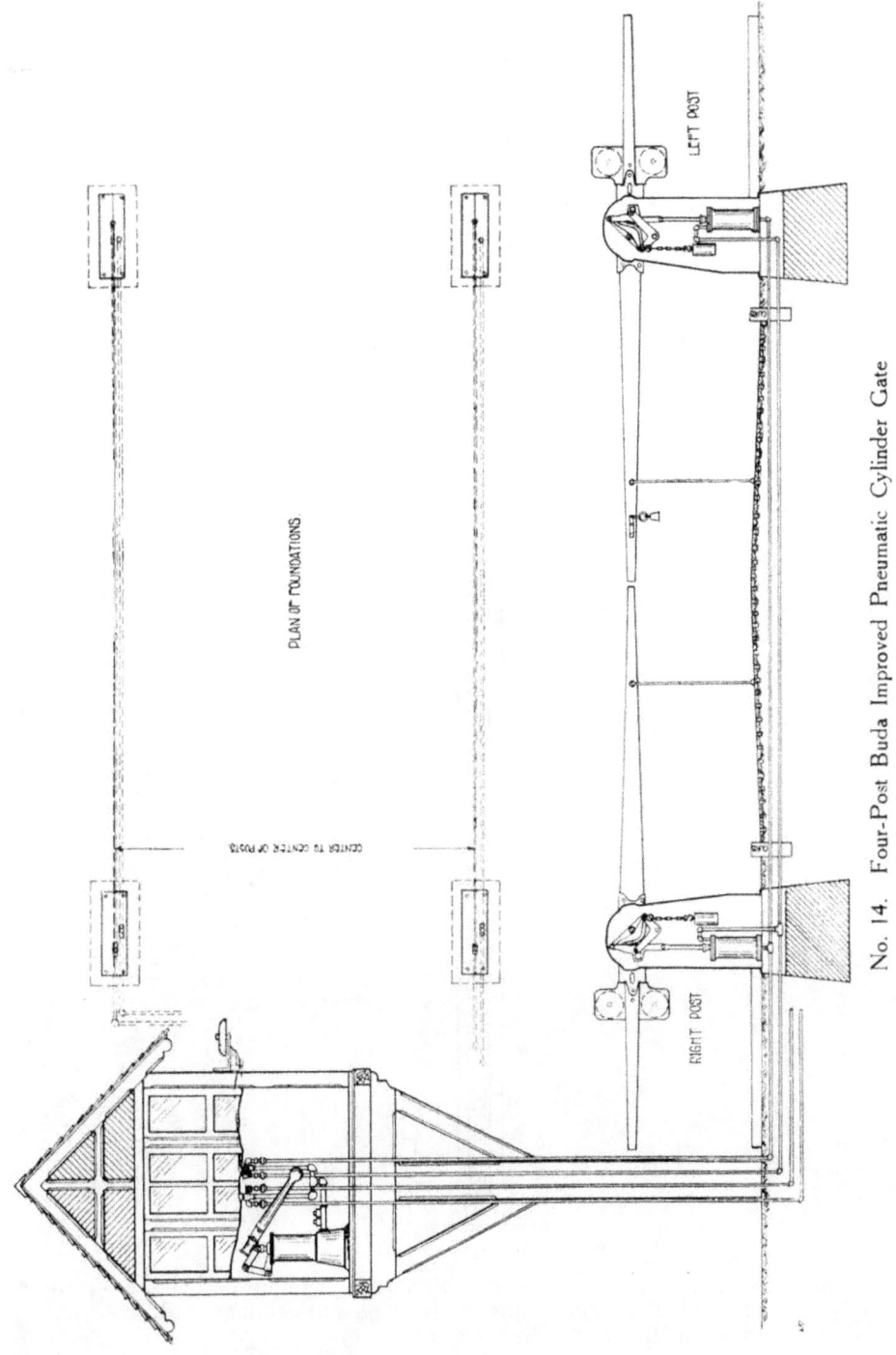

No. 14. Four-Post Buda Improved Pneumatic Cylinder Gate

Standard Single Steel-Post Tower

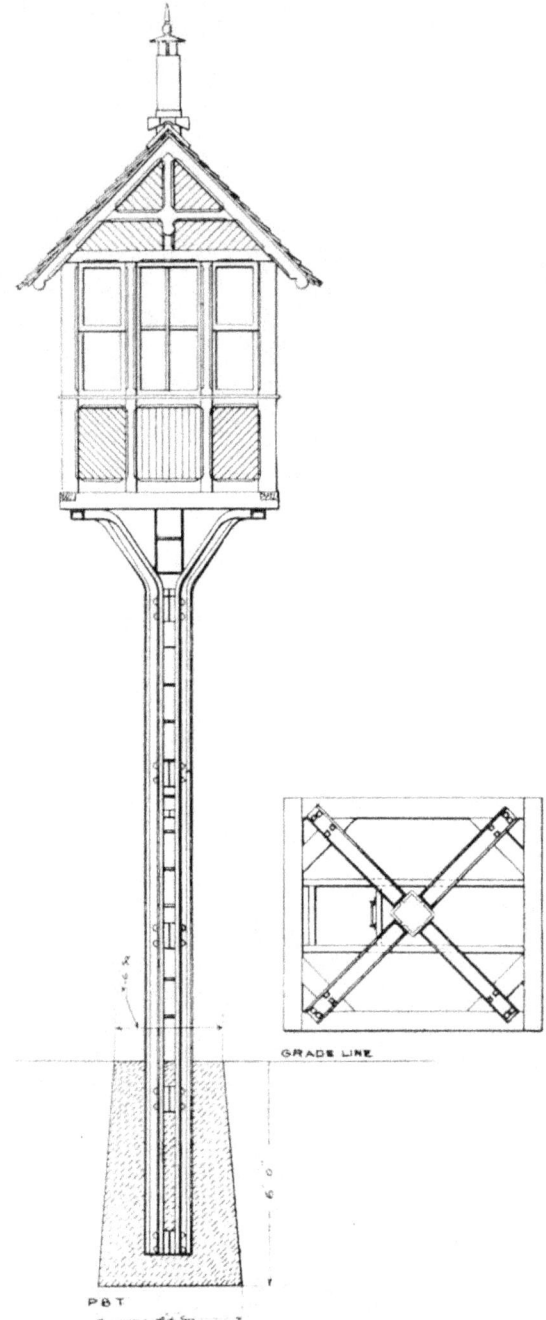

Where permanence is a consideration this style tower is taking the place of the wood post. The steel construction has all the advantages over wood, here, that it has in any other line of construction.

The steel post is imbedded in a concrete foundation as shown, and the result is substantial and lasting. The expense is little more than the wood style, but it represents economy in the end, doing away with the cost of maintenance. The house is of wood.

The Buda Foundry & Manufacturing Company

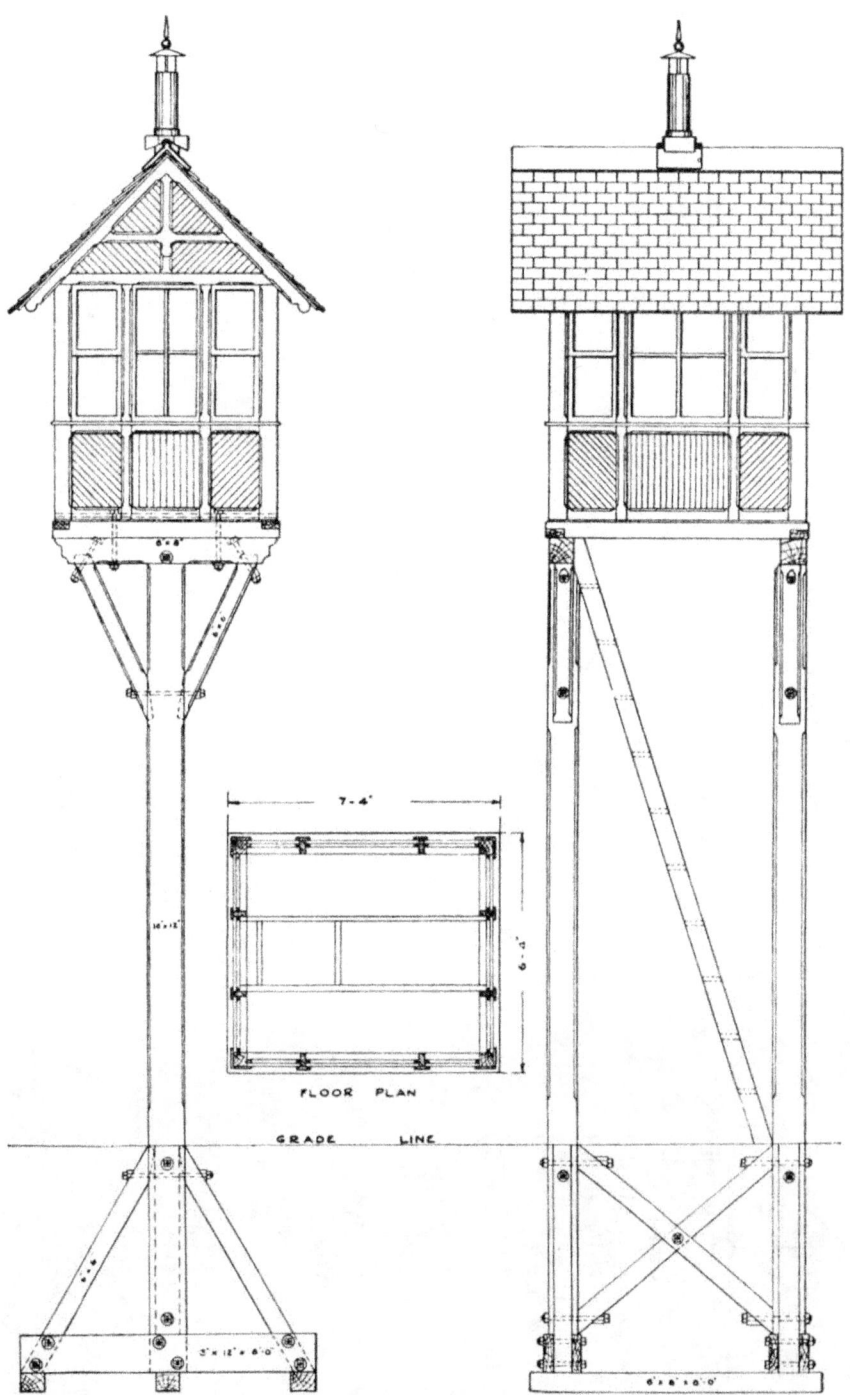

Standard Two-Post Tower for erection in dirt; but can be arranged for concrete base

The Buda Foundry & Manufacturing Company

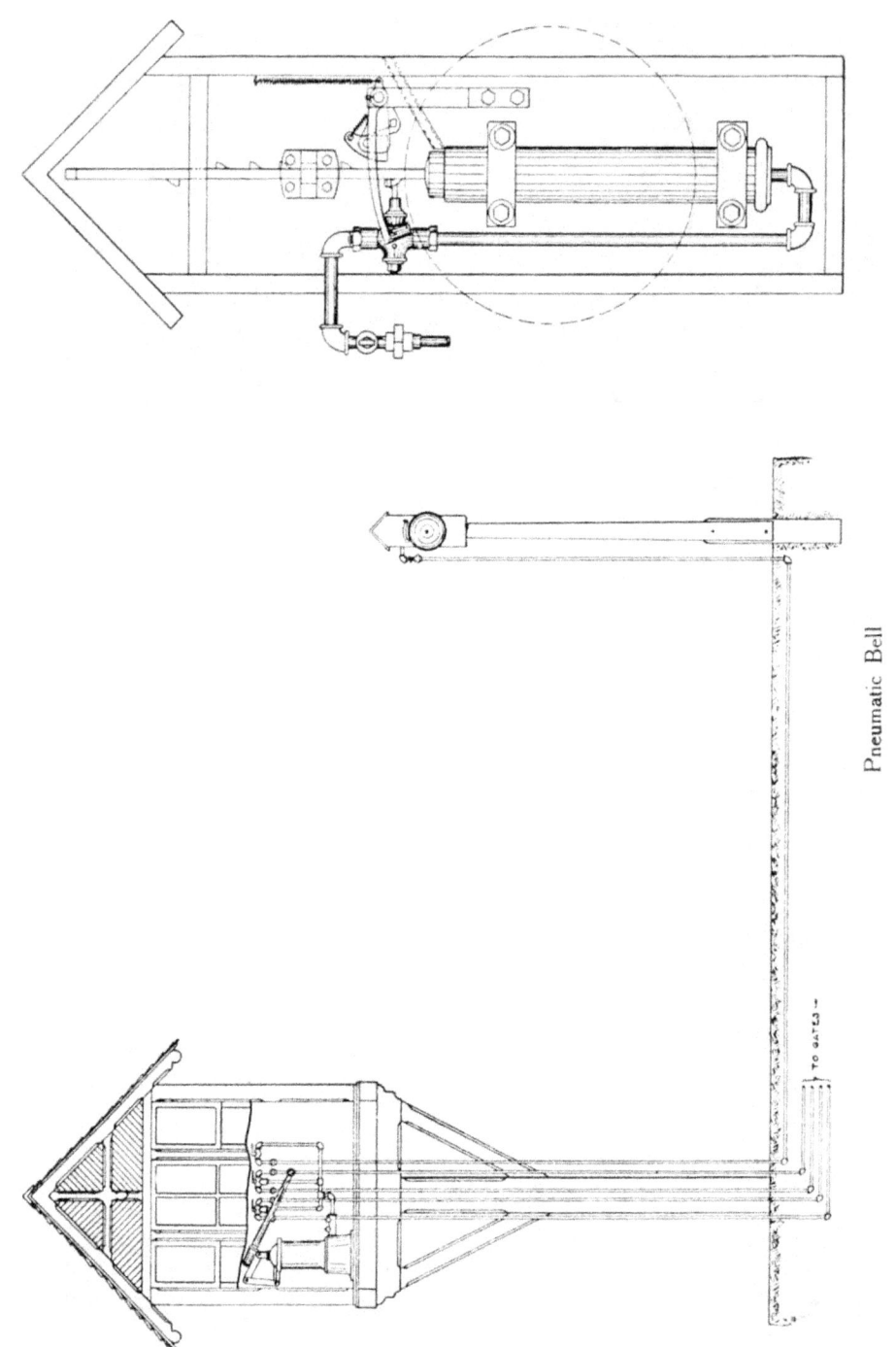

Pneumatic Bell

The Buda Foundry & Manufacturing Company

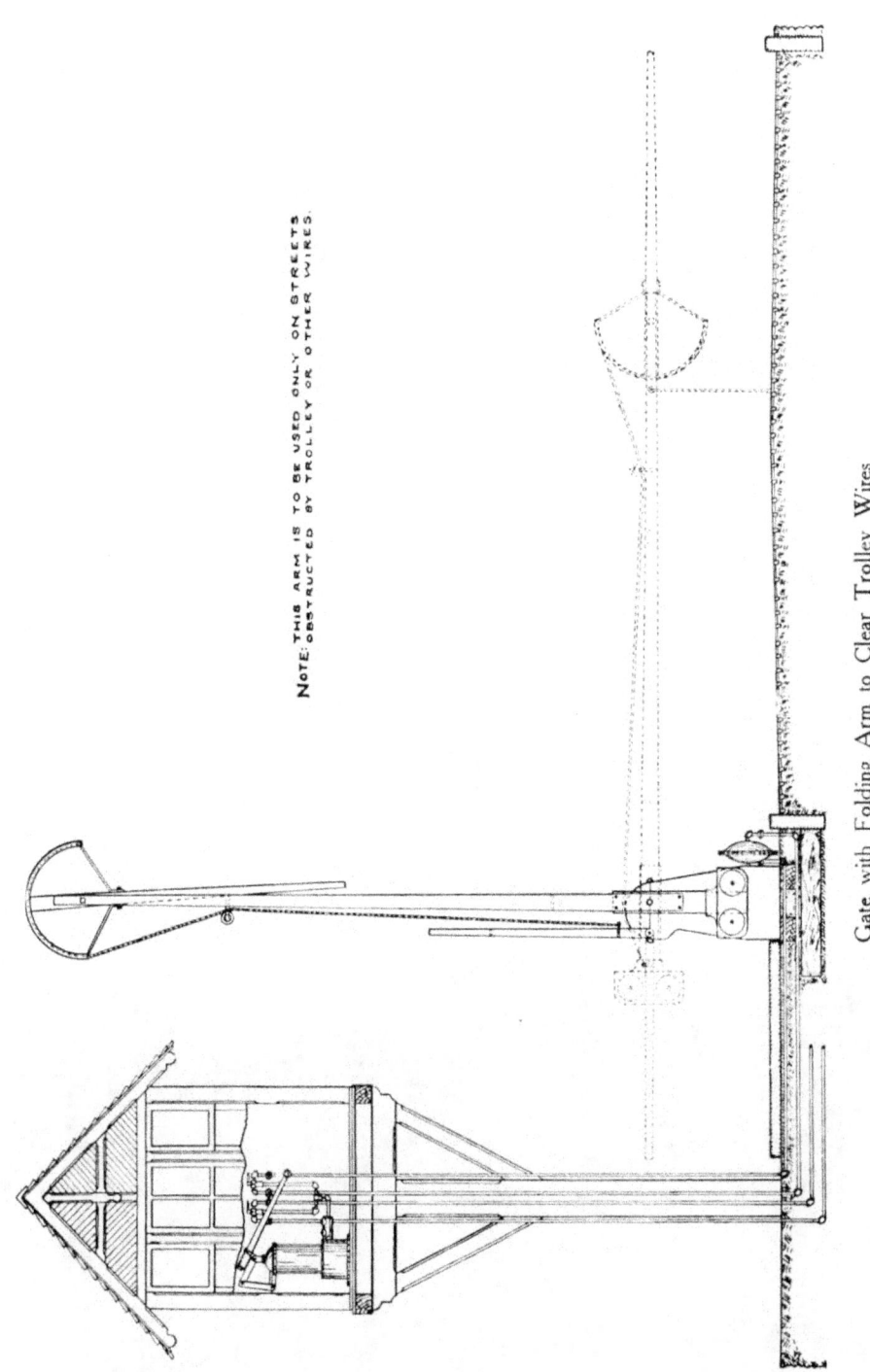

Gate with Folding Arm to Clear Trolley Wires

NOTE: THIS ARM IS TO BE USED ONLY ON STREETS OBSTRUCTED BY TROLLEY OR OTHER WIRES.

Repair Parts of Bogue and Mills Pneumatic and Mechanical Gates, Including Buda Improved Pneumatic Cylinder Gates

New Pattern No.	Old Pattern No.	Name of Castings, Finished	Price
		Posts and Internal Mechanism	
7100	B. B.	Post	$14.00
7101	B. A. A.	" Cover	2.00
7102	K.	" Door	.50
7103	K. 1	"	14.00
7104	K. O.	" Cover	2.00
7110	B. O.	Main Arm Shaft	2.50
7111	B. O. 1	" " "	2.50
7112	C. G. 3	" " "	2.50
7113	K. 2	" " "	3.00
7114		" " " for Cylinder Gate	2.50
7115		Connecting Link for Cylinder Gate	1.50
7120	B. 2	Auxiliary Arm Shaft	2.00
7121	B. 2 O.	" " "	2.00
7122	C. G. 14	" " "	2.00
7123	C.	" " Bracket	1.00
7130	B. 53	Double Sheave for No. 2 Post	2.00
7131	B. C. 3	" " " 1 "	2.00
7132	C. G. 4	Main	1.00
7133	C. G. 8	Guide	1.00
7134	24-A.	Double Sheave Shaft, 1⅛"x9¾" (Steel)	.50
7135	B. 33	"	2.00
7140	B. G.	Bell Crank for No. 1 Post	1.00
7141	B. F.	" " " " 1 "	1.00
7142	B. C.	" " " " 2 "	1.00
7143	K. 4	" " " " 12 inches	1.00
7144	B. G. G.	Upper Bell Crank	1.50
7145		Bell Crank for Cylinder Gate	1.00
7150	B. E.	Journal Cap	.25
7151	B. E. E.	"	.35
7152	B. E. O.	"	.50
7155	K. 7	Lock Diaphragm Bowl	.75
7156	B. H.	Back Diaphragm Large Bowl	2.00
7157	B. H. 1	Front	2.00
7158	31	Large Rubber Diaphragm	3.00
7159	32	Small	.50
7160	O.	Anti-friction bar	.20
7161	O. O.	"	.25
7162	C. G. 17	"	.50
7163	K. 9	"	.25
7170	5	Stuffing Box for No. 1 Post	2.00
7171	4	" " Gland for No. 1 Post	1.00
7172	54-A	" " complete with piston rod	4.00
7173	X.	Diaphragm Plate	.50
7174	54	Piston Rod for stuffing box No. 1 Post	1.00
7175	45	" " Fork for No. 1 Post	.75
7176		" " (complete) For Cylinder Gate	2.50
7176 A		" " Head "	.75
7176 B		" " Leather same as 7434 "	.50
7176 C		Dividing Plate "	.50
7177		Piston Rod (complete) "	1.10
7177 A		2" Rod "	1.00
7177 B		2" Rod Nut "	.10
7178		Cylinder (complete) with upper and lower covers	13.00
7178 A		6" " only "	7.00
7178 B		Lower Cylinder Cover "	1.50
7178 C		Upper Cylinder Cover (with stuffing-box gland) "	3.50
7178 D		Stuffing Box "	1.00
7179		Weight	1.50

The Buda Foundry & Manufacturing Company

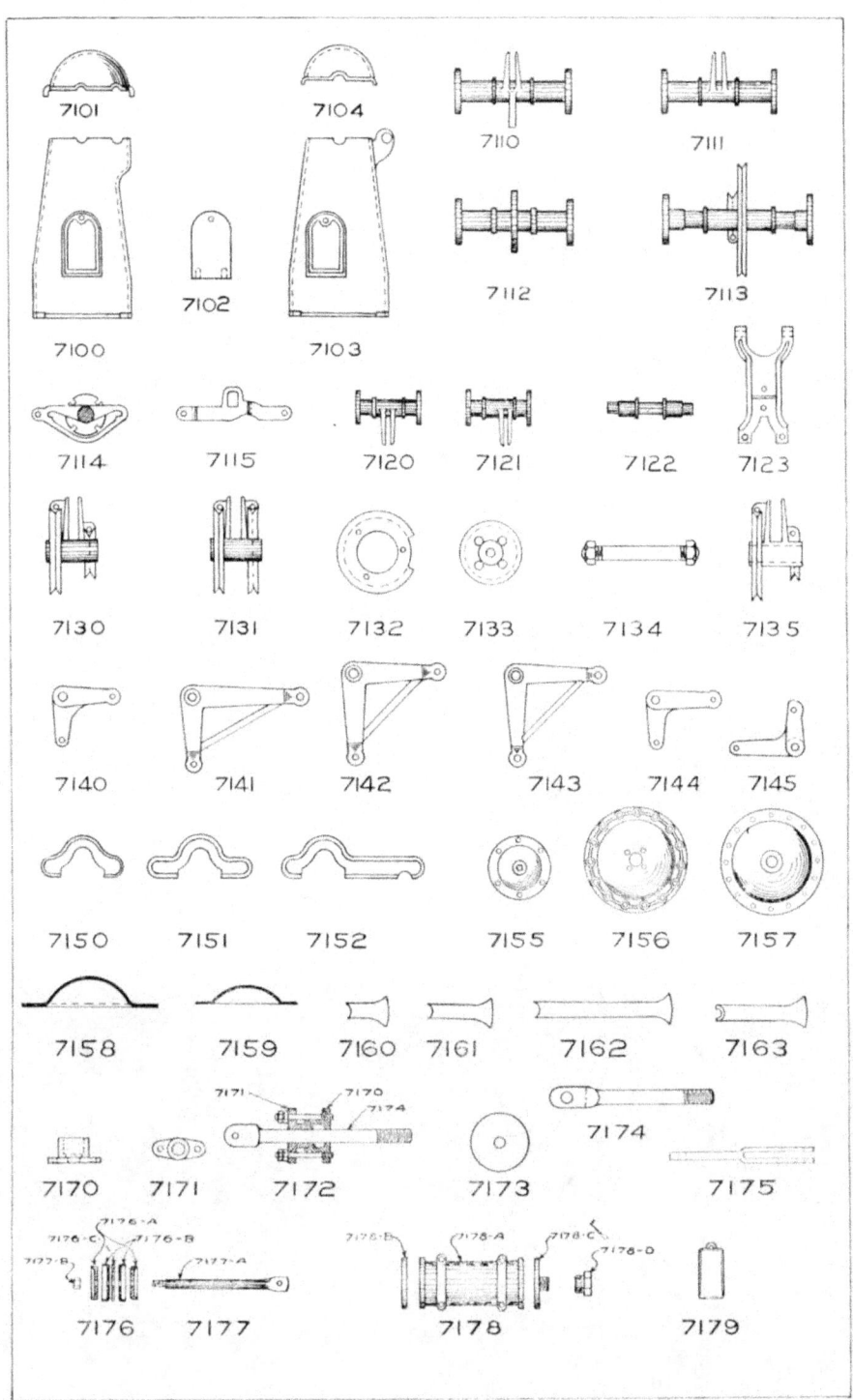

273

Repair Parts of Bogue and Mills Pneumatic and Mechanical Gates, Including Buda Improved Pneumatic Cylinder Gates
(Continued)

New Pattern No.	Old Pattern No.	Name of Castings, Finished	Price
7180	L.	Box Side, with Small Pinions for Open Post...	$7.00
7181	L. 1	Plain Side for Open Post..................	5.00
7182	L. 2	Box Side, without Pinion for Open Post.....	7.00
7183	R. 3	Cover for Large Hollow Post...............	2.00
7184	43	Bumper Bar 1"x1¼"x22" Stop for Arm......	1.00
7185	G. 100	Clevice for No. 2 Gate....................	.15
7186	M. 2	3" Pinion................................	1.00
7187	N.	Cog Lever................................	2.00
7188	N. 1	" "	2.00
7189	N. 11	" "	2.00
7190	M.	12" Cog Wheel...........................	1.50
7191	M. 1	" Wheels half reduced to 9".............	1.50
7192	14	¾" Open Link............................	.05
7193	42	⅝"x3" Flat Head Pin.....................	.10
7194	D. G.	Right or Left Post, complete, for No. 2 Four Post Pneumatic Gate........................	40.00
7195	S. G.	Pneumatic Post, complete, for No. 1 Two Post, or No. 5 Four Post Gates..................	50.00
7196	D. G. 5	Dead Post, for No. 5 Four Post Gate.......	30.00
7197	L. G.	Dead Post, for Lever or Crank Gate........	30.00
7198	C. G. A.	Power or Crank Post, complete, for Crank Gate	60.00
		Arm Fittings	
7200	B.	Main Arm Plate..........................	1.50
7201	B. 8	" " "	2.00
7202	B. 6	" " "	2.00
7203	B. 66	" " "	2.50
7204	B. 666	" " "	3.00
7205	K. 3	" " "	4.40
7206	K. 32	" " "	3.50
7207	K. 320	" " "	4.00
7208	K. 34	" " "	4.50
7209	B. 666-A.	" " "	3.50
7230	B. 7	Main Arm Plate Slide....................	2.00
7231	B. 77	" " " "	2.50
7232	B. 777	" " " "	3.00
7233	K. 31	" " " "	3.50
7234	K. 33	" " " "	4.00
7250	B. D.	Auxiliary Arm Plate.....................	.75
7251	B. 4	" " " (with lug).............	1.50
7252	B. 5	" " " " "	1.50
7253	B. 41	" " "	1.25
7254	B. 51	" " "	1.25
7255	B. 44	" " "	1.50
7256	B. 55	" " "	1.50
7257	B. 40	" " "	2.00
7258	B. 50	" " "	2.00
7259	B. 38	" " "	3.00
7260	B. 39	" " "	3.00
7261	B. 380	" " " (with lug)..............	3.50
7262	B. 390	" " " " "	3.50
7263	C. G. 18	" " "	.75
7264	C. G. 19	" " "	.75
7265	C. G. 180	" " "	1.00
7266	C. G. 190	" " "	1.00
7267	C. G. 20	" " " Segment Gear...........	.75
7268	K. 5	Auxiliary Arm Plate (with lug)............	.75
7269	K. 6	" " " (no lug)..............	.50

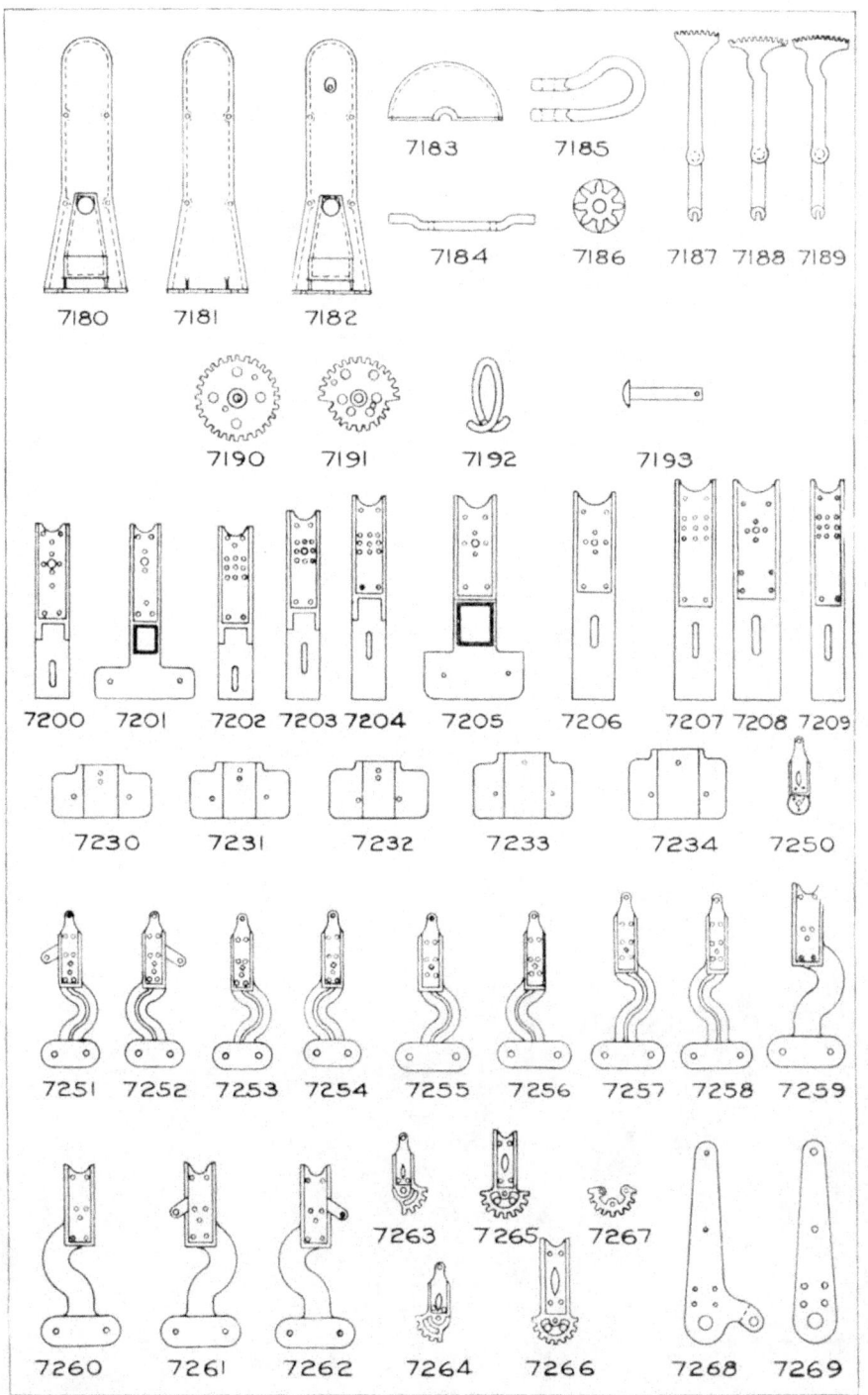

Repair Parts of Bogue and Mills Pneumatic and Mechanical Gates, Including Buda Improved Pneumatic Cylinder Gates

(Continued)

New Pattern No.	Old Pattern No.	Name of Castings, Finished	Price
7270	A. 10	Auxiliary Arm Plate (with lug)	$0.75
7271	A. 0	" " " (no lug)	.50
7272	S. 1	" " " with cogs	1.00
7273	S. 11	" " " "	1.00
7274	S.	" " " no cogs	.50
7275	K. A.	" " " Bracket for Old Crank Post	1.00
7280	A. R.	Arm Rest Connection Only	.50
7281	A. R. A.	Arm Rest, complete with Pipe	.75
7282	19	Lantern Hook (with snap)	.25
7283	17	" " Hook Snap only	.05
7284	16	" " Spring	.10
7285	18	" " Weight	.15
7286	B. O. A.	Crank for Arm Plate Bracket	1.00
7287	B. O. B.	Main Arm Plate Bracket	1.00

Sheave and Mechanical Connections

New Pattern No.	Old Pattern No.	Name of Castings, Finished	Price
7300	B. K.	Sheave Box Plate	1.00
7301	K. B.	Single Sheave Box, only	1.50
7302	K. K.	" " " Cover	.50
7303	20	" " " with Sheave and Gasket	3.00
7304	K. B. 1	Double Sheave Box, only	2.50
7305	K. B. 2	" " Box Cover	.75
7306	K. B. 1-A	" " Box with Sheaves and Gasket	5.00
7307	C. G. 10	" " Box only	2.50
7308	C. G. 10-A	" " Box with Sheaves and Gaskets	5.00
7309	9	1¼" Anti-friction Sheave	.75
7310	C. G. 26	Dividing Plate	.25
7311	B. K. 01	Sheave Box Plate for Concrete Foundation	1.25
7320	33	" " " Gasket for No. 20 (7303)	.35
7321	40	" " " " K. B. 1 (7304)	.50
7330	L. 6-A	Cross Arm Shaft, 1¼" x 12¼", No. 5 Gate	.50
7331	L. 67-A	Main Arm Strap, for No. 5 Gate	.75
7332	L. 7-A	Cross Arm Hook, for No. 5 Gate	.10
7333	L. 7-AA	Insulators for No. 5 Gate	.50
7334	L. 6	Cross Arm Header	.50
7335	L. 66	" " "	.75
7336	L.	24" Cross Arm	2.00
7350	21	Single Connecting Box, only	1.50
7351	22	" " " Cover	.50
7352	23	" " " complete	2.50
7353	C. G. 11	Double " " only	2.50
7354	C. G. 22	" " " Cover	.50
7355	C. G. 11-A	" " " complete	4.00

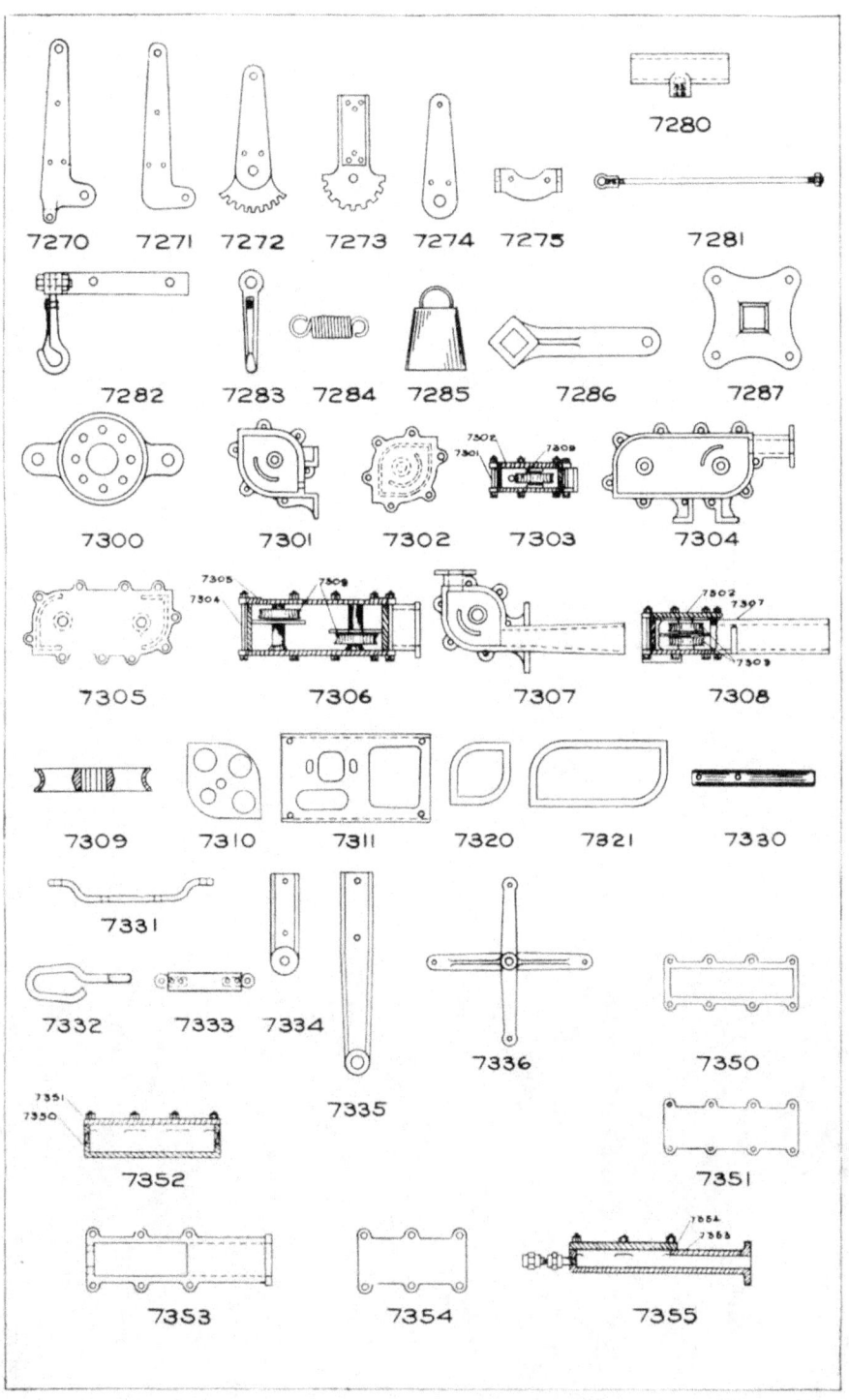

Repair Parts of Bogue and Mills Pneumatic and Mechanical Gates, Including Buda Improved Pneumatic Cylinder Gates

(Continued)

New Pattern No.	Old Pattern No.	Name of Castings, Finished	Price
7370	34	Connecting Box Gasket for No. 23 (7352)	$0.25
7371	38	" " " " C. B. C.	.35
7372	39	" " " " C. G. 11 (7353)	.35
7373	41	Flange Gasket for C. G. 11 (7353)	.25
7380	10	7/16" Turnbuckle	.50
7381	12	7/16" Rod Hook	.05
7382	13	7/16" S. Hook	.02½
7383	15	½" S. Hook	.02½
7384	30	¾" Pump Rod Coupling	.02½
7385	24	¼" Chain, per ft.	.10
7386	37	Open Post Gasket for L. 2 Post	1.00
7387	35	½" Union Gasket	.02
7388	36	1" Union Gasket	.03
		Pump and Air Connections	
7400	P. C.	Pump Cylinder, 8"	8.00
7401	P. C. 2	" " 10"	10.00
7402	P. C. 6	" Complete, 6"	15.00
7403	P. C. 8	" " 8"	20.00
7404	P. C. 10	" " 10"	25.00
7410	P. O.	" Top 8"	2.00
7411	P. T.	" " 8"	2.00
7412	P. T. 2	" " 10"	2.50
7420	P. B.	" Base 8"	4.00
7421	P. B. 2	" " 10"	5.00
7430	P. 4	" Follower, 8"	.75
7431	P. 42	" " 10"	1.00
7432	P. 7	" Spider 8"	.75
7433	P. 72	" " 10"	1.00
7434	P. P. 6	" Piston (leather) 6"	.50
7435	P. P. 8	" " " 8"	.75
7436	P. P. 10	" " " 10"	1.00
7437	P. P. R.	" " Rod (steel)	1.00
7450	123	Air Tap (Brass), with 1 handle and 2 ells	1.75
7451	123-A	" " Handle	.15
7452	1230	" " Complete with Nipples and Unions	2.00
7453	1231	" " Spring	.10
7454	1232	½" x ½" x ¾" Return Bend, made of fittings	.50
7455	2	Air Tap only (Cast Iron)	1.50
7456	1	" " Handle (Cast Iron)	.75
7457	25	" " with 2 handles fitted	2.50
7458	90	" " with 2 handles, 4 clamps, 3½ ft. Hose, Unions and Nipples	4.00
7459	3	" " only (Cast Iron)	2.00
7460	26	" " with 3 handles, fitted	3.50
7461	91	" " with 3 handles, 6 clamps, 5 ft. Hose, Unions and Nipples	5.00
7462	29	½" x ½" x ¾" Return Bend (Cast Iron)	.25
7463	6	¾" x 1¾" Double Check Valve (Cast Iron)	2.00
7464	7	½" Brass Cut-off	.50
7465	27	¾" Hose, per ft.	.12½
7466	28	¾" Hose Clamp (Brass)	.12½
7467	1230-A.	Air Tap, complete with Cut-off and Unions	3.00

The Buda Foundry & Manufacturing Company

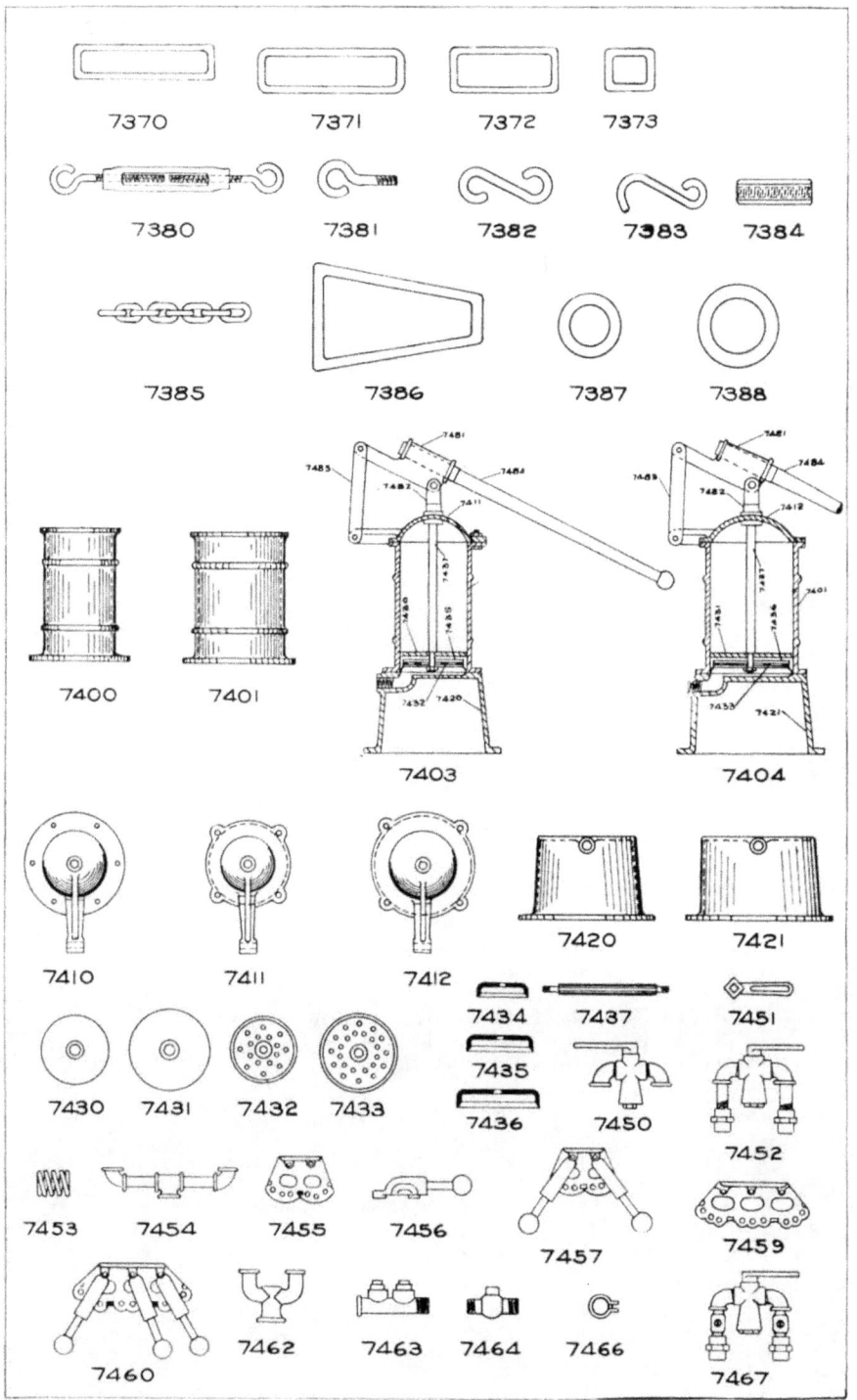

Repair Parts of Bogue and Mills Pneumatic and Mechanical Gates, Including Buda Improved Pneumatic Cylinder Gates
(Continued)

New Pattern No.	Old Pattern No.	Name of Castings, Finished	Price
7480	P. 1	Pump Handle Socket	$ 1.00
7481	P. 10	" " "	1.00
7482	P. 2	" Fork	.75
7483	P. 3	" Side Brace	.50
7484	P. H.	" Handle (wood)	.40
7485	P. S. B.	" Stud Bolt, ⅝" x 4" and 4½"	.25
Lever Gate Material			
7500	H. O.	Stand only	3.00
7501	A. 19	Lever Stand Shaft, 1¼" x 13½" steel	.50
7502	A. 20	" " Spring	.10
7510	H.	Stand Quadrant, Right Hand	1.00
7511	H. 1.	" " Left Hand	1.00
7520	A. 12	" Sheave, 15"	1.50
7521	H. 2	" " 20"	2.00
7530	R. H.	Lever for Stand, Right Hand	2.50
7531	L. H.	" for Stand, Left Hand	2.50
7550	L. S. 1	" Stand complete with 15" Sheave	12.00
7551	L. S. 2	" Stand complete with 20" Sheave	15.00
7580	A. 13	" Rod Guide	.15
7581	A. 14	" Latch	.25
7582	A. 15	" Stand Flange, 1¼"	.50
7583	A. 16	" Clamp	.15
7584	A. 17	" Dog and Rod	.50
Crank Gate Material			
7600	C. G.	Crank or Power Post	20.00
7601	C. G. 1	Dead Post	20.00
7602	C. G. 2	Post Cover	3.00
7620	C. G. 5	Split Sheave (Right Hand)	1.50
7621	C. G. 6	Split Sheave (Left Hand)	1.50
7630	C. G. 9	Pinion Gear	1.00
7631	C. G. 12	Ratchet Wheel	1.00
7632	C. G. 16	Segment Gear, 24"	2.00
7640	C. G. 13-R	Ratchet Dog (Right Hand)	.25
7641	C. G. 13-L	Ratchet Dog (Left Hand)	.25
7650	C. G. 15	Crank Shaft Bushing	.50
7651	C. G. 23	Gate Crank	.75
7660	C. G. 21	Auxiliary Arm Bracket	.75
7670	C. G. 24	Main Arm Plate, 9"	5.00
7671	C. G. 25	Main Arm Plate, 7"	4.00
Swing Gate Material			
7700	P. S. G.	Pneumatic Box Only	6.00
7701	P. S. G. 1	Pneumatic Box Cover	1.00
7710	P. S. G. 2	3" Pinion	1.00
7711	P. S. G. 3	Gear Bar	1.00
7720	P. S. G. 4	2" Roller	.50
7730	P. S. G. 5	Hinge Bracket	1.50
7740	P. S. G. 6	Drive Bar	1.50
7780	P. S. G. 7	Post Top	1.00
7781	S. G. 22	Hinge Strap	1.50

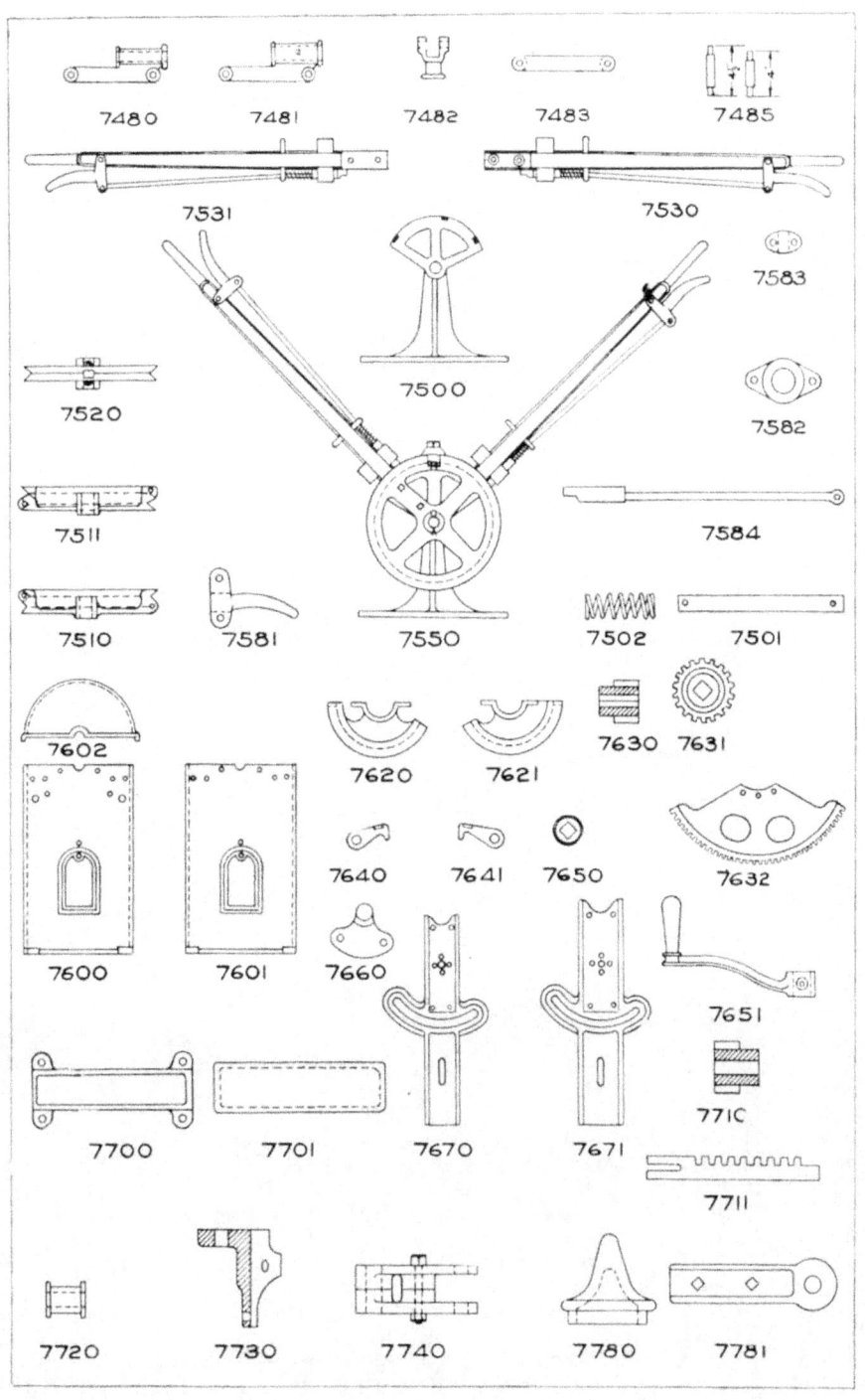

Repair Parts of Bogue and Mills Pneumatic and Mechanical Gates, Including Buda Improved Pneumatic Cylinder Gates

(Concluded)

New Pattern No.	Old Pattern No.	Name of Castings, Finished	Price
		Pneumatic Gong Material	
7800	E. O. O.	Gong Cylinder (Brass)	$ 2.50
7801	E. O.	" Piston Rod (Cast Iron)	1.00
7802	E.	" Piston Guide	.25
7803	E. 11	" Piston Follower	.10
7804	E. 86	" Piston Leather 2"	.25
7805	E. O. 1	Clamp for Pneumatic Bell Cylinder	
7806	E. O. 2	Cap for Pneumatic Bell Cylinder	.50
7820	E. 81	Gong Spring	.10
7821	E. 82	" Hammer	.35
7822	E. 83	" Ratchet	.50
7823	E. 1	" Hammer Stand	.25
7830	E. 84	" Cut-off (Brass)	.50
7840	85	Gong complete with Pole and Tower Fittings	15.00
		Automatic Gong and Farm Bell Material	
7900	E. 72	10" Steel Gong only	2.00
7901	E. 73	12" Steel Gong only	2.50
7902	A. 1	Bell only	1.25
7910	H. G.	Gong Frame complete for 10" or 12" Gong	2.00
7911	A. G.	Gong Frame only	1.50
7912	A.	Bell Frame for Swinging Bell	.50
7913	A. O.	" Yoke for Swinging Bell	.50
7914	69	" Frame for Stationary Bell	.50
7915	65	" Crank for Swinging Bell	.10
7920	H. G. 1	Gong Hammer for H. G.	.25
7922	A. G. H.	Gong Hammer with Dog Spring	.50
7923	66	Bell Clapper	.15
7924	A. G. R.	Gong Ratchet	.50
7930	H. G. 2	Gong Latch for H. G. (7910)	.25
7931	E. 79	Gong Latch for E. 74 (7941)	.35
7940	H. G. A.	Gong Frame complete for 10" or 12" gong	2.00
7941	E. 74	Gong Frame complete for 10" or 12" gong	2.50
7942	A. G. A.	Gong Frame complete for 10" gong	2.50
7950	H. G. 10	Gong complete with 10" steel gong	4.00
7951	H. G. 12	Gong complete with 12" steel gong	5.00
7952	E. 7410	Gong complete with 10" steel gong	4.50
7953	E. 7412	Gong complete with 12" steel gong	5.50
7954	A. G. 10	Gong complete with 10" steel gong and ratchet	5.00
7955	68	Swinging Bell, complete	2.50
7956	70	Stationary Bell, complete	2.00
7960	67	Bell Eye Bolt for Swinging Bell	.10
7961	71	Bell Eye Bolt for Stationary Bell	.10

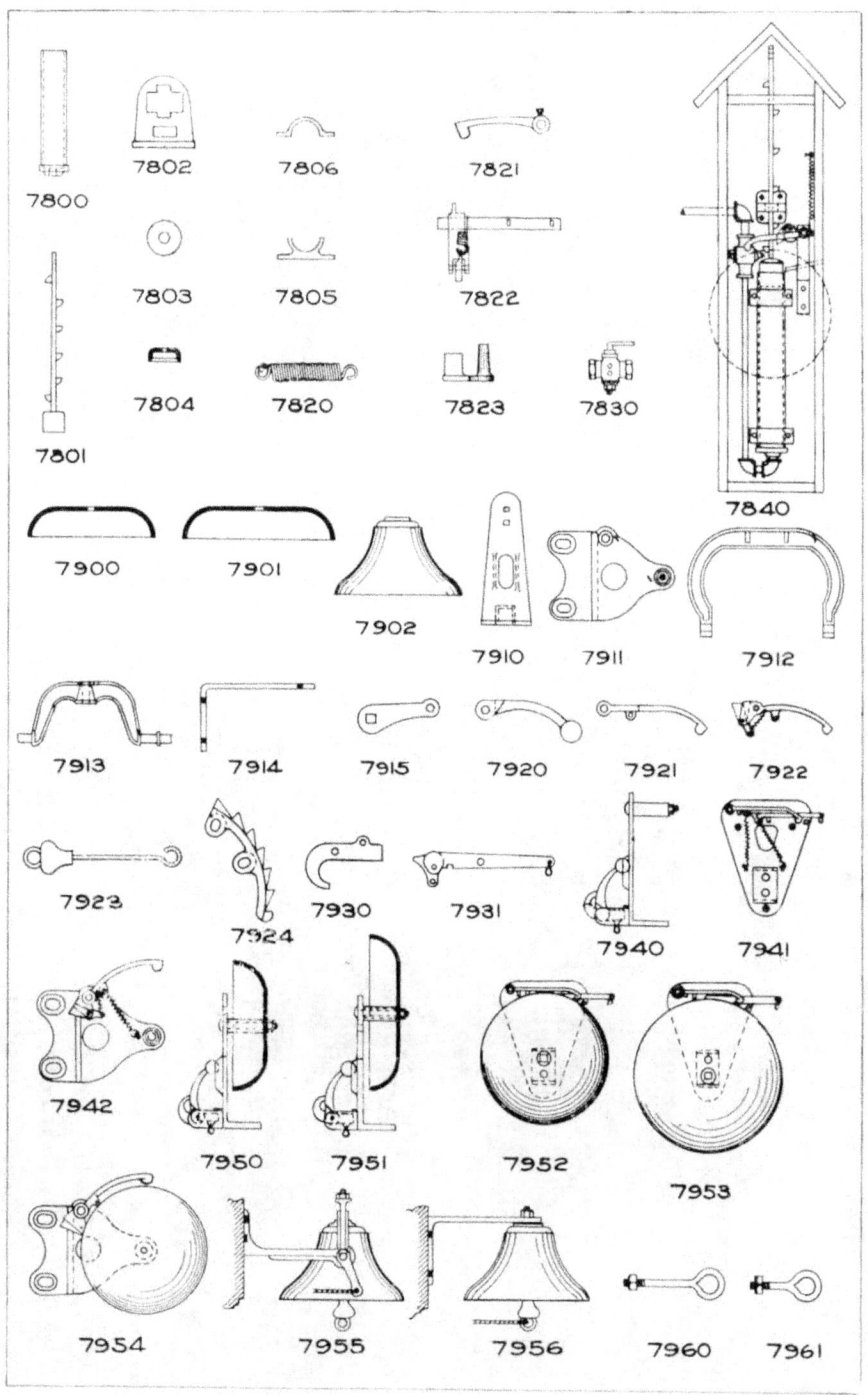

Fig. 1—Wheel spinning, jolting and damage to flange is avoided by using Buda replacers, the construction of which allows the tread instead of the flange to come in first contact, the broader surface of the tread giving a good frictional grip to start the ascent. This is particularly essential in replacing locomotives and a great advantage in the rerailment of cars.

Fig. 2—When the ascent is nearly made the wheel on the inner replacer gradually rises upon the flange and the deflection to the rail is positive. The flange on the outer wheel does not bear upon the replacer at any time.

Buda Car and Engine Replacers

Fig. 3—Inside replacer. This should not be placed so close to the rail that no space is left for flange to enter. Note gain cut in replacer that it may rest on base of rail also calks which press into the ties.

Fig. 4—Outside replacer. This should be placed close as possible to the rail. It is seldom that spiking becomes necessary but is sometimes advisable in cases of badly slewed trucks and poor road bed

Buda replacers are perfectly designed to accomplish replacements positively and with no damage to equipment. Their shape and general construction offer many advantages not found in other makes, the various features being herein described and illustrated. The replacers are furnished in three sizes and it is advisable to have the size and rail weight correspond. Particularly is it necessary to have the replacers large enough; for if the smallest size is used with the heaviest rail the wheels would not be raised high enough. Attention to the following table should, however, prevent any mistakes in ordering.

No. 1, for rail up to 60 pounds; weight per pair 197 pounds
No. 2, for rail 60 to 80 pounds; weight per pair 220 pounds
No. 3, for rail 80 to 100 pounds; weight per pair 240 pounds

As the load placed upon a pair of replacers is often tremendous, and as there is no way of determining in advance how often, or how severely they may be taxed in this respect, it requires no argument to make plain the fact that provisions should be made for any emergency. It is insufficient that replacers be strong enough only to effect a certain proportion of replacements. To so gamble on probabilities is to court delays, damage to equipment and what not, and to occasion useless expense.

Understanding this, most roads demand replacers heavy enough to be thoroughly substantial. We find, however, an occasional instance where lighter replacers are favored. Were we inclined to sell our replacers on claims of lightness, rather than serv-

No. 5—Inside replacer placed for rerailment of engine. Note gradual and easy incline. No interference with brake rigging.

Fig. 6—Same as Fig. 2 but photographed from different position.   Wheels are shown just sliding on rails

iceability, it would be a simple matter to reduce the amount of material we now use and effect, for ourselves, a substantial saving in the cost of production. Selling our replacers by the pair—and not by weight—it is obvious that our aim is to give the user what we know is required for reliable service even at a higher cost to ourselves.

Buda replacers are designed on correct scientific principles with proper provisions for weight to be supported on the arch; and the thickness of material is in proportion to strains and concussions encountered. Practical experience shows lighter construction, which may be cheaper in first cost, proves unsatisfactory in service.

While ample strength is secured by our construction, dead and useless weight is eliminated. The distribution of metal is seen on examination of the underside of the shell which is reinforced with six strong ribs and where also will be seen convenient handles provided to facilitate carrying. In the small size these handles are in the center. The two larger sizes have handles at each end as well, so that should the distance they are to be carried be considerable, the weight may be divided between two men.

The contour of Buda Replacers makes them the most successful of any other style in effecting replacements quickly and without damage to the track or equipment.

Unlike other replacers of this type, it will be noted that there is no abrupt arch at the end to be surmounted before the ascent is started. The slope is easy and gradual from start to finish. This prevents the usual jarring and jolting with the results which follow.

It will be observed that there is a groove at the end which protects the flange and allows the tread to first come in contact with the replacer, thus securing a better grip through the wider expanse of metal; the wheel not rising on the flange until it is ready to slide to the rail, and then the rise is accomplished so gradually that no injury occurs whatever. This arrangement which allows the tread to come in first contact is particularly valuable in replacing locomotives, as it does away with the wheel-spinning that ordinarily occurs in attempting to secure sufficient friction to start the ascent of those styles of replacers, blunt arched ends of which allow only the flange to come in contact.

The easy slope of the Buda Replacer, combined with the groove, which

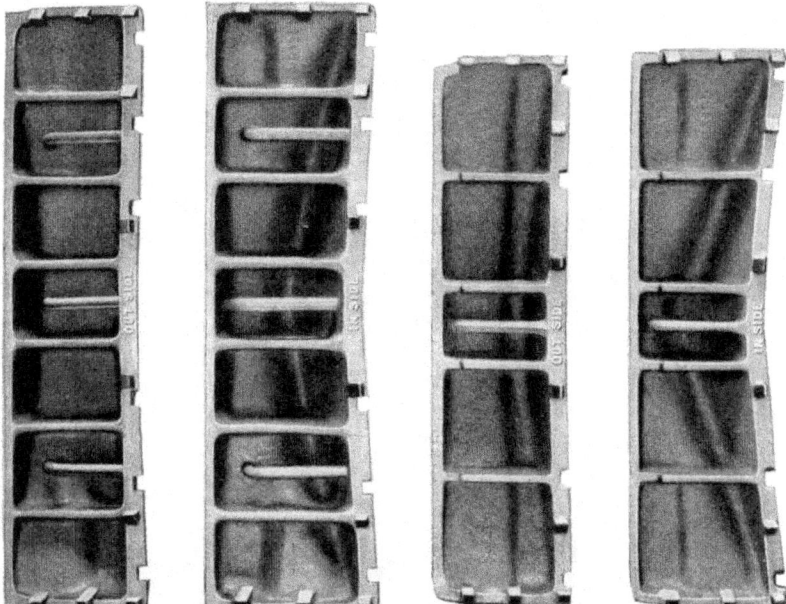

Underside of Replacers No. 2 and 3   Underside of Replacer No. 1

The strong construction of Buda replacers may be seen here. Six reinforcing ribs add to the natural resistance of the general form of shell. Also it may be seen that all dead weight is eliminated. We cannot recommend those forms of replacers which are too light to be serviceable.

makes it possible for the tread, instead of the flange, to secure the grip necessary to start the ascent, places our style far in advance of any other for re-railing locomotives or cars.

With many forms heretofore used, the complaint is common that wheels run across and drop on the opposite side. Such a thing is impossible with Buda Replacers. The deflection is absolutely positive. Repeated trials and extensive practical use have demonstrated perfect freedom from any trouble of this nature where our style is used.

Another feature which should not be overlooked is the gain cut into the inner wall, so that one side of the replacer can rest upon the rail. The proper relation between the height of the replacer and rail is therefore always maintained and overcoming at the same time the tendency of the derailed engine or car to loosen the ties from the rail during the process of replacement. This latter possibility is one that occasionally assumes considerable importance, particularly when the derailment occurs on trestles, bridges and the like.

It should be noted, also, that the Buda Replacers are equipped with long sharp calks which, under ordinary circumstances, fasten themselves firmly enough into the ties to make spiking unnecessary. If, however, the truck is badly slewed, or the derailment takes place where the track is low or filled with sand, mud or ice, spiking is advisable. To hold the spikes, square notches are cast along a rim provided for that purpose. We consider these notches have some advantage over complete holes, for the replacers may be more quickly released, and, as time is an important item on a railroad, anything that promotes even a small saving of it is to be considered.

Neither in length nor height do Buda Replacers interfere with brake rigging of cars or engines. They may be used on any equipment, including engines where the drivers are so close together as to prohibit the application of some styles.

We guarantee our style of replacers to be stronger and effect replacements more rapidly and satisfactorily than any other. Successful from the start, their sale has rapidly increased, and their merit has promoted their increasing use on those roads where small trial orders were at first placed.

They have never been abandoned after trial.

Wrecking Inclines

No. 1

No. 2

Wrecking Frogs—Old Style

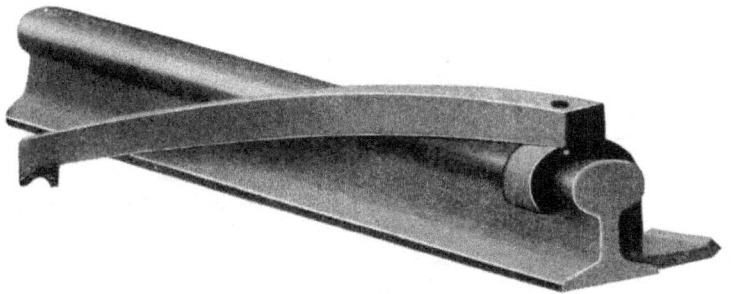

No. 1

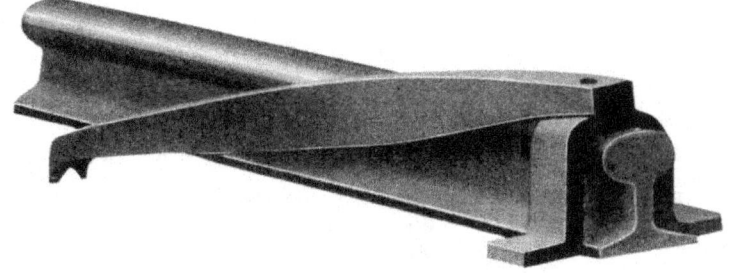

No. 2

Cinder Pit Ties

Style No. 1

Weight, 1600 Lbs.

Style No. 2

Weight, 1100 Lbs.

Made of Cast Iron.
Can be made for any section of Rail.

The Buda Foundry & Manufacturing Company

Buda Stoves

FOR STATIONS, ROUNDHOUSES AND CABOOSES

For many years we have made stoves for cabooses, roundhouses, railroad stations, watchmen's cabins, towers, factories and warehouses; the styles and sizes are shown in the following pages.

In purchasing stoves of this nature it is quite important to know that they are made of a substantial grade of iron and that they are well constructed throughout.

Our stoves may be ordered with every assurance of obtaining good material. They are neat in design and have an attractive appearance, which distinguishes them from ordinary stoves of this kind.

Our facilities for casting enable us to furnish stoves without delay, and as we make them in considerable quantities to supply the orders which come to us, we have arranged an economical system for handling the output, so that we can afford to quote somewhat lower prices than would be possible were we filling only an occasional order.

Our roundhouse pattern is made in one size only, it will be noted; but the other styles are made in several sizes to suit conditions.

Where a thoroughly reliable stove is desired, we recommend any we make. We do not, however, charge more for them on this account. Our prices will be found competitive with stoves made of lower grade iron.

Giant Stove

Roundhouse pattern. Fire-pot, 26 inches inside diameter. Weight, 1,100 pounds.

Buda Station Stove

Size	Largest Inside Diameter of Fire-pot	Weight
No. 1	17½ inches	570 lbs.
No. 2	15 inches	400 lbs.
No. 3	11½ inches	235 lbs.

Buda Stoves

"Volcano" Station Stove

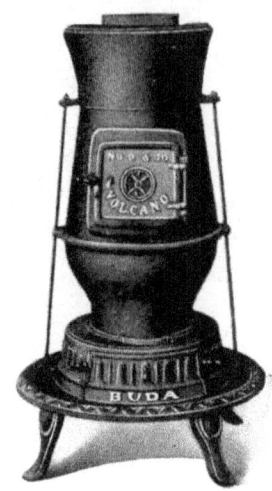

"Volcano" Way-Car or Caboose Stove

Size	Largest Inside Diameter of Fire-pot	Weight
No. 0	14 inches	275 lbs.
No. 1	17 inches	345 lbs.
No. 2	18 inches	450 lbs.
No. 3	20 inches	665 lbs.
Way-Car	14 inches	285 lbs.

"Lewis" Way-Car or Caboose Stove

Inside Diameter of fire-pot, 14 inches.
Weight, 350 pounds.

Paige Iron Works Department

MANUFACTURERS OF

Railroad Frogs, Switches, Crossings, Rail Braces, Etc., for Steam and Electric Railroads

Also Special Track Layouts for Street Railways, for either Trolley or Conduit Construction

We carry in stock and use Standard Section of T Rail, High T Rail and Girder Rail

The illustrations which follow are of a general nature and include a few standard designs as well. When desired we can furnish detailed blue prints.

The scope of work of this nature done by us is broad and compasses special layouts and work of every nature. Our equipment is perfectly designed with a view of economically handling every phase of construction from the plain rail to the finished product. This embodies liberal shop room, traveling cranes, electrically driven machine tools and other conveniences important to saving of time and expense. We are thus enabled to expedite deliveries and make quotations based on economies accomplished without detriment to the construction or quality of the work.

We have developed and maintained an extensive engineering force that devotes its time exclusively to this branch of our business and is therefore familiar with all the best practices in use in various parts of the country. Without expense to the purchaser we will send, upon application, an engineer to make survey, submit plans and specifications and furnish estimates of any special work required.

We desire to call particular attention to our "Hard Center Construction." The greatly increased traffic conditions call for increased strength of track special work. We use at point of maximum wear **a special steel, which is hard and tough** and all construction is reinforced and guaranteed. Before shipment all work is fitted, thus avoiding the delay and expense of getting it on the ground and discovering inaccuracies at a vital time when the work is wanted for use.

The Buda Foundry & Manufacturing Company

Special Layout Northwestern Elevated Railway, Chicago. Wilson Avenue Terminal

The Buda Foundry & Manufacturing Company

Special Layout Union Elevated Railway, Chicago. Fifth Avenue and Lake Street

The Buda Foundry & Manufacturing Company

Double Crossover. Fifth Avenue Station, Metropolitan West Side Elevated Railroad

The Buda Foundry & Manufacturing Company

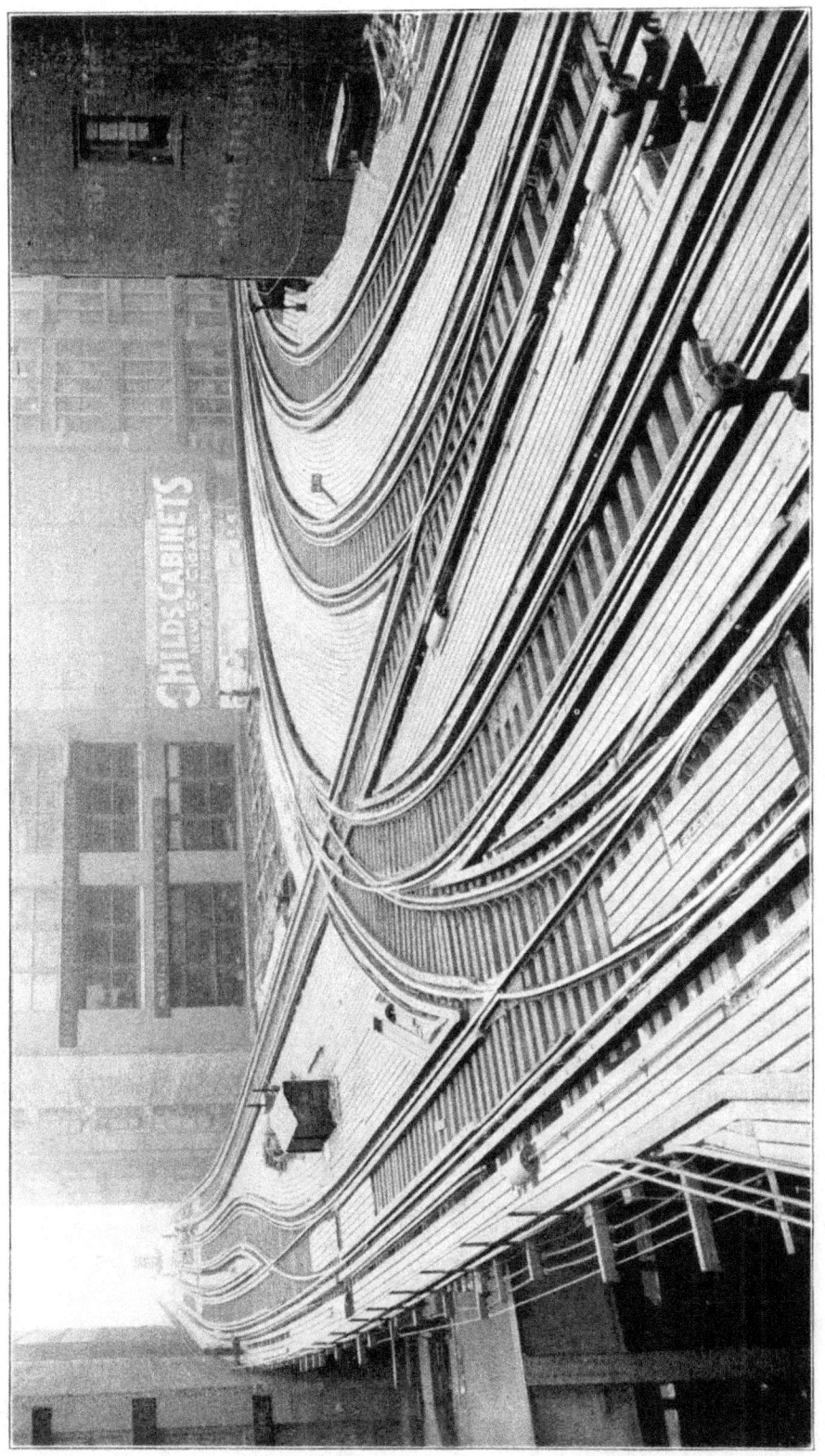

Special Layout. Market Street. Metropolitan West Side Elevated Railroad

The Buda Foundry & Manufacturing Company

Barn Layout at Wheaton, Ill. Elgin, Aurora and Chicago, Third Rail System

Hard Center Construction

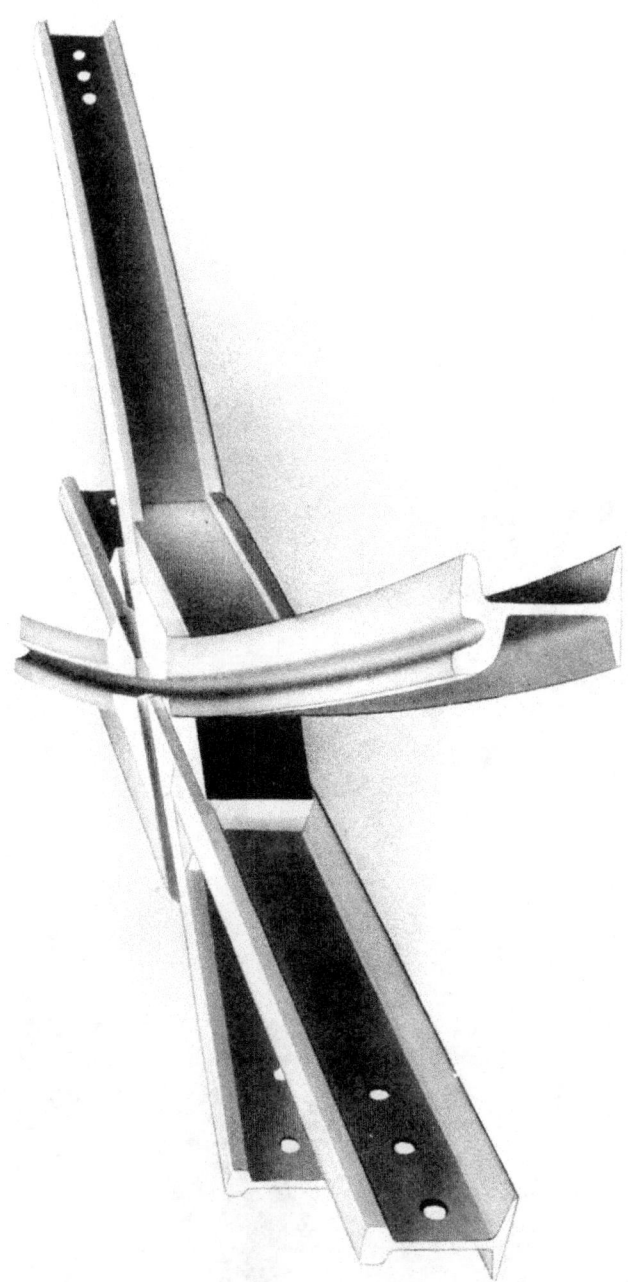

Special Work for Street Railways
TONGUE SWITCHES, FROGS, CROSSINGS, CURVES

Hard Center Construction
Removable Manganese Steel inserts at the points of maximum wear. The entire structure cast-welded into one integral piece.

Standard Construction
All wearing parts are of Rail. Bolted together.
STANDARD T-RAIL, HIGH T-RAIL, GIRDER GUARD RAIL

Buda Manganese-Center Frog

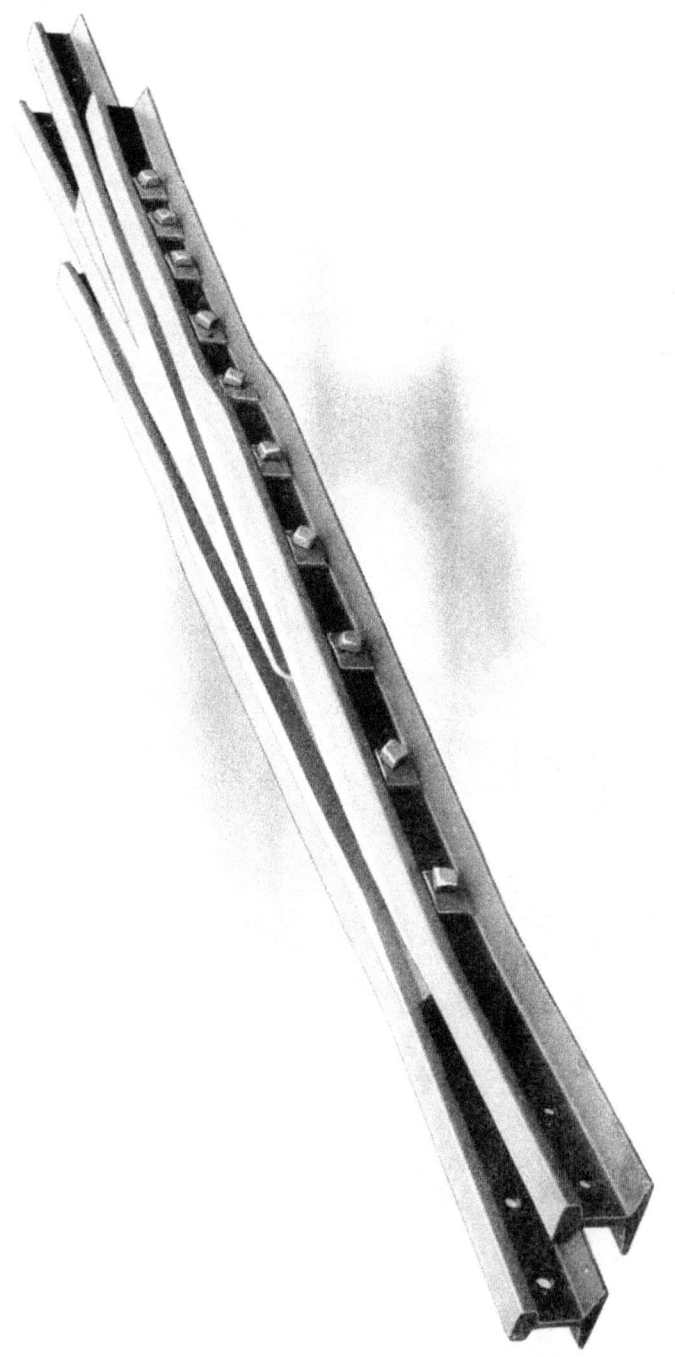

The Best Frog for Railroad Service

For High Speed Main Line Service. Will outwear three to five ordinary Frogs. We are prepared to furnish equal construction for crossings of all angles

Rigid Frogs

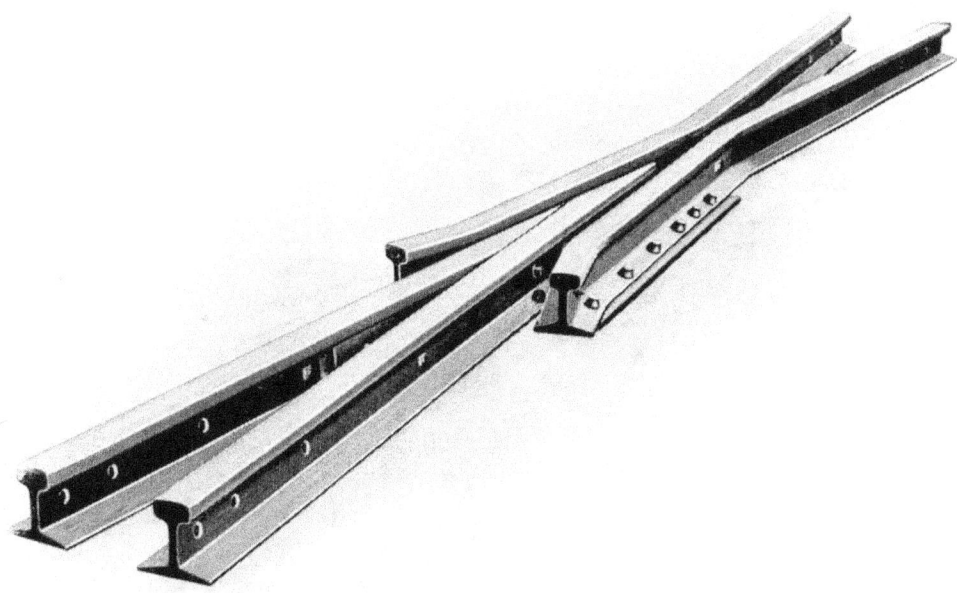

Style 38 H
Riveted.

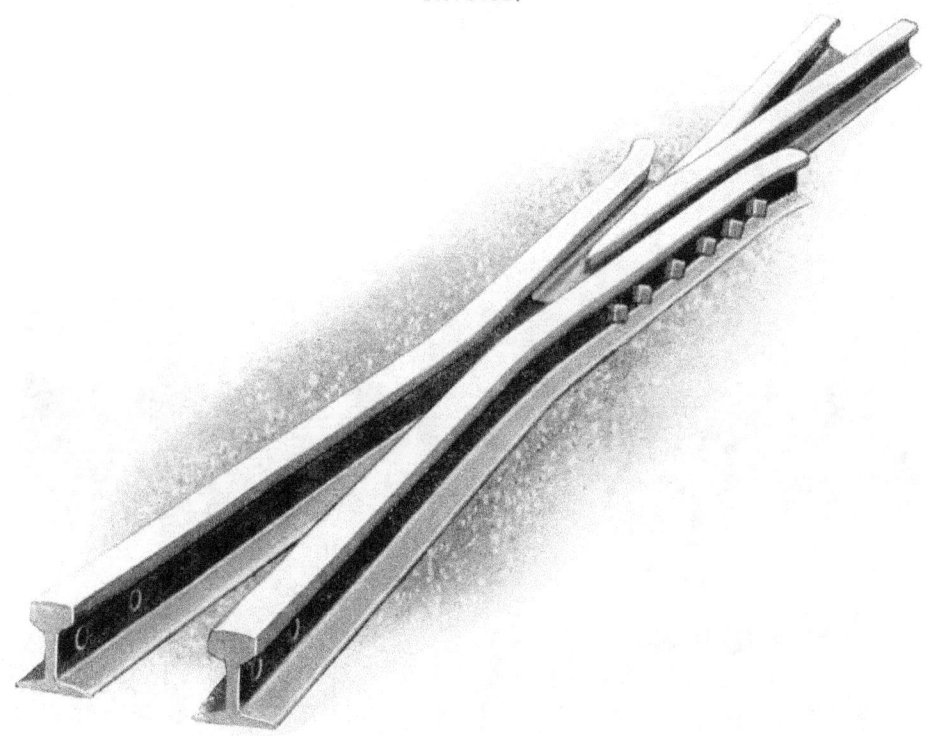

Style 39 H
Bolted and Filled.

Rigid Frogs

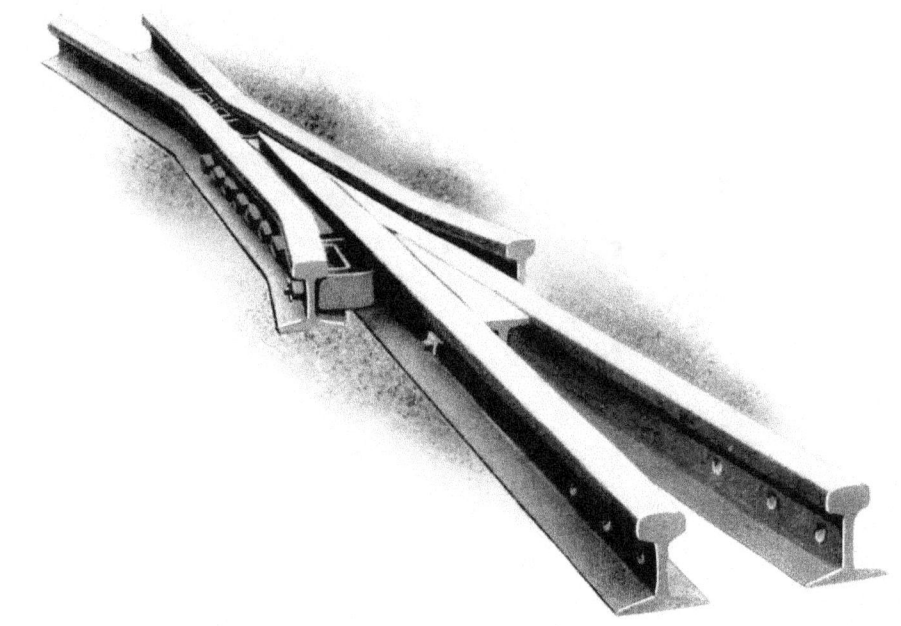

Style 39 H, with Crotch Filler and Foot Guards

Bolted and Filled.

Spring Washers

Made of spring steel. Beveled to fit angle of frog. Will take up stretch of bolt and prevent bolt turning.

Foot Guards

Pressed Steel.

Spring Frogs

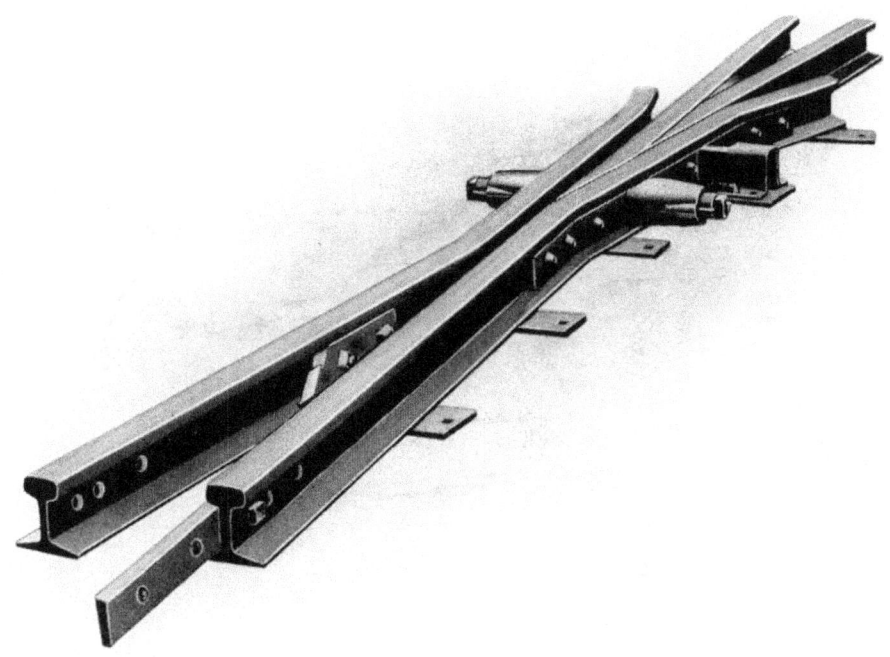

Style 40 H
Bolted Construction—Tie Plates Reinforced.

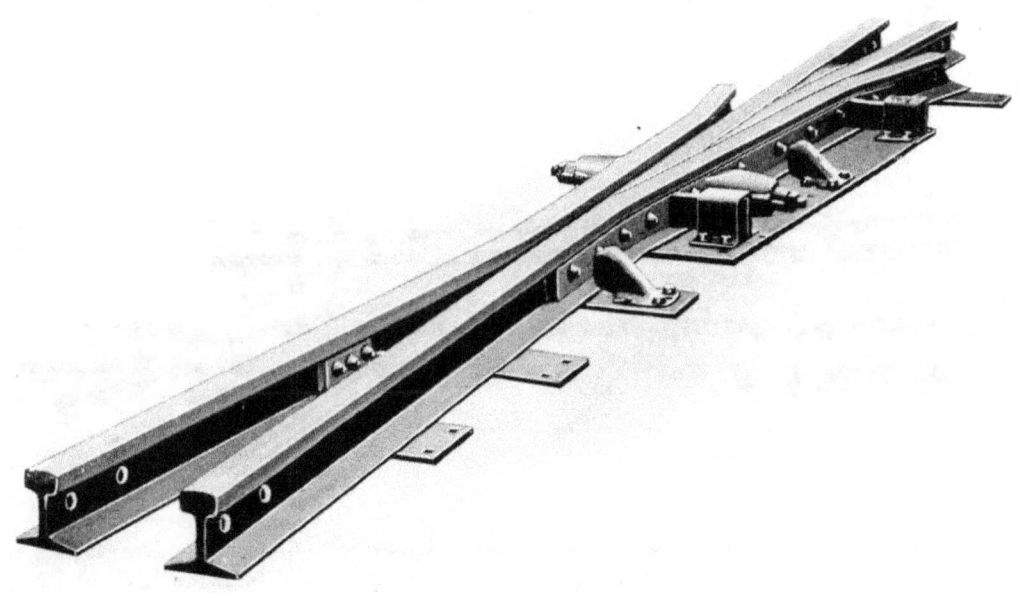

Style 151 H
Bolted and Filled—Riveted to Large Plate—Reinforced.

Crossings

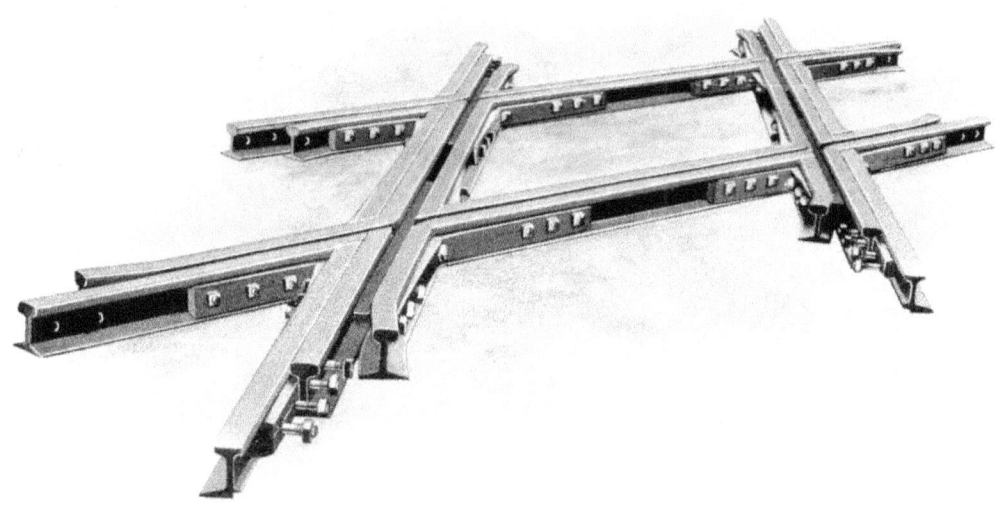

Style 115 H

Steam and Electric Crossing—Long Easing Rail—Forged Strap.

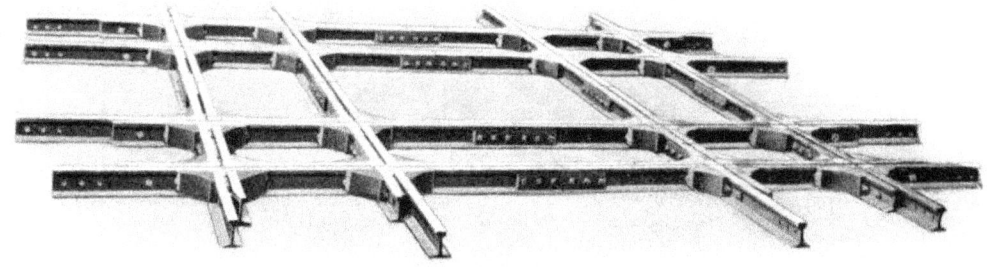

Double Track Electric Crossing

Hard Center Inserts at Point of Greatest Wear.

The Buda Foundry & Manufacturing Company

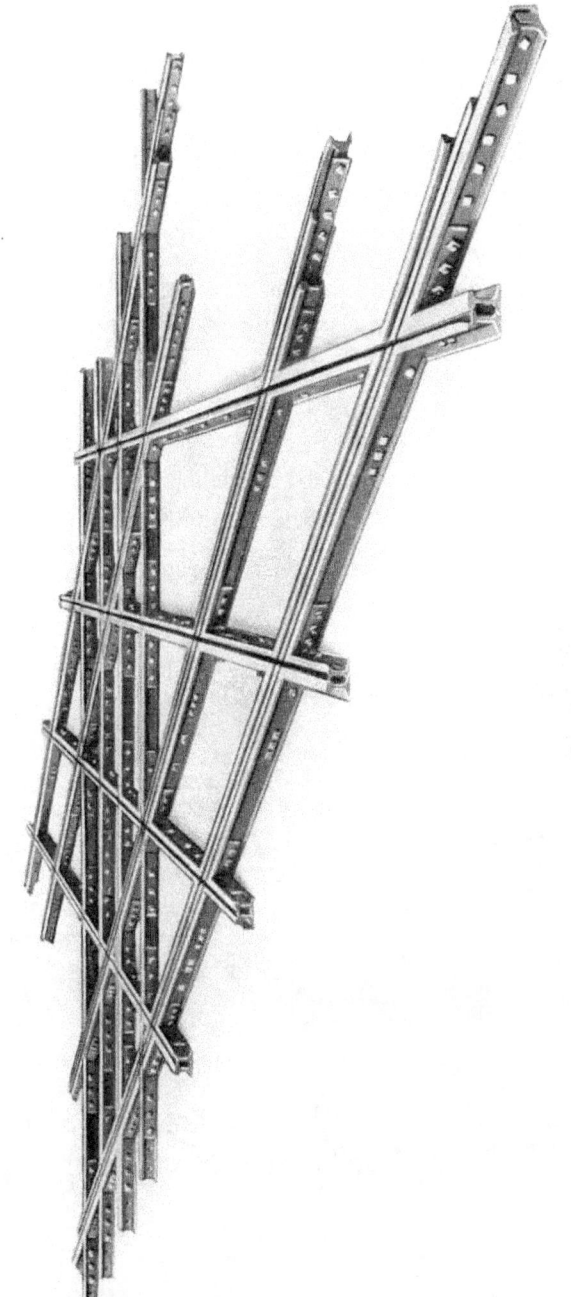

Special Layout

Double track steam R. R. crossing the intersection of two double track electric Railways, Division and Halsted Streets, Chicago.

The Buda Foundry & Manufacturing Company

Split Switches

WE ILLUSTRATE BUT A FEW STYLES OF CONSTRUCTION

We make no attempt to show all the styles of construction in the following pages, but illustrate a few general styles only. Style 73-H shown herewith can be used as a simple form of switch. In order to meet increased demand this style can, however, be added to. It can be made adjustable by use of the adjustable rods shown on page 309. Rail braces can be added; the point rails can be reinforced either on one side or on both sides of the web, for especially hard service. We recommend flat steel riveted to the web of rail. It is customary to omit the second and third rod on reinforced switches.

Style 73 H

With Horizontal Rigid Rods and Clips.

Split Switches

Style 154 H

With Special Rigid Horizontal Head Rod and Three Vertical Tie Rods and Eight Braces.

Style 153 H

Reinforced with 2½ x 4 Structural Angle—One Adjustable Insulated Head Rod. Ten Braces.

The Buda Foundry & Manufacturing Company

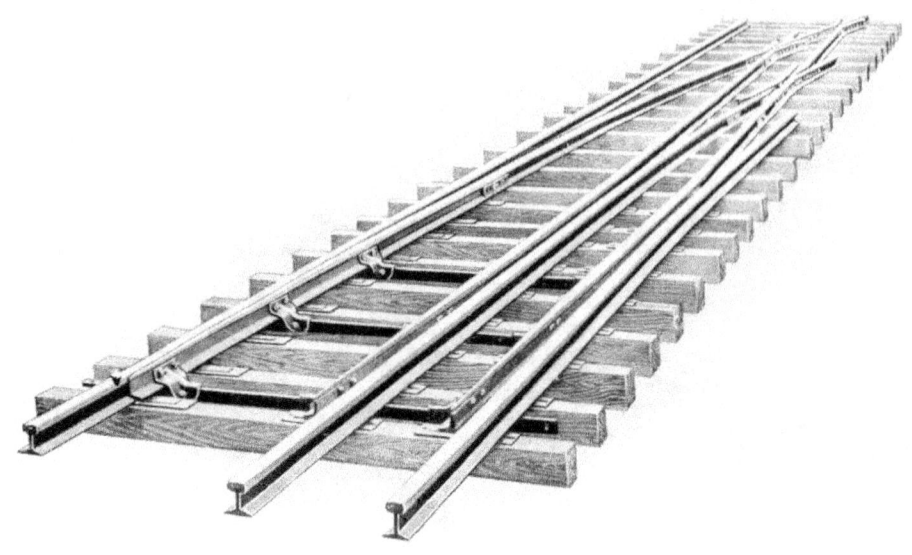

Style 28 H. 3 Rail
Vertical Rigid Rods.
For Standard and Narrow Gauges

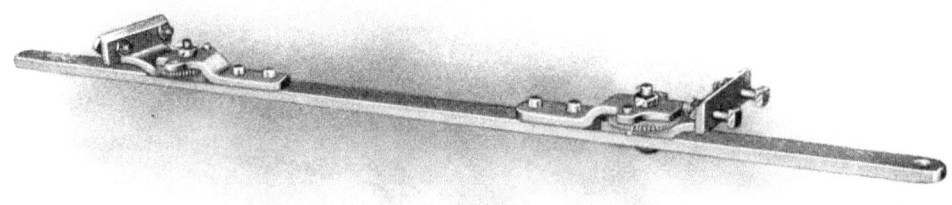

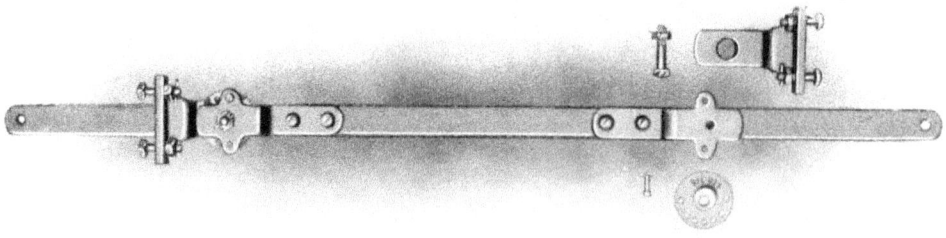

Eccentric Adjustments for Split Switches (Patented)

This type of adjustment has proven very successful and our latest form shown above is a great improvement over other forms. The switch can be adjusted without disconnecting the rails or stand.

Split Switch Plates and Rods

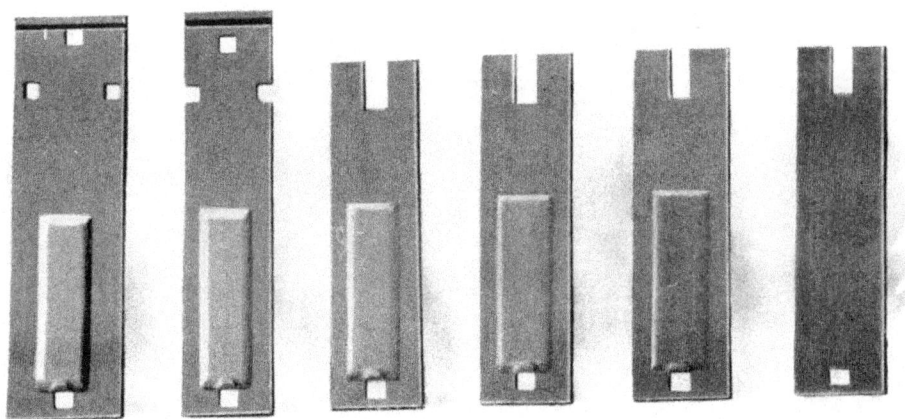

Slide Plates, pressed from one piece.
With or without braces.

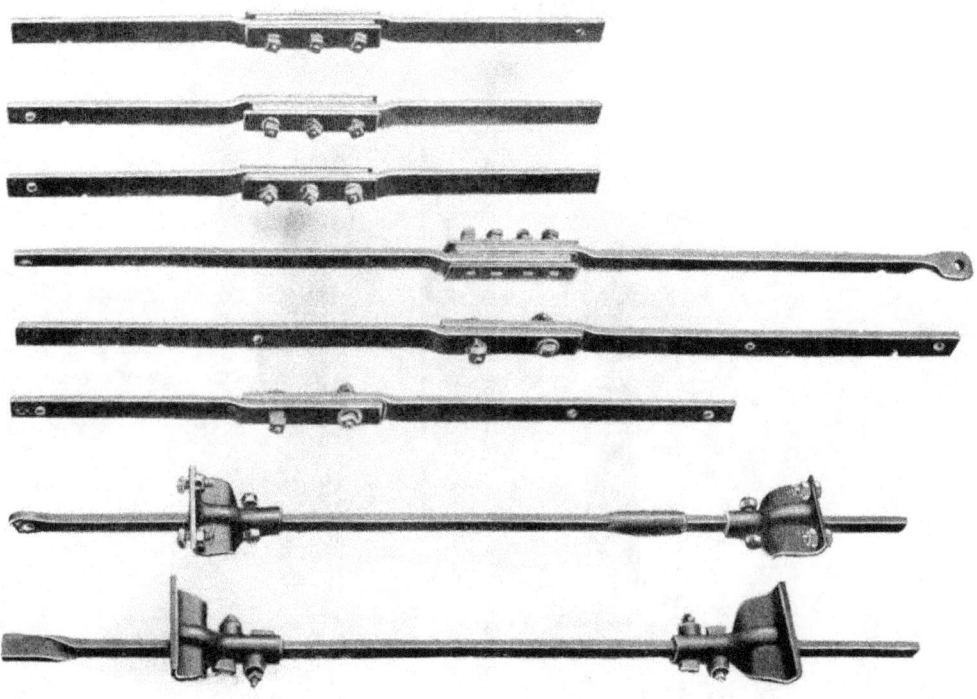

Insulated Rods.   Adjustable Rods.   Rigid Rods

Rail Braces

To fit any Rail, 30 to 100 pounds per yard.

Compromise Joints

Standard "T"   High "T"   Girder

To fit any sections of Rail.

Fixtures for Stub Switches

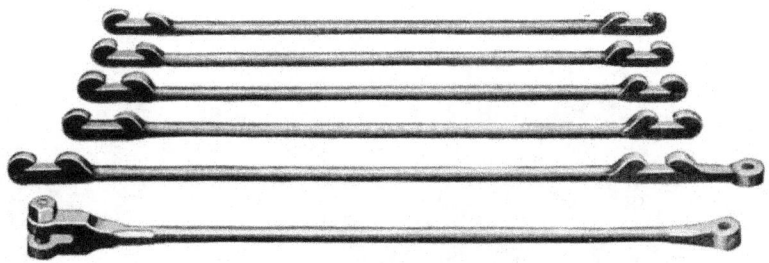

Eye Rods   Tie Rods   Connecting Rods

For Standard and Narrow Gauge.
Any section of Rail.

Head Chairs

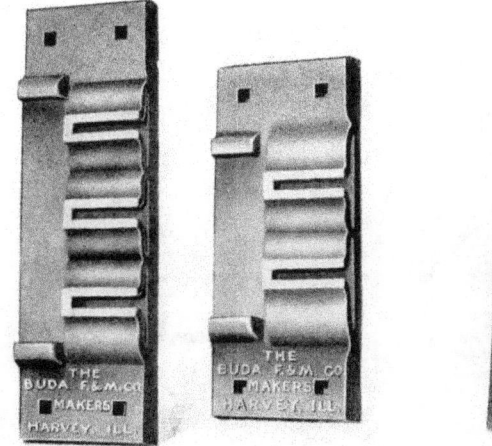  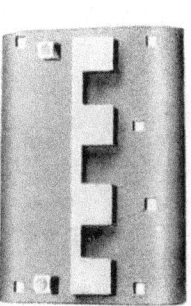

Cast Iron   Wrought Iron

For Two-way and Three-way Switches.
For any section of Rail.

Pressed Steel Switch Clips

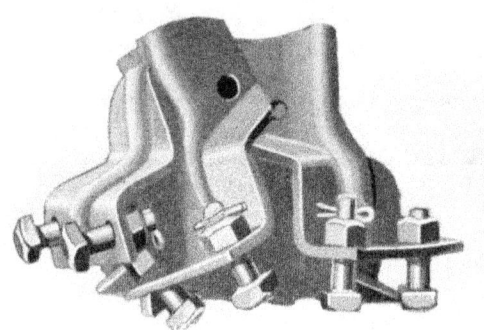 

For Vertical Rods

For Horizontal Rods

Useful Information

NAUTICAL MEASURE

A Nautical or Sea Mile (a knot) is the length of a minute of longitude of the earth at the equator at the level of the sea. It is assumed = 6086.07 feet = 1.152664 statute or land miles by the United States Coast Survey.

3 nautical miles = 1 league.

DRY MEASURE

UNITED STATES ONLY

Struck Bush.	Pecks.	Quarts.	Pints.	Gallons	Cubic Inch.
1	4	32.	64	8.	2150.
	1	8.	16	2.	537.6
		1.	2	0.25	67.2
		0.5	1	0.125	33.6
		4.	8	1.	268.8

A Gallon of Liquid Measure = 231 cubic inches.

A Heaped Bushel = 1¼ struck bushels. The cone in a heaped bushel must not be less than 6 inches high.

A Barrel of U. S. Hydraulic Cement = 300 to 310 lbs., usually, and of genuine Portland cement = 425 lbs.

To reduce U. S. dry measures to British imperial of the same name, divide by 1.032.

MEASURES OF LENGTH

FRENCH AND BRITISH

FRENCH.	BRITISH.			
	Inches.	Feet.	Yards.	Miles.
Millimetre	.039368	.00328		
Centimetre	.39368	.03280		
Decimetre	3.9368	.32807	.109357	
Metre	39.368	3.2807	1.09357	
Decametre	393.68	32.807	10.9357	
Hectometre		328.07	109.357	.0621346
Kilometre		3280.7	1093.57	.6213466
Myriametre		32807.	10935.7	6.213466

U. S.	French.	U. S.	French
1 inch	= .0254 metres.	1 yard	.9144 metres.
1 foot	.30479 "	1 mile	160.931 "

Circumference of circle = diameter x 3.1416.
Diameter of circle = circumference x 0.3183.
Side of square of equal periphery as circle = diameter x 0.7854.
Diameter of circle of equal periphery as square = side x 1.2732.
Side of an inscribed square = diameter of circle x 0.7071.
Length of arc = No. of degrees x diameter x 0.008727.

Table

Showing the Number of Feet, Board Measure, contained in a Piece of Joist, Scantling or Timber of the Sizes given

Size in Inches.	Length in Feet of Joists, Scantling and Timber.												
	12	14	16	18	20	22	24	26	28	30	42	44	45
2x 4	8	9	11	12	13	15	16	17	19	20	28	29	30
2x 6	12	14	16	18	20	22	24	26	28	30	42	44	45
2x 8	16	19	21	24	27	29	32	35	37	40	53	58	60
2x10	20	23	27	30	33	37	40	43	47	50	70	74	75
2x12	24	28	32	36	40	44	48	52	56	60	84	88	90
3x 4	12	14	16	18	20	22	24	26	28	30	42	44	45
3x 6	18	21	24	27	30	33	36	39	42	45	63	66	68
3x 8	24	28	32	36	40	44	48	52	56	60	84	88	90
3x10	30	35	40	45	50	55	60	65	70	75	105	110	113
3x12	36	42	48	54	60	66	72	78	84	90	126	132	135
4x 4	16	19	21	24	27	29	32	35	37	40	56	58	60
4x 6	24	28	32	36	40	44	48	52	56	60	84	88	90
4x 8	32	37	43	48	53	59	64	69	75	80	112	118	120
4x10	40	47	53	60	67	73	80	87	93	100	140	146	150
4x12	48	56	64	72	80	88	96	104	112	120	168	176	180
6x 6	36	42	48	54	60	66	72	78	84	90	126	132	130
6x 8	48	56	64	72	80	88	96	104	112	120	168	176	180
6x10	60	70	80	90	100	110	120	130	140	150	210	220	225
6x12	72	84	96	108	120	132	144	156	168	180	250	265	270
8x 8	64	75	85	96	107	117	128	139	149	160	224	234	240
8x10	80	93	107	120	133	147	160	173	187	200	280	294	300
8x12	96	112	128	144	160	176	192	208	224	240	336	352	360
10x10	100	117	133	150	167	183	200	217	233	250	350	366	375
10x12	120	140	160	180	200	220	240	260	280	300	420	440	450
12x12	144	168	192	216	240	264	288	312	336	360	504	528	540
12x14	168	196	224	252	280	308	336	364	392	420	588	616	630
14x14	196	229	261	294	327	359	392	425	457	490	686	716	735

Metals

Weight Per Square Foot

Thickness.	Wro't Iron.	Cast Iron.	Steel.	Copper.	Brass.	Lead.	Zinc.
	Lbs.	Lbs.	Lbs.	Lbs.	Lbs.	Lbs.	Lbs.
1/16 inch	2.51	2.34	2.55	2.89	2.67	3.69	2.34
1/8 "	5.03	4.69	5.10	5.78	5.35	7.38	4.68
3/16 "	7.58	7.03	7.66	8.67	8.02	11.07	7.02
1/4 "	10.07	9.38	10.21	11.56	10.7	14.76	9.36
5/16 "	12.58	11.73	12.76	14.45	13.37	18.45	11.7
3/8 "	15.10	14.07	15.31	17.34	16.05	22.14	14.04
7/16 "	17.62	16.42	17.87	20.23	18.72	25.83	16.34
1/2 "	20.14	18.77	20.42	23.12	21.4	29.53	18.72
9/16 "	22.65	21.11	22.97	26.01	24.07	33.22	21.08
5/8 "	25.17	23.46	25.52	28.90	26.75	36.91	23.44
11/16 "	27.69	25.81	28.08	31.97	29.42	40.60	25.80
3/4 "	30.21	28.15	30.63	34.68	32.1	44.29	28.13
13/16 "	32.72	30.50	33.18	37.57	35.19	47.98	30.49
7/8 "	35.24	32.85	35.73	40.69	38.28	51.67	32.81
15/16 "	37.76	35.19	28.28	43.35	41.37	55.37	35.17
1 "	40.28	37.54	40.83	46.25	43.75	59.06	37.50

Railroad Spikes

Size measured under head.	Average No. per keg of 200 lbs.	Ties 2 feet between centres, 4 spikes per tie, makes per mile.	Rails used, weight per yard.
5½ x 9/16	375	5870 lbs.—29⅓ kegs	45 to 70
5 x 9/16	400	5170 " —26 "	40 to 56
5 x ½	450	4660 " —23⅓ "	35 to 40
4½ x ½	530	3960 " —20 "	28 to 35
4 x ½	600	3520 " —17⅔ "	24 to 35
4½ x 7/16	680	3110 " —15½ "	20 to 30
4 x 7/16	720	2910 " —14¾ "	
3½ x 7/16	900	2350 " —11 "	16 to 25
4 x ⅜	1000	2090 " —10½ "	
3½ x ⅜	1190	1780 " — 9 "	16 to 20
3 x ⅜	1240	1710 " — 8½ "	
2½ x ⅜	1342	1575 " — 7⅞ "	12 to 16

Cast Iron Pipe

Weight of a Lineal Foot

Bore in Inches.	Thickness of Metal in Inches.									
	¼	⅜	½	⅝	¾	⅞	1	1⅛	1¼	1½
	Lbs.	Lbs.	Lbs.	Lbs.	Lbs.	Lbs.	Lbs.	Lbs.	Lbs.	Lbs.
2	5.52	8.74	12.27	16.11	20.25	24.70	29.45	34.52	39.88	51.54
2½	6.75	10.58	14.73	19.18	23.95	28.99	34.36	40.04	46.02	58.91
3	7.93	12.43	17.18	22.24	27.61	32.29	39.27	45.56	52.16	66.27
3½	9.20	14.27	19.64	25.31	31.29	37.58	44.18	51.08	58.29	73.63
4	10.43	16.11	22.09	28.38	34.98	41.88	49.09	56.60	64.43	80 99
4½	11.66	17.95	24.54	31.45	38.66	46.18	54.00	62.13	70.56	88.36
5	12.89	19.79	27.00	34.52	42.34	50.47	58.91	67.65	76.70	95.72
5½	14.11	21.63	29.45	37.58	46.02	54.76	63.81	73.17	82.84	103.08
6	15.34	23.47	31.91	40.65	49.70	59.06	68.72	78.69	88.97	110.45
7	17.79	27.15	36.82	46.79	57.06	67.65	78.54	89.74	101.24	125.17
8	20.25	30.83	41.72	52.92	64.43	76.24	88.36	100.78	113.52	139.90
9	22.70	34.52	46.63	59.06	71.79	84.83	98.18	111.83	125.79	154.63
10	25.16	38.20	51.54	65.19	79.15	93.42	107.99	122.87	138.06	
11	27.61	41.88	56.45	71.33	86.52	102.01	117.81	133.92	150.33	
12	30.07	45.56	61.36	77.47	93.88	110.60	127.63	144.96	162.60	
13	32.52	49.24	66.27	93.60	101.24	119.19	137 45	156.01	174.87	
14	34.98	52.92	71.18	89.74	108.61	127.78	147.26	167.05	187.15	
15	......	56.60	76.09	95.87	115.97	136.37	157.08	178.10	199.42	
16	......	60.29	80.99	102.01	123.33	144.96	166.90	189.14	211.69	
18	......	67.65	90.81	114.28	138.06	162.14	186.53	211.23	236.23	
20	......	......	100.63	126.55	152.79	179.32	206.17	233.32	260.78	
22	......	......	110.45	138.83	167.51	196.50	225.80	255.41	285.32	
24	......	......	120.26	151.10	182.24	213.68	245.44	277.50	309 87	

Note.—For each joint add a foot in length of the pipe.

Fish Plates and Bolts

Length of Rail.	No. Joints per mile.	No. Fish Plates per mile.	No. Bolts per mile.
24 feet	440	880	1760
25 feet	422	844	1668
26 feet	406	812	1624
27 feet	391	782	1564
28 feet	377	754	1508
30 feet	352	704	1408
33 feet	320	640	1280
45 feet	235	470	940
60 feet	176	352	704

Average Number of Track Bolts in a Keg of 200 Pounds

⅞ x 3½ with Hexagon Nuts	170 Bolts
¾ x 3½ with Square Nuts	210 Bolts
¾ x 3¾ with Hexagon Nuts	220 Bolts
⅝ x 2½ with Square Nuts	370 Bolts
½ x 2½ with Square Nuts	650 Bolts
½ x 3 with Square Nuts	600 Bolts

Cross Ties

Per Mile of Single Track

From Center to Center, 18 inches	3,520 Ties
From Center to Center, 24 inches	2,641 Ties
From Center to Center, 27 inches	2,348 Ties
From Center to Center, 30 inches	2,113 Ties
From Center to Center, 33 inches	1,921 Ties
From Center to Center, 36 inches	1,761 Ties

Melting Point of Metals

Name	Fahr.	Fahr.	Authority
Platina	4593°		
Antimony	955	842	J. Lowthian Bell.
Bismuth	487	507	"
Tin (average)	475		
Lead "	622	620	"
Zinc	772	782	"
Cast Iron	2010	{ 1922 2012 White. } { 2012 2192 Gray. }	Pouilet.
Wrought Iron	2910	2733	Welding Heat "
Steel	2370	2550	
Copper (average)	2174		

General Rules

For Determining the Weight of Any Piece of Wrought Iron

One cubic foot of wrought iron	=	480 lbs.
One square foot, one inch thick	= $480/12$ =	40 lbs.
One square inch, one foot long	= $40/12$ =	$3\frac{1}{3}$ lbs.
One square inch, one yard long	= $3\frac{1}{3} \times 3$ =	10 lbs.

Hence, the weight of any piece of wrought iron in pounds per foot is equal to $10/3$ times its area in square inches.

Example.—The area of a bar $3'' \times 1'' = 3$ square inches, and its weight is 10 quarter foot.

For round iron the weight per foot may be found by taking the diameter in quarter inches, squaring it, and dividing by 6.

Example.—What is the weight of $2''$ round iron?
$2'' = 8$ quarter inches. $8^2 = 64$.
$64/6 = 10\frac{2}{3}$ lbs. per foot of $2''$ round.

Example.—What is the weight of $\frac{3}{4}''$ round iron?
$\frac{3}{4}'' = 3$ quarter inches. $3^2 = 9$.
$9/6 = 1\frac{1}{2}$ lbs. per foot of $\frac{3}{4}''$ round.

The above rules are highly convenient, and enable mental calculations of **weight** to be quickly obtained with accuracy.

M. C. B. STANDARD WHEEL AND TRACK GAUGE

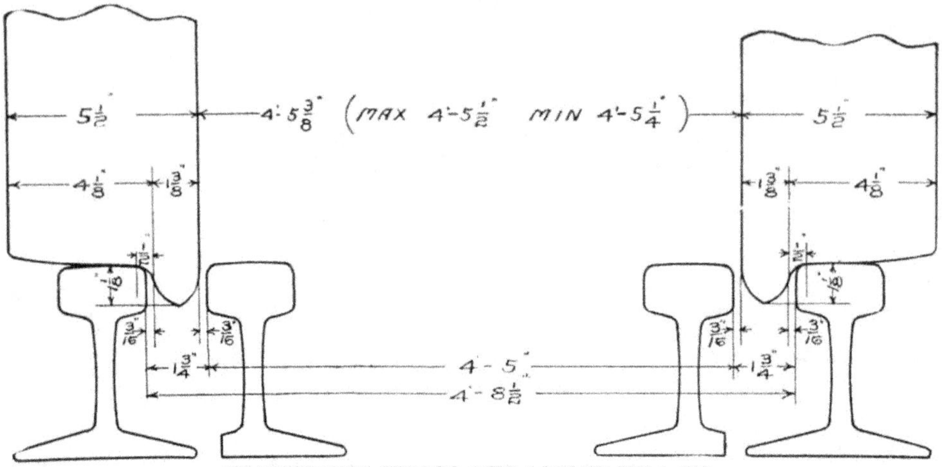

TURNOUTS FROM STRAIGHT TRACK

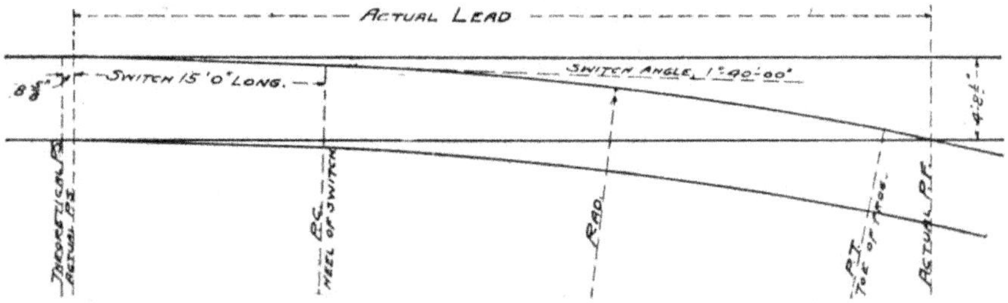

FROG NUMBER.	FROG ANGLE.	RADIUS OF CURVE.	DEGREE OF CURVE.	LEAD.	LENGTH OF CURVE.	MID. ORD. OF CURVE.
4	14° 15'	121.841'	48° 27'	43' $9\frac{1}{8}$"	26' $9\frac{1}{8}$"	$8\frac{13}{16}$"
5	11° 25'	193.991'	29° 52'	50' $4\frac{15}{16}$"	33' $0\frac{1}{8}$"	$8\frac{7}{16}$"
6	9° 32'	283.525'	20° 19'	56' 8"	38' $11\frac{1}{8}$"	8"
7	8° 10'	393.603'	14° 36'	62' $10\frac{5}{8}$"	44' $7\frac{13}{16}$"	$7\frac{5}{8}$"
8	7° 10'	516.219'	11° 8'	68' $2\frac{1}{4}$"	49' $6\frac{5}{8}$"	$7\frac{1}{8}$"
9	6° 22'	667.734'	8° 36'	73' $8\frac{1}{4}$"	54' $10\frac{13}{16}$"	$6\frac{3}{4}$"
10	5° 44'	841.083'	6° 49'	78' $11\frac{7}{16}$"	59' $8\frac{3}{8}$"	$6\frac{3}{8}$"

RIGID FROG

Name of parts and standard dimensions. Lengths to allow Anglebar Joints.

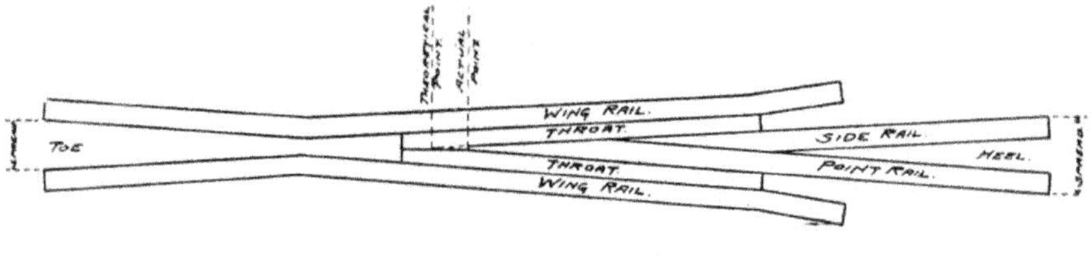

NUMBER OF FROG.	ANGLE.	LENGTH.	ACTUAL		THEORETICAL		SPREAD.	
			Point to Heel.	Point to Toe.	Point to Heel.	Point to Toe.	Heel.	Toe.
1 in 4	14° 15'	6' 0"	3' 7"	2' 5"	3' 9"	2' 3"	$11\frac{1}{4}$"	$6\frac{3}{4}$"
1 in 5	11° 25'	7' 0"	4' $3\frac{1}{2}$"	2' $8\frac{1}{2}$"	4' 6"	2' 6"	$10\frac{13}{16}$"	6"
1 in 6	9° 32'	8' 0"	5' 0"	3' 0"	5' 3"	2' 9"	$10\frac{1}{2}$"	$5\frac{1}{2}$"
1 in 7	8° 10'	9' 0"	5' $8\frac{1}{2}$"	3' $3\frac{1}{2}$"	6' 0"	3' 0"	$10\frac{5}{16}$"	$5\frac{1}{8}$"
1 in 8	7° 10'	10' 0"	6' 2"	3' 10"	6' 6"	3' 6"	$9\frac{3}{4}$"	$5\frac{1}{4}$"
1 in 9	6° 21'	11' 0"	6' $10\frac{1}{2}$"	4' $1\frac{1}{2}$"	7' 3"	3' 9"	$9\frac{5}{8}$"	5"
1 in 10	5° 44'	12' 0"	7' 7"	4' 5"	8' 0"	4' 0"	$9\frac{5}{8}$"	$4\frac{13}{16}$"

Middle Ordinates

Rad.	MIDDLE ORDINATE. 20' CH.	30' CH.	30' ARC.	CH. OF 30' ARC.	Rad.	MIDDLE ORDINATE. 20' CH.	30' CH.	30' ARC.	CH. OF 30' ARC.
30	1' 8 9/16"	4' 0 1/4"	3' 8 1/16"	28' 9 3/16"	78	0' 7 3/4"	1' 5 7/16"	1' 5 1/4"	29' 9 13/16"
31	1' 7 7/8"	3' 10 7/8"	3' 6 11/16"	28' 10 1/8"	79	0' 7 5/8"	1' 5 1/4"	1' 5 1/16"	29' 9 7/8"
32	1' 7 1/4"	3' 8 13/16"	3' 5 7/16"	28' 10 15/16"	80	0' 7 1/2"	1' 5 "	1' 4 13/16"	29' 9 7/8"
33	1' 6 5/8"	3' 7 1/16"	3' 4 3/16"	28' 11 3/4"	81	0' 7 7/16"	1' 4 13/16"	1' 4 5/8"	29' 9 15/16"
34	1' 6 1/16"	3' 5 7/8"	3' 3 3/16"	29' 0 7/16"	82	0' 7 3/8"	1' 4 9/16"	1' 4 7/16"	29' 10 "
35	1' 5 1/2"	3' 4 1/2"	3' 2 "	29' 1 1/16"	83	0' 7 1/4"	1' 4 3/8"	1' 4 1/4"	29' 10 1/16"
36	1' 5 "	3' 3 5/16"	3' 0 15/16"	29' 1 11/16"	84	0' 7 3/16"	1 4 1/4"	1' 4 "	29' 10 1/16"
37	1' 4 1/2"	3' 2 1/2"	3' 0 "	29' 2 1/4"	85	0' 7 1/16"	1' 4 "	1' 3 13/16"	29' 10 1/8"
38	1' 4 1/16"	3' 1 "	2' 11 1/16"	29' 2 3/4"	86	0' 7 "	1' 3 13/16"	1' 3 5/8"	29' 10 3/16"
39	1' 3 5/8"	3' 0 "	2' 10 1/16"	29' 3 3/16"	87	0' 6 15/16"	1' 3 5/8"	1' 3 1/2"	29' 10 1/4"
40	1' 3 1/4"	2' 11 "	2' 9 3/8"	29' 3 5/8"	88	0' 6 13/16"	1' 3 7/16"	1' 3 5/16"	29' 10 1/4"
41	1' 2 7/8"	2' 10 1/8"	2' 8 9/16"	29' 4 "	89	0' 6 3/4"	1' 3 1/4"	1' 3 1/8"	29' 10 5/16"
42	1' 2 1/2"	2' 9 1/4"	2' 7 13/16"	29' 4 3/8"	90	0' 6 11/16"	1' 3 3/16"	1' 2 15/16"	29' 10 5/16"
43	1' 2 1/8"	2' 8 7/8"	2' 7 1/16"	29' 4 3/4"	91	0' 6 5/8"	1' 2 7/8"	1' 2 13/16"	29' 10 3/8"
44	1' 1 13/16"	2' 7 5/8"	2' 6 3/8"	29' 5 1/4"	92	0' 6 9/16"	1' 2 3/4"	1' 2 5/8"	29' 10 3/8"
45	1' 1 1/2"	2' 6 7/8"	2' 5 3/4"	29' 5 5/8"	93	0' 6 1/2"	1' 2 5/8"	1' 2 1/2"	29' 10 7/16"
46	1' 1 3/16"	2' 6 3/8"	2' 5 1/16"	29' 5 5/8"	94	0' 6 3/8"	1' 2 7/16"	1' 2 5/16"	29' 10 1/2"
47	1' 0 15/16"	2' 5 1/2"	2' 4 1/2"	29' 5 15/16"	95	0' 6 5/16"	1' 2 1/4"	1' 2 3/16"	29' 10 1/2"
48	1' 0 5/8"	2' 4 7/8"	2' 3 7/8"	29' 6 1/16"	96	0' 6 1/4"	1' 2 1/8"	1' 2 1/16"	29' 10 1/16"
49	1' 0 3/8"	2' 4 1/8"	2' 3 5/16"	29' 6 3/8"	97	0' 6 1/16"	1' 2 "	1' 1 7/8"	29' 10 1/2"
50	1' 0 1/8"	2' 3 5/8"	2' 2 13/16"	29' 6 5/8"	98	0' 6 1/8"	1' 1 7/8"	1' 1 3/4"	29' 10 5/8"
51	0' 11 7/8"	2' 3 1/16"	2' 2 1/4"	29' 6 13/16"	99	0' 6 1/16"	1' 1 3/4"	1' 1 5/8"	29' 10 5/8"
52	0' 11 5/8"	2' 2 1/8"	2' 1 13/16"	29' 7 "	100	0' 6 "	1' 1 9/16"	1' 1 1/2"	29' 10 5/8"
53	0' 11 7/16"	2' 2 "	2' 1 5/16"	29' 7 3/16"	105	0' 5 3/4"	1' 0 15/16"	1' 0 13/16"	29' 10 3/4"
54	0' 11 3/16"	2' 1 1/2"	2' 0 13/16"	29' 7 3/8"	110	0' 5 7/16"	1' 0 5/16"	1' 0 1/4"	29' 10 7/8"
55	0' 11 "	2' 1 "	2' 0 3/8"	29' 7 7/16"	115	0' 5 1/4"	0' 11 13/16"	0' 11 3/4"	29' 11 "
56	0' 10 13/16"	2' 0 9/16"	1' 11 15/16"	29' 7 11/16"	120	0' 5 "	0' 11 5/16"	0' 11 1/4"	29' 11 1/16"
57	0' 10 5/8"	2' 0 1/8"	1' 11 9/16"	29' 7 7/8"	125	0' 4 13/16"	0' 10 7/8"	0' 10 13/16"	29' 11 1/8"
58	0' 10 7/16"	1' 11 13/16"	1' 11 1/16"	29' 8 "	130	0' 4 5/8"	0' 10 7/16"	0' 10 3/8"	29' 11 3/16"
59	0' 10 1/4"	1' 11 1/4"	1' 10 3/4"	29' 8 1/8"	135	0' 4 7/16"	0' 10 1/16"	0' 10 "	29' 11 1/4"
60	0' 10 1/16"	1' 10 7/8"	1' 10 3/8"	29' 8 1/4"	140	0' 4 5/16"	0 9 9/16"	0' 9 5/8"	29' 11 1/16"
61	0' 9 7/8"	1' 10 1/2"	1' 10 "	29' 8 3/8"	145	0' 4 1/8"	0' 9 3/8"	0' 9 5/16"	29' 11 3/8"
62	0' 9 3/4"	1' 10 1/8"	1' 9 11/16"	29' 8 1/2"	150	0' 4 "	0' 9 "	0' 9 "	29' 11 3/8"
63	0' 9 9/16"	1' 9 3/4"	1' 9 5/16"	29' 8 5/8"	155	0' 3 7/8"	0' 8 11/16"	0' 8 11/16"	29' 11 7/16"
64	0' 9 7/16"	1' 9 3/8"	1' 9 "	29' 8 11/16"	160	0' 3 3/4"	0' 8 1/2"	0' 8 7/16"	29' 11 7/16"
65	0' 9 5/16"	1' 9 "	1' 8 11/16"	29' 8 13/16"	165	0' 3 5/8"	0' 8 3/8"	0' 8 3/8"	29' 11 1/2"
66	0' 9 1/8"	1' 8 3/4"	1' 8 3/8"	29' 8 7/8"	170	0' 3 1/2"	0' 7 15/16"	0' 7 15/16"	29' 11 1/2"
67	0' 9 "	1' 8 3/8"	1' 8 1/16"	29' 9 "	175	0' 3 7/16"	0' 7 3/4"	0' 7 3/4"	29' 11 1/2"
68	0' 8 7/8"	1' 8 1/8"	1' 7 3/4"	29' 9 1/16"	180	0' 3 5/16"	0' 7 1/2"	0' 7 1/2"	29' 11 9/16"
69	0' 8 3/4"	1' 7 13/16"	1' 7 1/2"	29' 9 1/8"	185	0' 3 1/4"	0' 7 5/16"	0' 7 5/16"	29' 11 5/8"
70	0' 8 5/8"	1' 7 1/2"	1' 7 3/16"	29' 9 1/4"	190	0' 3 3/16"	0' 7 3/16"	0' 7 1/8"	29' 11 5/8"
71	0' 8 1/2"	1' 7 3/16"	1' 6 15/16"	29' 9 5/16"	195	0' 3 1/16"	0' 6 15/16"	0' 6 15/16"	29' 11 11/16"
72	0' 8 3/8"	1' 6 15/16"	1' 6 11/16"	29' 9 3/8"	200	0' 3 "	0' 6 3/4"	0' 6 3/4"	29' 11 11/16"
73	0' 8 1/4"	1' 6 11/16"	1' 6 7/16"	29' 9 1/2"	205	0' 2 15/16"	0' 6 9/16"	0' 6 9/16"	29' 11 11/16"
74	0' 8 1/8"	1' 6 7/16"	1' 6 3/16"	29' 9 5/8"	210	0' 2 7/8"	0' 6 7/16"	0' 6 7/16"	29' 11 11/16"
75	0' 8 1/16"	1' 6 3/16"	1' 5 15/16"	29' 9 5/8"	215	0' 2 13/16"	0' 6 1/4"	0' 6 1/4"	29' 11 11/16"
76	0' 7 15/16"	1' 5 15/16"	1' 5 11/16"	29' 9 11/16"	220	0' 2 3/4"	0' 6 1/8"	0' 6 1/8"	29' 11 3/4"
77	0' 7 13/16"	1' 5 11/16"	1' 5 1/2"	29' 9 3/4"	225	0' 2 11/16"	0' 6 "	0' 6 "	29' 11 3/4"

Degree of Curve.	Radius.	Mid. Ord. 20' CH.	30' CH.	Degree of Curve.	Radius.	Mid. Ord. 20' CH.	30' CH.
25	231.01	0' 2 5/8"	0' 5 13/16"	12	478.34	0' 1 1/4"	0' 2 13/16"
24	240.49	0' 2 1/2"	0' 5 5/8"	11	521.67	0' 1 1/8"	0' 2 9/16"
23	250.79	0' 2 3/8"	0' 5 3/8"	10	573.69	0' 1 1/16"	0' 2 5/16"
22	262.04	0' 2 5/16"	0' 5 1/8"	9	637.27	0' 15/16"	0' 2 1/16"
21	274.37	0' 2 3/16"	0' 4 15/16"	8	716.78	0' 13/16"	0' 1 7/8"
20	287.94	0' 2 1/16"	0' 4 11/16"	7	819.02	0' 3/4"	0' 1 5/8"
19	303.94	0' 2 "	0' 4 7/16"	6	955.37	0' 5/8"	0' 1 3/8"
18	319.62	0' 1 7/8"	0' 4 1/4"	5	1146.28	0' 1/2"	0' 1 3/16"
17	338.27	0' 1 3/4"	0' 4 "	4	1432.69	0' 7/16"	0' 15/16"
16	359.26	0' 1 11/16"	0' 3 3/4"	3	1910.08	0' 5/16"	0' 11/16"
15	383.06	0' 1 5/8"	0' 3 1/2"	2	2864.93	0' 3/16"	0' 7/16"
14	410.28	0' 1 7/16"	0' 3 1/4"	1	5729.65	0' 1/8"	0' 1/4"
13	441.68	0' 1 3/8"	0' 3 1/16"	..	......	......	......

Middle-Ordinates for Curving Rails

(Ordinates at the quarters are ¾ of Middle-Ordinates)

DEGREE OF CURVE.	LENGTH OF RAILS (Feet). INCHES.											DEGREE OF CURVE.
	30	28	26	24	22	20	18	16	14	12	10	
1°	$\frac{1}{4}$	$\frac{3}{16}$	$\frac{3}{16}$	$\frac{1}{8}$	$\frac{1}{8}$	$\frac{1}{8}$	$\frac{1}{16}$	$\frac{1}{16}$	$\frac{1}{16}$	$\frac{1}{16}$	$\frac{1}{16}$	1°
2°	$\frac{1}{2}$	$\frac{7}{16}$	$\frac{3}{8}$	$\frac{5}{16}$	$\frac{1}{4}$	$\frac{1}{4}$	$\frac{3}{16}$	$\frac{1}{8}$	$\frac{1}{8}$	$\frac{1}{16}$	$\frac{1}{16}$	2°
3°	$\frac{11}{16}$	$\frac{5}{8}$	$\frac{9}{16}$	$\frac{7}{16}$	$\frac{3}{8}$	$\frac{5}{16}$	$\frac{1}{4}$	$\frac{1}{4}$	$\frac{3}{16}$	$\frac{1}{8}$	$\frac{1}{16}$	3°
4°	$\frac{15}{16}$	$\frac{7}{8}$	$\frac{3}{4}$	$\frac{5}{8}$	$\frac{1}{2}$	$\frac{1}{2}$	$\frac{3}{8}$	$\frac{5}{16}$	$\frac{1}{4}$	$\frac{3}{16}$	$\frac{1}{8}$	4°
5°	$1\frac{3}{16}$	$1\frac{1}{16}$	$\frac{7}{8}$	$\frac{3}{4}$	$\frac{5}{8}$	$\frac{9}{16}$	$\frac{7}{16}$	$\frac{3}{8}$	$\frac{1}{4}$	$\frac{3}{16}$	$\frac{1}{8}$	5°
6°	$1\frac{7}{16}$	$1\frac{1}{4}$	$1\frac{1}{16}$	$\frac{15}{16}$	$\frac{13}{16}$	$\frac{5}{8}$	$\frac{1}{2}$	$\frac{7}{16}$	$\frac{5}{16}$	$\frac{1}{4}$	$\frac{3}{16}$	6°
7°	$1\frac{11}{16}$	$1\frac{1}{2}$	$1\frac{1}{4}$	$1\frac{1}{8}$	$\frac{7}{8}$	$\frac{3}{4}$	$\frac{5}{8}$	$\frac{1}{2}$	$\frac{3}{8}$	$\frac{1}{4}$	$\frac{3}{16}$	7°
8°	$1\frac{15}{16}$	$1\frac{11}{16}$	$1\frac{7}{16}$	$1\frac{3}{16}$	$1\frac{1}{16}$	$\frac{7}{8}$	$\frac{11}{16}$	$\frac{9}{16}$	$\frac{1}{2}$	$\frac{5}{16}$	$\frac{1}{4}$	8°
9°	$2\frac{1}{8}$	$1\frac{7}{8}$	$1\frac{5}{8}$	$1\frac{3}{8}$	$1\frac{1}{8}$	1	$\frac{15}{16}$	$\frac{3}{4}$	$\frac{5}{8}$	$\frac{1}{2}$	$\frac{1}{4}$	9°
10°	$2\frac{3}{8}$	$2\frac{1}{16}$	$1\frac{13}{16}$	$1\frac{1}{2}$	$1\frac{5}{16}$	$1\frac{1}{16}$	$\frac{7}{8}$	$\frac{11}{16}$	$\frac{9}{16}$	$\frac{3}{8}$	$\frac{1}{4}$	10°
11°	$2\frac{5}{8}$	$2\frac{1}{4}$	2	$1\frac{11}{16}$	$1\frac{7}{16}$	$1\frac{3}{16}$	$1\frac{1}{16}$	$\frac{3}{4}$	$\frac{5}{8}$	$\frac{7}{16}$	$\frac{5}{16}$	11°
12°	$2\frac{7}{8}$	$2\frac{1}{2}$	$2\frac{3}{16}$	$1\frac{13}{16}$	$1\frac{9}{16}$	$1\frac{1}{4}$	$1\frac{1}{8}$	$\frac{7}{8}$	$\frac{5}{8}$	$\frac{1}{2}$	$\frac{5}{16}$	12°
13°	$3\frac{1}{16}$	$2\frac{11}{16}$	$2\frac{5}{16}$	2	$1\frac{11}{16}$	$1\frac{3}{8}$	$1\frac{1}{8}$	$\frac{15}{16}$	$\frac{11}{16}$	$\frac{1}{2}$	$\frac{3}{8}$	13°
14°	$3\frac{5}{16}$	$2\frac{7}{8}$	$2\frac{1}{2}$	$2\frac{1}{8}$	$1\frac{13}{16}$	$1\frac{1}{2}$	$1\frac{3}{16}$	1	$\frac{3}{4}$	$\frac{9}{16}$	$\frac{3}{8}$	14°
15°	$3\frac{9}{16}$	$3\frac{1}{8}$	$2\frac{11}{16}$	$2\frac{1}{4}$	$1\frac{15}{16}$	$1\frac{9}{16}$	$1\frac{5}{16}$	$1\frac{1}{16}$	$\frac{13}{16}$	$\frac{5}{8}$	$\frac{7}{16}$	15°
16°	$3\frac{3}{4}$	$3\frac{5}{16}$	$2\frac{7}{8}$	$2\frac{7}{16}$	$2\frac{1}{16}$	$1\frac{11}{16}$	$1\frac{3}{8}$	$1\frac{1}{8}$	$\frac{7}{8}$	$\frac{5}{8}$	$\frac{7}{16}$	16°
17°	4	$3\frac{1}{2}$	$3\frac{1}{16}$	$2\frac{9}{16}$	$2\frac{3}{16}$	$1\frac{13}{16}$	$1\frac{7}{16}$	$1\frac{3}{16}$	$\frac{7}{8}$	$\frac{11}{16}$	$\frac{7}{16}$	17°
18°	$4\frac{1}{4}$	$3\frac{11}{16}$	$3\frac{3}{16}$	$2\frac{11}{16}$	$2\frac{5}{16}$	$1\frac{7}{8}$	$1\frac{9}{16}$	$1\frac{1}{4}$	$\frac{15}{16}$	$\frac{11}{16}$	$\frac{1}{2}$	18°
19°	$4\frac{1}{2}$	$3\frac{7}{8}$	$3\frac{3}{8}$	$2\frac{7}{8}$	$2\frac{7}{16}$	2	$1\frac{5}{8}$	$1\frac{5}{16}$	1	$\frac{3}{4}$	$\frac{1}{2}$	19°
20°	$4\frac{3}{4}$	$4\frac{1}{16}$	$3\frac{9}{16}$	3	$2\frac{9}{16}$	$2\frac{1}{8}$	$1\frac{11}{16}$	$1\frac{3}{8}$	$1\frac{1}{16}$	$\frac{13}{16}$	$\frac{9}{16}$	20°
21°	$4\frac{15}{16}$	$4\frac{5}{16}$	$3\frac{3}{4}$	$3\frac{3}{16}$	$2\frac{11}{16}$	$2\frac{3}{16}$	$1\frac{13}{16}$	$1\frac{7}{16}$	$1\frac{1}{8}$	$\frac{7}{8}$	$\frac{9}{16}$	21°
22°	$5\frac{3}{16}$	$4\frac{1}{2}$	$3\frac{15}{16}$	$3\frac{5}{16}$	$2\frac{13}{16}$	$2\frac{5}{16}$	$1\frac{7}{8}$	$1\frac{1}{2}$	$1\frac{3}{16}$	$\frac{7}{8}$	$\frac{9}{16}$	22°
23°	$5\frac{7}{16}$	$4\frac{11}{16}$	$4\frac{1}{16}$	$3\frac{7}{16}$	$2\frac{15}{16}$	$2\frac{3}{8}$	$1\frac{15}{16}$	$1\frac{9}{16}$	$1\frac{3}{16}$	$\frac{15}{16}$	$\frac{5}{8}$	23°
24°	$5\frac{5}{8}$	$4\frac{15}{16}$	$4\frac{1}{4}$	$3\frac{5}{8}$	$3\frac{1}{16}$	$2\frac{1}{2}$	$2\frac{1}{16}$	$1\frac{11}{16}$	$1\frac{1}{4}$	$\frac{15}{16}$	$\frac{5}{8}$	24°
25°	$5\frac{7}{8}$	$5\frac{1}{8}$	$4\frac{7}{16}$	$3\frac{3}{4}$	$3\frac{3}{16}$	$2\frac{5}{8}$	$2\frac{1}{8}$	$1\frac{3}{4}$	$1\frac{5}{16}$	1	$\frac{11}{16}$	25°
26°	$6\frac{1}{16}$	$5\frac{5}{16}$	$4\frac{5}{8}$	$3\frac{7}{8}$	$3\frac{5}{16}$	$2\frac{11}{16}$	$2\frac{3}{16}$	$1\frac{13}{16}$	$1\frac{3}{8}$	1	$\frac{11}{16}$	26°
27°	$6\frac{5}{16}$	$5\frac{1}{2}$	$4\frac{3}{4}$	$4\frac{1}{16}$	$3\frac{7}{16}$	$2\frac{13}{16}$	$2\frac{5}{16}$	$1\frac{7}{8}$	$1\frac{7}{16}$	$1\frac{1}{16}$	$\frac{11}{16}$	27°
28°	$6\frac{9}{16}$	$5\frac{11}{16}$	$4\frac{15}{16}$	$4\frac{3}{16}$	$3\frac{9}{16}$	$2\frac{15}{16}$	$2\frac{3}{8}$	$1\frac{15}{16}$	$1\frac{7}{16}$	$1\frac{1}{8}$	$\frac{3}{4}$	28°
29°	$6\frac{13}{16}$	$5\frac{7}{8}$	$5\frac{1}{8}$	$4\frac{3}{8}$	$3\frac{5}{8}$	3	$2\frac{7}{16}$	2	$1\frac{1}{2}$	$1\frac{1}{8}$	$\frac{3}{4}$	29°

DECIMAL PARTS OF A FOOT FOR EACH 1-16 OF AN INCH

Decimal Part of an Inch.		0"	1"	2"	3"	4"	5"	6"	7"	8"	9"	10"	11"
.0625	1/16	.0000	.0833	.1667	.2500	.3333	.4167	.5000	.5833	.6667	.7500	.8333	.9167
.1250	1/8	.0052	.0885	.1719	.2552	.3385	.4219	.5052	.5885	.6719	.7552	.8385	.9219
.1875	3/16	.0104	.0938	.1771	.2604	.3438	.4271	.5104	.5938	.6771	.7604	.8438	.9271
.2500	1/4	.0156	.0990	.1823	.2656	.3490	.4323	.5156	.5990	.6823	.7656	.8490	.9323
.3125	5/16	.0208	.1042	.1875	.2708	.3542	.4375	.5208	.6042	.6875	.7708	.8542	.9375
.3750	3/8	.0260	.1094	.1927	.2760	.3594	.4427	.5260	.6094	.6927	.7760	.8594	.9427
.4375	7/16	.0313	.1146	.1979	.2813	.3646	.4479	.5313	.6146	.6979	.7813	.8646	.9479
.5000	1/2	.0365	.1198	.2031	.2865	.3698	.4531	.5365	.6198	.7031	.7865	.8698	.9531
.5625	9/16	.0417	.1250	.2083	.2917	.3750	.4583	.5417	.6250	.7083	.7917	.8750	.9583
.6250	5/8	.0469	.1302	.2135	.2969	.3802	.4635	.5469	.6302	.7135	.7969	.8802	.9635
.6875	11/16	.0521	.1354	.2188	.3021	.3854	.4688	.5521	.6354	.7188	.8021	.8854	.9688
.7500	3/4	.0573	.1406	.2240	.3073	.3906	.4740	.5573	.6406	.7240	.8073	.8906	.9740
.8125	13/16	.0625	.1458	.2292	.3125	.3958	.4792	.5625	.6458	.7292	.8125	.8958	.9792
.8750	7/8	.0677	.1510	.2344	.3177	.4010	.4844	.5677	.6510	.7344	.8177	.9010	.9844
.9375	15/16	.0729	.1563	.2396	.3229	.4063	.4896	.5729	.6563	.7396	.8229	.9063	.9896
		.0781	.1615	.2448	.3281	.4115	.4948	.5781	.6615	.7448	.8281	.9115	.9948

PRODUCT OF FRACTIONS EXPRESSED IN DECIMALS

0	1	1/16	1/8	3/16	1/4	5/16	3/8	7/16	1/2	9/16	5/8	11/16	3/4	13/16	7/8	15/16	1
1/16	.0625	.0039															
1/8	.1250	.0078	.0156														
3/16	.1875	.0117	.0234	.0352													
1/4	.2500	.0156	.0313	.0469	.0625												
5/16	.3125	.0195	.0391	.0586	.0781	.0977											
3/8	.3750	.0234	.0469	.0703	.0937	.1172	.1406										
7/16	.4375	.0273	.0547	.0820	.1093	.1367	.1641	.1914									
1/2	.5000	.0313	.0625	.0938	.1250	.1562	.1875	.2188	.2500								
9/16	.5625	.0352	.0703	.1055	.1406	.1758	.2109	.2461	.2813	.3164							
5/8	.6250	.0391	.0781	.1172	.1562	.1953	.2344	.2734	.3125	.3516	.3906						
11/16	.6875	.0430	.0859	.1289	.1719	.2148	.2578	.3008	.3438	.3867	.4297	.4727					
3/4	.7500	.0469	.0938	.1406	.1875	.2344	.2813	.3281	.3750	.4219	.4688	.5156	.5625				
13/16	.8125	.0508	.1016	.1523	.2031	.2539	.3047	.3555	.4063	.4570	.5078	.5586	.6094	.6601			
7/8	.8750	.0547	.1094	.1641	.2187	.2734	.3281	.3828	.4375	.4922	.5469	.6016	.6563	.7109	.7656		
15/16	.9375	.0586	.1172	.1758	.2344	.2930	.3516	.4102	.4688	.5273	.5859	.6445	.7031	.7617	.8203	.8789	
1	1.000	.0625	.1250	.1875	.2500	.3125	.3750	.4375	.5000	.5625	.6250	.6875	.7500	.8125	.8750	.9375	1.000

Rails

Weight per Yard.	Tons per Mile of single Track.
8 lbs	12 $\frac{1280}{2240}$
12 "	18 $\frac{1920}{2240}$
16 "	25 $\frac{320}{2240}$
25 "	39 $\frac{640}{2240}$
30 "	47 $\frac{320}{2240}$
35 "	55
40 "	62 $\frac{1920}{2240}$
45 "	70 $\frac{1600}{2240}$
50 "	78 $\frac{1230}{2240}$
52 "	81 $\frac{1600}{2240}$
56 "	88
57 "	89 $\frac{1280}{2240}$
60 "	94 $\frac{640}{2240}$
62 "	97 $\frac{960}{2240}$
64 "	100 $\frac{1280}{2240}$
65 "	102 $\frac{320}{2240}$
68 "	106 $\frac{1920}{2240}$
70 "	110
72 "	113 $\frac{320}{2240}$
75 "	117 $\frac{1920}{2240}$
76 "	119 $\frac{960}{2240}$
78 "	122 $\frac{1280}{2240}$
80 "	125 $\frac{1600}{2240}$
85 "	133 $\frac{1280}{2240}$
90 "	141 $\frac{960}{2240}$
95 "	149 $\frac{640}{2240}$
100 "	157 $\frac{320}{2240}$
105 "	155
110 "	172 $\frac{1920}{2240}$

To find the number of tons (of 2,240 lbs.) per mile of single track, multiply the pounds per yard by 11 and divide by 7.

The Buda Foundry & Manufacturing Company

Area of Circles

Dia.	Area.	Cir.	Dia.	Area.	Cir.	Dia.	Area.	Cir.
1/8	0.0123	.3926	10	78.54	31.41	30	706.86	94.24
1/4	0.0491	.7854	10½	86.59	32.98	31	754.76	97.38
3/8	0.1104	1.178	11	95.03	34.55	32	804.24	100.5
1/2	0.1963	1.570	11½	103.86	36.12	33	855.30	103.6
5/8	0.3067	1.963	12	113.09	37.69	34	907.92	106.8
3/4	0.4417	2.356	12½	122.71	39.27	35	962.11	109.9
7/8	0.6013	2.748	13	132.73	40.84	36	1017.8	113.0
1	0.7854	3.141	13½	143.13	42.41	37	1075.2	116.2
1⅛	0.9940	3.534	14	153.93	43.98	38	1134.1	119.3
1¼	1.227	3.927	14½	165.13	45.55	39	1194.5	122.5
1⅜	1.484	4.319	15	176.71	47.12	40	1256.6	125.6
1½	1.767	4.712	15½	188.69	48.69	41	1320.2	128.8
1⅝	2.073	5.105	16	201.06	50.26	42	1385.4	131.9
1¾	2.405	5.497	16½	213.82	51.83	43	1452.2	135.0
1⅞	2.761	5.890	17	226.98	53.40	44	1520.5	138.2
2	3.141	6.283	17½	240.52	54.97	45	1590.4	141.3
2¼	3.976	7.068	18	254.46	56.54	46	1661.9	144.5
2½	4.908	7.854	18½	268.80	58.11	47	1734.9	147.6
2¾	5.939	8.639	19	283.52	59.69	48	1809.5	150.7
3	7.068	9.424	19½	298.64	61.26	49	1885.7	153.9
3¼	8.295	10.21	20	314.16	62.83	50	1963.5	157.0
3½	9.621	10.99	20½	330.06	64.40			
3¾	11.044	11.78	21	346.36	65.97			
4	12.566	12.56	21½	363.05	67.54			
4½	15.904	14.13	22	380.13	69.11			
5	19.635	15.70	22½	397.60	70.68			
5½	23.758	17.27	23	415.47	72.25			
6	28.274	18.84	23½	433.73	73.82			
6½	33.183	20.42	24	452.39	75.39			
7	38.484	21.99	24½	471.43	76.96			
7½	44.178	23.56	25	490.87	78.54			
8	50.265	25.13	26	530.93	81.68			
8½	56.745	26.70	27	572.55	84.82			
9	63.617	28.27	28	615.75	87.96			
9½	70.882	29.84	29	660.52	91.10			

Weights of Various Substances
PER CUBIC FOOT

Names of Substances—	Aver. Weight Pounds.
Anthracite, solid, of Pennsylvania	93
Anthracite, broken, loose	54
Anthracite, broken, moderately shaken	58
Anthracite, heaped bushel, loose	(80)
Ash, American white, dry	38
Asphaltum	87
Brass, (Copper and Zinc), cast	504
Brass, rolled	524
Brick, best pressed	150
Brick, common hard	125
Brick, soft, inferior	100
Brickwork, pressed brick	140
Brickwork, ordinary	112
Cement, hydraulic, ground, loose, American, Rosendale	56
Cement, hydraulic, ground, loose, American, Louisville	50
Cement, hydraulic, ground, loose, English, Portland	90
Cherry, dry	42
Chestnut, dry	41
Coal, bituminous, solid	84
Coal, bituminous, broken, loose	49
Coal, bituminous, heaped bushel, loose	(74)
Coke, loose, of good coal	27
Coke, loose, heaped bushel	(38)
Copper, cast	542
Copper, rolled	548
Earth, common loam, dry, loose	76
Earth, common loam, dry, moderately rammed	95
Earth, as a soft flowing mud	108
Ebony, dry	76
Elm, dry	35
Flint	162
Glass, common window	157
Gneiss, common	168
Gold, cast, pure, or 24 carat	1204
Gold, pure hammered	1217
Granite	170
Gravel, about the same as sand, which see.	
Hemlock, dry	25
Hickory, dry	53
Hornblende, black	203
Ice	58.7
Iron, cast	450
Iron, wrought, purest	485
Iron, wrought, average	480
Ivory	114
Lead	711
Lignum Vitae, dry	83
Lime, quick, ground, loose, or in small lumps	53
Lime, quick, ground, loose, thoroughly shaken	75
Lime, quick, ground, loose, per struck bushel	(66)

Weights of Various Substances—Concluded

PER CUBIC FOOT

Names of Substances—	Aver. Weight Pounds.
Limestones and Marbles	168
Limestones and Marbles, loose, in irregular fragments	96
Mahogany, Spanish, dry	53
Mahogany, Honduras, dry	35
Maple, dry	49
Marbles, see Limestones.	
Masonry, of granite or limestone, well dressed	165
Masonry, of mortar rubble	154
Masonry, of dry rubble (well scabbled)	138
Masonry, of sandstone, well dressed	144
Mercury, at 32° Fahrenheit	849
Mica	183
Mortar, hardened	103
Mud, dry, close	80 to 110
Mud, wet, fluid, maximum	120
Oak, live, dry	59
Oak, white, dry	52
Oak, other kinds	32 to 45
Petroleum	55
Pine, white, dry	25
Pine, yellow, Northern	34
Pine, yellow, Southern	45
Platinum	1342
Quartz, common, pure	165
Rosin	69
Salt, coarse, Syracuse, New York	45
Salt, Liverpool, fine, for table use	49
Sand, of pure quartz, dry, loose	90 to 106
Sand, well shaken	99 to 117
Sand, perfectly wet	120 to 140
Sandstones, fit for building	151
Shales, red or black	162
Silver	655
Slate	175
Snow, freshly fallen	5 to 12
Snow, moistened and compacted by rain	15 to 50
Spruce, dry	25
Steel	490
Sulphur	125
Sycamore, dry	37
Tar	62
Tin, cast	459
Turf or Peat, dry, unpressed	20 to 30
Walnut, black, dry	38
Water, pure rain or distilled, at 60° Fahrenheit	62½
Water, sea	64
Wax, bees	60.5
Zinc or Spelter	437

Green timbers usually weigh from one-fifth to one-half more than dry.

Index

A

Adjustable Rods	308
Automatic Feed Track Drills	88-113
Automatic Switch Stands	203

B

Ball-Bearing Jacks	135-164
Battery Chutes	238
Beams for Scales	16-30-31
Beams, Quick Weighing	31
Beetles	134
Benders, Rail	131-133

C

Caboose Stoves	290-292
Car Replacers	284-288
Cars, Hand, Push and Velocipede	51-87
Cinder Pit Ties	289
Coaling Station Scales	23
Compromise Joints	310
Cone-Bearing Journal Jacks	162-164
Crossing Gates	239-283
Crossings, Switches, Frogs	293-312

D

Depot Scales	20
Depot Stoves	290-293
Dollies, Timber	134
Dormant Warehouse Scales	37-41
Drills, Track	88-113
Drop Lever Portable Scales	43
Dump Scales (Wagon)	28

E

Engine Replacers	284-288

F

Fixtures for Stub Switches	311
Flat Bits (Rich)	114-118
Foot Guards	302
Foundations, Scales	11
Friction Jacks	198-199
Frogs, Crossings, Switches	293-312

INDEX—Continued

G

Gates, Crossing	239-283
Gauges and Levels	127-130
Girder Drills	101-102
Grain Hopper Scales	34-36
Grinders, Tool	121-126

H

Hand Cars	51-60
Hard Center Construction	299
Harvey Track Drills	107-113
Head Chairs	311
High Speed Steel	114

I

Inclines, Wrecking	288
Information, Tables of Useful	313-326
Iron Dealers' Scales	29

J

Jacks, Ball-Bearing and Cone-Bearing	135-164
Jacks, Geared Ratchet	165-166
Jacks, Ratchet	167-201

L

Levels and Gauges	121-130
Lining-Up Jacks	194-195

M

Miners' and Transportation Scales	25

P

Paulus Track Drills	88-102
Pillars for Scales	21
Pneumatic Gates	239-283
Pressed Steel Wheels	46-49
Prices of Twist and Flat Bits	120
Push Cars	62-69

Q

Quick Weighing Beams	31

INDEX – Continued

R

Rail Benders	131-133
Rail Braces	310
Rail Laying Cars	67
Railway Depot Scales	20
Ramapo Switch Stands	203
Recording Beams	16-31
Repair Parts, Drills	93, 97, 100, 106, 112, 113
Repair Parts for Scales	18, 32, 40, 41
Repair Parts, Hand Cars	68-73
Repair Parts, Push Cars	74-75
Repair Parts, Velocipedes	82-87
Replacers, Car and Engine	284-288
Rich Flat Bits	114-118
Roundhouse Stoves	290-293

S

Safety Crossing Gates	239-283
Scales	6-45
Scale Beams	16 and 30-31
Scale Foundations	11
Scale Repair Parts	18, 32, 40, 44
Scales, Depot	20
Scales, Dormant Warehouse	37-39
Scales, Dump	28
Scales, Coaling Station	23
Scales, Grain Hopper	34-36
Scales, Iron Dealers'	29
Scales, Miners' and Transportation	25
Scales, Pillars for	21
Scales, Portable Platform	42-43
Scales, Stock	27
Scales, Suspension Coal Tipple	24
Scales, Test Weights	45
Scales, Track	12-19
Scales, Wagon	26
Semaphore Stands	214-218
Slide Plates	308
Special Work	293-312
Split Switch Plates	308
Spring Washers	302
Steel Wheels, Pressed	46-49
Stoves	290-292
Stub Switch Fixtures	311
Suspension Coal Tipple Scales	24

INDEX—Concluded

Switch Clips, Pressed Steel... 312
Switches, Frogs, Crossings... 293-312
Switch Stands 202-237

T

Tables of Useful Information... 313-326
Tie Cars 66
Tie Plate Beetles 134
Timber Dollies 134
Tool Grinders 121-126
Track Drills 88-113
Track Gauges and Levels... 127-130
Track Laying Cars.. 67
Track Scales 12-19
Twist and Flat Bits, Prices of... 120

U

Useful Information 313-326

V

Velocipedes 76-87

W

Wagon and Stock Scales... 26-27
Warehouse Scales 37-39
Warehouse Stoves 290-293
Wilson Track Drills 103-106
Wood Center Wheels 50
Wrecking Inclines 288

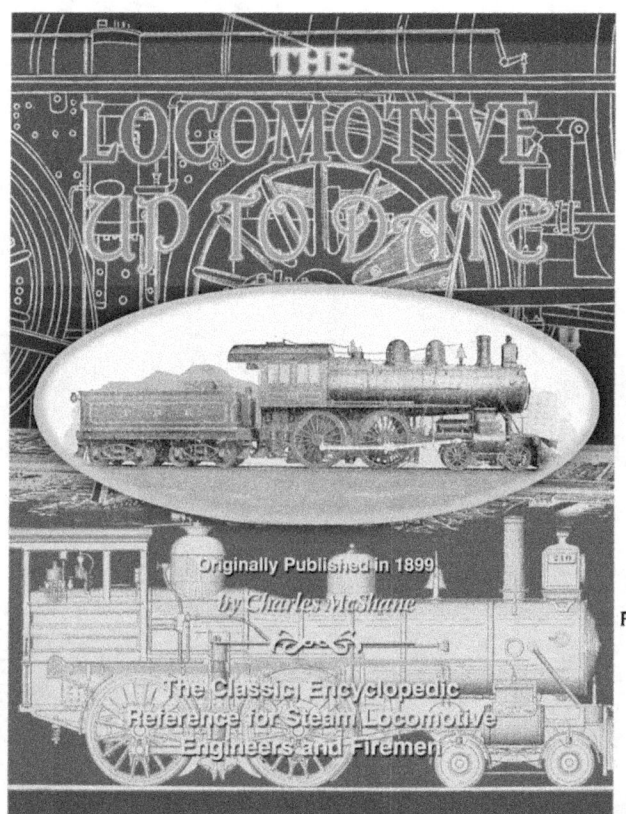

When it was originally published in 1899, **The Locomotive Up to Date** was hailed as "...the most definitive work ever published concerning the mechanism that has transformed the American nation: the steam locomotive." Filled with over 700 pages of text, diagrams and photos, this remains one of the most important railroading books ever written. From steam valves to sanders, trucks to side rods, it's a treasure trove of information, explaining in easy-to-understand language how the most sophisticated machines of the 19th Century were operated and maintained. This new edition is an exact duplicate of the original. Reformatted as an easy-to-read 8.5x11 volume, it's delightful for railroad enthusiasts of all ages.

Originally printed in 1898 and then periodically revised, **The Motorman...and His Duties** served as the definitive training text for a generation of streetcar operators. A must-have for the trolley or train enthusiast, it is also an important source of information for museum staff and docents. Lavishly illustrated with numerous photos and black and white line drawings, this affordable reprint contains all of the original text. Includes chapters on trolley car types and equipment, troubleshooting, brakes, controllers, electricity and principles, electric traction, multi-car control and has a convenient glossary in the back. If you've ever operated a trolley car, or just had an electric train set, this is a terrific book for your shelf!

ALSO NOW AVAILABLE FROM PERISCOPEFILM.COM!

THE CLASSIC 1911 TROLLEY CAR BUILDER'S REFERENCE BOOK

ELECTRIC RAILWAY DICTIONARY

By Rodney Hitt
Associate Editor, Electric Railway Journal

REPRINTED BY PERISCOPEFILM.COM

THE CLASSIC 1915 TROLLEY CAR
AND INTERURBAN RAILWAY BOOK

ELECTRIC RAILWAY ENGINEERING

By Francis H. Doane, A.M.B.

REPRINTED BY PERISCOPEFILM.COM

©2008-2010 Periscope Film LLC
All Rights Reserved
ISBN #978-1-935700-08-1

www.PeriscopeFilm.com

www.ingramcontent.com/pod-product-compliance
Lightning Source LLC
Chambersburg PA
CBHW080725230426
43665CB00020B/2619